W9-ALN-451

The Homevoter Hypothesis

The Homevoter Hypothesis

How Home Values Influence Local Government Taxation, School Finance, and Land-Use Policies

WILLIAM A. FISCHEL

HARVARD UNIVERSITY PRESS
Cambridge, Massachusetts
London, England 2001

Printed in the United States of America

Library of Congress Cataloging-in-Publication Data

Fischel, William A.

The homevoter hypothesis : how home values influence local government taxation, school finance, and land-use policies / William A. Fischel.

p. cm.

Includes bibliographical references and index.

ISBN 0-674-00609-7

1. Local government—United States—Citizen participation. 2. Local government—United States. 3. Homeowners—United States—Political activity. 4. Housing—Prices—United States. 5. Zoning—United States. 6. Local taxation—United States. 7. Education—United States—Finance. I. Title.

JS391 .F57 2001
338.973—dc21 2001024834

To the memory of Charles M. Tiebout,

for whom a sense of humor was an intellectual asset

Contents

Preface

I invented the portmanteau word "homevoters" (homeowners who are voters) to emphasize that residents who own their homes have a stake in the outcome of local politics that makes them especially attentive to the public policies of local governments. This book works out the implications of homeowners' concern about the value of their largest single asset. It explains why competition among local governments results in a race to the top in public education and environmental protection instead of, as is commonly alleged, a race to the bottom.

In *The Economics of Zoning Laws* (1985), I advanced the idea that local governments use their land-use controls in rational if not always admirable ways to maximize the value of owner-occupied housing in their community. Until then, most other economists had a Manichean view of zoning: It was modeled either as a wooden-headed constraint on urban development or as a sophisticated means of "internalizing externalities" by all-seeing planners. I sought to replace both of those approaches with a model that emphasizes the economic interests of residential voters as the best way to understand zoning.

My second book, *Regulatory Takings* (1995), investigated the role of the courts in refereeing the division of property interests between private owners of developable land and the public ownership that zoning implicitly confers on the rest of the community. I argued that the courts need to pay special attention to land-use regulation because local governments were too good at it. Their regulations have the potential to transfer too many property rights from the private to the public sector, making zoning unfairly and inefficiently restrictive.

In her *Yale Law Journal* review of my 1995 book, Carol Rose (1996, p. 1058) seemed somewhat perplexed by my focus on local government. "In distinguishing state or federal from local legislation," Rose wrote, "Fischel joins a mainstream tradition that can be described roughly as 'localism bashing.'" She pointed out that I am "certainly not the worst in this tradition; indeed, he defends local governments (especially the much-maligned suburbs) for the range of choice that they offer citizens and the efficiency with which they deliver services to the citizens that choose them." But she adds, "He argues that these governments' very efficiency—their satisfaction of their own 'median voters'—is linked to a predilection for unfairness to those who fall outside that category."

The present book might be viewed as a defensive response to Carol's comment. Really, I *do* like local government. That is why I spent so much time thinking of ways to correct its excesses and shortcomings. But simply retelling the virtues of local governance is not my objective in this work. I found an *explanation* for why local governments work better at providing local services than do larger-area governments.

The explanation is so simple that I stared at it for years without recognizing it. Everybody knows that homeowners care about the value of their major physical asset, their home. Most economists and nearly all homebuyers know that the good things and bad things that local governments do tend to raise or lower the value of that asset. Studies of political economy find that homeowners are the dominant political faction in all but the largest local governments. This book puts these three propositions together in a positive account of local political economy that shows how and why it differs from the state and national brand.

I wish to thank without implicating Tony Downs, Bob Ellickson, John Matsusaka, and Jon Sonstelie, who read and critiqued the entire manuscript, and Clay Gillette, Tom Heller, and Jon Teaford, who offered helpful comments on individual chapters. The year-long sabbatical leave during which the first draft of this book was written was sponsored by Dartmouth College and was supplemented by a grant from the college's Rockefeller Fund for Social Science Research. The Daniel

J. Evans School of Public Affairs at the University of Washington provided a hospitable environment for my sabbatical, and I am especially grateful to Bob Plotnick and Dean Marc Lindenberg for facilitating my stay. The Lincoln Institute for Land Policy underwrote earlier work that was the basis for several chapters, and Lincoln's Joan Youngman provided much-appreciated encouragement in this enterprise. The Homer Hoyt Institute provided a helpful forum for exploring early versions of this work, and I also benefited from seminars hosted by the Kennedy School of Government at Harvard University, Lehigh University, Marshall School of Business at the University of Southern California, Public Policy Institute of California, University of Virginia Law School, and Yale Law School as well as my home institution, Dartmouth College.

I am most indebted to my wife, Janice Goldberg Fischel, for her patient assistance in reading the manuscript and for her willingness to forsake home and career track for a year-long stay in Seattle. Okay, Seattle wasn't exactly hardship duty, but I do appreciate her tolerance for visiting burgeoning suburbs rather than more normal tourist spots. The sky seemed so much brighter when she was along.

Hanover, New Hampshire
March 2001

The Homevoter Hypothesis

1
An Asset-Market Approach to Local Government

THIS CHAPTER FRAMES the basic questions that motivate the book and outlines the homevoter hypothesis. The important facts are that home values are the largest part of most people's assets, and public events like taxes and spending affect the value of that asset. I describe the event that triggered the hypothesis, an insight I got at a zoning board hearing. The uninsurable riskiness of homeownership explains why homeowners dominate local politics.

The more debatable issue is where the homevoter model applies. Historically, owners of business property were the major players in local politics, but since about 1920, homeowners have become the dominant group of property owners. I conclude with a story that probes the moral limitations of the hypothesis.

1.1 Why Is This Book Different from Any Other?

Here are the four questions that motivate this book:

1. Should the property tax, long the mainstay of local government finance, be pooled among local governments or, alternatively, replaced by state taxes? Statewide tax base sharing has long been a staple of school-finance reform (Coons, Clune, and Sugarman 1970), and metropolitan property-tax base sharing has become a

cutting-edge idea among urbanists despite its long confinement in practice to Minnesota's Twin Cities (Myron Orfield 1997). Nor has the property tax been much admired among economists, who have traditionally seen it as a regressive tax on housing or as yet another burden on capital formation, somewhat like the corporate income tax (Dick Netzer 1966; Peter Mieszkowski 1972). Taxpayer surveys find that it is the least palatable tax to pay, and its use has been gradually supplanted by state taxes for much of the twentieth century (Glenn Fisher 1996; Alvin Sokolow 1998).

2. Should public education (the K–12 level) be funded primarily by state and national governments rather than mostly by local governments? Many serious economists, political scientists, and others interested in the public sector argue in favor of state or, better yet, national funding for schools, since the public benefits of education accrue to a much larger area than that encompassed by most local governments (Roland Benabou 1996; Ladd and Yinger 1994). This argument has been implicitly accepted by more than sixteen state courts, which have ordered legislatures to assume more of the burden of local school finance than the ordinary political process has traditionally allowed.
3. Must local governments be restrained from an environmentally destructive "race to the bottom" when they use zoning changes and fiscal incentives to attract commerce and industry? National environmental policy is founded on the idea that left to themselves, local governments will foul their own nests and those of their neighbors in an environmentally destructive downward spiral (Daniel Esty 1996). Even scholars sympathetic to local governments worry that they may be tempted to sacrifice the environment for jobs and tax base (Eric Monkkonen 1996; Oates and Schwab 1988).
4. Is the best remedy for the problem of "exclusionary zoning" to shift regulation of land use to metropolitan governments or statewide bodies? Most reformers believe that the insular zoning of modern suburbs can only be overcome by having higher governments make them accept their "fair share" of low-income housing and other unpopular land uses (Anthony Downs 1973;

Charles Haar 1996). Others have argued that city-wide zoning is an obsolete concept whose functions would best be shifted to the neighborhood (Robert Ellickson 1973; 1998; Robert Nelson 1999). Both sets of reforms regard local zoning as a power that is detachable from local government.

I take a contrary view:

1. The property tax must be analyzed as part of a system of local government that provides public services with less economic waste than others. Proposals to detach it from local units and distribute it on a metropolitan or statewide basis undermine this advantage.
2. Schools that are funded (not simply administered) locally perform better than those whose funds come largely from the state. The school-finance reforms initiated by state judges are a "natural experiment" in fiscal centralization, and the results are disappointing. The loss of local fiscal control has, according to many studies, resulted in declines in test scores and, in some important cases, diminished voter support for education.
3. Local governments are in fact so skeptical of the adverse environmental effects of new commerce and industry that their behavior is better characterized as a "race to the top" of the environmental pyramid. This race is propelled by risk-averse homeowners, who cannot insure their major asset from adverse neighborhood effects. Nor are homeowners in one community eager to degrade the environment of neighboring communities for their own fiscal benefits, in part because municipal neighbors are locked into a web of reciprocal relationships that are sensitive to unprincipled opportunism.
4. The history of local government formation demonstrates that zoning is an essential ingredient of municipal formation and function. Reforms of land-use regulation should recognize that no local government will surrender much of that authority to a metropolitan-wide government. The reforms more likely to succeed are those that address the fundamental reasons that homeowners are so skittish about neighborhood change. Financial carrots and sticks are essential to the orderly and equitable development of metropolitan areas.

1.2 Homeowners' Big Asset Grabs Their Attention

The reason that local governments perform better is that the benefits and costs of local decision making are reflected in the value of property in the jurisdiction. The homevoter hypothesis holds that homeowners, who are the most numerous and politically influential group within most localities, are guided by their concern for the value of their homes to make political decisions that are more efficient than those that would be made at a higher level of government. Homeowners are acutely aware that local amenities, public services, and taxes affect ("are capitalized in") the value of the largest single asset they own. As a result, they pay much closer attention to such policies at the local level than they would at the state or national level. They balance the benefits of local policies against the costs when the policies affect the value of their home, and they will tend to choose those policies that preserve or increase the value of their homes.

The importance of a home for the typical owner can hardly be overstated. Two-thirds of all homes are owner occupied. For the great majority of these homeowners, the equity in their home is the most important savings they have. Data from 1990 surveys show that "median housing equity is more than 11 times as large as median liquid assets among all homeowners; even for homeowners over 65, that ratio was still more than 3 to 1" (Engelhardt and Mayer 1998, p. 136).

It was reported that the 1990s bull market for corporate stocks has made the aggregate value of these stocks exceed the aggregate value of homes in the United States. But the 1990s increase in stock-market wealth was not widely shared. Examining the *Survey of Consumer Finances*, Joseph Tracy, Henry Schneider, and Sewin Chan (1999, p. 3) found "that the typical household in 1995 had 66 percent of its total assets in real estate and *no* portion of its assets in corporate equity." I point this out to emphasize why most residents have always been acutely concerned about public events that affect their homes' value. They do not really own much else.

I am arguing both positive and normative positions in this book. I think that, subject to some important qualifications, local governments perform localized services more efficiently than the state or national government would. But readers do not have to accept my normative contentions to find something useful here. The approach that yields the best understanding of local government behavior, and hence the best predictions about what happens when institutional arrangements are changed, is to see that behavior through the eyes of a homeowner.

1.3 Homevoters Think Holistically about Local Government

It is important to think of my thesis—that concern for home values is the central motivator of local government behavior—as being tied up in a package in which financing, regulation, and expenditure are all done by the locality. Local officials and voters are assumed to be capable of seeing the whole picture. The story makes little sense if each component—taxes, spending, and regulation—is examined by itself. Considered in isolation, the payment of $3,000 in property taxes to the locality to fund schools is just as painful to the taxpayer as the payment of $3,000 in income taxes to the state government to fund schools. (Actually, the property tax is probably more painful, since most income tax is withheld from paychecks.)

The same is true for expenditure: Parents of schoolchildren care as much about the quality of education when it is funded by the state as by the locality. And a regulatory change to accommodate a new dump excites as much neighborhood interest when it is proposed by an agency of the U.S. government as by the local waste authority. My hypothesis does not deny that a dollar is a dollar, a schoolbook is a schoolbook, or that a dump is a dump is not a rose.

But at the local level, none of these events can usefully be considered in isolation by those who make the decisions. An increase in local property taxes to add teachers for schools may make the community more attractive to homebuyers. This will, if the program is cost effective, add to the value of all homes in the community, not just of homes currently containing school-age children. The prospect of a capital gain (or the anxiety about a loss if the schools are left to deteriorate) makes the policy more palatable to the majority of voters, even those who do not have children in school. The added value to homes from an efficient program in turn increases the property-tax base.

My claim is not simply that everything goes round and round, however. There is a prime mover at the local level. In the foregoing scenario, both the costs and the benefits of the action—a tax increase, an extra teacher—are reflected in home values in the community when done at the local level, but not if they are part of a uniform state or national policy. Because of this particularized effect on all homes in their community, homevoters will, at the local level, want to adopt the mix of policies that maximizes the value of their primary assets.

Attention to home values will also guide regulatory policies. A town that is asked to rezone property for a low-level nuclear waste dump in exchange for $2 million a year in cash and benefits has to consider not just the value of the cash (which could be used to cut property taxes or to augment local services), but also the effect that harboring the dump will have on the community's reputation and health and hence the value of the voters' homes. This probably accounts for why the actual proffer of such a deal in New Jersey found no takers among that state's 567 municipalities (*New York Times*, December 9, 1995). The existence of the dump and its risk of spillover effects would be reflected in home values, and it apparently takes more than $2 million a year to offset that. The state commission formed to persuade localities to accept the fifty-acre facility was disbanded in 1998 after failing to persuade any municipality even to consider the details of the deal (Bergen County *Record*, February 15, 1998).

An example of the error that my approach avoids is much of the economics profession's analysis of "impact fees." These fees are levied on new development by local governments, and economists have typically analyzed them as if they were taxes. The taxes, it is said, add to the cost of the house in the same way that sales taxes add to the cost of consumer goods. Yet this analogy overlooks that impact fees are levied by a municipality that can withhold something that developers value if the fees are not forthcoming. If a court strikes down a sales tax, the state legislature that adopted it is unlikely to do anything that will affect the buyers or sellers of commodities. But if a court strikes down an impact fee, the municipal legislature is likely to respond by making it more difficult for developers to get their projects done. Impact fees cannot be thought of in the traditional tax framework because they are not taxes in the traditional sense. They are payments for permissions that can be withheld.

1.4 Terminology: Capitalization and Property-Tax Base

When I say that proximity to a dump is "reflected in home values," it is the same as saying that proximity to a dump "is capitalized in home values." Noneconomists are usually put off by the term "capitalization," but it is not a difficult concept. The term is borrowed from asset markets. It means nothing more than that the expected future flow of benefits or costs that accrue to something you own—a share of stock in Microsoft, a Russian government bond, your home—is systematically reflected in the present value of your asset. The present value is the price you could sell it for right now. Good news about Microsoft's expected earnings raises the price of that asset; bad news about Russia's economic reforms reduces the price of Russian bonds; reductions in local taxes, unaccompanied by reductions in local services, raise the value of your home.

The term "capitalization" puts people off because it evokes the messy algebra of discounting. The $10,000 benefit expected to be received twenty years from now is worth much less than $10,000 received right now, and the way to calculate that benefit is to apply a discount formula to the future benefit. But for the most part, it is not necessary to understand how this is done to use the concept of capitalization intelligently. (A step-by-step trip though the algebra can be found in Fischel 1991a.) People to whom I explain the concept for the first time usually respond with something like, "Of course the value of any asset is affected by anticipated events. Why would anyone think any differently?"

Because the property tax plays a large role in local government, it is important to understand its mechanics. The property tax is collected as a percentage of the tax base, which is the value of land and buildings located within the community. A local official called an assessor estimates the value of each taxable parcel to arrive at its assessed value, which in most states is supposed to be a uniform fraction of the estimated market value of the property. (It does not matter what fraction of market value is used as long as it stays the same from year to year, so examples in this book assume that property is assessed at 100 percent of market value.) Assessments thus determine the share of local taxes that each property owner must pay.

The amount of taxes to be collected is determined annually by the local governing bodies such as city councils and school boards. Property taxes pay for spending that is not financed by other means, such as (to mention the other two largest sources of local revenue) higher-government grants and local fees and user charges. The total amount to be collected divided by the tax base gives the property tax rate. A typical tax rate might be on the order of 2 percent, so that an owner of a home assessed at a market value of $200,000 would pay $4,000 annually in taxes. (Section 6.5 explains the difference between the tax rate and the "tax price," the latter being what the average voter has to pay for an increase in public services.)

For most local governments, the property tax is their largest single source of discretionary funds. As a result, public officials pay close attention to the tax base. The tax base of the average community is composed of, in the usual order of value, residential property (about 65 percent of the total), commercial and industrial property (25 percent), and "undeveloped" land such as farms, woodlots, and vacant lots (10 percent). The proportions vary considerably among communities. Some small suburbs are almost exclusively residential, and a few cities will have a large fraction of commercial and industrial property. Furthermore, several states allow communities to tax nonresidential properties at a higher rate, so that the residential share of taxes may be overstated by assessed value figures. As a result, there is considerable variation in property tax rates among local governments.

1.5 Risk Is the Key to Homevoter Participation

The idea behind the homevoter hypothesis was first advanced in a paper by Jon Sonstelie and Paul Portney (1978), "Profit Maximizing Communities and the Theory of Local Public Expenditures." That there is a financial motive for local political behavior now seems obvious. But it also presented a puzzle. We take care of our own homes because the benefit redounds to ourselves. Fixing the furnace makes sense, even if you are selling your home next year, because a nonfunctioning heating system would devalue your major asset. Prospective buyers would lower the price you would receive when you sold it.

But what special motivation would make people take care of the collective community benefits and costs that affect home values? Why wouldn't homeowners "free ride" on the efforts of others at zoning hearings, school board meetings, and city elections, with the result that only special-interest groups would be organized well enough to affect local politics? Here is how I discovered the special motivation.

I was chairing a meeting of the Hanover, New Hampshire, zoning board in 1997. A developer, who was a well-known native, was making a request for a routine special exception. (Unlike variances, which are hard to get, "special exceptions" are presumed to be granted if the applicant meets specific criteria set out in the ordinance.) He had purchased undeveloped land in a lightly populated residential district and subdivided it into lots larger than required by the zoning ordinance to build about a dozen single-family homes. The proposed homes would be nicer than those already in the neighborhood, and all of them would be out of sight of adjacent homeowners. All the developer needed from the board was permission to build his driveways across some intermittent streams that qualified as wetlands. He bent over backward to conform with the rules in that his proposed driveways exceeded the recommended drainage specifications at every crossing.

The opposition came from neighbors, particularly two who lived closest to the proposed driveway entrance. They raised "not in my back yard" (NIMBY) issues about flood control and character of the area, both of which I thought were likely to be improved by the development. It was an all-too-familiar litany for me after nine years on the board, and my mind started to go on autopilot.

As one opponent went on and on about the supposed ill effects of this project, I found myself brought up short: "Wait a minute," I thought. "I know this guy (the NIMBY). His son and mine are friends. I've seen him at school functions and talked with him. He's a sensible guy, salt-of-the-earth type. He's not crazy; he can't believe that this project is likely to harm him. So what's he worried about?"

Light bulb turns on in my head: He's not worried about the likely, *expected* effect of the development, which was benign. He's worried about the *variance* (statistical, not legal) in the outcome. He, like almost everyone else in town who appears at these hearings, owns his home. It constitutes nearly all of his nonretirement assets. He can insure it against fire and theft, but he cannot insure it against adverse neighborhood effects. So Tom (the NIMBY) was doing his best in the absence of insurance to reduce the possibility that some unlikely event would adversely affect the value of his home.

NIMBYism is weird only if you think solely about the rationally expected outcome from development. NIMBYism makes perfectly good sense if you think about the variance in expected outcomes, and the fact that there is no way to insure against neighborhood or community-wide decline.

As often happens with my great ideas, I soon found that someone else had thought of it earlier. In an obscurely published paper that I nonetheless had in my files (and so maybe my zoning-board epiphany was just my subconscious at work), Albert Breton (1973) invoked economic theory to explain the existence of zoning and the difficulties it posed for developers. He identified the cause of residents' aversion to development as an incomplete insurance market. Since residents cannot insure against neighborhood change, zoning offers a kind of second-best institution. If homeowners were insured against neighborhood decline, they wouldn't worry so much about unlikely scenarios and behave like NIMBYs.

If homeownership is such a risky portfolio choice, why is it so common? Pride of ownership is one factor, and tax advantages are another. The imputed income (the amount you would have to pay to rent your own home) from owning a house and the capital gains realized from ownership are now completely untaxed at the federal and state level. No other widely available asset has both advantages. And in one sense, owning a home rather than renting does reduce risk. As a housing consumer, having a predictable stream of cash payments in the future is valuable, even if the value of the underlying asset fluctuates. So the risk I am concerned with is asset risk, not cash-flow risk.

1.6 Why Homeowners Are Different from Others

In further support of the idea that the risks of homeownership are the key factor, I would point out that both apartment owners and apartment dwellers are rarely NIMBYs, even after accounting for their lower numbers. I do not have numbers on this, but in my experience on a zoning board and my frequent attention to other disputes, it appears that the opposition to land-use change is usually by homeowners. The only systematic exception is opposition by existing businesses to potential competitors, and even then they usually try to clothe their naked protectionism with appeals to environmental issues that primarily affect homeowners.

Lack of NIMBYism by apartment owners seems strange only if we attribute NIMBYism simply to expected effects of the proposed development rather than the variance of those effects. In absolute dollars, owners of multifamily housing have even more to lose from adverse neighborhood effects than most homeowners. And apartment-building owners could be effective NIMBYs if they cared to, since they could round up tenants and business allies to oppose the land-use change. But such opposition is rare. The reason is that owners of multifamily homes can spread their risks of ownership much more easily than homeowners. They cannot insure against devaluation of their assets from neighborhood change, but they can divide ownership of rental housing among many owners much more easily by forming a REIT (real estate investment trust) or some other multi-investor form of ownership.

Homeowners cannot similarly divide their assets among locations. A proposal to divide home equity between owner-occupants and distant investors is described in Andrew Caplin et al. (1997). This arrangement, which would be similar in many respects to REITs, would reduce homeowner exposure, though not the risk of ownership. The authors of the proposal concede, however, that dividing ownership is considerably more difficult for owner-occupied homes than for apartment houses and office buildings. A more direct way to assuage NIMBYism is home equity insurance, which has been advocated by Karl Case, Robert Shiller, and Allan Weiss (1993). Their scheme, however, would cover only swings in metropolitan-wide values, not individual communities or neighborhoods. Shiller and Weiss (1998) conceded that even this coarser insurance market would be dauntingly difficult to establish. Zoning may be the best insurance for now.

Another method of diversification, suggested to me by a rueful California real-estate investor, might be for homeowners to get a second mortgage and use the proceeds to invest in safer assets. If the home's value goes down too much, the homeowner can just walk away from the mortgage. Many states, however, allow the lender to haul a defaulting homeowner into court to obtain a "deficiency judgment" (Michael Schill 1991, p. 494). the lender obtains the difference between the home's foreclosed value and the unpaid debt, which puts the homeowner's supposedly safer assets at risk. Some states disallow this remedy—though usually only for first, not second mortgages—but even then the homeowner suffers relocation costs and a much poorer credit rating from a default. Second mortgages are a risky way to spread asset risk.

After a while, it occurred to me that my zoning-board insight applies to more than just land-use regulation. Concern about the vulnerability of their largest asset also explains why homeowners are more likely to participate in school board meetings, vote in local elections, and otherwise participate in community affairs. There is hard evidence that they do so. Denise DiPasquale and Edward Glaeser (1999) analyzed a national survey of citizen participation in local affairs. Even after controlling for other economic and demographic differences between homeowners and renters, they found that homeowners were more conscientious citizens and were more effective in providing community amenities.

The importance and vulnerability of their asset are not the only reasons that homeowners are more likely to be the major local political actors. Living in a home for a long time creates a personal attachment for which changes in the neighborhood and community are upsetting. Surveys indicate that long-term residence by both renters and homeowners is an important factor in community participation (Verba, Schlozman, and Brady 1995, p. 452). But length of residence does not always mean more protectiveness. Kent Portney (1991, p. 94) found that long-time residents were *less* opposed than newcomers to the establishment of proposed waste-disposal sites in Massachusetts. Less systematically, I have observed that people who have just moved into the neighborhood are often most concerned about proposed land-use changes. Maybe noneconomic attachments to neighborhoods and community are formed that quickly, but I suspect that the size of the down payment and the newly acquired mortgage make new homeowners especially watchful of local activity. The uninsurable-asset aspect of homeownership still seems like the key factor.

1.7 Homeowners Have Not Always Been Prime Movers

People to whom I have explained the homevoter hypothesis often agree with it but point out that it neglects the influence of other property owners in the political process, particularly development-minded interests such as employers, homebuilders, and chambers of commerce. Historically, it certainly seems better to focus on development interests. The "quiet enjoyment" of land was not what land-hungry pioneers were after in any stage of the settlement of the American continent.

In the phrases made famous by economic historian Willard Hurst (1956), American pioneers and settlers of the West eagerly transformed "land at rest" into "land at risk." The paths of the common law and constitutional protections of property were both turned to facilitate this widespread demand for development (Harry Scheiber 1989). Entrepreneurial landowners founded towns and cities, not just farms and ranches, to make money for themselves and their investors. Even the Puritans had mixed motives, as the title of John Frederick Martin's work suggests: *Profits in the Wilderness: Entrepreneurship and the Founding of New England Towns in the Seventeenth Century* (1991).

Town founding flowered after the American Revolution. Alan Taylor's fascinating *William Cooper's Town* (1995) is a fine-grained account of the profit-minded activities of the New York town founder who also sired the novelist James Fenimore Cooper. The senior Cooper laid out lots, provided financing for new farms, and established a public school, all with an eye toward attracting settlers in the 1790s.

Nor was Cooper's careful planning unique, as John Reps's (1965) wonderfully illustrated history of American town planning establishes with numerous examples. A 1790s reporter described an Ohio Valley town founder's strategy, which rivals the sophistication of modern e-commerce entrepreneurs:

> In order to found a colony at first, he holds out an encouragement to settlers by giving them a town lot and four acres of ground for nothing . . . This he does only to the first twelve or twenty that may offer themselves . . . In order to manage this concern to the best advantage, the [founding] landowners will always take care and not sell all their land contiguous to each other, but only at certain distances, so that the whole face of it may be cultivated, and the intermediate uncultivated parts consequently rise in value. (p. 358)

It is thus difficult to read the development of American towns in the 1800s as other than a competitive contest among development-minded landowners. Eric Monkkonen (1988; 1995) persuasively argues that the municipal corporation, an American invention of the early 1800s, was an important vehicle for economic development throughout the nineteenth century.

1.8 Commuters Vote Their Homes, Not Their Jobs

Why are things different now? One reason for the prodevelopment impetus of local politics in the 1800s is that most people lived and worked within the same jurisdiction, and often on the same parcel of property. Being a homeowner had little to distinguish itself in municipal affairs from being a farmer, a business owner, or an employee. It was not that the business owner was indifferent to his home. It was that his town was also his place of work, and he would make trade-offs to promote both his business interests and his interests as a homeowner. Commuting from one town to another on a daily basis was not feasible for most people. Until the late 1800s, even the biggest cities were walking cities, and the upper classes lived closest to work, in contrast to twentieth-century suburban patterns where the rich live in the far suburbs (LeRoy and Sonstelie 1983).

As I shall demonstrate further in Section 9.3, the local political framework changed to favor homeowners in the first three decades of the twentieth century. Intraurban commuting became widespread first with streetcars (Sam Bass Warner 1962) and soon after with buses and automobiles. Urban homeownership also increased considerably in the same period.

Commuting and homeownership created a new urban politics. Where people worked and where they resided were no longer the same, and their political loyalties became divided. The growth of homeownership and owners' demand for protection of their assets from the threat of commercial intrusions brought zoning into being in the 1910s and 1920s (Section 9.4). The further expansion of the voting franchise, particularly women's suffrage, and impatience with big-city political machines brought control of politics ever closer to the voters.

1.9 Big Cities and Developer-Elites Are Lesser Players

The homevoter is a twentieth-century political phenomenon whose importance has been hidden from most scholars by their fixation with the machinations of big-city politics. Influential books such as Paul Peterson's *City Limits* (1981) have delved into the politics of large places. Peterson's outlook is similar in many ways to mine, especially his views that cities compete with one another in an economic context. He also notes, as I do, that cities are different from states in that "urban politics is above all the politics of land use" (p. 25). But Peterson arrived at pessimistic conclusions about cities' ability to solve their own problems. As a result, he proposed some extraordinarily centralizing reforms, such as fiscal equalization by the federal government (p. 219).

Peterson's pessimism arose, I suspect, because of his focus on the largest municipalities. He was writing in the shadow of New York City's brush with bankruptcy in the 1970s, when all large cities seemed to be in trouble. Although I am inclined to the more optimistic view of Bernard Frieden and Lynn Sagalyn's *Downtown, Inc.* (1989), which revealed much entrepreneurial bootstrapping by such places, my main response is that big cities by themselves are not all that important anymore.

Political scientists have begun to recognize that urban issues require an understanding of the political economy of the suburbs, in which more than half the American population now resides (Danielson and Lewis 1996; Mark Schneider 1989). Only about a quarter of the U.S. population lives in a municipality with more than 100,000 people (Monkkonen 1995, p. 3). The fraction peaked in 1930 at about 30 percent. As I will argue in Section 4.13, smaller size usually means that homeowners get their own way.

In the places where most people live—suburbs, towns, and small cities—homeowners have become the dominant political force. This trend was accelerated by the U.S. Supreme Court's 1960s reapportionment decisions, which held that state legislatures had to be apportioned on the one-person, one-vote rule. Although the classic malapportionment was the overrepresented rural county, the decisions actually helped the suburbs gain representation at the expense of both central cities and rural areas (James Reichley 1970, p. 172; Danielson and Lewis 1996, p. 206).

Sociologists have suggested that cities and suburbs can be characterized as "growth machines," to use the term first deployed by Harvey Molotch (1976). Prodevelopment elites are said to be barely ruffled by growth controls and other municipal manifestations of homeowners' muscle (Warner and Molotch 1995). Although I think their claim that growth controls do not raise housing prices is contradicted by the evidence (Fischel 1990), I must concede that developers and their allies are active players in municipal affairs even in smaller cities.

My thesis, however, is not that developers are powerless. They do have influence in local affairs. But in the smaller jurisdictions in which most of the population and developable land are located, theirs is the influence of supplicants and salesmen. They need to get the approval of local officials—officials responsive to voters whose local economic stake is in the value of their homes and only indirectly in the value of new development. Even in larger cities, where developers have more traditionally had special influence, the establishment of strong neighborhood associations makes developers dance to the tune of local homeowners (Berry, Portney, and Thomson 1993, p. 287).

Nor can developers sweep away opponents with the aid of the courts. Builders' "right to develop" in the teeth of opposition from nearby homeowners has been tenuous, at least since the U.S. Supreme Court put its seal of approval on zoning in Euclid v. Ambler (1926). Other judicial doctrines that might protect developers have been anesthetized for almost as long (Robert Ellickson 1977). The resurgent "regulatory takings" doctrine offers what I think is a useful tool to discipline local zoning's excesses (Fischel 1995). I must concede, however, that there is little evidence that state courts have yet grasped this possibility. As a result, most developers know that it is by the sufferance of the homevoters that they get their projects approved. The nearby homeowners must be persuaded that the development does not leave them worse off, and the homeowning taxpayers must likewise be satisfied with the fiscal impact.

1.10 Conclusion: Doing Good and Doing Well

Thomas S. Stribling's novel *The Unfinished Cathedral* (1934) was set in Florence, Alabama, in the early 1930s. The scenario, location, and timing correspond to the facts of the infamous incident in Scottsboro, Alabama. Its opening chapters describe a lynching in the works. Six black youths were rousted from a freight train on which they had stolen a ride. They were accused of raping two white women, who had also been nonpaying guests of the railroad.

As the news spreads of the alleged rapes and the arrest of the youths, a lynch mob descends on the town. They surround the jail and demand that the boys be given up to them. Just as the mob seems ready to overwhelm the law, a group of local Rotarians marches out from a nearby building and stands between the mob and the jail. Their leader persuades the mob to disperse.

Rotarians? No, the local Rotary Club had not suddenly become an agent of the NAACP. Its entirely white membership included the owners of most of the developable property in the town. Florence (like Scottsboro) is on the Tennessee River, and the Tennessee Valley Authority's dams were being built at the time. Property values were rising near dam sites as land speculators from the North were expected to buy up prime locations for new industry and related development. The Florence Rotarians believed that a lynching, however well justified in their minds, would result in bad press for Florence in northern newspapers. Any perception that the city was a lawless place might, they feared, put an end to the ongoing property boom and leave them holding worthless assets. So they risked their lives in a daring and successful maneuver to stop the lynching. Concern about property values saved the lives of the accused boys.

Accounts of the real Scottsboro case, which was a national cause célèbre (the accused were convicted but later exonerated), do mention a lynch mob, but it was dispersed after the sheriff called in the National Guard, not the Rotary Club (James Goodman 1994, p. 6). Stribling's novel added the Rotarian twist to the story, but it was not a fanciful addition. In his highly regarded work *The Mind of the South*, historian Wilbur J. Cash indicated that lynchings declined in the 1920s and '30s as the Southern population gathered into towns whose material prosperity made them sensitive to "the frown of the world" (1941, p. 306). Stribling's fictional scenario was intended both to illustrate this fact and to deploy it as an indicator of attitudes in the small Southern city. (Both Cash and Stribling indicated that the lynch mobs were most often rural folk who, I would point out, had less to lose from the "frown of the world." Townspeople's fortunes were tied to local reputation; farmers' output was sold in anonymous markets.)

I originally intended to include Stribling's vignette as an indicator of the power of property to motivate men to organize for collective action and to respond to the opinions of the outside world. I think the story does that well enough, although Stribling neglected to say much about homeowners. But the story also raises a question about the merits of the motive around which I have organized this book. According to his literary biographer, Stribling's use of this example was intended to show the shallowness of the commitment of white Southern society to the rights of blacks even as the worst manifestations of oppression—mob violence—were declining (Edward Piacentino 1988, p. 103). His theory certainly sounds consistent with the rest of *The Unfinished Cathedral*, which takes Southern Babbittry unsparingly to task. Stribling would have preferred, I assume, to have written about a group of whites who stopped a lynching for more noble motives than to protect local property values, but that would not have been true to the world as he saw it.

In the present book, I am going to show how mercenary concern with property values, especially that of homeowners, motivates citizens to organize and make personal sacrifices for such things as public schools and amenable environments. But I want to dilute the seeming cynicism of that proposition. I don't mean to say that people who are concerned about these good things act solely because of how it affects their property values. Nor do I mean that if good schools and other public amenities did not map into higher home values that they would not be good things (though I guess I would take a second look at them in that case). What I am arguing as a normative matter is that the world will get more of these good things if the motive to do good is lined up with the motive to do well.

2
Local Government's Corporate Form

THIS CHAPTER casts local governments in their corporate role and contrasts them to business corporations. Most economists view corporations exclusively as vehicles for conducting private businesses. Even those who write about nonprofits neglect the municipal corporation. Yet for more than a century, the laws of municipal and business corporations ran in parallel, and many state constitutions still treat them under the same section.

I submit that local governments can be better understood if we examine them with the same economic lens with which business corporations are studied. The crucial difference is that the principal "shareholders" of most municipal corporations, homeowners, cannot diversify their assets like the shareholders of most business corporations do. Having all their assets in one location makes homeowners painfully attentive to the affairs of their municipality. They are not content to sit back like diversified shareholders of business corporations and let the market take care of corporate affairs. Local politics is thus driven by real-estate economics.

An approximate measure of a sector's importance to the economy is employment. In 1999, total civilian employment in the United States was about 135 million, of which 20.2 million (15 percent) worked for a government. Of this 20.2 million, 13 percent worked for the federal government (not counting uniformed military personnel), 24 percent for state governments, and 63 percent for local governments, which include school districts (Joint Economic Committee 2000).

This overstates the importance of local governments because state governments provide much of the revenue and thus much of the direction for local government employees. The national government also sets much of the agenda for both states and localities and provides full-time employment for many people through contracts. Nonetheless, civilians who get paychecks from local governments outnumber state and federal employees by a wide margin. The pyramid is an apt metaphor for federalism: The national government is at the top and commands the most attention, but the local-government base is both broader and closest to the people.

2.1 A Lexicon of Local Government Law

The major concerns in this book are with municipalities and school districts, but they operate in a legal framework that varies from state to state. Homevoters are most effective in units of local governments that are relatively small, regardless of their official designation as city, town, school district, or county. Though I will use "local government" and "municipality" as generic terms, understanding the official nomenclature can help readers to translate these ideas to real institutions. (My generalizations are distilled from publications by the U.S. Advisory Commission on Intergovernmental Relations [ACIR 1992; 1993] and Gillette and Baker [1999].)

Counties blanket the entire land area of the United States, and number 3,043. (They are called "parishes" in Louisiana and "boroughs" in Alaska.) Counties originated as administrative units of state governments, and they are the basis for regional courts and the legal-records system in almost all states. They are created solely by the state legislature, but in the twentieth century many states have allowed counties to acquire "home rule" charters and thus serve as large-area municipalities in some urban areas. County boundaries rarely change, and then only by special acts of the state legislature.

Unincorporated areas: About a third of the U.S. land area, mostly in mountainous and arid areas of the West, is owned by the federal government and is not subject to state and local taxes and regulations. Almost nobody lives in these places year-round. A large amount of the remaining, nonfederal land is still unincorporated. Most of this extra-municipal territory, which contains about a fifth of the U.S. population, is in states west of the Mississippi and south of the Ohio rivers. In these states it is possible to live in a densely populated suburb—usually near an incorporated central city—in an unincorporated area. In these places, the urban services of firefighters and police officers—the latter often nostalgically called "sheriff's deputies"—are provided by the county.

One of the complications of county governance of unincorporated areas is that its officials are elected by all county residents, including those of incorporated and unincorporated areas. Although residents of the unincorporated areas may have the most interest in county decisions, they cannot be allotted more than their per capita share of votes in county elections. Some states formerly gave rural districts disproportionate representation in county elections, but this was held to be unconstitutional by the U.S. Supreme Court in Avery v. Midland County (1967).

Special districts are one means of matching residents' voting, taxes, and services in unincorporated areas (Nancy Burns 1994). Water and sewer districts are often set up by the original developers of the area. Special districts typically have limited municipal powers of taxation to accomplish specific ends, though in arid areas the "limited power" over water may be crucial. Irrigation districts are one of the few local governments that are sufficiently limited in scope that the U.S. Supreme Court is willing to exempt them from the *Avery* rule of one resident, one vote. Salyer Land Co. v. Tulare Lake Basin Water Storage District (1973) let stand a California arrangement that apportioned votes by value of land holdings.

Aside from their role in providing services in unincorporated areas, special districts are often used to sidestep state-constitutional constraints on local government fiscal powers. If the city's constitutional borrowing limit has been reached, its elected officials may ask the legislature to establish a special district to undertake, say, airport development. Such districts are the fastest growing category of local governments in urban areas. Yet they are not especially important for my story. The interesting aspect of local government in the United States is its ability to do things independently of the will of its creator, the state. Most special districts are closely bound by state law in purpose and scope, and their functioning is, with some justice, ignored by most voters unless something goes badly awry in them.

Municipalities: Although most are called cities, smaller units with the same powers may be called boroughs or villages in some states. (Towns and townships are described in the next section, where I argue that many should be counted as municipalities.) Incorporation of municipalities is largely the product of bottom-up government. In most states, local residents and landowners form them by a process that is specified by state constitutions and enabling legislation. The usual rules require a minimum population, a contiguous area, and an election of the people in the area to approve the incorporation. (I describe in more detail the fairly typical procedures of Washington State in Section 10.4.) Many states with extensive unincorporated areas now require higher-government review of the reasonableness of incorporation and the viability of the proposed city (ACIR 1992).

School districts are a hybrid of municipality and special district in most states. They can tax and spend but do not have general regulatory authority. Most are corporate in the sense that they are "legal persons" in the eyes of the law. They numbered 14,556 in 1992. Consolidation of rural school districts has reduced their aggregate numbers, but they are still thick on the ground in most urban areas.

Most school boards are chosen in direct elections and are independent of municipal government. (Those that are not are designated "dependent" districts in U.S. Census nomenclature.) The authority of school boards is more circumscribed by state law than that of municipalities. I describe in Chapter 5 the centralization of public schools that has emerged from the school-finance reform movement that began in the 1970s. In a growing number of states, school districts are treated like counties once were, as mere administrative units of the state.

School-district boundaries are often different from those of municipalities, especially outside of the Northeast. A single district may encompass several small municipalities and some unincorporated area. Very small cities may have an independent elementary school district but join with others in providing a high school. Occasionally a large city has two or more school districts. It is rare, however, for school districts to have no perceptible overlap with municipalities. Despite their separate origins and governance, school districts and general-purpose municipalities are closely identified with one another. A municipality that is touting its charms usually mentions that it has "good schools."

2.2 Twenty-Five Thousand Municipal Corporations

Corporations: City governance is more like that of business corporations than it is like state government. Municipalities are corporate in the sense that they are recognized as legal persons. Their corporate nature permits them to make contracts and own property, and, on the flip side of those legal benefits, be liable for tortious behavior and breach of contract. Like business corporations, a municipality's continued existence is not dependent on the inclusion of any named resident or official. In this sense, they are "immortal," to use the term that always seems so scary when applied to business corporations. Like businesses, the municipalities in which most Americans live have the power to choose and reorganize their governing arrangements, and they often do so by amending their corporate charters (Renner and DeSantis 1993).

Government organization: Two off-the-shelf organizational types dominate the basic form of municipal government. The older form is an elected mayor and city council, with the council often elected by submunicipal districts called wards. The mayor-council form looks most similar to state government, with its independently elected governor and a legislature selected from geographic districts. (The commission form of municipal government, which combines executive and legislative powers in elected officials, has become rare with the professionalization of municipal management.)

The council-manager form of city government dates from about 1910. Voters in wards or in citywide elections select a city council, which then hires a professional manager as the city executive. The council-manager government was promoted by Richard S. Childs, a tireless reformer who worked through the National Municipal League. Childs explicitly sought to make local government follow the model of business corporations, analogizing the elected council to the board of directors and the hired manager to the chief executive officer (John East 1965, pp. 36, 67). Medium-sized municipalities most often choose the council-manager arrangement, and by the 1990s it had become the dominant form of organization among all urban municipalities (Renner and DeSantis 1998, p. 32). School districts typically have a similar structure, in that elected school boards hire a district superintendent who acts as chief executive officer.

Childs's managerial movement also influenced cities that have retained the old mayor-council organization. In many of them, the division of authority between the mayor and the council is now much less distinct. Modern mayors often participate in city councils in ways that a governor never would with the state legislature, and a third of mayor-council cities also have a professional, nonelective city administrator, just like council-manager cities (Renner and DeSantis 1993, p. 61).

Public and private governments: Municipalities are unlike most business corporations in that they have the power to tax, the ability to impose regulations within their territory ("the police power"), and the power to take property by eminent domain. To my mind, the telltales for general government powers are that the locality can vary its own revenues and choose its own zoning laws. These government powers have analogs in private corporations, particularly condominium and residential community associations. Their "C, C, and R's" (covenants, conditions, and restrictions) establish rules by which owners and occupants can be regulated and assessed for improvements.

Much has been made recently of these "private governments" as replacements for municipalities (Robert Dilger 1992). Although private governments are growing rapidly, they show little sign of actually displacing established municipalities. Private associations sometimes perform municipal services for themselves, for which they may negotiate a rebate from the municipality, but their regulatory and "taxation" powers are limited to those contractually agreed upon in advance. The crucial difference between them and municipal corporations is that the latter contain at least some involuntary members, since their formation requires less than unanimous consent of those who fall within their territory (Robert Ellickson 1982). In contrast, no parcel of real estate within a private community association can be included without the consent of its owners at the time the association was formed.

Towns and townships: Above the Mason-Dixon line and in the states carved from the original Northwest Territories, most counties have subunits called towns and townships. In New England, where towns were the original units of settlement, towns almost always have full municipal powers. Indeed, the term "municipal corporation" was invented by Massachusetts judges in the early 1800s to distinguish New England towns from English "borough corporations," a few of which had been established in America during the colonial period (Joan Williams 1985). As New Englanders moved west, they sowed the democratic ideals of the town in their settlements (Jon Teaford 1975), though the mass participation of the "town meeting" was mostly displaced by representative government.

Townships and towns in New York, New Jersey, and Pennsylvania also have municipal powers, although it is still possible in these states to form a separate municipality such as a borough or city within the territory of the township. (Such subdivision is much rarer in New England.) Townships in Ohio, Michigan, and Wisconsin can have general government powers, but they are often shared with the county. In other U.S. regions where townships exist, they are usually no more than county administrative units.

Old-world contrast: Although American local government traditions borrowed from the English church parish and, to a lesser extent, the "borough corporation," the traditions parted soon after the American Revolution (Hendrik Hartog 1983). The British Municipal Corporations Act of 1835 greatly centralized the chartering of local government (Hardy Wickwar 1970, p. 22). This step was regarded as a liberalization measure in that it undermined the medieval privileges of the English borough corporation. Adam Smith, for one, had criticized the limitations on trade imposed by such corporations in *The Wealth of Nations* (1776 [1937, p. 124]). Smith conceded that the boroughs had originally been a liberalizing force in that they undermined the power of the landed lords (p. 376), but their use as a counterweight to manorialism had long since passed. To undermine these remnants of privilege, the 1835 act put Parliament in charge of local charters, and British cities have lacked ever since the degree of self-governance that those of America have.

In Europe, city creation and governance has long been a top-down matter. As Tocqueville observed (perhaps for rhetorical effect) in *Democracy in America* (1835, vol. 1, chap. 2), "The political existence of the majority of the nations of Europe commenced in the superior ranks of society and was gradually and imperfectly communicated to the different members of the social body. In America, on the contrary, it may be said that the township was organized before the county, the county before the state, the state before the union."

Number of municipal corporations: The U.S. Census unfortunately treats all American townships as if they had no general municipal powers. For this reason, the ACIR (1993) counts 19,296 "cities." This is too low a count of local governments whose authority is general, as opposed to limited-authority special districts and independent school districts. I have attempted to remedy this deficit by adding the Census count of cities to a count of townships in states where they have general taxing and regulatory authority. The municipal corporations (exclusive of independent school districts) of relevance to this book number about 25,000.

2.3 Cities Can Grow by Annexation and Consolidation

Existing cities add to their territory, especially in the West, by annexation of unincorporated territory and, much less often, by consolidation with another municipality. There is a great deal of land for the expansion of existing cities or the establishment of new ones. Although we are an urban nation, the vast majority of our land is rural, including most of the land area within metropolitan statistical areas, the Census Bureau's county-based method of tracking urban activity. Even under a generous definition of "built-up" area, no more than 4 percent of the contiguous (non-Alaskan) U.S. land area is urban or built up (Fischel 1982; Vesterby and Heimlich 1991).

For the most part, annexation must be desired by voters in both the preexisting municipality and the residents or property owners of the area to be annexed. Although some states still allow unilateral annexation (that is, by the will of the city alone), the trend is toward mutual consent. Whose vote counts as consent can vary, and the "one-person, one-vote" rule is again allowed some variation at the local level. Many states allow a city to annex unincorporated territory if owners of 60 percent (to give a typical figure) of the property value in the proposed territory petition the city.

A city can also grow by consolidation with an adjacent, already incorporated municipality. This, too, must usually be mutual, so that residents—not, in this case, property owners—of both places must approve. Some writers use the term annexation to include consolidation, but the two are legally distinct. Consolidation involves more legalisms than annexation because one unit of government is dissolved and its corporate assets and liabilities must be transferred to the other. A central city that is surrounded by other incorporated municipalities can usually expand its territory only by consolidation. This usually means that the land area of such cities is not likely to change (Epple and Romer 1989).

Some consolidations have merged a central city with its surrounding county, which may have previously consisted of small municipalities and unincorporated territory. These are often engineered by the state legislature rather than being entirely consensual. Nineteenth-century examples of these hybrids of consolidation and annexation over county areas are New York, Philadelphia, and San Francisco. Post-1950 examples are Indianapolis, Jacksonville, and Nashville. Once thought to be the wave of the metropolitan future, city-county consolidation is now rare (Jon Teaford 1997).

Once established, municipalities hardly ever go out of business except by consolidation with an adjacent city. In contrast to business corporations, municipal corporations seldom go bankrupt, and when they do, the restructuring rules are far more gentle (McConnell and Picker 1993). This should hardly be surprising, given that the city's shareholders live within its borders and consume most of its services.

2.4 Legally Circumscribed but Politically Powerful

The rules for the behavior of municipal corporations have long been more circumscribed by the state than those for private corporations have been. Local governments are said by all legal commentators to be "creatures of the state." As such, their boundaries, powers, and even their very existence can be altered without consent or compensation by the instrument of their creator, the state legislature or the state constitution. The leading case for the "creature" rule is Hunter v. City of Pittsburgh (1907), in which the U.S. Supreme Court declined to intervene on behalf of taxpayers disgruntled by the forcible consolidation of their former city with Pittsburgh.

The contrary rule for business corporations is said to have arisen from Dartmouth College v. Woodward (1819), in which the U.S. Supreme Court prohibited state legislatures from changing the charters of colleges and other private corporations after they had been issued. Chief Justice John Marshall mentioned specifically that municipalities and other "public" corporations were not similarly protected by the contract clause from ex post legislative change. Gerald Frug (1980, p. 1100) takes this aspect of the decision as a foundation for his thesis that municipal corporations are powerless compared to business corporations and state governments.

The distinction is less stark than it sounds, though. The *Dartmouth College* opinion also said that state legislatures could, at the time they issued private corporate charters, reserve the right to amend them in the future, and many states did exactly that (Merrick Dodd 1954, p. 29). As I shall argue in Section 2.8, the legal limits on municipalities seem more like self-binding restraints than judicial shackles.

The subordinate role of municipalities before the law also appears in the rule of statutory construction called Dillon's Rule. Articulated by the influential judge and treatise author John F. Dillon in 1871, it holds that (as quoted in Gillette and Baker 1999, pp. 275–276):

> A municipal corporation possesses and can exercise the following powers, and no others: First, those granted in express words; second, those necessarily or fairly implied in or incident to the powers granted; third, those essential to the accomplishment of the declared objects and purposes of the corporation,—not simply convenient, but indispensable. Any fair, reasonable, substantial doubt concerning the existence of power is resolved by the courts against the corporation, and the power is denied.

There is more, but the reader surely gets the picture of Dillon as Dutch uncle, giving something with one hand and then doing his best to restrict its enjoyment with the other.

Dillon's Rule remains the rhetorical focus of modern debate about the legal powers of local government, but its practical effect has been undermined by municipal innovations. Since Dillon set out the last edition of his famous treatise in 1911, most states have set up home rule or charter cities whose powers are broader and less subject to judicial sniping than Dillon thought wise (Neil Littlefield 1962). Not all cities have home-rule charters, but the movement by itself telegraphed to judges and legislators that Dillon's constricted view of municipal functions had become outmoded. And Dillon never anticipated zoning, an innovation of the 1910s and 1920s that revolutionized local governments by allowing them to control their future development.

A more general rule also constrained local governments. The "public purpose" principle holds that municipalities (as well as state governments) may not spend their revenue solely for the benefit of private individuals. It is analogous to, but not the same as, the "public use" doctrine in eminent domain, which supposedly prevents governments from using eminent domain to transfer property from one private owner to another (Thomas Merrill 1986). While some have seen these doctrines as motivated by plutocratic opposition to the redistribution of wealth (Morton Horwitz 1982), they seem to be more than that.

Local governments themselves might seek such rules to assure prospective investors in a home or a business in the community that their assets will not be stripped from them by local changes in taxation or eminent domain (Eric Monkkonen 1995). In this respect, the public purpose doctrine is similar to the uniform tax-assessment principle (Richard Epstein 1985, chap. 18). Both require that the burdens and benefits of local government be shared according to a predictable formula. Although these doctrines have fuzzy boundaries, they do raise the cost of simple wealth transfers by requiring that they be made through the subsidization of public activities. As I will discuss in Section 6.5, this doctrine is most important in its effect on local school finance.

While Dillon's Rule and the "creature" theory seem to rein in the powers of American local government, forces besides home-rule provisions promote local autonomy. During the nineteenth century, many state constitutions were amended or rewritten to limit the ability of legislatures to tinker with local affairs (Charles Binney 1894). The provisions are typically described as requiring uniformity of laws among all classes of subjects, including locations, and banning local and special legislation that would benefit or burden only a single city. Among the interferences to be forestalled was the practice by some state legislatures of granting exclusive street-railroad franchises to favored enterprises in particular cities, much to the dismay of the city's residents.

State legislatures have found their way around these constraints by making narrow classes of cities. A state's three or four largest could all be in separate population-size classes on which the legislature could then impose "general" laws that affected only one. But as Gillette and Baker (1999, pp. 253–274) show, many courts still strike down state legislation that is narrowly tailored to fit a single city.

2.5 Risk Distinguishes Municipal from Business Corporations

In his influential book about American corporate history, Mark Roe summarizes the distinct governance of modern American business corporations as "distant shareholders, a board of directors that has historically deferred to the CEO, and powerful, centralized management" (1994, p. ix). Roe does not breathe a word about municipal corporations, though.

It is not difficult to see why. Private business corporations have far-flung and diverse stockholders who are nonetheless united by their desire to maximize the present value of the enterprise. Their shares are traded daily in stock markets. While business shareholders are often "rationally ignorant" of managerial quality, managers are induced to maximize profits by feedback from the stock market (Henry Manne 1965). Poor managerial performance results in threats of bankruptcy, takeovers, and job losses, and good performance is rewarded by stock options and pay bonuses. These disciplines are nearly absent in municipal markets.

I submit that municipal corporations are different mainly because of the economic position of their shareholders. Homeowners are the primary stockholders of municipal corporations. Like business stockholders, the value of their assets (their homes) goes up and down with the efficiency by which municipal services are selected and delivered. The crucial difference, however, is that homeowners bear an inordinate amount of risk in owning their homes. They cannot diversify it, as stockholders of business corporations can, nor can they insure it by selling some of the risk to someone else, except for such losses as occur by fire or theft. As I argued in the previous chapter, the key to understanding municipal corporations, in contrast to business corporations, is that homeowners are stuck with a large, indivisible asset whose value they cannot insure.

This large asset makes homeowners anything but distant shareholders. They elect municipal "boards of directors" who closely monitor municipal managers. Although state and national government managers may resemble William Niskanen's (1971) independent bureaucrats, local government managers have far less power than their business counterparts. Municipal managers do not need the same punishments and rewards as those of businesses because the stockholders of municipalities consume most of the managerial product.

Homeowners and their elected officials can monitor managerial performance themselves, since they see it every day. If the roads are not maintained, it is usually clear to local voters. And because poor municipal service adversely affects the value of their homes, homeowners have strong reasons to bring it to the attention of their elected officials and municipal managers. Stockholders of far-flung businesses usually know little about what their managers do or how well they do it. If a manager allows her employees to produce an inferior product, few stockholders know about it directly. Most spend little time worrying about such shirking, though, since they have diversified portfolios and because stock-market specialists discipline inefficient businesses by selling or refusing to buy them.

2.6 Municipalities Never Allocated Votes by Share

The most obvious difference between stockholders of municipalities—the homevoters—and those of businesses is that municipal voters never get more than one vote per resident. Almost all business corporations choose to allocate voting rights by shares, so that someone who holds ten shares has nine more votes than someone with one share. Municipalities allocate votes so that each resident has the same number—one—regardless of how large or how valuable his or her property is. This is different even from the municipality's closest private analog, the residential community association, which usually chooses to allocate voting rights for collective decisions along the lines of unit ownership, though sometimes by unit size or value (Ellickson and Been 2000, p. 703; Barzel and Sass 1990). They almost never enfranchise tenants, and, where unit ownership is the basis of voting, always permit an owner of multiple units to have multiple votes.

The municipal corporation's voting cannot be accounted for by a top-down scenario, in which local-government democracy supposedly evolved by imitating the democratic trends of the state and national governments. For much of the nineteenth century, local governments distributed their voting rights more widely than the state (Adrian and Griffith 1976, p. 114). If priority established causality, the democratization of state governments flowed from local models.

Cities once excluded tenants from voting, though many of the larger American cities remedied that on their own by the mid-1800s (Mary Ryan 1997). The focus on property qualifications for voting, however, has obscured an important point. General-purpose municipalities never granted voting power to residents in proportion to their property holdings. The rule has always been *no more than* one vote per resident.

Why municipalities never adopted share voting is not clear. State constitutions seem not to have been the barrier, and, if they were, they could have been modified to allow share voting in municipalities had there been much demand for it. The proprietors of development companies that established New England towns in the seventeenth century had adopted the share-voting model, so it cannot be that the form was unfamiliar to inhabitants who then formed town government (John Martin 1991, p. 183). The federal courts did not address the issue until 1967, when the U.S. Supreme Court made one vote per resident the national rule for municipalities in Avery v. Midland County. Yet I have not found a single instance of municipal share voting in any of the histories of American local government that I consulted.

Proving a negative is always dicey, but I found no evidence of it in the American municipal histories of Charles Adrian and Ernest Griffith (1976), Hendrik Hartog (1983), Eric Monkkonen (1988; 1995), Mary Ryan (1997), or Jon Teaford (1975; 1979). The closest thing to an exception was Teaford's passing remark about New York City in the early 1800s, where reformers complained that those who owned property in several wards could vote in each of them (1973, p. 62). But even in that hidebound city, with its limited corporate voting membership, there is no evidence that the size or value of holdings (as opposed to its location in different wards) entitled anyone to more than a single vote (Hartog 1983). Municipal corporations are among America's most persistently democratic institutions, and the puzzle is why they never imitated their business-corporate cousins.

2.7 Did Location Risks Keep Municipal Voting Democratic?

One reason share voting might not have taken hold in municipalities is that owners of *smaller* properties might have worried that owners of larger properties would impose disproportionate burdens on them. Owners of larger properties might have formed an oligarchy that would use taxation and regulation to transfer resources from the smallholders to themselves. Indeed, the Jacksonian Democrats of the nineteenth century feared that a powerful federal government would enable the rich to oppress the poor, given the greater political influence at the national level by moneyed interests (Paul Carrington 1997).

This sounds odd to modern ears. We normally think of the risk of "majoritarian oppression" as flowing from the many owners of smaller assets using their democratic voting powers to redistribute wealth held by only a few largeholders. But majoritarianism does not disappear if votes are allocated by the value of one's holdings. In that case, the largeholders might combine to redistribute wealth from smallholders, or at least neglect the smallholders' interests in governing the corporation.

Dollar-based majoritarianism was in fact an anxiety of small shareholders of early American *business* corporations (Colleen Dunlavy 1999; Pauline Maier 1993). For this reason, nineteenth-century business corporations did not immediately adopt the share-voting principle. Instead, they often voted by shareholder (like municipalities) or adopted hybrid voting schemes that gave more votes to large shareholders, but put a ceiling on how many votes any single shareholder could have. Only by the last quarter of the 1800s did share voting become the dominant norm for businesses.

Why didn't municipal corporations go down the same road toward share voting? One possible reason is that smallholders in municipalities had no means of diversifying their risks. Whether they owned homesteads or business property, residents of municipalities typically had all or a large fraction of their assets in one place. Thus if the largeholders were going to oppress them, as they might under share voting, the smallholders just had to endure it.

The risk of this "other majoritarianism" applied initially for business corporations as well, which is why many did not embrace share voting right away (Dunlavy 1999). People who invested in business corporations could not easily purchase a variety of unrelated stocks to diversify risk, and smallholders would be understandably wary of share voting. As R. C. Michie (1987, p. 171) points out, "For much of the first half of the nineteenth century the U.S. stock exchanges that existed were little more than local markets." Even the largest of them, the New York Stock Exchange, in 1820 listed only thirty securities, of which twenty-eight were local enterprises.

I suspect that smallholders' anxiety began to dissipate as business corporations became more numerous and stock markets developed over the course of the nineteenth century. Railroad investment and the invention of the telegraph in 1845 were major factors in both trends. With an active stock market in fractional shares of business, smallholders in business corporations could more easily diversify their risks, including the risk of majoritarian oppression. Diversification and the related principle of share liquidity remain the main protection of smallholders in business corporations from majoritarian "freeze-outs" of minority shareholders from value-enhancing transactions (Easterbrook and Fischel 1991, p. 119).

Municipal stockholders, however, never obtained similar opportunities for diversification. Their assets continued to be concentrated within a single corporation simply because it is too costly to live or run a business in more than one place. Owners of commercial property can now diversify to some extent among municipalities by means of corporate ownership or, more recently, real estate investment trusts. Almost all homeowners, in contrast, are stuck with all their holdings in a single municipality. Thus it makes some economic sense for homeowners to resist share voting in municipal affairs, even if local governments had the latitude to call their own shots on this matter. The long and continuous history of one-resident, one-vote in municipalities may owe less to democratic ideals or constitutional rules than to the risk aversion of local property owners and, especially in this century, homeowners.

2.8 Municipal Corporations Sought Constraints

The downside of democratic voting within municipal corporations was the risk that largeholders might be exploited by the smallholders. Nineteenth-century cities had corporate powers that could bind all residents to contracts with outsiders. This made it possible for smallholders or, where they could vote, tenants to transfer wealth within the municipality. The hazard was that the municipality would agree by majority vote to undertake a risky venture, such as subsidizing a private railroad, to promote local development. The gains and losses of such risks, however, were not uniformly distributed. Tenants might want the better jobs, and small businesses might want the greater trade, but most of the taxes would be paid by larger property owners. Indeed, if the deal went sour, the property owners might find that they were personally liable for the city's debts and lose their own property in a sheriff's sale (Joan Williams 1986).

The aforementioned "creature of the state" view and Dillon's Rule, as well as the public / private distinction, can be thought of as attempts to curtail these excesses. By limiting the enterprise functions of local government and the ways in which it could exercise its powers, legal and constitutional constraints kept municipal majorities from going overboard in their economic enthusiasms. The state-imposed constraints are a logical means by which cities can conduct a more limited but crucial set of public business in a democratic setting. Because they could not use the share-voting arrangements that forestall largeholder exploitation in business corporations, municipal corporations had to resort to a set of external constraints.

Most modern commentators regard Dillon's Rule and related constraints as "top-down" rules that state judges and state legislatures imposed on their unruly children, the local governments. Yet there is a paradox in this view. The heyday of Dillon's Rule—roughly 1870 to 1910—corresponded to the period of the greatest power of local government. Local spending outstripped that of both the state and the national government during that era (John Wallis 2000; Wallace Oates 1999). Why would the same era produce the apotheosis of Dillon's Rule?

Eric Monkkonen (1988, p. 129; 1995, p. 15) has suggested an interesting explanation. His investigations show that local governments themselves sought these constraints. The Illinois Constitution of 1870, which was a landmark in embodying Dillon-like provisions to limit local government, was heavily influenced by representatives of local governments. They in effect complained that they had too much power.

Outsiders were unwilling to invest in local projects if the investors' property could later be subject to crushing taxes or municipal debts that they did not agree to incur. An unrestrained ability to tax and incur debt was harmful to the interests of all residents who sought economic development, but they could not unilaterally forswear it. So they sought (or at least acceded to) legislation, constitutional changes, and court rulings to limit what they could do. Having the higher sovereign—the state—constrain municipal sovereignty assured investors that local majorities would not later go after their assets. Local government wanted to tie its hands so as to attract residents and business that would otherwise be wary of majoritarian exploitation after they had committed to locate there. (Similar rationales for the rise of independent institutions that enriched the sovereign by restraining its powers are offered by Yoram Barzel [1997] and North and Weingast [1989].)

This is not to say that the constitutional restraints have overcome the problems that democratic voting presents for local governments. Municipalities in the early 1900s found that they had to undertake their own gas works because private investors could not be assured that their assets would be secure from unreasonable regulation (Werner Troesken 1997). For private companies to get past this risk, states had to preempt local regulation with statewide boards, which better protected gas company interests. Modern California municipal water companies appear to have underpriced (and thus overused) domestic water in order to spread the wealth among homeowners (Christopher Timmins 1999). Municipally owned electric companies also tend to underprice their output and thus redistribute wealth from the larger taxpayers who subsidize it (Sam Peltzman 1971). These examples demonstrate the rationality of rules that attempt to restrict municipal enterprise to a relatively narrow category.

Historians besides Monkkonen have pointed out that state legislatures have always been highly attentive to the demands of local governments (Burns and Gamm 1997). And small wonder. State legislatures have always been locally elected. At-large voting at the state level is usually limited to candidates for governor and other executive positions. The proportionate voting methods of Europe, in which the party winning, say, 25 percent of the vote gets 25 percent of the legislative seats, has never taken hold in America. Older state constitutions went out of their way to guarantee representation by city, towns, and county. Even after Reynolds v. Sims (1964) ruled that state legislatures had to be apportioned by population rather than geography, voting districts are usually formed along local government boundaries. It can formally be said that local governments are creatures of the state, but as a political matter, states are more often creatures of the local governments.

2.9 Why Do Private Governments Vote by Share?

The obvious counter to my explanation for municipal corporate voting is the governance structures of condominiums and similar residential community associations. Their votes are normally allocated more like business corporations (most typically, one dwelling unit, one vote), yet these are the very private corporations that most resemble local governments (Robert Ellickson 1982). Private governance seems to run counter to my suggestion that democratic voting in local government could be an evolutionary winner, not simply something imposed by states and courts.

When looked at more closely, however, condominium governance does not just allocate votes by unit ownership (analogous to share voting). The same governance rules also specify rules for assessments (taxes) and supermajority voting rules that usually forestall opportunistic transfers by the big owners against the small (Barzel and Sass 1990; Ellickson and Been 2000, pp. 690–721). Condominium rules don't just protect the few-but-rich from the many-but-poor. The network of governance works both ways to protect both the large and the small investor.

The reason such elaborate rules can be used in residential community associations is that they deal with a more limited and foreseeable set of issues than municipalities. Private community associations do not control much undeveloped land. Indeed, during the development process, the developer is careful to retain a majority of voting shares, lest she find her early buyers adopting rules that frustrate her plans (Uriel Reichman 1976). Rules for private community associations seldom contemplate major changes in land use. Such entities do not educate children or put people in jail. In such a circumscribed setting, the optimal governance structure is probably different from the ideal for municipal corporations, which have plenary powers to tax, take property, spend money, and regulate behavior. To put it another way, the municipal corporation controls a larger fraction of residents' assets—their life and liberty as well as their real property—and so allocating votes on the basis of real-property ownership is less appropriate.

Good point, my libertarian friends say. Why not run with it? Some advocate the replacement of existing municipal corporations by consensual, private community associations (George Liebmann 2000; Robert Nelson 1999). This would limit the government's ability to tax, take property, and spend money.

Aside from the holdout problem of getting landowners to join an association, which is especially acute when the holdout remains as an immovable neighbor, privatizing municipalities would create a governmental vacuum that would necessarily be occupied by higher units of government. Private governments lack police power, taxing power, and eminent domain. Such powers would then be the exclusive domain of the state government or its administrative units, typically the county. A program to privatize local government risks undermining an institution that has the ability to displace state powers. Turning local police into security guards necessarily increases the reach of the state police, since only they will be able to actually make arrests and prosecute criminals. Making local zoning into a purely contractual arrangement would invite the state to do the zoning, with effects that may be even less attractive to classical liberal thinking.

2.10 Conclusion: Corporate in Deed as Well as in Name

I have in this chapter expounded the idea that municipal corporations still deserve the name. The historical divergence of business and municipal corporations may be an example of evolutionary adaptation. Shareholders in business corporations did not need the protections of per capita voting once they could diversify their holdings among corporations in an efficient stock market. As a result, business governance may have evolved to promote firm value by share voting, letting the risks of plutocratic majoritarianism be handled mainly by the market. (I invoke "evolution" without a rigorous model of how it happens, hoping to stimulate more investigation.) I have not proved it in any formal sense, but owners of assets that are large and uninsurable, such as owner-occupied homes, seem less likely to accede to the one-dollar, one-vote method of decision making. The most important difference between municipal and business corporations, their voting structures, may be functional rather than historical.

Cleaving to the one-resident, one-vote method does create other problems for municipal corporations. The more conventional aspects of per capita majoritarianism surely explain the existence of judicial doctrines such as Dillon's Rule, the public purpose rule, and regulatory takings. I shall explore in Chapter 11 the ongoing need for such disciplines, particularly in the area of land-use regulation.

The homevoter hypothesis does not, however, hinge on any particular explanation for the democratic nature of local government. Undiversified assets and one vote per resident are facts of life, regardless of what one has to do with the other. The next chapter will present the "generic" model of local government that is now dominant among most economists and many political scientists. I will show its power but also its incompleteness as a persuasive explanation for local government behavior. The homevoter hypothesis attempts to complete the economic model of local government first started by a young economist named Charles Tiebout.

3

Capitalization, Zoning, and the Tiebout Hypothesis

THIS CHAPTER explores the essential ingredients of the Tiebout hypothesis, in which residents "vote with their feet" among communities to select their preferred bundle of public services. It is the economic superstructure for the homevoter hypothesis. The critical features examined here are the principle of capitalization, the effectiveness of zoning, and the realism of the Tiebout model's assumptions.

Capitalization is critical because if home values do not reflect conditions that local governments have control over, there is not much left to my hypothesis. Local voters need to feel the financial pain or gain of local decisions. I establish that capitalization does happen and that zoning is the necessary condition for it. I then move on to the Tiebout model to anchor this finding in the modern economic theory of local public economics.

Most economists will regard this sequence as backward. They would expect to see the Tiebout model presented first, the empirical evidence about capitalization next, and zoning as an afterthought or a footnote. My sequence, however, is deliberate. I want to take capitalization out of the shadows of public economics. Instead of being the derivative sideshow, capitalization should be the main event. Concern about home values is what motivates most local government actions. It explains why, if one wants to maintain what I see as the virtues of local government, reforms should not attempt to divorce the collection of taxes from the decisions to spend and regulate. Local tax collection is an inseparable part of the efficiency of local government.

3.1 Intermunicipal Tax Capitalization without Much Math

My favorite example of tax capitalization was provided by a homebuilder in Concord, New Hampshire. He had built homes all along a street that ran through a semirural part of Concord and into the next town, Bow. The builder wasn't very imaginative—he must have had two basic styles of houses—but he was productive, for there were several homes of the same style on both sides of the border. The reason this was useful to me was that Bow and Concord have quite different fiscal conditions. Concord, the state's capital and its third largest city (at about 36,000 population), has the full range of city expenditures but a large amount of untaxable, state-owned property. So taxes there are pretty high, even by New Hampshire's we-tax-only-property standards. Bow, on the other hand, is small (about 6,000) and has a large and eminently taxable electric-power generating plant within its borders. So its property taxes are rather low.

Bow is so small that it did not have its own high school. (In New Hampshire, as in other New England states, the school district is almost always coterminous with the town or city.) At the time of my study, Bow sent its children to Concord High School, with which it had an agreement to pay tuition based on the number of pupils sent. Thus Bow and Concord got pretty much the same public education, but had very different tax rates.

My interest in Bow and Concord was the result of my job as an expert witness in Claremont v. Governor (N.H. 1997), a school-finance case. The plaintiffs in *Claremont* were five old mill towns whose property tax base had declined with the migration of textile mills to the South in the 1950s, but much of whose population remained behind. All five towns had high property taxes—for schools and other town services—and relatively low family incomes.

All of the plaintiff districts received a disproportionate share of New Hampshire's state education aid because of their low family incomes, low property-tax values per pupil, and high tax rates. The amount of state aid, however, was modest by national standards. Through the 1990s, New Hampshire had no broadbased income or sales tax. Candidates for the governor's office who failed to pledge to veto any broad-based tax, in the unlikely event the legislature would pass one, were not taken seriously because they did not get elected.

The claim by the five towns in Claremont v. Governor was that their constitutional rights were being violated because of the high tax rates required to fund schools, which, the plaintiffs argued, was unfair to their taxpayers and their schoolchildren. My task as an expert for the state was to point out that at least one of these allegations, unfairness to taxpayers, was mooted by capitalization. If comparatively high tax rates cause housing prices to be lower in those towns, the economic burden of living in these towns and paying taxes there is equalized.

The Bow and Concord comparison, which state officials had come up with at my behest, was a graphic example of how the tax burden was equalized. I will report a stylized example in Figure 1, rather than reproduce the photographic pairs of houses and actual tax rates that we employed. It is worth keeping in mind that the houses, lots, and neighborhoods were practically identical; you could easily imagine homeowners walking into the wrong house on a foggy night.

The 5 percent tax rate applied to the Concord house, according to this example, is two and a half times larger than the 2 percent rate in Bow. But this does not imply any disparity in the ability of the homebuyer in Concord to pay for schools and other public services. Capital-

House in Bow	House in Concord
Tax rate: 2%	Tax rate: 5%
Price: $200,000	Price: $160,000
10% Mortgage: $20,000	10% Mortgage: $16,000
Property taxes: $4,000	Property taxes: $8,000
Total annually: $24,000	Total annually: $24,000

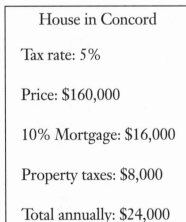

Figure 1 An example of tax capitalization in adjoining towns with identical homes

ization has taken care of that. The house in Bow costs $200,000. With a mortgage at an interest rate of 10 percent (the number is easy to compute), the annual mortgage payment on the Bow house is $20,000. The taxes on the Bow house are $4,000, so the total cost of owning a house in Bow is $24,000 a year.

The house in Concord cost the homebuyer $160,000. The 10 percent mortgage costs $16,000 annually, and the annual tax bill is $8,000, so the total cost of owning the Concord house is also $24,000. The total cost of owning the home in Concord is exactly the same as it is in Bow. Full capitalization equalizes the burdens of the different tax rates. The $40,000 reduction in the buying price left the owner in high-tax Concord with exactly enough money to pay the extra $4,000 in annual property taxes.

3.2 Some Objections to Capitalization

I have run this example past some skeptical audiences, including economists, attorneys, state tax judges, and Dartmouth and University of Washington students, who have offered the following questions and observations:

Why didn't the developer build everything in Bow, the low tax place?

He must have paid less for land on the high-tax Concord side. The capitalization effect accrues to land, the only truly immobile factor of production. If one of the homes were to burn down and the owner decided to sell the lot and let the buyer rebuild, the value of public services and the burdens of taxation would still be capitalized in the price of the lot, assuming the home can be rebuilt.

The examples assume, unrealistically, that both homes are fully mortgaged. What if people paid cash for some or all of the homes? Wouldn't the low-tax Bow buyer be better off over the years, since she has to pay only half as much in taxes, and thus be able to sock away more money in other investments?

The wealth position of buyers of both houses would be the same, regardless of whether they took out mortgages on 100 percent, 80 percent, or none of the purchase price. Suppose both buyers had $300,000 in wealth before the purchase. The buyer of the Concord house pays $160,000 in cash (no mortgage) at the beginning of the period. He has $140,000 left over. If he invests this at 10 percent interest, the $140,000 yields an annuity of $14,000 per year. He can pay his $8,000 in taxes and have $6,000 annually left over to invest in the stock and bond market. The buyer of the Bow house pays $200,000 in cash, leaving her with $100,000 in liquid assets. At 10 percent interest, she can get an annuity of $10,000, from which she has to pay $4,000 in taxes, leaving her with $6,000 to invest in the stock and bond market, the same amount that the Concord buyer has. The equality of outcome is the same for any mortgage / cash split, and it is not sensitive to the amount of wealth at which each starts.

Wait a second. The example does not work out if you plug in another interest rate, say 5 percent.

Correct. This particular example, in which the Bow house is worth $40,000 more than the Concord house, depends on the 10 percent rate of interest I used. But the same example could be done with a 5 percent rate of interest, or any other number. The difference in the value of the houses rises if interest rates are lowered. At a 5 percent interest rate, an annual tax differential of $4,000 would not be worth $40,000 in house value, but $80,000. But this also changes the tax rates needed to finance any particular level of public expenditures. To work out a fully general example, we economists must solve a simultaneous equation system for interest rates, tax rates, and house values.

Maybe economists solve simultaneous equations, but homebuyers don't do that.

People do not actually have to do the math to make the market work. All they have to do is realize that there is a net advantage—lower tax or lower mortgage—to living on one side of the town border or the other. They head for the house on the side with the greater financial advantage, and that drives the price up there and down in the less-favored side. The dynamics are exactly the same as those of any other asset market. You do not have to be a financial genius to make money by buying what you expect to be a high-yielding stock at a low price and selling (or declining to buy) a low-yielding stock at a high price. In doing so you help the market equalize the net rate of return of owning stocks.

When you ask people why they bought a particular home, most would not give tax differences as the key factor. Isn't the example unrealistic for that reason?

No. The example is drawn from real life. These differences are exactly what we observe either from paired examples (the "comparables" that real estate appraisers look for) or from statistical regressions. The reason these markets work so well is that some people do care about fiscal differences, and in buying a home, you have to bid against those people. In real estate, as in other asset markets, some people with money are well informed, and they are the buyers that must be bid against.

If you really do not care about the tax difference (or do not know about it), the seller of the Concord (the high tax) house could raise the price higher than I have supposed in the previous section's example. But not much higher, unless you are silly enough to tell the seller that you would pay just as much for the house in Concord as for the identical one down the street in Bow. (Okay, some people are that silly, but the fool-and-his-money theorem assures us that they are not influential in most markets.) The house seller in Concord cannot count on folks like you to come by right away. He has to price to sell eventually, and having a price too close to its twin in Bow is bound to deter some potential buyers from looking. After all, the seller in Bow is not likely to be shy about pointing out the great tax advantage that her house has over its twin in Concord. Markets can work well even if only a few people are attentive to differences in the quality of assets, as Friedrich Hayek (1945) proposed and as Vernon L. Smith (1982) confirmed with experimental data.

What happens if Bow's population grows? Won't that and other future changes in fiscal conditions dilute the tax base (more homes but same fiscal-cow of a power plant) and reduce capitalization?

Capitalization results from forecasts about future fiscal differences as well as those differences that prevail right now. If homebuyers in Bow expect the town to grow and the tax base to be diluted (since the new homes would probably not be accompanied by a new power plant), they would take that into account when buying their homes. Of course, if the dilution occurs a long time in the future, it will not affect current prices much. The sum of $1,000 due next year affects the selling price of a house much more than does $1,000 due twenty years from now.

Moreover, Bow homeowners control the land use in their town (remember, the town and the school district occupy the same land area), and they can use zoning and exactions to make new homes pay their own way, as I will describe in Section 3.9. To the extent that a certain amount of homebuilding cannot be charged for the dilution of the tax base, I would expect that this fact would already be incorporated in the home price difference. But the odds favor the existing homeowners. Not too many would vote for land-use laws and subdivision procedures that would reduce the value of their most valuable single asset.

3.3 Everything Seems to Be Capitalized

Property-tax differentials are not the only things that are capitalized. Econometric studies of single-family housing markets show capitalization of an amazing variety of location characteristics. Here is a selective list with a few of the possible sources:

- Toxic waste dump announcements reduced values in Woburn, Massachusetts, the site of Jonathan Haar's *A Civil Action* (Katherine Kiel 1995), but toxic waste dump cleanups restored values in Houston (Janet Kohlhase 1991).
- Having one's home in a historic district raised values in Baltimore (Deborah Ford 1989), but historic designation reduced apartment house values in Philadelphia because of restrictions on conversion (Asabere, Huffman, and Mehdian 1994).
- Large public housing projects reduced nearby home values in New Haven (Grether and Mieszkowski 1980) but small, dispersed projects did not have any effect on neighboring home values in Portland, Oregon (Rabiega, Lin, and Robinson 1984).
- Higher neighborhood crime rates reduced values in Baltimore (Ralph Taylor 1995).
- Through traffic on neighborhood streets reduced home values in Baton Rouge (Hughes and Sirmans 1992).
- A wide dispersion of commercial developments (as opposed to concentrating commerce in fewer districts) reduced home values in Boston suburbs (Lafferty and Frech 1978).
- Localized air pollution reduced home values in Pittsburgh (Paul Portney 1981).

- Having homeowners rather than renters as neighbors raised home values in various cities (Rohe and Stewart 1996).
- Adoption of municipal growth controls raised home values in the San Francisco Bay Area (Katz and Rosen 1987).
- Good schools raise home values almost everywhere (Section 6.14). This has even seeped into the consciousness of that chronicler of everyday Americana, *USA Today.* "Home Buyers Go Shopping for Schools," read a headline of May 15, 1996. The accompanying article noted that even buyers without children sought homes in good school districts "because of greater appreciation and pride of ownership."

The lesson from these studies is simply that the value of owner-occupied homes is a remarkably sensitive barometer of the expected benefits and costs from events influenced by local public policies. This list should not be taken to mean that the effects listed are good or bad because they raise or lower the value of single family homes in the community. One would need additional information to evaluate the policies that are at issue. For example, the exclusion of landfills, which might benefit individual homes near the sites, might cause municipal trash collection costs to rise so much for others that the net effects on all local home values could be negative. Urban growth boundaries might monopolize the housing market, so that their seemingly beneficial effects on homeowners may not be net benefits to society.

3.4 How Efficient Is the Housing Market?

The capitalization that I have talked about so far concerns differences among communities within a single housing market, which usually would be a metropolitan area. These markets are generally confined to areas that are a reasonable commuting distance from workplaces. My claim has been that this market works thoroughly to price the advantages and disadvantages of living in a particular community. But is there evidence that this market in general works well?

Economists have examined the larger, national housing market and asked how efficient it is when compared to other asset markets, such as the stock and bond markets. The housing market's efficiency as a national market is obviously less because of the transaction costs of gathering information and making trades. Opportunities for low-priced houses in North Carolina are difficult to take advantage of if you are located in Oregon.

What is surprising is that the evidence suggests the market is not all that inefficient. Economic studies indicate that during some periods of unusual housing price increases (such as the 1970s), housing market participants seemed to have missed making an easy buck, and many people got windfall gains (Hamilton and Schwab 1985). The 1980s saw periods of price bubbles in regional housing markets that cannot be explained easily in terms of expected returns (Case and Shiller 1989). But these short-term conditions do not persist. Over the long haul, housing prices seemed to have incorporated expected capital gains all across the country (Guntermann and Smith 1987; Gyourko and Voith 1992). Persistent price differences between regions of the country seem to have reflected the relative attractiveness of these places (Blomquist, Berger, and Hoehn 1988) and the effects of land-use regulation (Stephen Malpezzi 1996).

My concern in this book, however, is primarily with how well housing prices reflect differences in public service quality and taxes among communities within a metropolitan area, not among widely separated areas. The underlying issue, after all, is not whether we should have national governance of cities. Congress's governance of Washington, D.C., is at least somewhat cautionary in this regard. The issue is whether a metropolitan or state government would do better than local governance. The case for localism hinges in large part on how well the housing market conveys the proper information and incentives to the political actors in local communities. A critical issue, then, is the extent of capitalization of differences in municipal services, taxes, and regulations within a metropolitan, rather than a national, housing market.

3.5 How Extensive Is Capitalization?

The extent of fiscal capitalization within local housing markets was addressed in a detailed and econometrically sophisticated study called *Property Taxes and Housing Values: The Theory and Estimation of Intrajurisdictional Property Tax Capitalization* by John Yinger, Howard Bloom, Axel Börsch-Supan, and Helen Ladd (1988). A chapter of that book reviewed in detail thirty published studies of property-tax capitalization by professional economists. The studies used a variety of samples from states and metropolitan areas around the country in which property taxes were the main means of financing local schools. All but three of them show statistically significant evidence of capitalization of property taxes.

The Yinger book is a convenient compendium of studies and an excellent guide to capitalization principles, but its original research presented, as many people have read it, a challenge to the tax-capitalization claim. It is almost universally agreed that, all other things being equal, a higher property tax will lower the value of housing and other property in the community. The critical question is, how much? If the degree of capitalization is 100 percent, then 100 percent of the differences in tax rates among communities is offset by other housing costs. The seeming $800-a-year tax break in a low-tax town is offset by an $800-a-year higher mortgage payment or other cost of buying a home, such as forgoing interest and dividends on other types of investment. If capitalization is only 50 percent, then the seeming $800-a-year tax break on the house in the low-tax town is offset by an extra $400-a-year mortgage payment.

Yinger's group examined a large sample of homes in several Boston suburbs that had been underassessed relative to newer homes in the same community. After a Massachusetts court decision ordered uniform assessments in the 1970s, the tax bills on the underassessed homes rose and those on the formerly overassessed homes fell. By observing sale prices of the same homes over a period of time, the study estimated how much the tax changes affected ("were capitalized in") the value of the homes.

Their Boston-area study found that there had been capitalization of tax advantages to underassessed homes in every community, but much less than they expected. In their best sample, only about 20 percent of the previous tax differences (which were wiped out by court-ordered reassessment) had been reflected in the price of housing. A $300 annual tax break for a favored (older) property should have resulted in a $10,000 premium over a disfavored (newer) home, using the Yinger group's infinite time horizon and a 3 percent discount rate. But in fact the tax break yielded, in their preferred sample, only about a $2,000 value differential. In this seemingly ideal experiment, little capitalization of tax differences took place. Moreover, capitalization varied a great deal in their sample, ranging from 9 percent in Arlington to 79 percent in Belmont. If capitalization is supposed to guide public policy, it seems both weak and uncertain in its effect.

The reason for incomplete capitalization in the Yinger study had nothing to do with the failure of participants in the housing market to notice tax differentials. The failure had to do with the design of the study. On reflection, the authors concluded that participants in the housing market had anticipated, well before the court decision that ordered the reassessments, that the tax differentials would not be permanent (Yinger et al. 1988, p. 125).

Homebuyers did not necessarily know that there would be a judicial mandate to reassess at market value. They simply did not think that such blatantly unfair and illegal assessment differentials would last long. Imagine that you are looking to buy a home in Wellesley, Massachusetts (one of the towns in the sample) in the early 1970s. You look at some homes there and notice that the taxes on similar properties varies considerably. You ask why, and someone—the homeowner, the realtor, the tax assessor—will have to admit that not only is it unfair, but it is contrary to state law and the state constitution.

How long would you expect such differentials to last? One sure answer is, not forever. Indeed, you might have gotten wind of a lawsuit that was in the works to rein in these practices. But the answer you get could vary from town to town, depending on the opinions of the real estate professionals who specialize in particular places and the politics of individual towns. It should be no surprise that the tax differential should be capitalized as if it were not going to last and that capitalization should vary from town to town.

3.6 Capitalization of *Anticipated* Taxes Is 100 Percent

I have reviewed the Yinger group's flawed (by its authors' admission) study because I have encountered several economists who cite it as evidence that capitalization is weak, and my own reading of their book initially left me with that impression, too. Without capitalization, the homevoter has less incentive to do the right thing; doing good is not aligned with doing well. Here I describe two studies whose samples did not suffer from homebuyers' uncertainty about future policy changes. Both find nearly 100 percent capitalization of tax differences.

A clever study by A. Quang Do and C. F. Sirmans (1994) looked at homes in San Diego County in the 1980s that had been built by developers who had agreed to the terms of a "Mello-Roos" bond. This special bond (named for its legislative sponsors, not for laid-back marsupials) was designed to assist growing California communities that were strapped by the constraints of Proposition 13, which rolled back property taxes in 1978. (More details on this to come in Section 4.8.) Both the tax-rate and assessment limitations of the initiative made it difficult to provide for new schools in growing communities after 1978. Because Proposition 13 did not allow the older homes to be taxed more, the new homes had to bear the entire burden of building new schools through special taxes to finance the Mello-Roos bonds. But kids from the older homes could attend these new schools just like everyone else.

Mello-Roos bonds were paid for by a tax on the new homes, not the old ones, but the public services the bonds financed were the same for all. Do and Sirmans found that the value differences between old and new housing were 100 percent capitalized at a 4 percent rate of interest applied over the twenty-five-year life of the Mello-Roos bond. Because 4 percent is within a point of other estimates of the real (inflation-taken-out) interest rate at the time, I take this study as evidence that a fully anticipated tax differential will, in an active local housing market, be fully capitalized.

The reason for the difference between Do and Sirmans's result and that of the Yinger study is that the Yinger group erroneously supposed (as they began their study) that homebuyers in the Boston area thought the tax favoritism would last forever. It did not; the Massachusetts courts ordered reassessments as required by state laws that had been flouted in practice. In California, the ultimate source of the tax differential was Proposition 13, an amendment to the California Constitution that has proved immutable since it was approved in 1978. Thus the homebuyers in Do and Sirmans's California sample could look at a \$700 difference in taxes between two otherwise identical houses—one in the Mello-Roos district, and the other outside of it but in the same school district—and figure the difference in present-value terms over twenty-five years, which amounted to about \$13,500. They thus paid \$13,500 less for the new home than they would for an otherwise similar home outside the Mello-Roos district.

This is the same sort of calculation that homebuyers can make when examining homes in different jurisdictions outside of California. Oded

Palmon and Barton Smith (1998) challenged the Yinger study directly, noting that its theoretical capital cost was set too low, which led the Yinger group to expect more capitalization than they found. For their empirical work, they found a Houston-area sample of special taxes for various planned communities whose service levels (mainly water and sewer) were identical. The taxes were different, however, because the bonds that financed the improvements had been issued at different times. Some had interest rates higher than others, and rates did not change for the life of the bond. Subsequent homebuyers thus faced different tax liabilities for the same services. Palmon and Smith found that anticipated differences in tax liabilities among the different communities were 100 percent capitalized in home prices. The differences in tax liabilities were expected to be permanent because they were perfectly legal.

I conclude from these studies that persistent property tax differences among homes within the same housing market will be fully capitalized. Less than full capitalization can usually be explained by two factors: Potential homebuyers may not expect the current annual differences in taxes to last long (as in the Massachusetts case examined by the Yinger group), or relevant differences among the communities, such as school quality or attractive views, are known to buyers and sellers but not to econometricians.

3.7 House-Value Capitalization Implies Zoning

It is important to understand that the existence of capitalization implies a critical precondition. To discover that especially high (or low) public-school test scores are capitalized in the value of owner-occupied housing, as many studies have found, implies that access to schools in that community is not free. Since access to schools is typically governed by residence in the community, it follows that capitalization is evidence of an inelastic supply of developable sites. (This means that home construction in the community does not respond readily to increases in their price). This implies in most cases that someone besides the private landowners has to give the go-ahead to develop additional housing units.

Zoning and related land-use controls generate this community-wide inelasticity. To see why, consider the analogous stock-market condition. When stock-market followers learn that a drug company is about to get FDA approval for its new treatment for cancer, the news is quickly translated into higher prices for the ownership of this stock. This could not happen if ownership in the company were perfectly elastic in supply. The supply is limited to those who had previously purchased the stock.

This does not mean that the stock cannot be traded. Indeed, an extensive market in stocks is necessary for capitalization of the good news into the higher price. Exclusion from ownership is always a conditional exclusion: People who do not own the stock have to get the current owners' permission to obtain shares. Furthermore, the existing owners retain the right to limit the issuance of new stock in most corporations. They will approve it if the issuance will raise the value of their ownership shares by, for example, obtaining funds (at a lower cost than borrowing) to acquire more capital to produce the new drug.

A drug company's ability to conditionally exclude new owners is analogous to a local government's ability to exclude new residents. At one level, simple ownership of property allows each individual homeowner to exclude potential occupants. This is analogous to the individual stockholder's ability to exclude potential buyers of her shares. More critical for my purposes is the collective ability by homeowners to control net additions to the number of housing units in the community, just as stockholders can collectively control (via voting or via their elected board of directors) net additions to the number of ownership shares. Collective control is necessary because some desirable characteristics of the community are subject to congestion by additional residents. If a local public project—a park, for instance—is subject to crowding, which lowers its value as more people use it, the local government must be able to limit net additions to the housing stock in order for the benefits of the park to be reflected in existing home values. Zoning and other strands in the web of land-use controls are a way of doing that.

3.8 Local Governments, Not the States, Can Capitalize

Stuart Gabriel raised an important objection to my focus on local government. He pointed out that the many quality-of-life studies by economists seem to demonstrate that the good and bad things that states did in the public sector showed up in home values. Unlike the many popular studies of "best places to live," which rank places by a laundry list of qualities, economists focus on housing prices and, to a lesser extent, wage rates as clues for where in the country people want to live (Jennifer Roback 1982). The idea is that nice places will attract immigrants and raise housing prices there. (The effect of wages is more complicated. Attracting more workers may depress wages, but firms may also move to amenable areas to take advantage of the labor pool, thus bidding up local wages.)

My reasons for neglecting states are three. First, the states are large in land area. Most economic activity occurs in urban areas, which account for less than 4 percent of the lower forty-eight's land area. More of the land in every state—including densely populated Rhode Island, Delaware, and New Jersey—is covered by forests, cropland, pastures, and open space than by urban and transportation uses. States would have to be able to severely limit development on the vast majority of their land area in order to "conditionally limit" additional development that was attracted as a result of policies that had a positive net benefit on land values. Now some states, most notably Oregon, Vermont, and Hawaii, have moved in the direction of limiting development outside of their urban areas. But even in these three states the amount of land still available for development is huge compared to that within even the largest municipalities.

The second reason that the states are different has to do with their politics. Because they are large in land area and population, the median-voter model, which applies well for local government (as will be shown in Section 4.11), is more likely to be compromised by interest-group activity in the state capitol. Employment-based interests will be more influential in state politics and less so in most local governments. States are eager to attract and retain high-paying employers (DeBartolome and Spiegel 1995), and there is evidence that better schools and other public services are an effective bait (Jay Helms 1985). But the benefits from statewide success in attracting employers usually accrue to groups organized around employment categories rather than to property owners. Statewide taxes to finance the better schools are diffused to a larger group of voters than at the local level, and the benefit / cost discipline that homevoters impose on locally financed schools is largely absent at the state level.

A final reason to exclude the states is that their ability to capture net benefits in land values is limited by the U.S. Constitution, which does not permit states to restrict immigration from other states or direct statewide benefits exclusively to preexisting residents (Edwards v. California 1941). This ban is not absolute—in-state university tuition can be less than for out-of-staters, for example—but it inhibits implementation of the "visit and then go home" campaign associated with Oregon's governor Tom McCall in the 1970s. Local government regulations, however, get pretty much a free pass on the same issue. An insightful lawyer, Malcolm Misuraca, once argued that local government growth controls in California should be treated as if they were impediments to "freedom to travel" among the states. Misuraca succeeded in district court, but the argument was firmly rejected by a federal appeals court in Construction Industry Association v. City of Petaluma (9th Cir. 1975). No one has successfully raised it since.

3.9 Zoning Is an Elastic Community Property Right

Robert Nelson (1977) and I have said for a long time and in many places that zoning is best thought of as a collective property right whose benefit inures to the politically dominant group of the municipality that does the zoning (Fischel 1978; 1985). The text of zoning laws, however, does not lend much support to my assertion that the laws offer existing homeowners the ability to "conditionally exclude" additional land uses.

A typical American zoning ordinance looks as if it is setting the use of land for all time. The ordinance adopts a map that divides the municipality into various districts in which certain activities and structures are permitted and others are excluded. The details of what is permitted can be mind-numbing and so convoluted as to confuse even the people who are supposed to administer it. The number of structures permitted on the lot, their placement on the lot, building height, parking requirements, water and sewer connections, number of unrelated renter-occupants, and frontage on public streets are all subject to regulation.

Some uses are permitted at the discretion of administrative boards (zoning and planning commissions), but their discretionary authority is not so large as to suggest an easy transfer of development rights from the community to a development-minded landowner whenever the landowner is willing to offer in-kind compensation. My local zoning and planning boards did a little bargaining with developers, but always within the confines of an ordinance that set close parameters on our discretion. We could not allow an apartment house in a single-family district, even if the neighbors would not have had a conniption over such an idea. Nor is there much in the planning documents that supposedly guide the zoning regulations to suggest property value maximization as the goal. The usual catalog of goals in master plans reads like a child's wish list, assembled without recognition that one goal, say, affordable housing, might conflict with another, say open-space preservation.

Focus on the characteristics of the documents and administration of ordinances obscures the most important aspect of any zoning law: It can always be changed. It is, after all, a *local* law. If the local government wants to change its regulations, there is precious little in the state enabling legislation, the state constitution, or judge-made law to prevent it from doing so. Zoning laws are continually amended, and most are rewritten entirely every few decades. A zoning law that fails to conform to the demands of the body politic is a temporary law.

Change may be slowed by procedural requirements. For example, some courts are hostile to "spot zoning," a zoning change that affects only one or two parcels. Changes are also slowed by elaborate notice requirements and, in some jurisdictions, the requirement of an environmental impact statement. But the very existence of procedural requirements makes it clear that change is expected. A few developers may get the benefit of an unintended loophole in an old zoning law, but once the law is changed, as it soon is after the loophole is discovered, the town has no obligation to allow developers in otherwise similar circumstances to do the same thing as their lucky (or foresighted) compatriots.

Some developers do anticipate the changes and build before the ink is dry on the more stringent regulations in order to vest their rights (David Dana 1995). (Most zoning laws permit previously established, nonconforming uses to continue if they are not otherwise noxious.) My favorite for candor was the landowner who put up several buildings at the edge of Lake Washington in Kenmore, a growing suburb of Seattle: "It was more a defensive move than anything else," he said. "If we were to do nothing, we could end up with a wetland and a wildlife area"

(*Seattle Post-Intelligencer*, December 12, 1998, p. D4). But the cost of building and maintaining currently unprofitable structures keeps most other landowners from using this option.

3.10 Zoning Is a Powerful Constraint on Development

Most of the evidence in support of the property-rights view of zoning is indirect. One source is the many capitalization studies, which show that zoning classifications do make a difference in the value of property (Fischel 1990). In Southern California, for example, a rezoning from agriculture to single-family residential can raise the land's value enormously (Brownstone and DeVany 1991). If zoning were a will-o'-the-wisp, malleable at the mere request of developers, it is difficult to see why zoning classifications should contribute to differences in the value of otherwise similar properties.

Some economists have explored the theoretical conditions in which the unzoned land market is capable of doing the work that zoning is alleged to do (Epple and Platt 1998; William Wheaton 1993). If the demand for housing and public services by various income groups is sufficiently different, the groups may sort themselves naturally into different communities. If such conditions hold, "exclusionary" zoning would just be validating the market. But empirical studies of whether zoning follows the market in other respects indicates that it does not (McMillen and McDonald 1991; James Thorson 1994; 1997).

Thorson, for example, found that after McHenry County, a Chicago suburb, adopted agricultural zoning, the previously permitted pattern of single-family development was radically changed. (The case validating the rezoning is Wilson v. McHenry County [Ill. App. 1981].) After an initial spike of rural building, induced by developers who anticipated the new restrictions and got their permits before the rezoning took effect, development was moved toward existing towns that did not have such restrictions. It is difficult to believe that developers in a previously hot market for homes would have moved in this direction without the visible hand of government regulation.

Even without the aforementioned empirical studies, the idea that zoning is an ineffectual constraint on development is completely at odds with the attention paid to it by otherwise rational people. Zoning is regarded by most scholars of local government, not just your zoning-conscious author, as the most important municipal function (Richard Briffault 1990a, p. 3). A dominant reason for municipal incorporation in Los Angeles in the 1950s was to transfer zoning from a prodevelopment county government into the hands of local homeowners (Richard Cion 1966). As I will describe in more detail in Chapter 10, 1990s incorporations in King County (Seattle) likewise were motivated primarily by a desire to obtain local control of zoning.

Local control of zoning is so popular that even the most vigorously interventionist courts have had little success in reforming it. The New Jersey Supreme Court was in the forefront of legal attacks on "exclusionary" zoning during the 1970s and 1980s. The *Mount Laurel* decisions aroused enormous political resentment. They were so unpopular that legislative leaders threatened not to reappoint the state's chief justice if he did not lay off. The threat appeared to work. In Hills Development v. Bernards Township (1986), Chief Justice Wilentz affirmed the legislative response that actually undermined most of the *Mount Laurel II* (1985) remedy by removing the courts from the fair-housing scene. Shortly thereafter, Governor Kean stretched his political capital to induce legislators to approve the chief justice's reappointment, although there is no record of a specific quid pro quo (Kirp, Dwyer, and Rosenthal 1995, pp. 137–143).

Chief Justice Wilentz may have had in mind his judicial predecessors' difficulty in controlling the popular demand for local land-use controls. Back in the 1920s, when zoning was spreading rapidly, the New Jersey courts bravely bucked the trend by construing the police power to encompass only traditional nuisances, thereby striking down attempts to separate commercial and residential uses (State v. Nutley 1924). Even after the U.S. Supreme Court put its imprimatur on zoning in Euclid v. Ambler (1926), the New Jersey Supreme Court distinguished its string of prodeveloper decisions from both *Euclid* and those of other states (Oxford Construction v. Orange 1926). Within a year of the *Oxford* decision, however, the state had passed a constitutional amendment specifically reversing the New Jersey Supreme Court's narrow construction of the police power in zoning (National Municipal Review 1927; Lumund v. Board of Adjustment 1950, 584).

3.11 Shopping for Communities in the Tiebout Model

A second precondition for capitalization of local community characteristics is that homebuyers must have a choice of different communities and be aware of differences among them. The famous Tiebout model posits that there are numerous communities and that households can shop around among them for the mix of services they prefer. This process of "voting with one's feet" was advanced by Charles Tiebout (1956) as a way for people to reveal their preference for local public goods. He regarded this as a solution to the theoretical problem posed by Paul Samuelson (1954) and Richard Musgrave (1939).

The difficulty, according to Samuelson and Musgrave, is that public goods—the kind that are equally available to all if they are provided—cannot be supplied by the market because of the "free rider" problem. We free ride on aerial fireworks displays when we decline to pay for them by private subscription, knowing that if they will be paid for by someone else we can still enjoy them. Many of us do the same for public radio and TV.

Whether Tiebout resolved this theoretical problem is not entirely clear, but his model nowadays stands for the proposition that local government provision of geographically isolated public goods is superior to provision of the same goods by larger, more centralized units of government. Tiebout's model is the touchstone of that part of public economics that deals with any aspect of local government. I shall describe the assumptions and their relevance to experience, at least in the United States. I think that the important assumptions do correspond to reality and that Tiebout's omission of political behavior is easily fixed by adding homevoters.

A key assumption is that there must be a large number of autonomous communities. This is not much debated. As I showed in Section 2.2, there are about 25,000 general purpose, local governments in the United States, and almost as many school districts. School districts are more constrained by state law in what they can do, but except in those states that have become highly centralized in their financing of education, such as Hawaii, California, and New Mexico, there are fiscal as well as qualitative differences among them. That school districts do not correspond perfectly with municipal boundaries is less compromising of the model than it sounds. Municipalities are capable of dealing with their neighbors to promote their joint school district's interests.

Most of the U.S. population lives in metropolitan areas of more than 500,000, and most of these areas have at least a score of local governments. Several of the largest metropolitan areas (more than 1 million population) have hundreds of local governments. I once attempted to get a count of local governments in large metropolitan areas to get a sense of whether, by traditional industrial organization standards, the four largest local governments had any kind of market power over the supply of new housing based on their control of land area (Fischel 1981). In only a handful of metropolitan areas, such as Baltimore, Washington, and Miami, where county governments often supplant cities, did the four largest local governments control more than 30 percent of the land in the built-up part of the metropolitan area. If local government were thought of as an "industry," its industrial structure would look far more competitive than the major manufacturing industries in the United States. Even in rural areas, it is rare for potential residents not to have at least three or four local governments and school districts within a half-hour drive of their jobs. (Most rural residents nowadays are not farmers, so they are usually not tied to living where they work.)

3.12 Homebuyers Are Aware of Community Differences

Aside from assuming a choice of numerous municipalities, Tiebout applied ideas about the nature of consumers from standard economics. Potential residents of these many communities are numerous, mobile, and knowledgeable about the conditions of public services in these communities. They select the community that best matches their preferences. This set of assumptions is also uncontroversial among economists, though it is not hard to satirize: "Oops, I just noticed that the shade-tree commission is not doing its job. Time to sell the house and move to Arborville."

My defense of Tiebout's assumption about mobility is that people move for reasons that typically have little to do with local government. Tiebout shoppers may begin their search when they graduate from school and take a job; when they get married; when they take a new job too far away to stay in their present home; when they have children and need a larger home; and when they retire and want a warmer climate or a smaller home. On all of these occasions people have an opportunity to shop for a community and a school district as well as for homes with larger lots or more bathrooms. Since Americans make these moves about once every four years, there is an active market in communities as well as in homes.

The primary economic evidence that homebuyers are aware of fiscal and public service differences among communities is, of course, capitalization. Wallace Oates (1969) was the first to make this point and to provide the econometric evidence. (In so doing, Oates gave an enormous boost to Tiebout's 1956 article, which had previously been given a cool reception.) Using a 1960 sample of northern New Jersey communities, Oates concluded that "if a community increases its tax rates and employs the receipts to improve its school system, the coefficients indicate that the increased benefits from the expenditure side of the budget will roughly offset (or perhaps even more than offset) the depressive effect of the higher tax rates on local property values" (1969, p. 968).

Oates's study has been replicated using different samples, time periods, measures of school quality, local services, and econometric techniques (Dowding, John, and Biggs 1994). Capitalization studies are now an undergraduate exercise, and it is difficult to interest journal editors in new studies without a major twist. Political scientists, however, have wondered how homebuyers know to gravitate, Tiebout-style, to the better school districts. It is true that information that allows homebuyers to compare communities' public services is abundant. Real estate salespeople provide it upfront in booklets and websites about schools and amenities and on the listing sheet for individual properties.

Do homebuyers actually use such information? The direct evidence is surprisingly slim. Teske, Schneider, Mintrom, and Best (1993) surveyed residents of Long Island, New York, suburbs to test their awareness of fiscal differences. They asked respondents to rank their own town's tax rate and spending per pupil with two others nearby and found that only 21 percent got the rankings right. Teske and company argued in defense of the Tiebout model that the glass was half full: When the sample was winnowed of people less likely to care about schools, their awareness score rose to near half.

In a related study, Schneider, Teske, Marschall, and Roch (1998) found that low-income parents seem able to select schools on the basis of educational quality, even though the parents' objective knowledge of school differences was even more limited than that of participants in the Long Island study. As the subtitle of their article put it, "In the land of the blind, the one-eyed parent may be enough." These political scientists, who cited no capitalization studies, have discovered for schools what I argued in Section 3.2 was true for capitalization of tax differences: It does not take many knowledgeable buyers for markets to work.

Still, it does seem puzzling that markets can work with such apparently limited information. Political scientists Kenneth Bickers and Robert Stein (1998) took up this issue. They suggest that homebuyers do not rely on formal data as much as on "informational heuristics" to locate preferred schools. Heuristics involve things like looking for neighborhoods whose residents are likely to demand better schools, such as, to use their examples, academics, Jews, or wealthy people. ("Forget the Boston area school guide; just give me Paul Samuelson's address.") Bickers and Stein's telephone survey of households in the Houston area found that recent movers, and especially those with children, did gravitate toward schools with higher test scores, even though most respondents could not rank their school's scores accurately. Homebuyers, as opposed to renters, were especially savvy in ferreting out the higher-scoring school districts.

Bickers and Stein's heuristics seem analogous to the way I purchase a computer. I do not learn much about technical specifications. I mainly ask colleagues whose work and habits are similar to mine what they have purchased and how they have liked it. It seems reasonable to suppose that many people deal with complex goods in this way. Selecting a community on the Tiebout end of the house-hunting trip is less complicated than it sounds.

3.13 Tiebout's Model Allows for Commuting and Size Limits

A third set of Tiebout's assumptions is usually dismissed as being patently unrealistic but irrelevant for most of the tasks at hand. Potential residents were said by Tiebout to have no employment, only income from nonlabor sources. This assumption served to divorce the choice of community from a specific location within the metropolitan area. The standard urban economics model (not Tiebout's) assumes that people have to go to work daily, and this forces them to trade off the cost of commuting longer distances to their jobs with the desire to have larger lots and cheaper (per square foot) housing. If residents had to locate near their jobs, their choice of communities would be limited. This would not work for the Tiebout model, and so Tiebout had to get rid of work.

In the real world of work and commuting, the number of accessible communities in most metropolitan areas is nonetheless large. Don't think in terms of people commuting from "the suburbs" to "the central city." Jobs in most metropolitan areas are now enormously dispersed. Bruce Hamilton (1982) found that commuting patterns appeared to be almost random when compared with the predictions of the standard suburb-to-city-and-back model of urban economics. Urban households have for more than half a century been able to select jobs in multiple locations, not just in a central business district, and this has increased the number of communities among which homebuyers can shop.

The more problematic of Tiebout's "unrealistic" assumptions is that each community's public activities are enjoyed (or endured) within the community's boundaries, but not outside it. This is not literally true, of course. You can enjoy the streets and parks in other communities, and their traffic can spill over the usually invisible boundaries into yours. One can take this in two directions. The first is to argue that most local activities affect only their residents most of the time, and so that is the point worth focusing on. But the lasting questions in local public economics concern the role of the community in the larger world. Island municipalities in a boatless sea are not especially interesting.

The other approach, which was taken up most systematically by Wallace Oates (1972), is to use Tiebout's no-spillovers assumption as a springboard for discussion of what Oates titled *Fiscal Federalism.* I am going to follow the Oates path in trying to integrate communities into their larger economies. Unlike Oates, I will dwell on the internal incentives for local governments to adjust to the demands of the outside world instead of, as Oates emphasized back then, the external fiscal mechanisms that higher governments might use to get the locals to behave. For example, I will show in Section 8.7 that intermunicipal pollution problems are usually restrained by a locally generated spirit of reciprocity.

Another of Tiebout's assumptions concerned the size of the community. If communities could provide public services at a cost that was insensitive to how many residents enjoyed them, there would be no reason to have more than one community. So Tiebout assumed that the communities had some fixed asset that was valued by residents—a beach was his most used example—that could not be easily reproduced. Thus the primary public attraction could become congested as more residents moved in. This allowed Tiebout to suppose that any given community had first a falling cost per resident for providing public services as its resident population rose, and then a rising cost as the population became still larger. Small communities would thus encourage growth to get more people to share the cost of services, and larger communities, which were close to their minimum average cost per resident, would discourage growth. They would manage growth by zoning, Tiebout supposed, though he did not describe in any detail how it would work.

3.14 Why Are Fiscal Advantages Persistent?

One problem with Tiebout's model, which he recognized, was that in a world where space and hence transportation costs mattered, a system of communities with fixed boundaries would be insufficient to accommodate all tastes for public services. There would have to be as many different communities as there were different demands for public services, and the variety of demands could be large. This means that for an ideal world, the ability to incorporate one's own community should be much easier than it is.

The theoretical objection to the Tiebout model is that in a world in which all preferences are satisfied, we should observe no systematic capitalization of differences among communities (Ross and Yinger 1998). After all, capitalization means that an acre of land is higher in value on one side of a municipal or school district border than an otherwise identical acre on the other side. It would seem that there would be gains from trade to be had by moving the border or by creating another jurisdiction that could replicate the desirable qualities of the more valuable jurisdiction.

Yet the evidence is that municipal boundaries, once established, are in fact difficult to change when they rub up against another city. Both consolidation and secession are rare (Epple and Romer 1989). The differences in value between communities indicate that people have to buy a more expensive home than they would otherwise want in order to get schools or other local services of a quality they are willing to pay for. It's like the inefficiency of a tie-in sale: You have to buy the service contract along with the car, even though you might want only one of them.

I have two answers for this objection. One is the corporate model that I have adapted for municipalities. We do not find it theoretically objectionable that investment in business corporations should yield different rates of return. The higher rate of return of a dollar invested in Xerox in the 1960s or Microsoft in the 1980s provides an incentive for other companies to enter those businesses. Thus the high value of municipalities that manage their assets well and give the voters what they want at a low cost is a reward for homeowners in those places and a signal to other places that they should emulate them.

This is not an entirely satisfactory response, though. In the business world, competition and entry by other firms should eventually cause the profitability of firms to converge to a normal rate of return, so that we observe over the long run little systematic capitalization. Xerox now gives ordinary returns, and Microsoft may soon, too. But there appear to be persistent differentials among municipalities, especially with regard to their schools. Several generations of ivy-league admissions directors have known that New Trier High School, located in a suburban-Chicago district, is as reliable a supplier of talented students as any pricey prep school. One would expect that advantage to be eroded as other Chicago-area districts figured out how New Trier does it.

The other answer to why municipalities do not proliferate like amoebas is that homevoters have better reasons than business shareholders to be reluctant to divide existing municipal boundaries. In most metropolitan areas, secession is the only way to create the additional competition that would eliminate capitalization. As I have repeatedly emphasized, most municipal shareholders—homeowners—cannot diversify their risks. Aside from promoting political participation by homevoters, this high degree of risk makes voters reluctant to change institutional structures. An investor in a business corporation can easily change her portfolio if she feels that returns are too low. But she can do so without radically changing her risks of investment. She knows that she has to take some additional risk to get higher returns, but she can do that without putting her entire portfolio on the line.

The typical homeowner is in no such position. To alter the boundaries of municipalities or school districts is to put much of his net worth on the line. There's no way to put half of his home in one district and half in another. It should not be surprising, then, that nearly all states make it next to impossible for voters to secede from existing municipalities to form their own communities. Formation of municipalities from unincorporated, county-governed land is easier to do, but, as I will demonstrate in Chapter 10, even those potential organizational advantages are usually grasped only after a concerted campaign to convince homeowners that their lot (figuratively and literally) will be improved under the new government.

The down side of the institutionalized aversion to entry in the municipal services business is that it retards competition. This means that some municipalities that work themselves into favorable fiscal positions will not find as many imitators as they would in the business world. Differences in home values due to fiscal advantages will persist longer than they do in the business world. I find this constraint less troubling than some—having a limited menu is better in most cases than a metropolitan-wide prix fixe. From the homeowner's point of view, fixed boundaries offer the security of knowing that the community that provides many of the essential services to your largest and most durable asset will be the same in the next decade as it is in the present. (Section 11.13 offers some "on the other hand" considerations for allowing municipal secession.)

3.15 Hamilton Introduced Fiscal Zoning and Exactions

The major amendment that the Tiebout model required was to match zoning, which Tiebout mentioned only in passing, with local taxation, which he ignored entirely. Most local governments use property taxes to fund local services. Property taxes are typically uniform per unit of value, but the right to enjoy the services financed by the tax is not tied to the payment.

Developers thus have some incentive to build units that will pay less in property taxes than the users of the units will get in services. The developer would be able to sell such units at a higher price that reflected the fiscal gain. (The gain would be tempered by her customers worrying that their fiscal benefits would be eroded by subsequent unchecked development.) If there were no constraint on such enterprise, the

Tiebout system would implode as communities found themselves unable to finance a distinctive level of services.

Bruce Hamilton (1975) repaired Tiebout's omission by proposing that municipalities could use zoning to indirectly specify the taxable property for each new development. If the average home in the village was worth $200,000, then the new average home would have to be worth at least $200,000. (No zoning law can legally specify a minimum dollar value, but the matrix of lot size and quality standards that are legal can come pretty close.) Under the Tiebout-Hamilton conditions, the local property tax becomes an unavoidable fee for services rendered. New construction "pays its own way" in municipal costs. The property tax has no deadweight loss because homebuyers get exactly what they pay for (since they have a choice of many communities' service packages), and they pay for exactly what they get (since local zoning sees to it that they cannot shirk by building a smaller than average house).

Critics of this model concede that if zoning did work so perfectly, it would indeed give the result that Hamilton claimed, but they argue that zoning is too crude to make such fine distinctions (Mieszkowski and Zodrow 1989). I argue that the critics greatly underestimate the creativity of local governments (Fischel 1992). In the previous example, suppose that the village had $100,000 per household worth of commercial and industrial tax base in addition to its average home values of $200,000. Now the new home would have to bring with it $300,000 in tax base. It would seem that it could do this only by demanding that new homes cost $300,000, which could upset the Tiebout sorting mechanism.

But in reality, developers and municipal governments can find their way around such problems. For example, the developer might propose a "mixed use" development of commerce and homes that worked out to $300,000 per new household so that the fiscal impact would be nil. But if such a deal could not be worked out and the proposed use was not anticipated to pay its own way from property taxes alone, the developer might be asked to provide financial benefits to the community to make up the fiscal deficit. These might be dedicated facilities that benefit the entire community, or they might be side payments called "exactions" or if regularized by a schedule, "impact fees" (Blaesser and Kentopp 1990).

Such payments are controversial not because they charge too little, but typically because they charge more than the development seems to add to the municipality's fiscal costs. Courts have paid some attention to them by finding that the more imaginative arrangements constitute an unconstitutional "regulatory taking." In Dolan v. Tigard (1994), the U.S. Supreme Court tried to limit exactions to amounts that were "roughly proportional" to inconvenience caused by the new developments. Commentators worry that this will inhibit transactions and end up making zoning more exclusive (Lee Fennell 2000). Wise developers know, however, that it is better to pay reasonable exactions than to litigate them. Community demands for specific side payments are likely to be struck down in some state courts as illegal "contract zoning" (Judith Wegner 1987). To deal with this, developers will offer to "donate" something of value to the community, knowing that if they do not, no rezoning or other regulatory accommodation will be forthcoming.

Many commentators nonetheless claim that local governments continue to subsidize sprawl because property taxes do not cover the cost of infrastructure development. The Real Estate Research Corporation's study *The Costs of Sprawl* (1974) was a pioneer in promoting this myth, which continues to be an article of faith among the antisprawl set. It overlooks entirely the exactions process, which has been a widely used tool in American land-use controls for at least half a century (Heyman and Gilhool 1964). Alan Altshuler and Tony Gómez-Ibáñez (1993), who examine the exactions process and review the literature, conclude that, if anything, exactions extract payments in excess of the social costs of development.

Nor are there any special mysteries about how to do fiscal zoning. For local public officials who want development to pay its own way (as all who wish to retain their jobs typically do), how-to manuals such as *The Development Impact Assessment Handbook* (Burchell, Listokin, and Dolphin 1993) are widely available. And the process works to the advantage of established homeowners. Marla Dresch and Steve Sheffrin (1997) undertook a nuanced study of how market conditions determine who pays for exactions in California: When the housing market is strong, the buyers pay in the form of higher prices, but otherwise the burden is shifted back to developers and landowners. Established homeowners are insulated from the burden in either case.

3.16 Communities Can Have Heterogeneous Housing

Hamilton's original (1975) amendment to the Tiebout model characterized the communities as insisting on a degree of homogeneity of housing styles and family income that is both appalling and unrealistic. Homogeneity does have its advantages. Benham and Keefer (1991) found that the rare group of firms that successfully operated under democratic management and ownership, voting per capita rather than per share, had to be small and homogenous. Homogeneity reduces the temptation for majoritarian transfers of assets within municipalities that Dillon's Rule and other state limitations on municipal activities were concerned about.

Nonetheless, homogeneity can be taken too far. The homogenized, plain-vanilla suburb that the Tiebout-Hamilton model contemplates is everywhere under fire. But critics overlook that Hamilton (1976) quickly modified his model to allow for heterogeneous communities. Rich and poor can live in the same community in the revised Tiebout-Hamilton model, provided that the potential stock of each type of housing is foreseeably limited. This helps explain why local governments in fact can have a fairly wide variety of income classes and housing types within them, as Howard Pack and Janet Pack (1977) found, and still conform to the Tiebout-Hamilton model.

To see why the model is unaffected by limited heterogeneity, suppose that a community is zoned such that half of the homes will be for the rich, and half will be for the poor. Because the schools and other public services will be equally available to all, this results in a transfer of wealth from owners of rich homes to owners of poor homes. (Actually, if the zoning is foreseen before construction of the homes, the transfer will be from one set of landowners to another, but I will stick to "rich" and "poor" homeowners to make the argument clearer.) If the annual transfer amounts to $1,000 from rich homeowner to poor homeowner, homes for the rich will eventually cost the present value of $1,000 a year less than homes in a homogeneous rich community. (At an interest rate of 5 percent and a long time horizon, this would be about $20,000 less). Homes for the poor in the mixed community will cost about $20,000 more than those in another benchmark community of all poor people.

The key to this calculation is that the number of homes in each category must be fixed for the economic future. If the rich can remove their homes to avoid the transfer, it will not work, nor will it work if the poor can pour into the community without restriction. The zoning laws must not only restrict the poor from entering beyond some anticipated number, but also prevent the rich from subdividing their homes to accommodate the poor and then leaving. Zoning laws accomplish both of these requirements by having limited districts for smaller homes and by preventing larger homes in single-family home districts from converting to apartments or two-family homes. The homes do not even have to be built for this to happen, as long as the zoning laws are in place and are expected not to change much. (How do I reconcile this with my previous paean to zoning's plasticity? Although it is easy to finetune a zoning ordinance with annual amendments to close loopholes and deal with unforeseen contingencies, most general zoning categories persist for decades.)

The people who gain or lose from rezonings are those who owned the land prior to the anticipated implementation of the new zoning laws. After a rezoning from large lots to smaller lots, which would accommodate the poor, the buyers of "rich" homes pay less for the land, and they have money left over to pay their somewhat higher property taxes. The buyers of "poor" homes pay more for them, and so have less money left over after paying their mortgage. Capitalization levels the economic field for all subsequent players (Hamilton 1979).

3.17 Heterogeneity May Increase Home Values

My assumption in the foregoing analysis has been that the transfer is zero-sum—what the original poor gain is what the original rich lose. It does not have to apply if there are beneficial peer-group effects from mixing rich and poor, as some economic theorists have argued (Fernandez and Rogerson 1996; Roland Benabou 1996). A community or a school district with a mix of residents from various income levels or other characteristics may be more valuable to potential homebuyers than a plain-vanilla jurisdiction.

Most of the large, privately planned "new towns," such as Reston, Virginia, Columbia, Maryland, and Foster City, California, have a mix of building types to appeal to a heterogeneous market (Richard Brooks 1974; Lynn Burkhardt 1981). The developer of Foster City strongly implied in a conversation that such a mix was a profit-maximizing strategy (Fischel 1994). Celebration, Florida, which was developed by the Disney Corporation, likewise sought a mix of housing types in order to promote a mix of income levels within the community, although its live-in chroniclers, Douglas Frantz and Catherine Collins (1999, p. 219), still fault it for not offering subsidized low-income housing within its borders.

There is also some evidence that judicious mixing of students makes for a better education (Henderson, Mieszkowski, and Sauvageau 1978). Most selective, private colleges and prep schools recognize this benefit by offering scholarships to lower-income families and attempting to admit a mix of students from various backgrounds. It is my impression that many affluent buyers are eager to avoid the modern stigma of living in a white-bread suburb. Public planners and private developers are more than willing to cater to that taste. Suburbs such as Oak Park, Illinois (west of Chicago), Shaker Heights, Ohio (south of Cleveland), and Maplewood, New Jersey (west of New York City), proudly advertise their successful strategy of maintaining a racially integrated community, and the casual evidence is that it has done nothing bad to their housing prices.

This is not to say that "exclusionary" zoning—regulations whose effect is to preclude mixing of rich and poor—is a problem that can easily be left alone. My point in these last two sections is only that localities are not uniformly opposed to heterogeneity of homes and population. There is much variation within most suburbs already, and a sizable fraction of the suburban population seems to think that is just fine.

3.18 Conclusion: The Tiebout Model Works Okay

My goal in this chapter has been to persuade the reader that the homevoter hypothesis rests on plausible behavioral and institutional foundations. The capitalization of differences in local taxes, amenities, and public services is well established. The housing market may not be as efficient as the stock market, but its imperfections are not so great as to make the comparison irrelevant. Municipalities are capable of controlling and channeling the broad flows of their urban growth, and there is plenty of evidence that these controls have real bite.

The Tiebout model is likewise a decent description of reality. Indeed, it is a good description of *realty.* The old saying that real estate's three rules are "location, location, and location" is also a summation of what drives the Tiebout model. People moving to a new community pay close attention to the quality of local public services and the taxes they expect to pay.

I will readily concede that many municipal decisions do not seem to fit the rational mold in which I have cast them. Few municipal officers would say that their job is to maximize property values. But close examination of the declared objectives of supposedly profit-maximizing business managers can also uncover a gulf between theory and practice, a fact that economists have wrestled with since its revelation by Richard Lester (1946). Compared with the messy decision processes that go on in business corporations, municipalities do not look so irrational, especially when we keep in mind that municipalities have to make most of their decisions in full view of the public. It might be best to judge both types of corporations by what they do, not by what they say.

4
The Median Voter in Local Government Politics

THE PREVIOUS CHAPTER described and defended the Tiebout-Hamilton model of local government. Yet this is almost an oxymoron. There is hardly any government in the model. Its engine is mobility of the population, not politics. In this chapter, I integrate into the Tiebout model my view of municipal corporations as deliberate, value-maximizing agents of homeowners.

Economists have for years shamelessly poached on the territory of political science in addressing the governance of business corporations. Their shyness about the governance of municipal corporations is the product of their unnecessary quest for a nonpolitical solution to the problem of public goods. This quest started with Charles Tiebout himself, as I will explain using the biographical information I obtained about him.

The rest of the chapter is dedicated to showing that a fairly straightforward political model, the median voter, is applicable to almost all local governments. The major exceptions are large cities, but even in these places homevoters are a force to be reckoned with. They are among the reasons that rent control is such an uncommon policy in the United States.

4.1 Podiatric Politics: Exit or Voice?

When I was at Princeton in the early 1970s, the graduate students used to put on skits at the annual economics department holiday party.

Wally Oates, who had put Tiebout's model on the map with his evidence about capitalization (1969), was one of the more genial members of the Princeton faculty, and we were confident that he would take the following skit in good humor:

> *Narrator:* We're here on election day at the Borough of Princeton's polls. We've noticed an odd event. Professor Oates has gone into the voting booth, and he is taking off his shoes and socks. Professor Oates, what's going on?
> *Student impersonating Oates:* Well, it's hard to pull the levers with my shoes and socks on.
> *Narrator:* Why don't you use your hands?
> *Oates impersonator:* Oh, I do use my hands for state and national issues, but for local issues, I have to vote with my feet.

The metaphor of "voting with one's feet" is older than Tiebout's economic exposition of it. (Tiebout did not actually use the term.) It has an honorable history for most Americans, who are not many generations removed from ancestors who voted with their feet against an oppressive regime, or at least against a society that was unresponsive to their political, religious, or economic aspirations. But there is also a seemingly different American tradition, which is to stand your ground and try to change the system from within. The tension between these traditions was nicely caught by the title of a book that is an enduring classic in social science, *Exit, Voice, and Loyalty: Responses to Decline in Firms, Organizations, and States,* by Albert Hirschman (1970).

It is worth emphasizing that when we economists use the term "exit," we do not confine its meaning to the obvious case of removing one's person and assets from an unsatisfactory jurisdiction. We also mean the unwillingness of outsiders to enter a jurisdiction because of the unappealing conditions there. If the latter seems like a strange use of the term "exit," the reader should keep in mind that it comes from the tribe of social scientists who insist that a prospective benefit forgone is a "cost." Likewise, an exit is an entrance forgone.

Moreover, when we think about it, leaving a municipality is by itself harmless if the exiting family or firm is replaced by another with the same essential characteristics. That's just "turnover." Thus when we say that "exit" is a way of penalizing a local decision to raise taxes without simultaneously improving services, we must mean that there are fewer or less satisfactory replacements for the taxpayers who have left. There has to be some net loss imposed on municipal authorities for exit to be any sort of discipline.

There are cases in which exit is encouraged, as when Kansas prohibitionists said "good riddance" to the beer-drinking German immigrants who veered off to the wetter climes of Missouri and Nebraska in the 1800s (Robert Bader 1986, p. 111). But that only points to the benefits of a having a variety of independent jurisdictions to accommodate differences in taste. Exit has to hurt to be a meaningful discipline.

Although Hirschman's work is often cited by economists in support of the Tiebout model, Hirschman himself was ambivalent about reliance on mobility. In a follow-up article (1978), he opined that having too easy an exit would make it more difficult to accomplish desirable income redistribution in some jurisdictions. His example of undesirable mobility was that of the modern, multinational corporation, whose inclination to leave high-tax jurisdictions he thought inequitable. Among political scientists and legal scholars, the Tiebout model is suspect for the same reasons. Too much mobility is said to promote too little politics (Richard Briffault 1990b, p. 414; Gary Miller 1981, p. 3).

4.2 Homeownership Causes Exit to Amplify Voice

I think there is an error here on both sides, that of the Tiebout-admiring economists and the Tiebout-skeptics such as Hirschman, at least when considering local governments. "Exit" from a local government is regarded as equivalent to selling stocks in a corporation, the usual way by which stockholders who are unhappy with management's decisions can leave (Vicki Been 1991). The stock-selling discipline only works if the sale results in a lower price for the stock, which leaves inefficient managers with less-valuable stock options, makes them vulnerable to hostile takeovers, and reduces their ability to raise new capital. The exit discipline—selling the stock—hurts the seller as well as the wayward managers, insofar as the price is made lower upon leaving. But most stockholders have diversified portfolios, so the hurt is seldom acute, and the capital loss is likely to be offset by capital gains elsewhere. Examination of managerial ability by stock pickers uncovers potential buy orders as well as sell orders.

The owner of a home, by contrast, has a large fraction of her wealth tied up in the property. To sell it at a loss has much greater consequences than selling the stock of an incompetently managed company. Owners of homes cannot diversify their portfolios by spreading out ownership of their asset among more risk-neutral investors.

As a result of this enormous concentration of wealth in one asset, people who buy houses are more careful about it than almost any other episodic transaction, save perhaps getting married. Such care is reflected in the evidence that public benefits and costs are capitalized in the value of owner-occupied housing. But this creates what may seem like a paradox: Evidence of Tiebout mobility from the capitalization studies is actually support for the idea that, once you buy the house, you are stuck with it, and you then have an incentive to exercise as much voice as you can to protect and enhance its value. "Exit"—unwillingness by prospective homebuyers to enter—promotes "voice" (political participation) by would-be homesellers.

It is rare for homeowners to move just because the public service mix is not to their liking. One reason for this is that the knowledge that taxes have become unexpectedly high or schools are worse than anticipated is seldom limited to the homeowner in question. Because the new knowledge is likely to be public, moving in response to bad news is more difficult because the seller would get a lower price for her house than otherwise. This reduction in wealth—the bank does not reduce your mortgage obligation just because taxes go up—is apt to make it more difficult to move.

Reduced mobility as a result of capitalization has a distinct upside: It makes homeowners—the dominant municipal stockholders—eager to organize to prevent the unhappy events that reduce their home values. Once you have made the purchase, your only protection against community decline is watchfulness and activism. No one sells insurance against the risk of community decline.

The prospect of being stuck with a devalued asset makes those who are mobile into very careful shoppers, and this makes the housing market an unexpectedly accurate indicator of community qualities. This resolves the seeming paradox of voice being promoted by exit. They are not really contradictory disciplines. After the house has been purchased, the best hope of maintaining or improving one's investment is "voice," involvement in the political process. The capital loss that the owner might suffer upon exit in fact is what encourages so much voice by homeowners in local government, and it is what makes prospective buyers of homes so eager to be informed about local conditions.

4.3 Charles Tiebout Challenged the Free-Rider Theory

I have written for years about the Tiebout model and occasionally wondered what the author of the idea was like and how he came up with it. Tiebout died in 1968. When I was in Seattle in 1998, Dick Morrill, a retired geography professor, mentioned that Tiebout had spent the last six years of his fourteen-year academic career at the University of Washington. In the autumn of 1999, I contacted several of his friends and colleagues and talked with his son, Bruce Tiebout, to obtain some of the facts about his life. (Bruce confirmed that the family name is pronounced *Tee*-bow, the latter syllable rhyming with the bow of arrows and cellos.)

Charles Mills Tiebout was born on October 12, 1924, and grew up in Greenwich, Connecticut, a suburb of New York City. He was the second of the three children of Harry Morgan and Ethel Mills Tiebout. Harry was a psychiatrist and was famous as the first of his profession to endorse the methods of Alcoholics Anonymous.

After service in the navy during World War II and graduation from Wesleyan University, Charlie Tiebout began working on his PhD in economics at the University of Michigan in 1950. Richard Musgrave, the doyen of American public economics, was at Michigan at the time, and Tiebout took his course. But Musgrave's influence was indirect. Tiebout published his famous 1956 article after he had taken a job as an assistant professor of economics at Northwestern in 1954. The article was not based on Tiebout's Michigan dissertation (1957), which had been directed by Daniel Suits and which analyzed Keynesian multiplier effects in local economies.

Musgrave, however, did inspire Tiebout's article. While Tiebout was at Michigan, Musgrave was putting together his landmark work, *The Theory of Public Finance* (1959). He had years before written an influential article, "The Voluntary Exchange Theory of Public Economy" (1939). Musgrave showed that such a theory, advanced by some European economists of the late 1800s, was untenable because of human nature. People would not reveal their true valuation for public goods if the goods would be provided regardless of whether they paid. A market-based "voluntary exchange" mechanism would simply not work. Paul Samuelson embedded this pessimistic assumption in his seminal article, "The Pure Theory of Public Expenditures" (1954), in which he showed that an optimal level of public expenditures existed in principle, but it could not be attained by ordinary market processes.

The upshot of the Musgrave-Samuelson view of public goods was that economists conceded that politics, not the market system, necessarily determined the level and composition of collective goods. It was this deference to politics that Tiebout set out to challenge. The title of Tiebout's work, "A Pure Theory of Local Expenditures" (1956), obviously paralleled Samuelson's title, but its inspiration was more likely the work of his Michigan professor, Musgrave. Tiebout's avowed objective was to suggest a model by which public goods could be provided efficiently without politics.

4.4 Tiebout Had to Be an Out-of-the-Box Thinker

Although Tiebout did not write about his idea while at Michigan, it did occur to him while he was there. Richard Musgrave told me in 1994 that Tiebout had orally presented his hypothesis in his Michigan seminar (which I infer was around 1952). As Musgrave recalled for me in a conversation in 1994, however, Tiebout had presented his ideas in a lighthearted, joking manner. That Musgrave did not take it too seriously is suggested by the fact that there is only passing mention of it (p. 132) in his 1959 book. The "voting by feet" idea, attributed to Tiebout, is described briefly in Musgrave and Musgrave's text, *Public Finance in Theory and Practice* (1989, p. 453), but it is dismissed as "unrealistic" in most settings.

Tiebout's lighthearted presentation of his theory in Musgrave's class was initially puzzling to me. Why would someone come up with a good theory and not be serious about it? But as I interviewed more people who knew him, I found that humor was one of Tiebout's most notable traits. Almost everyone remarked on this, and many of his contemporaries have stories about his capers. Even Tiebout's children thought he was funny, an accomplishment any parent can envy. Bruce Tiebout told me that his father's Christmas cards were legendary. After moving from Evanston to Los Angeles in 1958 to take a job at UCLA, he sent as his card a photograph of his family on the beach. The three young children are smilingly reading economics texts, while Charlie and his wife Betty are poring over comic books with looks of great concentration.

My point in this digression is to suggest that Tiebout's insight into the problem of public goods was a product of his out-of-the-box way of looking at things. Such a viewpoint may have been essential. Government centralization was the watchword of the 1950s, whose adults remembered all too clearly two world wars and the Great Depression they bracketed. The focus on national governments, the only institutions believed capable of responding to such cataclysms, was everywhere. In his wide-ranging survey of fiscal federalism, Wallace Oates (1999, p. 1142) pointed out that centralization of governments reached its worldwide high point in the 1950s. For those intellectuals who thought about it at all during that era, America's fragmented system of local government was regarded as an embarrassment (Jon Teaford 1997, p. 85).

One might suspect that the town-meeting tradition of Tiebout's New England hometown (Greenwich, Connecticut) led him to think more seriously about local government, but his best friend from his youth, Philip Worn (who married Tiebout's sister), recalled no such interest. I like to suppose instead that Tiebout's anarchical sense of humor, his ability to look at the world with the off-center detachment that humor both requires and engenders, had something to do with formulating his revolutionary hypothesis.

4.5 Tiebout's Work Remained Unfinished

Tiebout's model did not have a political sector because his primary objective was to show that it was possible to obtain a market-like determination of the ideal level of public goods. He did insert "municipal managers" in his model, but they were assumed to be entirely nonpolitical. They simply offered a set of services, and people then selected a community. To avoid the need to inquire about how the managers got direction, Tiebout (1956, pp. 417, 420) alluded to the Darwinian possibility suggested by Armen Alchian (1950). Deliberate profit maximization by such managers was not necessary for them to achieve the effect of profit maximization and, hence, the least-cost level of public services. A competitive process analogous to biological natural selection would ensure that the surviving firms' objectives would appear to be profit maximizing. This would occur even when managers were radically uncertain about future market conditions.

But, as many scholars have concluded, Tiebout's model still seems to require politics to ensure that its municipal managers will not behave inefficiently, at least when landowners cannot secede from jurisdictions and municipalities are not infinitely divisible (Epple and Zelenitz 1981; Vernon Henderson 1985). I concur. The evolutionary process of winnowing out unprofitable firms that Alchian suggested as a substitute for profit maximization seems less applicable to municipalities. They seldom go out of business, secession from existing municipalities is rare, and new towns and cities are created only episodically (Sections 2.3 and 3.14). Moreover, the uncertainties of the market, which led Alchian to propose his evolutionary theory, seem less important for local public services. It takes less entrepreneurial guesswork to know the demands of community residents for municipal services. Unlike corporate shareholders, resident "owners" of municipal corporations are the consumers of the product. If the public works director fails to maintain local roads, municipal shareholders feel it in their shock absorbers.

Tiebout did not publish or even suggest an empirical test of his 1956 hypothesis. Perhaps for this reason, it did not get much attention until Oates published his 1969 study showing that local government taxes and spending were reflected in house prices. It is probably more accurate to call it the Tiebout-Oates hypothesis. Tiebout did not even mention property taxation in his model, though, to be fair, he was responding to Musgrave's and Samuelson's theories of expenditure determination, not taxation. It was not until Bruce Hamilton (1975) introduced zoning into Tiebout's model that one could answer the criticism of Buchanan and Goetz (1972), among others, that the poor would endlessly chase the rich around the metropolitan area in a Tiebout model.

Tiebout wrote only a few other papers about local government, and only one of those, coauthored with Vincent Ostrom and Charles Warren (1961), has had much influence. The larger part of his research focused on regional economic development, and he achieved considerable success in this area as a scholar and as a high-level consultant. He devoted most of his professional time at the University of Washington, to which he had moved in 1962, to its distinguished geography department. The department maintains a Tiebout website listing his publications, and the Western Regional Science Association has a dissertation prize in his memory. But his writing in regional science had almost no connection with his now-famous 1956 paper.

The fame of the "Tiebout hypothesis" is primarily among social scientists with an interest in local government and fiscal federalism. His name appears in a whopping 1,500 articles in the Social Science Citation Index between 1975 and 1999. Of the most recent one hundred citations (as of 1999, covering less than a year), all are to his 1956 article. He died in Seattle from a sudden heart attack on January 16, 1968, at age forty-three. His wife, Betty, survived him by thirty-one years, and his three children, Charles, Bruce, and Carol, still live in the Seattle area.

4.6 Homeowners Rule (and Renters Do Not)

I have proposed to remedy Tiebout's omission of a political sector by inserting homeowners as the prime movers of the model, and this section defends my focus and its neglect of renters. The largest and most active group of voters in all but a few cities consists of homeowners. (I am counting, as the U.S. Census does, owner-occupants of condominiums, row houses, cooperatives, and mobile homes—not just detached, single-family homes, though this is by far the largest category.) National data indicate that about 67 percent of all households are in owner-occupied units. This actually understates the pervasiveness of homeownership as an institution. A study by Jim Berkovec and Peter Zorn (1998) concluded that between 80 and 90 percent of Americans own a home at some time in their lives.

Nearly every study has shown that renters participate in local affairs in disproportionately low numbers compared to homeowners. In a national survey, 77 percent of homeowners said that they voted in local elections during the period 1984–1992, while only 52 percent of the renters did (Rossi and Weber 1996, p. 23). Evidence from individual cities confirms the national data. A New Orleans referendum on homestead tax exemptions was examined by Pamela Moomau and Rebecca Morton (1992). They found that homeowners know and vote their interests. Renters did not participate much even when there appeared to be gains to them from doing so. And studies of apartment-rental differences among communities find that renters do not appear to pay close attention to the quality of local public services (Carroll and Yinger 1994), in contrast to the overwhelming evidence that homeowners do (Martinez-Vazquez and Sjoquist 1988).

Low renter participation in politics is not confined to municipal governance structures. Most private homeowner associations, which regulate the affairs of condominiums and "planned communities," do not enfranchise renters in their governance structures. It is especially interesting, then, that the progressive-minded developers of Columbia, Maryland, one of the largest and most successful of the recent privately developed communities, did allow tenants to vote and permitted them to run for community-association offices. As Lynne Burkhardt (1981, p. 27) documented, however, renters' participation in community affairs in Columbia remained much lower than that of owner-occupied units. Asset ownership matters.

4.7 Rent Control Is Rare Because of Homeowners

If renters lack political influence, why, my friends from New York ask me, do we have rent control? That policy certainly serves renters who already live in the city, even as it denies those not there access to the cheaper units (since with the lower rents, tenant turnover is much reduced). I choose to turn the question on its head and ask, why don't most cities have rent control? Stringent rent control is rare except in places like New York City, which in 1980 had 7.8 percent of the nation's rental stock and a supermajority (75 percent) of renter-voters.

As of 1983, a high point for rent control, only 10 percent of all rental units in the United States were subject to rent control (mostly in New York City), and about half of those ordinances allowed market-rate rents to be charged to new tenants once the previous tenants departed (Kenneth Baar 1983). As of 1991, a little more than two hundred municipalities had rent-control ordinances (Edgar Olsen 1991, p. 931). Although some states have constitutional constraints that prevent local governments from adopting rent control, two hundred still seems like a tiny fraction of the more than 25,000 local governments with police-power authority under which rent control could be adopted.

Rent control's scarcity is a political puzzle. Even in the suburbs, renters greatly outnumber landlords. A local politician seeking votes could tip the balance in her favor by promising to enact rent control and related tenant-security legislation whose effect is to transfer at least some of the value of apartments from their nominal owners to the current tenants. It could be, of course, that landlords offer something even more valuable than votes to politicians: cash for their campaigns. But the jingle of that voice is muted in smaller communities, in which the positions of the candidates are pretty clear to everyone. Yet rent control, at least its more stringent brand, is nearly absent in small communities even in states where its adoption is entirely a matter of local option. (Rent control is "stringent" if it is supplemented by regulations restricting conversion of apartments to other uses, thus foreclosing landlord exit, and if it keeps rents below market levels even when new tenants move in [Olsen 1991].)

Stringent rent control is rare, I submit, because it is usually bad for homeowners. There are two effects they might worry about. Rent control almost always results in some physical deterioration of buildings because owners have less incentive to maintain their structures if rents are low. Some excess depreciation is offset by informal tenant contributions and by the force of habitability laws, but the consensus is that the net effect of rent control on building quality is negative (Joseph Gyourko 1990; Moon and Stotsky 1993). Because this neighborhood blight might spill over to owner-occupied homes, homeowners have reason to oppose rent control.

Another reason that homeowners do not like rent control is that it shifts the burden of taxation from apartment owners to homeowners (Anthony Downs 1983, p. 141). Although moderate rent controls do not seem to reduce apartment house values by much, stringent rent control in Berkeley and Santa Monica clearly did so (Michael St. John 1990). Such reductions in value can have insidious consequences. A profile of Robert Moses, New York's highway builder of the 1950s, noted that his infamous demolition of the East Tremont neighborhood in the Bronx to make way for the Cross Bronx Expressway was financially rational. The apartment houses of East Tremont, in which thousands of tenants lived, were cheaper to purchase than nearby commercial property because the apartments were subject to rent control. Their landlords were eager to be rid of them (Robert Caro 1998, p. 48). As these examples suggest, the reductions in value of apartments by rent control mean that owners of other properties, chiefly owner-occupants, must shoulder more of the local property-tax burden.

4.8 Proposition 13 Promoted Rent Control

My view that homevoters restrain rent control is supported by the sudden increase in the number and stringency of local rent control laws in California after Proposition 13 (Jeffrey Chapman 1981). This famous 1978 voter initiative figures large elsewhere in the present book. It is the most important fiscal event at the state and local levels since the Great Depression, so it is worth two paragraphs to explain what it did. (Readable legal reviews of its background and consequences are Joseph Henke [1986] and Henke and Woodlief [1988].)

In a statewide election on June 6, 1978, the California constitution was amended, by a popular vote of nearly 2–1, so as to limit the ad valorum (monetary value) taxation of any property in the state to no more than 1 percent of assessed value. The only exception was to pay for previously adopted bond issues. No statewide property tax of any sort was thereafter allowed, but new local taxes not on the dollar value of property are permitted as long as they are approved by a two-thirds majority of the jurisdiction. The latter taxes are called "parcel taxes." They typically tax each parcel the same amount and are most commonly used in affluent suburbs to provide modest supplements to local school spending (Brunner and Sonstelie 1997).

More critical for my argument about rent control is that Proposition 13 rolled back all assessed values to their 1975 levels. This by itself was a significant tax break, since nominal home values in California had grown by about 20 percent per year between 1975 and 1978. As long as the owner did not sell the property, her assessment could grow by no more than 2 percent per year. Upon sale of the property, it was reassessed at market value, but this assessment could then rise by no more than 2 percent per year. Homeowners who had purchased prior to Proposition 13's passage in 1978 and have not sold their homes often have tax liabilities of less than one-tenth of otherwise identical homes that have sold recently. The average California effective property tax rate (the ratio of taxes paid to true market value) in the early 1990s was a shade over one-half of 1 percent because so many homes were not sold (O'Sullivan, Sexton, and Sheffrin 1995, p. 137).

The spread of rent control among California cities after 1978 was widely attributed to the supposed promise by Proposition 13's garrulous promoter, Howard Jarvis, that property tax reductions would benefit tenants as well as homeowners. This was seemingly made more credible by Jarvis's day job as lobbyist for an apartment owners' association in Los Angeles. When the rent reductions did not materialize, the story goes, cities were urged to enact rent controls to spread the benefits of the tax cut to tenants.

The holes in this story are gaping. Apartment owners had strenuously denied Jarvis's claims in full-page newspaper advertisements prior to the vote (*Sacramento Bee*, May 12, 1978). Jarvis himself was hardly a credible source. He claimed that a wide range of benefits would occur on passage of Proposition 13 that were palpably untrue. For instance, he claimed that school funding would not be harmed by Proposition 13, despite the fact that the statewide reduction in property taxes just about equaled the sum of all school budgets for the entire state. And the theory also supposes that California rent-control activists had somehow been restrained prior to Proposition 13 by the notion that rent controls could not be adopted because rent levels were determined by property taxes. I never encountered a rent-control activist who thought that rents were determined by anything other than the greed of landlords.

A more logical explanation for the spread of rent control is that after Proposition 13 passed, homeowners had much less to lose by allowing tenant-activists to push for rent control. Under Proposition 13's assessment rules, property tax liabilities on individual homes no longer depended on the value of other property in the community. A reduction in the value of apartments no longer shifted the burden of taxation to homeowners, because homeowners' assessments were maxed out by the 1975-plus-2-percent rule. Even for homes that were sold and reassessed, the 1 percent maximum rate meant, in most communities, that additional funds could not be extracted from homeowners. Thus apartment-house owners lost their best allies—homeowners—to fiscal indifference, and the rent control debate took the lopsided form of tenants versus landlords.

I concede that California homeowners retained their anxiety about blighted apartments, and reductions in property-tax revenue from devalued apartment buildings may have worsened local fiscal conditions, even if it did not raise homeowners' taxes. But this only explains why rent control is not universal in California. It is the sudden uptick in rent control after Proposition 13 that was unusual. The spread of rent control after 1978 is consistent with my view that homeowners are the dominant political faction in most places and that local politics can be predicted to a large extent by a policy's effect on home values.

4.9 The Commonwealth of the Property Tax Base

My account here is not simply a different story about rent control. It also shows that property taxes are a relatively sensible local source of revenue. (This section anticipates a theme I will expand on in Section 8.2.) Rent control can be an enormously destructive force for part of the community, blighting areas much like placement of an unmanaged waste dump could. By making apartment values part of the community's commonwealth, normal ad valorum property taxation makes the more extreme forms of rent control and other opportunistic transfers of wealth less attractive to homeowners. Proposition 13 tore down that commonwealth system, and policies such as rent control became more attractive.

I hesitate to make the following addendum about rent control, because I worry that it could be used out of context, sort of like the rare economic case against free trade. There is an economic case for rent control, though, that does not rely on what I regard as silly theories about the imbalance of power between landlord and tenant. (Silly because the tenant has at least as many ways to inflict extralegal pain on an unfair landlord as vice versa.) The case is that rent control turns tenants into homevoters. One reason that tenants do not vote or participate in local affairs as much as homeowners is that renters do not have as much stake in the outcome. It is nice if schools get better or neighborhood amenities improve, but it also means that landlords get to raise the rents (Timothy Bartik 1986). If the tenant is protected from rent increases, though, he gets to enjoy the local improvements without having to pay more, and he might therefore become a more involved citizen.

Two qualifications are in order. One is that most landlords have an implicit rent-control policy for seated tenants. Rents are seldom adjusted upward for them to market levels, at least in noninflationary times (Robert Ellickson 1991b, p. 951). The reason is that turnover of financially reliable, well-behaved tenants is the second-last thing the landlord typically wants. (Last is formal rent control.) Thus most long-term tenants do have some self-interested incentives to participate in local affairs, and that may account for why they do participate to some extent, even though their voting rates are well below those of homeowners.

The more important qualification is that it is not difficult for landlords to convert apartment buildings to condominiums, so that renters can become owners if there is demand for it. If we really think that owner-occupancy makes better citizens, there are lots of ways to encourage it. But stringent rent controls almost always do the opposite. Among the most onerous burdens of stringent rent controls are regulations that prohibit condo conversion, even when seated tenants are protected from eviction. As I suggested in an article about regulatory takings and rent control (Fischel 1991b), such laws prevent the exit remedy that would ordinarily temper rent regulations, and, in such instances, the only protection for apartment owners may be the courts.

4.10 Does Homeownership Cause Unemployment?

I cannot not leave homeownership without mentioning at least one potential downside. Andrew Oswald (1996) has cross-country and cross-state evidence that high rates of homeownership seem to cause unemployment. This odd-sounding result is explained not so much by homeowners themselves becoming unemployed as by policies that discourage the rental market. Lack of rental apartments discourages migration from job-poor to job-rich areas because, apparently, out-of-region job seekers have no place to stay during their search and trial periods.

Unemployed people who own homes are reluctant to leave because of the transaction costs of selling a home and attachment to their community. For example, L. F. Dunn (1979) found that permanently laid-off textile workers in a rural town would accept a wage 14 percent lower in their town rather than move for work in another city. Reluctance to leave, however, seems less important than inability to find temporary quarters at the prospective destination. After all, the reluctance to leave is caused in part by something that many find admirable: loyalty to one's community and neighbors.

Scarcity of rental housing seems to have less worthy spillover effects. Among those policies that restrain the apartment market (and thus, by default, stimulate homeownership rates that are too high) is rent control. Developers of multifamily housing eschew the rental market when rent control is anticipated, and those that do brave it have to be rewarded for their risk-taking with higher rents (Avinash Dixit 1991; Fallis and Smith 1984). Thus Oswald's finding is not so much an indictment of homeownership—it's no great compliment, either—as it is yet another argument against rent control and similar legislation that restricts consensual exchange in the housing market.

We may at least conclude from Oswald's work that the fact that homeowners might be better citizens does not warrant a policy of encouraging ownership at the expense of rental units. Even if we put aside the financial difficulties that poor people have in purchasing a home, national and regional unemployment issues may warrant a more active rental market than any individual community might want. Newcomers often need rental units to get their feet in the job-market door. Sawing off the bottom rung on the housing ladder does not make it easier for people to climb to the top.

4.11 Median Voters Work Best in Local Governments

My discussion of municipal corporations in Chapter 2 emphasized the active role of homeowners in governing municipalities. Business corporations do not have such active shareholders, I argued, in part because the divisibility of share ownership allows stockholders to spread their risks. With only a small stake in any given firm, business stockholders have little incentive to pay attention to their internal governance. Now it is time to defend my emphasis on the role of homeowners in municipal affairs.

The median-voter model of politics, which is the social-science name for majority rule, was first elaborated by Howard Bowen (1943). His hypothesis was that under majority rule, the householder who had the median income, or, I would add, median home value, in the community would get the public services and taxes he demanded. This would be true by definition if all residents simply voted on all issues that had an economic effect. But the median-voter model goes further and asserts that this result will hold even in representative governments. Elected officials select budgets and taxes "as if" they had been voted on in a plebiscite. (To be precise, the model should be called the "median-income-voter" or the "median-home-value voter" model, but I will continue to use the economists' shorthand and omit the precise economic characteristic along which voters are lined up.)

The median-voter model has been subjected to an extensive set of statistical tests in the economics literature, and most of these tests have involved samples of local governments. The consensus as I read it is that the median-voter model holds up quite well in comparison with its alternatives. The alternatives are (1) that bureaucrats expand the level of public services to increase their own wealth and power (William Niskanen 1971), (2) that concentrated economic interests lobby successfully for a set of goods of little interest to the median voter (George Stigler 1971), or (3) that some combination of bureaucrats and special interests set all-or-nothing voting agendas so that the median voter has to select more than she wants (Romer and Rosenthal 1979).

Thomas Borcherding and Robert Deacon (1972) and Ted Bergstrom and Robert Goodman (1973) were among the first to test whether the median-income voter actually got the level of public goods that Bowen hypothesized. Both studies used samples drawn from cross-sections of American local governments. They found that expenditures on various municipal services seemed to vary among them according to the economic characteristics of the median-income voter. Their results, appropriately hedged and qualified, indicated that the median-voter approach worked well. The level of public services seems to have been set "as if" a referendum among the voters had been held on every issue, even in jurisdictions in which referenda are never held.

The evidence since then is overwhelmingly in favor of the median voter at the local level. William McEachern (1978) found that the levels of bonded indebtedness of jurisdictions that voted directly on them and those in which the city council had the final say were not significantly different. Robert Inman (1978) examined fifty-eight Long Island school districts and similarly found that the median voter accurately predicted differences in school spending. Bergstrom, Rubinfeld, and Shapiro (1982) found a similar result for Michigan school districts: Decisions by plebiscites closely matched those by elected representatives. Other studies were reviewed by Randall Holcombe (1989), who found the results sufficiently persuasive that he proposed the median voter as an appropriate benchmark for all government decisions, the analog to perfect competition in private markets.

Although the empirical evidence for the median voter is impressive, a nagging question remains: How does representative politics at the local level actually work to give the median voter what she wants? I submit that it works because of local government's corporate template. Unlike the states and the national government, whose antimajoritarian institutions include bicameral legislatures, independent executives and judiciaries, and difficult-to-amend constitutions, municipal corporations are structured to give the majority what it wants (Ellickson 1977, p. 405). Cities seldom have more than a single legislature, and many dispense with separately elected executives altogether. The most common governance structure in smaller cities is the council-manager form, in which voters elect a council and the council selects the city's chief executive officer (Section 2.2).

Saul Levmore (1992) offers an explanation for the apparent lack of fear of majoritarianism at the local level: The threat of exit keeps government excesses in check, so there is less need for institutional constraints. The discipline of the market, of the smiles and frowns of the rest of the world, usually motivates homevoters in cities to forgo value-reducing behavior. The discipline of exit apparently influences the evolution of political institutions as well as ordinary politics. If exit is easy, majoritarian political institutions are easier to tolerate, and those forms come to dominate. This is why the median-voter model works so well at the local level.

4.12 Low Turnouts Can Be Signs of Satisfaction

Critics of the median-voter model note that few jurisdictions vote directly on public services. We have representative government in all but small New England towns. Even most town meetings are attended by only a small fraction of the eligible voters, and voters usually decide a carefully limited range of issues. And it is well established that voter participation is generally lower in purely local elections than in national elections (Verba and Nie 1972, p. 31).

Low political participation, however, could also be a sign of satisfaction by adult residents who, in nearly all cases, deliberately chose to live in a particular town. A national study of cities by Eric Oliver (1999) finds that more homogeneous communities, both rich and poor, have lower rates of participation in voting and other local political activity than cities with heterogeneous populations. Oliver argues that the lower participation in homogenized communities is caused by having less conflict to be resolved. Tiebout-sorting among preferred communities seems to induce lethargy in local politics. (Robert Dilger [1992, p. 140] reports similar lethargy among private homeowner associations.) To invert the conclusion, as Bill Niskanan suggested to me, higher participation at the national level reflects the lack of "exit" options from that jurisdiction.

Focus on average voting rates is misleading in any event. At the local level, there are many ways besides voting to influence public officials. Letter writing, buttonholing, attending meetings and hearings, and organizing neighborhood groups are all more effective and frequent at the local level than at the state and national levels (Verba, Schlozman, and Brady 1995, p. 453). Besides, average voting rates mask the variation in local voting turnouts from year to year. For example, New England town-meeting attendance, which involves a larger time commitment than just voting, fluctuates according to the intensity of the issue involved (Joseph Zimmerman 1999). A serious controversy can easily double or triple the participation rate at the local level, while it seldom does more than jiggle the state and national voting rates. Frank Easterbrook and Daniel Fischel (1983, p. 415) make the same argument in defense of voting in business corporations. Average participation in stockholder meetings is low, but it can rise dramatically when an important issue, such as a takeover, is on the table.

4.13 The Size of the Government Makes a Difference

Thomas Romer and Howard Rosenthal (1979) were not so impressed with the median-voter model. To them the econometric evidence was not convincing because the ideal level of public spending could be some multiple of what the median voter actually prefers. An agenda-setting school administrator might offer an all-or-nothing proposal to voters that would force them to agree to a larger amount. Thus one could find statistically significant variation in spending according to median-voter characteristics, but average spending might actually be 50 percent more than what the voters actually want.

Much of the controversy about the applicability of the median-voter model can be resolved by noting that the size of the jurisdiction seems to make a difference. Geoffrey Turnbull and Peter Mitias (1999) compared the median-voter model's predictions with an open set of alternative explanations for government tax and expenditure patterns. They found that the median-voter model dominated others in a sample of municipalities, but when applied to counties and state governments in the same region as the municipalities (the upper Midwest), no particular model consistently explained spending variations.

Another approach was employed by John Matsusaka (1995; 2000), who compared states that permitted voter initiatives, in which the median voter would seem to prevail by definition, with states that do not. (The split is about half-and-half, with most of the initiative states in the West.) He wanted to see if the initiative states had fiscal policies that were different from those of states whose legislatures made all the statewide laws. In the noninitiative states, the voters cannot second-guess their legislatures. If there was no difference between the two groups of states, then state legislatures might best be considered as faithful agents of the median voter. Matsusaka's extensive studies found, however, that the initiative states had smaller (1995) and more decentralized (2000) public sectors. This suggests that in normal, representative state politics, the will of the majority does not always prevail, which is why initiatives were adopted in the first place (Thomas Cronin 1989).

Other evidence about the influence of jurisdiction size comes from Howard Bloom and Helen Ladd (1982). They asked whether budgets of Massachusetts towns and cities were opportunistically increased after property assessments were raised. The median-voter model would predict that an increase in property assessments would simply cause tax rates to decrease, which would keep revenues constant. Most of the model's competitors would say that bureaucrats or special interests would take advantage of the apparent windfall and spend more.

Bloom and Ladd found evidence for both ideas. In bigger cities, legislative councils did take some liberties with the nominally larger tax base and spend more, but in small towns, tax rates were dutifully cut. In small towns, the voters get what they want. One price of residence in a big city is greater slippage between want and get, in part because, as William Hoyt (1999) theorized, lack of capitalization makes voters careless about local government efficiency. Perhaps this explains why large cities continue to build fixed-rail transit systems despite evidence that they will not solve any urban problem except unemployment among construction workers (Kenneth Small 1992).

A result similar to Bloom and Ladd's was found by Dennis Holtz-Eakin and Harvey Rosen (1989). Their study of capital budgeting in New Jersey municipalities found that suburban and rural jurisdictions behaved as if governed by the rational median voter. The smaller towns used appropriate discount rates and time horizons, while large cities did not. And even Romer, Rosenthal, and Munley (1992), the first two of whom had cast doubt on the median-voter model, found that the median-voter model worked well in smaller New York State school districts, but not (as they expected) in the larger, urban districts.

4.14 Bigger Cities Are Smaller Players

The evidence in the previous section suggested that homeowning shareholders have problems governing large municipal corporations. This is similar to the Berle and Means (1932) hypothesis, which says that large business corporations are imperfectly responsive to shareholders. The modern answer to Berle and Means is that the stock market takes care of the problem of managerial discretion by making firms run by managerial slackers ripe for takeovers (Easterbrook and Fischel 1991, p. 171). Here I suggest that the size problem is less important in municipalities because, unlike big businesses, big cites are not all that important, and because many big cities have adopted governance structures that protect homeowners.

As I mentioned in Section 1.9, only about 25 percent of Americans live in cities with more than 100,000 people. I regard that size as a rough threshold at which voters find it difficult to know what is going on in city hall. For larger places, the median voter model shades into the interest-group model. As a benchmark for academics, I note that Ann Arbor, Berkeley, and Cambridge are municipalities with about 100,000 residents.

The foregoing 25 percent statistic is a little misleading. About 20 percent of the U.S. population in 1990 lived in "unincorporated" areas of counties. Most of these people are nonetheless supplied with municipal services by county governments, and some of these counties have populations that exceed 100,000. Unincorporated areas, however, can become incorporated as new cities, or they can be annexed by existing cities, so it is not proper to count them as if their present status were immutable. Although the declining demographic importance of large cities is mostly caused by depopulation of central cities, some of it is also caused by the incorporation of new, smaller cities.

There are two complementary reasons for why homevoters have more influence in small rather than large jurisdictions. The more obvious is that smaller size itself makes it more likely that voters will know what is going on in local government. The issues are fewer and political figures are more accessible in smaller jurisdictions. It is well established that political participation is greater in smaller cities, which offsets the lower participation caused by homogeneity (Eric Oliver 1999). More important, I believe, is that most voters in smaller jurisdictions are homeowners. They have an incentive to pay attention to politics: Good decisions will increase the value of their major asset, and bad ones will reduce it.

4.15 Big Cities Can Decentralize to Empower Residents

Unlike shareholders in large business corporations, the shareholders of big cities cannot deal with their agency problems by resorting to stock market diversification. Ownership in their homes cannot be divided into fractional shares. So city dwellers resort to political reforms that appear to make municipal operations different from those of business corporations. For example, almost all cities have laws requiring easy public access to the decision process of both elected officials (the "board of directors") and hired managers. Sunshine laws, freedom of information, and open-meeting rules all promote shareholder information. Specialists in exploiting this information—local newspaper reporters, political gadflies, and would-be office holders—reduce the cost of monitoring for the average citizen. While such openness can inhibit some otherwise efficient transactions, it should be seen as part of the process by which municipal corporations are made more responsive to their shareholders.

The voter initiative is another device by which large cities are made more responsive to their resident shareholders. Although most scholarly writing about initiatives concerns their use in dealing with statewide issues, the vast majority of cities with populations larger than 50,000 permit voters to initiate laws independently of city councils and vote on them in a citywide election. As Tari Renner and Victor DeSantis (1993, p. 69) indicate, the initiative is most popular in the larger cities. All of the cities with populations greater than 500,000 that responded to their extensive survey had the initiative.

A structural reform that makes big cities more responsive to homeowners is ward voting. Ward voting is most common in large cities, especially in the eastern and central United States. It declined during the first two-thirds of the twentieth century as part of the municipal-reform movement that opposed big-city bosses and political machines (Renner and DeSantis 1993, p. 57). This trend reversed itself when federal enforcement of the Voting Rights Act of 1965 caused many cities to replace at-large election of city councils with elections by wards or districts. Tim Sass and Stephan Mehay (1995) found that adoption of electoral districts did increase council representation by minorities.

Ward representation also has quantifiable results on the land-use front. Evidence from Atlanta indicates that black neighborhoods were no longer peppered with unwanted commercial development after ward representation was adopted and blacks were elected to city council (Hinds and Ordway 1986). Ward-based cities behave more like suburbs in land-use decisions. Siting locally unwanted activities like group homes becomes everywhere more difficult in ward-based cities than in those with at-large councils (James Clingermayer 1994). Clingermayer (1993) also found that early zoning laws were adopted most frequently in cities with ward representation, which is consistent with the greater influence in ward-based systems of homeowners, who occupy the apex of the zoning pyramid. A survey of 1,400 cities by Mark Schneider and Paul Teske (1993, p. 732) found that cities with ward representation were less prodevelopment than those that elected councils at large.

Election of city councils by wards in many ways turns the cities into collections of small towns, and homeowners become more influential. Ward-based politics means that each councilmember pays close attention to local issues. Describing the ward-based city of Los Angeles, Edward Banfield (1965, p. 84) quoted a local politician as saying, "By custom, the councilman is considered the administrator of the city services in his district."

4.16 Logrolling and Special Districts Also Decentralize

I should not give the impression that neighborhood (ward) politics in big cities gives the wards and the cities the same fiscal incentives as independent suburbs. Tax rates must usually be uniform throughout the city, and this makes an important difference in the wards' political economy. If a ward were an independent taxing district (like a separate municipality), its decision on whether to expand the size of the local library would have to account for both sides of the financial scale. The improved library would raise home values, but the increased property taxes would depress them. Only if the beneficial appreciation effect exceeded the depressing effect of higher taxes would homeowners favor it. This would promote an efficient number and size of libraries. But in the big city, a neighborhood library is paid from taxes in all wards, not just in the one in which it is located. The benefits accrue to the neighborhood, but the costs are borne citywide.

The library example may overstate the differences between big and small cities. In big cities, political deals will be made to satisfy various neighborhoods. Larger cities may actually establish formal neighborhood associations (rather than wards) to broker public services (Berry, Portney, and Thomson 1993). Deals may involve spreading the libraries and parks and road improvements around or trading one for another—a park in this area, a library in that one. Thus even in relatively large cities it may be possible to obtain many of the efficiency advantages of property-tax financing of services. And submunicipal business- and neighborhood-improvement districts, which are rapidly growing in large cities, do restrict taxes and spending to particular areas (Richard Briffault 1997; Ellickson 1998). Such areas should be treated as if they were smaller municipalities, at least for the services that they finance.

Business improvement districts are financing services in much the same way that special assessment districts finance capital improvements. My town has a "sidewalk district" for which urban property owners are taxed and rural dwellers are not. Special assessment districts were common in the 1800s (Stephen Diamond 1983). They have become less prevalent since zoning and planning rules have permitted localities to oblige developers themselves to finance capital improvements (Heyman and Gilhool 1964). The transaction costs of setting up informal logrolling deals and formal improvement districts, however, seem higher in larger, multiward cities, so it would be Pollyannaish to suggest that bigger cities are just as efficient as the smaller units of government. I want only to suggest that the differences are not so great as to treat most larger cities as if they were states.

4.17 Conclusion: Tiebout Can Coexist with Politics

I submit that Tiebout's neglect of local government politics requires only modest amendment of his model. In most local governments one just has to replace Tiebout's invisible municipal managers with the median-voter model. The median voter will want to do most of the same things that an entrepreneurial private manager would want to do. The major difference is that the median voter cannot as easily accommodate major changes in the character of the community. Personal attachments and collective decision-making will make it harder to "take the money and run" when an apparently value-increasing change in the community is in the offing. This personal attachment is among the factors that, as I will explain in Chapter 7, make a competitive "race to the bottom" in local environmental affairs among the least plausible scenarios.

Homeowners are clearly the dominant political faction in the communities in which the great majority of Americans reside. Because majority rule, rather than rule by special interests, seems to apply in most local governments, the prospect of capital gains and losses to homeowners is the most consistent motivator of local government activity. The normative aspects of the homevoter hypothesis depend also on the applicability of the Tiebout model to actual government structures. I think the fit is better, at least, than the view that treats local government as a scaled-down state government.

The novelty of my presentation is to take the capitalization of home values out of the sideshow and display it on the midway. In a sense, I am turning the capitalization studies upside down. It is not just that local taxes, schools, and zoning affect home values. It is that this fact makes homeowners organize to be the masters of taxes, schools, and zoning.

A few researchers, most prominently Jan Brueckner (1982; 1983; Brueckner and Joo 1991) and Jon Sonstelie and Paul Portney (1978; 1980b) have developed this connection and shown its relevance with clever empirical studies. But their work has been neglected in much of the policy arena, in part because it has been subjected to economic theory's enervating perfectionist criteria. Harold Demsetz (1969) has derided the criteria as the "nirvana" condition: Because it might be possible for an all-knowing planner to deal with some spillover effect or uncertainty, either of which upset efficiency conditions, the institution in question must be given a failing grade. (For an example, see Truman Bewley [1981] on the theoretical failings of the Tiebout model when compared to the outcomes that might be achieved by an all-knowing central planner.)

Caroline Hoxby (1999) has indirectly addressed this criticism. In the context of a Tiebout-Oates model, she asks whether home-value capitalization by itself generates enough information for voters to choose the efficient level of local services compared to the information that a centralized agency could realistically acquire. She demonstrates with a theoretical model that centralized agencies would have to be nearly omniscient about local demands for services in order to match the performance of housing markets in providing relevant information. The reason that housing markets work better is that they are not subject to the free-rider problem. If you don't pay for the house, you don't get the house and all of the local public services and amenities that are tied to it. Centralized administrators cannot recreate that information because residents have no incentive to reveal it, given that the service will be provided regardless of their inclination to pay.

Even without Hoxby's elegant theoretical argument, my view has been that localism's performance should be compared to the likely performance of the same tasks by national, state, or metropolitan-area bodies. For this comparison, we do not need much theory, since there is an ongoing experiment in replacing local financing with larger-government financing under the rubric of school-finance reform. The next two chapters explore the evidence regarding this modern twist in fiscal federalism.

5

Serrano and the California Tax Revolt

THIS CHAPTER and the next offer an extensive example of how focus on homeowners' interests affords a better account of local government than the traditional public-finance approach, which normally separates spending decisions (in this case, for schools) from taxing decisions. I start with my hypothesis of how California's *Serrano* decision, which equalized school spending in the 1970s, caused Proposition 13, which dramatically cut property taxes in the state in 1978.

Causation is important for my argument because Proposition 13 is regarded by many as an example of the failure of local voters to appreciate their own interests or control local spending. If, as I argue, the median voter is really the power behind the throne in local government, why did all of those California voters rise up with pitchforks in 1978 and pass Proposition 13, which imposed a ham-handed limitation on the main source of local government revenue? I propose to rescue the median-voter model (and the reputation of California voters) by showing that the *Serrano* decision, which was not something desired or anticipated by elected officials and voters, made it perfectly rational for home-value-maximizing voters to jettison more than half of the property tax.

The more general proposition explored in this chapter is that voters tolerate property taxes only when the public services financed by them are capitalized in home values. The spread of *Serrano*-like court cases around the country has, I submit, contributed to a disaffection with local property taxation. In the following chapter I apply this insight to explain why the centralization of education finance induced by the courts has produced such disappointing results.

5.1 *Serrano* Divorced Local Property Taxes from Schools

In August of 1971, the California Supreme Court issued a decision that has continued to reverberate in both California and the rest of the nation. Serrano v. Priest (1971) held that the then-current system of reliance on local property taxes and state aid—a system common throughout the nation—was unconstitutional if disparities in locally taxable property among school districts led to disparities in educational opportunities, which the court apparently took to mean spending per pupil.

The court illustrated the source of its dissatisfaction with the system by pointing to two communities in Los Angeles County. Baldwin Park was a low-income, largely Hispanic city with a meager property-tax base. Beverly Hills was, needless to say, a high-income, "property-rich" city. Although Beverly Hills's tax rate was less than half that of Baldwin Park, it was able to spend more than twice as much per pupil. The *Serrano* plaintiffs had consistently used this pairing to illustrate the unfairness of the property-tax system for funding public education. (For an explanation of how Baldwin Park got to be "property poor," see Section 9.11.)

The 1971 court decision did not specifically find that California's system was unconstitutional as it operated, since only the legal issue, not the facts, had been argued. But the California Supreme Court remanded the case to a lower court with an opinion that more than implied that any variation in spending among districts was to be viewed with great skepticism. Public education was declared to be a "fundamental interest" (96 Cal. Rptr. at 608). Inequalities in public education were, as a result, subject to "strict scrutiny" by the court instead of the usually flaccid standard of "rational basis" for evaluating the legislature's actions. Education funding was by this language put on the same footing as racial discrimination, and the political branches were thus on notice that the courts would tolerate far less inequality, as the courts perceived it, than had been the norm in the past.

The California Supreme Court initially suggested several alternatives to localism in education funding, including full state assumption of funding (which was eventually adopted after Proposition 13 passed in 1978), interdistrict sharing of commercial and industrial tax bases, and a scheme called district power equalization. The last plan would equalize "only" the tax base per pupil among the districts—a sort of consolidation of tax bases without actual merger of districts—after which districts could spend more or less per pupil. The merits of these suggestions in meeting the court's demands were debated in both popular and scholarly tracts, but no one could miss the highly equalitarian rhetoric of the court's 1971 decision.

While the subsequent trial was proceeding, the California legislature attempted to revise its aid formula to reduce the effects of local tax bases on spending. It gave more aid to the property-poor districts, and it tried, with limited success, to restrain local spending in property-rich and high-spending districts in the hope of forestalling the court from implementing a more drastic approach. Much of the state's equalization aid was undone by inflation, however, which made many districts look richer than they were, and by local voter overrides of the state's spending ceilings (Sonstelie, Brunner, and Ardon 2000, chap. 3).

The legislature's efforts were to no avail. In December 1976, the California Supreme Court in *Serrano II* validated a remedial approach that had been crafted by the lower court to which the original decision had been remanded. Judge Jefferson of Los Angeles Superior Court had looked at the possible remedies and the 1971 *Serrano I* decision and concluded that whatever the state did, it had to require that no district spend more than $100 per pupil more than any other, unless the additional spending could be shown to be unrelated to differences in property tax base. Few districts could sustain the latter burden, and the 1976 *Serrano II* decision was widely, and I believe correctly, perceived as requiring essentially equal spending per pupil from all public sources throughout the state (Friedman and Wiseman 1978). The only variations allowed were categorical grants, such as special education, whose categorization did not relate to tax base per pupil.

5.2 *Serrano*'s Centralizing Remedies Influenced Other Courts

As of this writing, about seventeen other state courts have followed *Serrano*'s lead in overturning their state's school-finance arrangements.

I call these cases "*Serrano*-like" or "*Serrano*-inspired," regardless of whether they cite *Serrano* as a leading precedent. For readers who lack legal training, I should point out that state courts often borrow from the decisions of other courts to find both common-law and constitutional precedents (Paul Carrington 1998; Alan Tarr 1998). The deployment of such precedents buttresses the courts' authority in that it suggests they are not making new law but are instead interpreting laws and constitutional provisions that have been around for many years. It does not explain why their judicial predecessors had overlooked the ancient constitutional provisions on which the modern courts have based their decisions.

The characteristic that unites the *Serrano*-style cases is not so much their legal and constitutional reasoning, which changes to fit local circumstances. It is the thrust of their remedies. The *Serrano*-inspired cases have moved their school systems toward more equal expenditures (Evans, Murray, and Schwab 1997) and centralization of funding at the state level (Alan Hickrod et al. 1995), with reduced reliance on local property taxation (Bahl, Sjoquist, and Williams 1990).

Equalization and centralization are logically separate. States could centralize funding but distribute the money unequally, and there are schemes that tend to equalize spending but continue to rely on local property taxation. In practice, however, the two tendencies go together. It is difficult to imagine a stable system in which states collect most of the money for public schools and distribute it in a way that systematically favors one locale over another. And, as I will show by yoking *Serrano* with Proposition 13, voters will not long stand for a system that ships their local property taxes to the state in order to equalize school expenditures. As a behavioral matter, equalization has inevitably led to centralization.

5.3 *Serrano* Was Not Driven by Local Dissatisfaction with Schools

Aside from its equalizing and centralizing effects, the other important aspect of the *Serrano* litigation is that it was not the product of local dissatisfaction with schools in California. As James Lee and Burton Weisbrod (1978) described it, the plaintiffs were essentially stage dummies for a concerted and well-funded effort by reform-minded lawyers. John Serrano was a college-educated social worker. The public education of his son, also named John, was going well after the Serrano family moved, Tiebout-like, from East Los Angeles to a better school district. (East Los Angeles, a poor, unincorporated part of the county, was nonetheless in the enormous Los Angeles Unified School District and, as a district matter, had property values per student and expenditure per student that exceeded the state average.)

Mr. Serrano agreed for ideological reasons to be the lead plaintiff (*Los Angeles Times*, December 31, 1976, p. 3). Perhaps as a side benefit to those bringing the case, his Hispanic name did induce some reporters and scholars to suppose that he was a poor Chicano in a property-poor, low-spending district. School-district plaintiffs were also recruited by lawyers, who supposed that they were continuing the courageous work of the NAACP attorneys that culminated in Brown v. Board of Education in 1954 (Arthur Wise 1967; Peter Enrich 1995).

The foregoing facts are not presented to expose the public-relations spin of the litigation, though that isn't the least of my motives, either. It is important for my theory that the litigants and the California courts were not responding to popular dissatisfaction with schools and property taxes. The *Serrano* decision thus appears to have been a "natural experiment."

5.4 Why "Natural Experiments" Are Important

Evidence in the social sciences (as opposed to that in the natural sciences) is often problematic because most of it is generated by events that people more or less deliberately undertake. The "con" in econometrics of which Edward Leamer (1983) complained is that his fellow econometricians were treating these purposeful acts as if they were forces of nature. Classical statistical theory works only if variations in data occur randomly, that is, as if people had no control over them. Leamer's explication of this problem has caused economists to look for the rare "natural experiment" in which some truly exogenous force changes the usual rules.

If equalization and centralization of school funding along *Serrano II* lines had been the decision of the California legislature, we should suspect that the downside of these policies had been considered and rejected by the elected representatives of voters. It would still be interesting to study and explain such an event, but I could not as plausibly claim that the reform caused the tax revolt. I would have to explain why the same people who voted for legislators who enacted a centralizing school-finance bill in 1977 voted a year later for Proposition 13, which pulled the plug on half of the revenue source that the legislature had dedicated to school funding.

Thus the *Serrano* decision is the closest thing we will get to a natural experiment in education finance. It is not a pure experiment, since school finance had been centralizing since the Great Depression (David Beito 1989). *Serrano* also touched an equalitarian nerve in an area that even conservatives conceded was more ripe for judicial intervention than others (Ralph Winter 1972). But it is also clear that the courts have gone farther in undermining localism than almost any legislature wanted to go. In fact, *Serrano* was the beginning of a trend in California's supreme court whose activism in the 1970s "left little room for doubt that it had overtaken the state legislature as the place where state policy was most likely to be made" (Paul Carrington 1998, p. 84).

The California legislature clearly did not want to go all the way down the *Serrano* road. School-finance equalization had been on its agenda immediately before the first *Serrano* decision, but the legislature never went as far toward equalization and centralization as the *Serrano II* court did. School bills that verged on it were considered by the legislature prior to *Serrano I* in 1971 and rejected (Arnold Meltsner et al. 1973). Nor was there evidence that a cabal of "property-rich" districts was holding up otherwise popular reforms. In this respect, the state legislature seemed to be adhering to the median-voter model.

5.5 *Serrano* Was Not Foretold by *Brown* or State Constitutions

In opposition to my "natural experiment" view, one might argue that voters and legislators could have foreseen how the California judges would act, given the active intervention of the courts in school desegregation cases following Brown v. Board of Education in 1954. The *Serrano* lawyers and their counterparts in other states often invoked *Brown* both for its equalitarian ideals and its focus on public education. If *Serrano* was a politically popular progression from *Brown* and related desegregation decisions, the "naturalness" of the *Serrano* experiment is suspect.

The analogy between the civil-rights and school-finance cases, however, seems far-fetched. Most African Americans outside the South live in central cities, which usually have near-average or even above-average property value and spending per student. This was conceded even by *Serrano*'s intellectual architects, Coons, Clune, and Sugarman (1970, p. 357). It is telling that the NAACP Legal Defense Fund has not participated in the legal onslaught on education finance (Jack Greenberg 1994, p. 439).

Nor were there any serious voting-rights issues at the time of *Serrano I* in 1971. Equal access to the ballot at the state and local level was cemented by 1960s decisions on state legislative reapportionment (Baker v. Carr 1962) and by Congressional voting rights legislation. The *Serrano* litigants could not seriously claim a denial of political representation for residents of low-spending districts. Arthur Wise's (1967) catchy "one-dollar, one-scholar" motto was easily within the reach of legislators apportioned on the "one-person, one-vote" principle. Indeed, for courts to adopt dollar / scholar equalization thwarts the equalitarian voting principle, since it was clear that most properly apportioned legislatures did not wish to equalize expenditures per pupil. (There are occasional claims that because children cannot vote, they are unrepresented, which seems right if one believes that storks drop babies down chimneys for unsuspecting and unwilling parents to raise.)

Residents of "property-poor" districts are "discrete and insular minorities"—a test that civil rights advocates took from U.S. v. Carolene Products (1938, n. 4) to justify judicial trumping of legislative enactments—only in a numerical sense that trivializes the intellectual thrust of the Warren Court's civil rights decisions. The judges of that court struggled to reconcile minority rights with the equally compelling principle of a democratic, majority-rule government (John Hart Ely 1980). In fact, as the school-finance cases are often argued, the class of "property-poor" districts expands to include most of the population of the state. Looking at the factual and legal gulf between the desegregation decisions and the *Serrano* claims, it is unlikely that the California legislature, dominated in 1970s by liberal Democrats, would have thought itself at the same risk of court intervention as Southern state legislators were in the heyday of civil rights.

The California Constitution likewise conveyed almost no hint that

Serrano's equal-spending remedy would be forthcoming. Dissents in *Serrano II* point this out without any retort from the majority other than a disdainful aside about the "compendious, comprehensive, and distinctly mutable state Constitution" from which the judges supposedly derive their authority (135 Cal. Rptr. at 368). Although the constitutions of several other states do suggest special concern for education, their exhortations to the legislature to provide a "thorough and efficient" education and the like are seldom placed in the bill of rights section, whose provisions have been the source of most of the "fundamental rights" revealed by the courts.

Even scholars who admire state court intervention concede that there is at best a tenuous fit between a state constitution's language and history and the decisions in *Serrano*-inspired cases (Molly McUsic 1991; Peter Teachout 1997; Julie Underwood 1994). McUsic's classifications of constitutional provisions that might support a *Serrano*-style decision were entered in an econometric study of the post-*Serrano* decisions (to 1992) by David Figlio, Thomas Husted, and Lawrence Kenny (2000). They found no connection between a state's constitutional provisions and the state courts' decisions to uphold or overturn the state's school-finance system.

5.6 *Brown*'s Aura Forestalled Anti-*Serrano* Amendments

Several people have asked me why there have been no constitutional amendments to reverse *Serrano*. Voters and legislatures in other states have also dealt with *Serrano*-like decisions without changing their constitutions to restore fiscal sovereignty to the legislature. While constitutional change is more difficult than ordinary legislation, states have amended their constitutions over 5,000 times (Lawrence Friedman 1988, p. 35). Several states, including California, have constitutions that can be amended by majority vote in an initiative. Indeed, Proposition 13 is an example, in that it did amend (coincidentally) Article XIII of the California Constitution. Other California initiatives have reversed specific court rulings, so it would not have been unprecedented to put an anti-*Serrano* amendment on the ballot. This raises the possibility that the *Serrano* court accomplished what the legislature would have eventually done on its own.

While this is an important objection to my contention that *Serrano* is a natural experiment, I remain unpersuaded. As a broadly historical matter, public acceptance of ambitious U.S. Supreme Court rulings has always been high, and few decisions have been reversed by Constitutional amendments (William Ross 1994). This may be because, as surveys show, most citizens think that inventive court decisions (for example, about privacy) are supported by explicit constitutional texts (Michael Klarman 1991, p. 779). The deference that the U.S. Supreme Court gets from the electorate surely spills over to the state courts.

I think that it is here that Brown v. Board of Education has been most influential. *Brown* is now enormously popular. Rather than being seen as a long-overdue reversal of the U.S. Supreme Court's approval of racial segregation in Plessy v. Ferguson (1896), *Brown* is viewed as a heroic decision. Even unsparing critics of Warren Court decisions such as Robert Bork (1990) have felt compelled to carve out an exception for the case that supposedly ended segregated schools. That it did not actually do so, as Gerald Rosenberg (1991) persuasively argues, is beside the point in the court of public opinion. The U.S. Supreme Court led the way in tearing down the mountain of segregation, serving up *Simple Justice*, as the title of Richard Kluger's (1975) still-popular account of the ruling has it.

As a result of its popularity, *Brown* has enabled state judges to assume a cloak of moral guardianship in any matter that touches education inequalities. The problem with such clothing is that it tends to smother critical thought. For example, the Kentucky Supreme Court declared at the outset of its 1989 decision to throw out the state's entire system of school finance:

> The goal of the framers of our constitution, and the polestar of this opinion, is eloquently and movingly stated in the landmark case of Brown v. Board of Education: "education is perhaps the most important function of state and local governments. Compulsory school attendance laws and the great expenditures for education both demonstrate our recognition of the importance of education to our democratic society." (Rose v. Council, 790 S.W.2d at 190 [Ky. 1989], citing *Brown*, 347 U.S. at 493)

The Kentucky court's deployment of this quotation has two non-sequitur-like qualities. First, it implies that *Brown*'s main legacy was to elevate public schools beyond normal political discourse. But the U.S. Supreme Court focused on schools primarily because they already were so important. *Brown*'s enduring legacy was its burial of the separate-but-equal doctrine as a matter of law. It reversed *Plessy*, which had upheld segregation of railroad passengers by race. *Brown* no more changed the importance of public schools than it did passenger railroads.

The other non sequitur of the Kentucky court was to neglect that the importance of schools was the product of legislation. The "great expenditures" that the *Brown* court invoked as evidence for education's importance were undertaken by the *elected legislators* of "state and local governments." Courts of law had not ordered the construction of a vast public school system against the wishes of voters and their representatives. Use of the success of the legislative branch (as suggested by *Brown*'s dicta) as a reason for the Kentucky court to order a complete overhaul of the system can only be explained by the reverential haze that *Brown* evokes.

The same passage from *Brown* that the Kentucky court deployed appears in school-funding decisions in California, Connecticut, New Jersey, Tennessee, Texas, Vermont, and Wyoming, all of which overturned school funding arrangements that had been in place for some time. (Other state courts that overturned school-finance systems also usually cite *Brown*, but without quoting this passage.) And only the New Jersey court acknowledged the dissonance of the phrase "most important function of state *and local* governments," with the plaintiff's request for judicial intervention to supplant localism (Robinson v. Cahill, 303 A.2d at 284 [1973], my italics).

It is impossible to know whether judges' deployment of *Brown* in the school-finance cases was to convince themselves of the rightness of their task or was calculated to disarm would-be constitution amenders. Judges do think about the latter possibility. "You wouldn't reverse *Brown*, would you?" is an unanswerable retort in debates about constitutional amendments to reverse *Serrano*-style decisions.

To concede that *Serrano* was not easily reversed by explicit amendments is still consistent with the contention that normal political processes would never have produced it. As I shall demonstrate in Section 5.12, when voters in California and other states were actually asked whether they would like to shift school funding from the locality to the state in order to accomplish *Serrano*-style goals of equalization, they always declined. The *Serrano* court's decision still seems as close to a natural experiment as we are likely to get on a major local government issue.

5.7 Proposition 13 Challenges Median-Voter Models

Eighteen months after *Serrano II* was issued in December of 1976, California voters upended local financing of schools and everything else by voting in Proposition 13 in June 1978. Proposition 13 rejected local financing of most services by capping the property tax rate at 1 percent and holding assessment increases well below inflation. (Proposition 13 was described in more detail in Section 4.8.) The property tax quickly yielded less than half of its previous revenue, and the yield has not drifted up with inflation because of the assessment ceilings. Because of *Serrano* and Proposition 13, property taxes in California are now administered as if they were statewide taxes (O'Sullivan, Sexton, and Sheffrin 1995, p. 139).

And Proposition 13 is durable, despite substantial evidence that it is responsible for the state's inadequate schools and other public ills. The ongoing damage provoked *Sacramento Bee* editor Peter Schrag to invoke a Miltonian lament as the title of his book *Paradise Lost: California's Experience, America's Future* (1998). Yet attempts to reverse Proposition 13 get nowhere. A modest erosion of its constraints on local officials' fiscal discretion was reversed by a 1996 initiative, Proposition 218, which now requires what were formerly classified as land-use exactions to be approved by the voters (Stacey Simon 1998). Voters in California appear to have done something horrible to themselves in 1978, and they don't show any sign of regretting it.

In a 1979 symposium on Proposition 13, Geoffrey Brennan and James Buchanan offered Proposition 13 as evidence that the median voter does not prevail in local politics. In their view, local politicians are no more likely than state or national politicians to give the voters what they really want. Proposition 13 was evidence that local governments were spending much more than the median voter actually demanded. If I am to retain any credibility for my thesis that the property tax is a preferred method of financing local schools and that majority rule is the way to look at local politics, I need to explain Proposition 13, which seems to reject all of those ideas in the nation's largest state. My story must account for why California voters were so unhappy with property taxes.

The explanation is simple. The level of property taxes in 1978 was not what their local or state officials would have chosen without *Serrano*. The taxes were imposed by the state legislature acting under the gun of the California Supreme Court. Proposition 13 is popularly compared to the Boston Tea Party, and the analogy has some validity. Both were rebellions against a tax imposed by an unelected potentate.

5.8 Homevoters Were Disfranchised by *Serrano*

My first explanation for Proposition 13's appeal to the voters invoked the Tiebout model (Fischel 1989). In Serrano v. Priest, the California Supreme Court essentially threw out the connection between local property tax payments and the local schools. The California legislature's compliance with this mandate converted that half of the local property tax that went for schools into the sort of tax payment whose benefits were divorced from how much homeowners paid. Since everyone agrees that property taxes, taken in isolation, are unpleasant to pay, Californians decided en masse to cut property taxes in half.

Alan Post (1979, p. 385), the California legislative analyst at the time Proposition 13 passed, noted that it was not such a bad thing in one respect, since it would now require the state-funded system that was necessary to comply with *Serrano*. *Serrano*'s fiscal relation to Proposition 13 is also suggested by some strange political bedfellows. Jonathan Kozol (1991, p. 220), who is well to the left of center, noted that *Serrano*'s insistence on equality of spending may have provoked Proposition 13. On the other side of the political spectrum, Joel Fox, head of the Howard Jarvis Taxpayers Association, has invoked *Serrano*'s equalitarian goals as a reason to suppress evasions of Proposition 13's constraints (*Los Angeles Times*, January 14, 1999, p. B11).

I actually thought of the *Serrano* connection almost as soon as Proposition 13 passed in 1978, but I did not have much evidence. The first good evidence on Proposition 13 was a study by Kenneth Rosen (1982), which was, as the reader might have guessed, a tax-capitalization study. After Proposition 13 passed, Rosen proposed to use the dramatic tax cut as what he regarded as a natural experiment to see how much property values would rise when property taxes were reduced. The key to this was that local services did not change immediately after Proposition 13 because the state legislature used the state's accumulated budget surplus to bail out local governments and school districts. Thus service levels did not change, and property taxes were reduced. Rosen found that at prevailing interest rates, about half of the property tax reduction was capitalized in higher home values. (How much capitalization should be normally expected was discussed in Section 3.5.)

Rosen's inferred capitalization rate was low, I believe, because homebuyers did not expect the bailout to last, and it did not. After the state's accumulated budget surplus was exhausted, it had to rely on existing revenues to fund schools. Its *Serrano II* response (described later) had depended on property taxes as well as the state's budget surplus to implement it. Spending on schools soon declined because legislators were disinclined to raise state income and sales taxes to offset the loss in property taxes. More importantly for my story, school spending became highly equalized in order to conform to the still-binding *Serrano II* decision of 1976.

But the tax capitalization that Rosen found was still puzzling to me. In the Tiebout world that Californians seemed to have inhabited in the early 1970s, a state-mandated property tax cut should have generally reduced property values. A good number of capitalization tests confirming the Tiebout model used 1970 data from California municipalities (Gerald McDougal 1976; Sonstelie and Portney 1980a). Gutting the fiscal mainstay of municipal and school-district choice should have made most people worse off and driven property values down, not up. The state's post–Proposition 13 bailout of localities would have delayed this only by a year or two, and the homebuyers in Rosen's sample would surely have been aware of its short-term nature.

Even more peculiar was Rosen's finding that high-income communities in his Bay Area sample were especially benefited by Proposition 13. The median home values in the richest communities in Rosen's sample rose more than the average after Proposition 13 passed (Fischel 1989, p. 468). Even if most California voters had been unhappy with local property taxes, the affluent communities, with what had been good schools, seemed least likely to join the tax revolt or gain from it. Yet property values in affluent places increased much faster in Rosen's Bay Area sample after Proposition 13 passed.

The only explanation for Rosen's results that made any sense to me is that local voters in general, and voters in high-income communities in particular, had been knocked off their local Tiebout equilibrium by *Serrano.* In a Tiebout world, the taxes and housing payments they made bought them the level of local services, including schools, that were better than they could get elsewhere. But such an equilibrium had in effect been declared unconstitutional in California by the *Serrano II* court.

The erosion of the Tiebout equilibrium did not happen all at once. As the legislature tried to deal with the obviously equalitarian intent of *Serrano I* (1971), high-spending districts found it increasingly difficult to tax themselves for their schools. The final solution for *Serrano II* (decided in December 1976) was Assembly Bill 65, drawn up by the legislature in the summer of 1977. AB 65 would have raised average spending for the state, but it did so in a way that, for most districts, disconnected their local property tax payments from their local schools. It implemented the Coons, Clune, and Sugarman (1970) district power equalization formula, which meant that "property-rich" districts would have to ship some of their local taxes to the state for redistribution if they wanted to spend more on their own schools. "Recapture," this was called, as if property-rich districts had previously plundered their neighbors for tax base.

Had AB 65 been fully implemented, the high-income districts' home values would have fallen, and to some extent, the implementation of previous reforms must have depressed home values in such districts (relative to the average district—home values everywhere were rising at the time because of national inflation). Thus the beneficial effects on housing values from Proposition 13 (as detected by Rosen) are best seen as a partial restoration of home values from the depressing effects of complying with *Serrano.*

5.9 *Serrano* Explains the Vote Swing from 1972 to 1978

My modest empirical venture into explaining Proposition 13 addressed the question of why voters had in 1972 rejected an initiative that would have done much the same thing as Jarvis's Proposition 13 did in 1978 (Fischel 1996a, pp. 616–619). The 1972 Watson initiative (named for the Los Angeles County assessor who put it together) would have cut back property taxes to a maximum of 1 percent, just like Proposition 13, though Watson did not propose limits on reassessments. Watson's initiative would have sent most of the fiscal responsibility for schools and welfare (the latter funded in part by counties) to the state. He in fact mentioned that it would be a good way to comply with the just-issued *Serrano I* decision.

Voters rejected Watson's initiative by a 2–1 margin in 1972, as they had rejected a similar initiative he had proposed in 1968. The legislature had in 1972 come up with an alternative that offered property tax relief, and, as Anthony Barkume (1976) found, voters in high-spending school districts were especially opposed to having the state do the financing. The Watson initiative, I submit, would have reduced the home values of at least the high-spending districts.

I looked at the "swing" in votes from the 1972 Watson initiative, which had failed by 2–1, to the 1978 Jarvis initiative (Proposition 13), which passed by 2–1. A whole lot of voters must have changed their minds in six years, and I wanted to know if voters who had switched positions were in school districts with unusual characteristics. So I looked up the vote by city within Los Angeles County, and I selected the twenty-nine cities whose name corresponds to a "unified" school district. (Unified districts, which enroll most students, operate schools from kindergarten through grade twelve.) Most of the county's population was in my sample, even allowing for the dominance of the city of Los Angeles.

I ran a simple correlation between two variables. First was the "swing," the change in the vote on Watson in 1972 to the vote on Jarvis (Proposition 13) in 1978. If a city had given Watson's proposal 40 percent of its votes (and, necessarily, had 60 percent opposed), but then voted for Jarvis by 70 percent, the swing to be explained was 30 percentage points. (I calculated it as a percentage of the original, so the datum here would be 30 / 40 or a 75 percent swing.)

The second variable was the percentage of each district's local school expenditures that were to be financed by local property taxes in 1978. Those with the highest percentage were the "property-rich" districts (many populated by not-so-rich people) that were the stronger candidates to have at least some of their tax base "recaptured" by the state. I found an impressively high (r =.71) simple correlation between the 1972–1978 vote swing and the indicator of local property-tax reliance.

(The correlation would have been much higher but for a single outlier, the city of Compton, which, alone among all Los Angeles County cities, voted against Proposition 13.) This implies that half (.71 squared = .50) of the interdistrict variation in the swing of votes from the 1972 Watson initiative to the 1978 Jarvis (Proposition 13) initiative can be explained by a single variable, the percent of school funding from local sources in 1978.

Explaining half of the variation in a single vote, say in 1972, is to admit that you cannot explain much. You could flip a coin and do as well. But explaining the *change* in votes from 1972 to 1978 is much more difficult to do. Voter's preferences seldom change as radically as they did between the Watson and Jarvis initiatives, so most of what one gets when looking at changes in votes is random noise. Indeed, some explanations of Proposition 13 viewed it as essentially an irrational choice, a desire to get "something for nothing," to quote the subtitle of one influential book that examined voter surveys (Sears and Citrin 1982). I was really impressed that I could explain half of the variation in the swing vote for my sample of twenty-nine communities with but one variable. In fact, I could not (and still cannot) think of anything else to add to the determinants of the vote swing in order to undertake a multiple regression analysis.

This simple statistic fits my theory well. The property-rich, high-spending districts had much opposed Watson's 1972 initiative, as Barkume (1976) had also found. In 1972, they preferred local property taxes and local school spending to the state-funded school spending that Watson offered. (In 1972, no one knew how the 1971 *Serrano I* decision would work out, so I think it is reasonable to assume that the radical equalization required by *Serrano II* in 1976 was not anticipated by homebuyers, especially since California was the pioneer in this litigation.) But by 1978, the *Serrano II* remedy had left the formerly high-spending districts with even higher property taxes. These taxes now had little connection with the quality of their schools.

What in 1972 had been a tax closely tied to benefits that were capitalized in home values had by 1978 become just another tax. After *Serrano II*, property taxes were no more connected to home values or school quality than any other tax, and they were considerably more obnoxious to pay. So the districts that were stuck with high local property taxes in 1978 swung disproportionately to Jarvis's tax limitation, shifting the funding burden to the state. *Serrano II* had killed the Tiebout system for schools, so the formerly high-spending districts joined with voters who had always disliked property taxes to kill the property tax.

5.10 *Serrano II* Effectively Blocked Property Tax Relief

In response to some skepticism by Jack Coons when I described my first article about *Serrano* and Proposition 13 (Fischel 1989) in Berkeley in 1991, I undertook documentary research about how the California legislature responded to *Serrano* (Fischel 1996a). I found that the 1977 legislature was fully aware of the voters' rising dissatisfaction with property taxes, but legislators were hog-tied by the need to respond to *Serrano II.* I will not go through that story again in this space, where the focus is on homeowner capitalization. The story is not complicated—Sacramento just did not have the dollars to respond to both the tax revolt and *Serrano II*—but I needed to dispose of several other theories of Proposition 13 in explaining why the *Serrano* explanation fits best. While I do not claim to have nailed down every corner of the connection between *Serrano* and Proposition 13, I remain unpersuaded by alternative explanations that I have heard before and since my 1996 article. (My claims that are unaccompanied by citations in this and the next section are supported in my 1996a article.)

The easiest to dismiss are those that focus on the supposed political acumen of Howard Jarvis, the garrulous leader of the Proposition 13 movement (Daniel Smith 1999; Robert Kuttner 1980). His rough-and-ready manner may have had some popular appeal, but this does not explain why Jarvis's four previous property-tax initiatives were complete failures. His post–Proposition 13 initiative in 1980 and his foray into elective politics were likewise unsuccessful. It seems most charitable to describe Jarvis as one of those perennial gadflies who just happened to have a ready-made cure when the wages of *Serrano* came due.

John Kenneth Galbraith described Proposition 13 as "the revolt of the rich." This shows that he can turn an alliterative phrase better than Robert Kuttner, who subtitled his 1980 book on it "the revolt of the haves." Neither author explains why the "rich" did not revolt before 1978, despite being presented with plenty of fiscal initiatives that would have cut overall taxes.

The catchy characterization is misleading in any case. Although affluent voters and residents of "property-rich" districts did support Proposition 13 more than others, the initiative passed with huge majorities in nearly every community in the state. Even poor Baldwin Park, the low-income and property-poor poster child of the *Serrano* litigation, gave Proposition 13 a 70 percent majority. Proposition 13 was not a close vote, which is all the more remarkable given that, from 1960 to 1978, every *fiscal* initiative in California had failed (Rabushka and Ryan 1982, p. 14). Something had so completely changed the fiscal landscape that the usual rules did not apply. That something, I submit, was *Serrano*.

Another common explanation centered on a local miscalculation. The Los Angeles County tax assessor sent out huge increases in tax bills just before the Proposition 13 vote, and this is said to have swung the margin toward Jarvis's initiative (Martha West 1999, p. 305). The assessor explained—reasonably, I would say—that he did so to avoid being accused of hiding the bad news until after the election (Alexander Pope 1979). But property taxes had begun rising well before 1978, and the importance of Mr. Pope's timing seems greatly overrated. Proposition 13 passed by the same margin in Los Angeles County as in most of the state's other counties, whose assessors were not so imprudently forthright.

Peter Schrag (1998) and Tony Downs (in a personal communication) suggested that Proposition 13 was caused by local political failures to reduce taxes in the face of assessment inflation. Schrag wonders why local school boards did not lower taxes if voters were upset, and Downs suspects that municipal officials were simply too tin-eared to hear the voters' concerns.

I don't know what features of California school finance at the time may have prevented local boards from reducing local expenditures and taxes. I strongly suspect that local boards were responding to rules from Sacramento rather than blithely spending local revenue that they had the power to give back to dissatisfied taxpayers. The basis for my suspicion is the complete absence of any *local* property tax revolts during the period. California empowers citizens of its local governments to propose initiatives. If free-spending local officials were the cause of Proposition 13, I would expect many local initiatives to try to curb them. There weren't any in the two years before Proposition 13 passed. I looked explicitly for them in the indexes of the *Los Angeles Times* and the *San Francisco Chronicle*, both of which had good coverage of local politics. Nor were there stories of local school boards being ousted in elections for their free-spending ways. Taxpayers' anger was directed at politicians in Sacramento, and newspaper stories at the time indicate that state, not local, officials were facing the voters' wrath.

Another indication that Proposition 13 was related to state-imposed school-finance reform rather than bloated municipal budgets comes from a list in a briefing book for the California State Assembly (1980), which analyzed the fiscal condition of the state's thirty-one "No-Property-Tax Cities." These mostly small cities had sufficiently large commercial tax bases to be able to fund all municipal expenditures from sales taxes instead of property taxes. If out-of-control municipal property taxes had been a contributing cause of Proposition 13, then voters in these thirty-one cities should have had less inclination to favor it. But twenty-six of them gave Proposition 13 a larger majority than did the state as a whole. As a population-weighted group, the thirty-one cities voted 74 percent for Proposition 13, compared 65 percent for the state as a whole. The reason cannot have been municipal extravagance in property taxation, since these cities had none. Their greater support for Proposition 13 is evidence that municipal (as opposed to school) spending was not the problem.

5.11 Budget Surpluses Did Not Cause the Tax Revolt

A more sophisticated explanation for Proposition 13 is that voters were disgusted with the state legislature for allowing the state's budget surplus to pile up without giving them any property tax relief. As I found, however, the legislature was aware of the surplus and the voters' demand for tax relief, and leaders of both parties were eager to ease property taxes. But the form of the relief was complicated by *Serrano II*'s insistence that any property taxes that were used to fund schools had to be unrelated to a given district's spending per pupil. Some homeowners could get property tax relief, but many others with the same complaints could not. And the amount of the state funds available for property tax relief was shrunk by AB 65 (the *Serrano-II* response), which was expected to spend all of the state's budget surplus on the new school funding plan.

AB 65 relied heavily on property taxes, and any substantial cut in property taxes would have made it moot (as in fact Proposition 13 did). Legislators were told this clearly by the respected legislative analyst Alan Post (*Los Angeles Times*, August 1, 1977). As a result of not having enough money and an inability to direct it satisfactorily to constituents, the legislature in 1977 adjourned without having passed any property tax relief. The 1978 state budget surplus turned out to be even larger than expected, and the legislature did offer an alternative to Proposition 13 that relied on it, but even that amount was no match for Proposition 13's massive cut.

Another explanation is that AB 65, the *Serrano II* response, was a political miscalculation. The legislature would have had enough money to head off the tax revolt, goes this theory, if it had selected a statewide school expenditure that was closer to the existing average spending. (David Kirp said this in a phone conversation in 1992, but he would not elaborate on it.) I did not deal with this claim in my 1996 article, but I recently came across a detailed analysis of the legislative process at the time by Richard Elmore and Milbrey McLaughlin. In *Reform and Retrenchment: The Politics of California School Finance Reform* (1982), they concluded that the AB 65 "level-up" approach was the only way to get enough votes for passage of a bill that satisfied *Serrano II* (p. 162). Legislators from high-spending districts were unwilling to accept a bill that pulled them down to the preexisting mean.

"Level up" was what nearly all advocates of *Serrano* assumed would happen (Charles Benson 1972; Lawyers' Committee 1971). To "level down" would seem contrary to the intent of *Serrano*. The plaintiff's lawyer in *Serrano II* reinforced this sentiment with the threat of a suit even after AB 65 was passed in 1977, thundering that the legislature, which had just committed all of its anticipated surplus to *Serrano II* compliance, had not done nearly enough. The notion that the legislature could have satisfied the court by spending no more than had been spent before the decision is not credible.

The non-*Serrano* explanation for Proposition 13 that does make some sense is that from 1975 to 1978 housing prices were rising more rapidly than nonresidential property prices, and California assessors were compelled by law (as they are in other states) to raise homeowners' assessments. Thus even if tax rates had been steady, homeowners would have borne a larger share of the property tax. This shift surely did complicate the legislature's response to homeowners' complaints, but it is not by itself a satisfactory answer. The legislature knew how to fix that problem early in 1977. It in fact did submit a constitutional amendment (Proposition 8) as an alternative to Proposition 13.

Proposition 8 would have allowed (not required) the legislature to reduce residential property tax rates below that of other property. The bill that was a companion to this constitutional change, however, protected homeowners' property taxes only from nonschool assessments. This suggests to me that reduction in homeowners' assessments for school purposes was ruled out because of worries either that it would conflict with *Serrano* or that it would take away revenues needed for the already passed *Serrano* response bill, AB 65. (Proposition 8 lost in the same election that Proposition 13 passed.)

5.12 Voters in Other States Prefer Local Funding, Too

Several published comments that have addressed my hypothesis wonder why contemporary opinion polls did not show that voters were unhappy about school taxes because of *Serrano* (Peter Schrag 1998, p. 148; Daniel Smith 1999, p. 205). One response is that it takes social science insight to see the true relationships. If the test of a social science hypothesis is that its implications must be transparent to the public, why would it take any special skill to generate it? (No smart answers, please.)

The lack of evidence from opinion polls has an easier response: You don't get the right answer if you don't ask the right question. None of the polls I read made the connection between court-ordered school-finance reform and property taxes. As I will show in this section, when voters in statewide referenda *are* asked the right question—Do you want to continue local property-tax financing for education, or do you want to shift the obligation to the state?—voters almost everywhere choose localism.

The clearest and cleanest evidence comes from statewide referenda and initiatives prior to the *Serrano* decision. The issue of whether school financing should be shifted from the local property tax to a statewide tax was actually put on the ballot in several states. It was not an incidental test. The reformers who quickly flocked to the courts after *Serrano* had actually proposed the same centralizing reforms to the voters. As Paul Carrington (1973, p. 1245) pointed out, voters rejected these proposals in 1972 in California (the "Watson initiative" discussed in Section 5.9), Colorado, Michigan, and Oregon. A proposed constitutional amendment to centralize school financing was also rejected by voters in Michigan in 1971 (Elwood Hain 1974). A few years before the court-ordered reform of 1979, voters in the state of Washington rejected two referenda that proposed an income tax and a corporation tax to relieve local districts of the obligation to fund schools (Diana Gale 1981, p. 149; Theobald and Hanna 1991).

Even after *Serrano*, referenda that asked voters to approve the taxes required by *Serrano*-style decisions were rejected. West Virginia voters were asked in 1984 to approve a revenue-equalization bill that responded to its court's *Serrano*-style decision of Pauley v. Kelly (W.Va. 1979), and the voters defeated it: "The people wanted local control of taxes," according to an analysis by J. J. Flanigan (1989, p. 234). On May 5, 1998, Ohio voters rejected by a four-to-one margin a proposal to replace local property taxes, whose variations were found unconstitutional by the Ohio Supreme Court in Derolph v. State (1997), with a two percentage point increase in the state sales tax.

I do not claim to have checked every source, but I cannot locate a single statewide initiative or referendum in the post–World War II era that proposed anything like *Serrano*—equalize school spending or taxable resources by centralizing funding—and came anywhere close to passing. This is consistent with, as I mentioned in Section 4.13, the work of John Matsusaka (1995; 2000), who found that initiative states have had more decentralized control of government expenditures throughout the twentieth century. When they are asked about it directly, voters prefer local control.

The issue also comes up in ordinary state politics. Deborah Arnessen, a well-funded Democratic candidate for governor of New Hampshire in 1992, proposed to create a new state income tax and substitute it for local property taxes to fund schools. As Colin Campbell and I (1996) and Lisa Shapiro (1995) demonstrated, the voters rejected Ms. Arnessen primarily because of her school-funding platform. Her chief campaign advisor was also the plaintiffs' attorney in a New Hampshire school-finance case, Claremont v. Governor (N.H. 1993), which eventually mandated (*Claremont II* 1997) what the voters had rejected at the polls. That the New Hampshire court was not protecting a "discrete and insular minority" is suggested by the fact that voters from four of the five plaintiff school districts failed to give Ms. Arnessen a majority in the 1992 gubernatorial election.

5.13 Locals View the Property Tax Base as Their Own

Without an understanding of why local governments are different from state governments, it is hard to explain statewide voters' aversion to having the state equalize local property tax bases. If one just counts potential fiscal gainers, statewide taxation of property (or a similar redistributive scheme that takes from the "property-rich" and gives to everyone else) ought to win every time. Property value per student is unusually high in a few communities. Small-population communities may have resort properties that are owned by out-of-staters; they may have electric power generating plants or dams that are attractively immobile targets of taxation; or they may have been unusually successful in attracting shopping centers or industrial development. Many states have something like California's straightforwardly named City of Commerce, incorporated as a tax haven and run by a small group of residents whose public needs (very broadly construed) are well taken care of (Gary Miller 1981, p. 45). Voters who reside in districts with less than the mean amount of tax base per student easily outnumber those in the property-rich districts.

If all that voters cared about was keeping their own taxes low, intercommunity property-tax transfers should be the rule rather than the exception. Yet such expropriation is hardly ever undertaken without a judicial prod when local property taxes fund the bulk of schools and other local services. In such situations, I submit that people view their property taxes as different from other taxes. They are part of their own city's or town's property. Voters are almost as loathe to grab neighboring communities' "property" as they would be to use the power of the state to take their neighbors' homes without compensation.

When Kansas, responding to *Serrano*-like litigation, "recaptured" the tax base of the rural town of Burlington, which has a power plant, the town and others in its situation sued the state (Unified School District No. 229 v. State [Kansas 1994]). One of the town's claims was that the state had "taken" its property without just compensation. Takings claims are normally made by *individuals* whose property is burdened by state actions. By invoking the takings claim (which, like all the other claims, was not successful), the community was invoking the principle that its local tax base, unlike other tax bases to which Burlington residents contribute, was its own property.

5.14 Maine Tried and Rejected a Statewide Property Tax

Status-quo bias could have influenced the aforementioned statewide votes that rejected *Serrano*-style tax base sharing. People are used to local property taxation, and so their reluctance to redistribute the tax base might be attributed to a more general reluctance to change long-time habits. One could, perhaps, suggest that human beings have for good reasons been reluctant to change long-standing institutions, but I do not actually have to resort to that argument. The experience of the state of Maine offers a compelling counterexample.

In 1973, the Maine legislature adopted a uniform statewide property tax designed to "recapture" taxable values in property-rich towns and transfer them to other towns and cities to pay for schools. Because only a few districts (mostly resort towns along the coast) had unusually high taxable property per resident, the net effect of Maine's statewide tax was to take property tax revenue from a small number of towns and give the proceeds to towns and cities within which a great majority of the state's population resided. The tax and the distribution scheme thus "forced some communities to support the education system in others" (Perrin and Jones 1984, p. 486).

The 1973 Maine legislation was not the product of popular dissatisfaction with schools or local property taxation. It was explicitly motivated by the school-finance litigation that began with *Serrano I* in 1971. A *Serrano*-style suit had made its way to the Maine Supreme Court. At the time (1973), the U.S. Supreme Court was hearing the federal version of *Serrano*, which was San Antonio v. Rodriguez (1973). The Maine court specifically delayed its decision to see how the U.S. Supreme Court would rule (Norton Grubb 1974).

The Maine legislature, however, decided not to wait. It adopted the statewide property tax plan in anticipation of an adverse ruling. The U.S. Supreme Court ultimately ruled in San Antonio v. Rodriguez that states were not compelled to equalize school finance, and the Maine court, as a result, backed off (Kermit Nickerson 1973). But the Maine legislature decided to keep the law on the books. After all, it looked like a politically attractive thing to do, at least if one simply counted noses. The statewide property tax and the related school-funding distribution formula allowed the state to transfer property-tax wealth from a few towns to other places in which the vast majority of the year-round population lived.

Despite the apparent fiscal benefits of the 1973 program to most Maine residents, the statewide tax and the related school-funding reform were highly controversial. After four years of contentious tinkering with the distribution formula, legislators agreed to hold a statewide referendum on the tax in 1977. The vote to repeal it passed with an overwhelming majority. Although the small "property-rich" towns that bore the brunt of the statewide tax did vote disproportionately for repeal, a majority of voters in districts that supposedly benefited from the state tax also voted to repeal it (Perrin and Jones 1984).

The importance of the vote in Maine on this issue is that it started from a different status quo position. The "status quo" in 1977 was that one town's property tax base was obligated to fund schools in other towns. Four years' experience with such a regime is admittedly less of a status quo than a hundred years of experience with local taxation, which is the approximate pedigree of local taxation for schools. But Maine in 1973 did take property taxes away from local control, and it did offer a taste of statewide funding to its electorate. It may not have been as "natural" an experiment as California's, since the threat of a court decision that prompted Maine's legislation faded away, but it stands as a strong counterexample to the idea that voters would reject local funding if only they experienced its alternative.

5.15 *Serrano* Influenced Other States' Behavior

I've actually convinced, I think, a good part of the local-public-finance community to take the *Serrano*–Proposition 13 connection seriously. Even economists who like the equalization idea behind *Serrano* admit that the California Supreme Court went too far in undermining local fiscal control (Fernandez and Rogerson 1999). But the usual question then is, what about other states? There have been sixteen other state supreme courts that have gone in the *Serrano* direction (by my count, as of 1999). Did they get a Proposition 13 for their trouble? And what about other property tax revolts? Many seem to have occurred in states whose courts did not have anything like *Serrano*. Fair questions.

My answer is that *Serrano* itself changed the national political landscape, so it is in fact difficult to chart the influence of other courts on fiscal arrangements without a detailed historical knowledge of individual states. California is such a large state—one of every seven Americans lives there—that it necessarily generates an enormous amount of litigation. So much law emanates from California that its court decisions have considerable weight in other states. Moreover, the litigation group that put together the *Serrano* case was well organized and well financed (Lee and Weisbrod 1978). And after Serrano v. Unruh (Cal. 1982), the lawyers did not even need foundation financing, since the California Supreme Court ordered the state to pay the legal expenses of the victorious plaintiffs. Attorneys general in other states had good reason to advise their governors and legislatures that the seemingly novel interpretation of the hortatory education clause in their constitutions could be a license for judges to redirect the financing of education.

Their best defense might be an orderly surrender in advance to the forces of equalization and centralization. Even if elected officials succeeded in defending their system once in court, turnover of supreme court justices and creative reformulation of complaints—first "equity," then "adequacy"—made anything less than full state control and absolute equality of expenditure a constitutionally risky path. (No state actually went that far, but that is the outcome consistent with most plaintiffs' positions.) While the nominal complaints have varied over time, the centralizing and equalizing *remedies* remain essentially the same, as even the advocates of classifying them as distinct "waves" of litigation admit (Peter Enrich 1995, pp. 128–143). In other words, after *Serrano* there were no more natural experiments.

The U.S. Supreme Court's *Rodriguez* decision derailed the *Serrano* train at the federal level, and the original *Serrano* advocates were certainly disappointed by it. But the U.S. Supreme Court decided no more than that inequalities in local tax bases did not offend the U.S. Constitution's Equal Protection Clause. Perhaps because the vote in *Rodriguez* was a razor-thin 5–4, the majority opinion explicitly gave the state courts freedom to deploy their own constitutions, and even their own equal protection clauses, to do whatever they wanted to school financing.

In case the states did not get the message, Justice William Brennan, who wrote a dissent in *Rodriguez*, went on the lecture and law review circuit to extol the virtues of an independent and expansive state court interpretation of their own constitutions (Brennan 1977). Former Connecticut chief justice Ellen Peters (1997) gratefully acknowledged Brennan's influence on her and other state-court justices, specifically mentioning the school-finance decisions of her court. In closing the doors of the federal courthouse to such suits, *Rodriguez* pointed to a wide-open door in the state courts.

5.16 The Threat of Litigation Induced Legislation

The evidence for *Serrano*'s extrajudicial influence is necessarily episodic. One can generate from case reporters Lexis and Westlaw lists of court victories and defeats, but not of legislative committee compromises and out-of-court settlements on school finance. Nonetheless, the stories that I relate in this section clearly demonstrate the immediate and persistent influence of *Serrano* in other state legislatures.

I am not alone in this observation. A well-traveled team of school-finance consultants observed, "Even where litigation has not occurred or has not succeeded, the prospect of litigation has prompted revisions of state funding policies" (Augenblick, Myers, and Anderson 1997, p. 63). As I described in Section 5.14, Maine's statewide property tax legislation was the result of an anticipated state supreme court decision. The Maine legislation, which both centralized and equalized school funding until the voters revoked it, can thus be directly tied to *Serrano*.

New Mexico. According to a history of school finance in New Mexico by David Coulton (1996), legislators there were told in 1974 that their state supreme court was about to issue a *Serrano*-style decision, and they responded with legislation to preempt it. New Mexico's school finance, already highly centralized, became almost completely so after this action. In due time, the legislature also further reduced reliance on property taxation in response to popular dissatisfaction with it. Thus New Mexico did a *Serrano* and a Proposition 13, but with neither a recorded court decision nor a popular tax revolt. As in California, the crucial fact is that the legislation was induced by the court, not the voters, and the subsequent property-tax cut was a logical and popular response by the legislature to the new fiscal regime.

Michigan. The Michigan Supreme Court decision in Governor v. State Treasurer (1972) was clearly *Serrano* inspired and directed at getting the legislature to pass an equalitarian school-finance bill (Elwood Hain 1974). The bill was passed, and its features were highly redistributive in that it took from the property-rich and gave to the property-poor districts (Paul Rothstein 1992). After the legislation was passed, the Michigan Supreme Court withdrew its decision, and so Michigan is counted as a state whose school-finance arrangements have been untouched by the courts. That the original decision was intended to nudge the legislature was specifically mentioned in Justice T. E. Brennen's tart dissent (203 N.W.2d at 475): "The majority opinion . . . is a political position paper, written and timed to encourage action by the state Legislature through the threat of future court intervention."

Ohio. Ohio's *Serrano*-style *DeRolph* decision (1997), actually mentions (78 Ohio St.3d 193 at p. 218) in the majority opinion that the legislature and the court had been playing in the same fiscal sandbox for many years: "In *Walter* [a 1979 case that upheld Ohio's system], this court reviewed the constitutionality of the Equal Yield Formula for school funding and, in 1979, upheld that formula as constitutionally acceptable. There is a body of thought," the court coyly goes on in *DeRolph*, "that the General Assembly created the Equal Yield Formula in anticipation of the filing of the *Walter* case."

Kansas. The experience of Kansas, as related by Charles Berger (1998), shows that from 1972, when a trial court invoked *Serrano*-style principles, to the present, the state courts have set the agenda for school-finance legislation. The judge in the most recent case held meetings with the governor and legislative leaders to plan the state's most recent reform. Separation of powers is not something that appears to worry this court.

5.17 Did *Serrano* Cause the Massachusetts Tax Revolt?

The Massachusetts Supreme Judicial Court, which found for the reform-minded plaintiffs in McDuffy v. Secretary (1993), likewise sets out a history of legislation induced by the threat of litigation. The previous litigation was Webby v. Dukakis. *Webby* was brought in 1978 when the legislature was considering what Edward Morgan (1985) describes as a equalitarian and centralizing school-finance bill. The bill, which was sponsored by Governor Michael Dukakis, was having a rough time in the legislature. The lower house was balking, and the plan looked dead in the water. Then the *Webby* litigation was filed. As a Brandeis University doctoral dissertation by Bruce Perlstein (1980, p. 569) points out, "The suit was officially filed before the state's Supreme Judicial Court on May 9 [1978], on the eve of the House vote, in an attempt to influence the outcome." The House promptly caved in and adopted the Dukakis reform, and the litigation was immediately dropped (*Boston Globe*, May 16, 1978, p. 16).

Perlstein, who was an active advocate of the Massachusetts reform as well as its most detailed chronicler, appears to be of two minds about the influence of the litigation threat. On the one hand, he notes that "the specter of possible court intervention was frequently cited by reform proponents as a major reason" for the reform vote, especially in light of Boston's wrenching experience with court-ordered desegregation (1980, p. 571). On the other hand, Perlstein points out that the vague, seventeenth-century language in the state's constitution about "wisdom and knowledge, as well as virtue," which was deemed to be the education cause, seemed like a weak anchor for the litigation. (This did not deter the Massachusetts court in 1993 from deploying it on behalf of a sweeping reform edict in *McDuffy*.) Moreover, the length of time it would take to get a court decision meant that "the prospect of judicial intervention therefore had only a limited credibility in the more immediate legislative effort" (Perlstein 1980, p. 571). Perlstein is more inclined to give credit for the passage of the bill to the interplay of political personalities, which he describes abundantly. But it is also clear in his thesis that the state's overall school-finance agenda was much influenced by *Serrano* and its judicially induced legislation in other states (pp. 186–215).

The 1978 school-finance bill greatly increased property taxes and centralized state spending in Massachusetts (Perlstein 1980; Avault, Ganz, and Holland 1979). It may seem a tad tendentious of me to point out that two years later, Proposition 13's most famous imitator, Proposition 2.5, was approved by the voters of Massachusetts. This property-tax revolt was not as severe as California's, but like Proposition 13, it did most of its damage to local school spending (Herman Leonard 1992, p. 21), and it effectively gutted the equalizing legislation that was passed in the shadow of the state's *Serrano*-like litigation in 1978 (Morgan 1985).

Unlike my *Serrano*–Proposition 13 connection, I do not have a recorded political connection between Dukakis's school-finance reform bill and the tax revolt. I have found no Massachusetts analog to Alan Post telling the 1977 California legislature that their *Serrano*-response bill had eaten up all the funds for property tax relief. But the circumstances seem similar, and I have encountered no other rational explanation for why Massachusetts voters decided to shoot themselves in the foot in 1980.

I would not be surprised to find similar circumstances behind most of the other property tax revolts around the country. It might resolve a puzzle. David Figlio (1997) concluded that most property-tax revolts have damaged school quality. This seems monstrous in a nation that has always put so much stock in education. Have modern voters gone mad? Perhaps not. Maybe they are rationally responding to the alienation of local property taxes from school quality that is the chief legacy of *Serrano*.

5.18 Conclusion: Causation and the Median Voter

The homevoter hypothesis offers an explanation for one of the most important subnational fiscal events of the twentieth century, Proposition 13. The *Serrano* decision caused Proposition 13 in the following sense. Without the *Serrano II* decision, which disconnected local property taxes from school spending, the property tax revolt would not have gotten any more steam than it had in 1968 or 1972, and the state legislature would have had a much easier time heading it off.

Trying to establish a single cause for a major event is an unfamiliar enterprise for an economist. My tribe of social scientists is most comfortable with many observations of small events, to which we can apply our refined methods of statistical analysis. Even historians have become less comfortable with stories of causation. ("Slavery could have had something to do with the Civil War, but we don't have enough observations to do a cliometric study.") I have been drawn into this enterprise because Proposition 13 is so often thrown up as evidence against all of the foundations of the homevoter hypothesis. Without *Serrano* as a first cause, Proposition 13 indeed does stand as an enduring contradiction of the median voter and the relative efficiency of property-tax financing of education. In the next chapter, I will explore what we know about the educational effects of the outcome desired by the *Serrano* litigants and their legion of successors in other states.

6
The Fruits of School-Finance Centralization

I ARGUED in the previous chapter that *Serrano* constituted an unexpected "natural experiment" in education funding. It greatly centralized and equalized education funding in California, and its influence on other states, both direct and indirect, also changed their direction. This chapter examines what we know about the effects of *Serrano*'s legacy on spending and educational quality.

The evidence on average spending is indeterminate because *Serrano* caused other states to adjust without having a court decision. What seems clearer is that the decisions are fiscally regressive and hurt average educational quality. The decisions have not helped poor people generally because so many of them live in the "property rich" places whose wealth was the focus of litigation. Centralization of funding responsibilities, the outcome desired by *Serrano* and its progeny, seems to have reduced average public school quality and, to some extent, driven educationally ambitious families to private schools.

These outcomes are balefully consistent with the homevoter hypothesis, since the very intention of the *Serrano* movement was to disconnect property value from school taxes. I demonstrate that voters are aware of this connection, and that statewide funding especially alienates the majority of the population who have no children in the public school system. Localism is not dead in school finance, but it has been wounded by a movement whose equalitarianism seems misplaced.

6.1 Has *Serrano*'s Legacy Raised School Funding?

The previous chapter demonstrated that the *Serrano* decision has promoted equalization of spending and centralization of funding throughout the country, even where state courts ostensibly did not interfere with existing arrangements. Thus in one sense we now have a national experiment in school funding theory. The state judiciary has provided an experiment in what happens when school funding responsibilities are shifted from local districts to the state to a degree not demanded by the electorate. The first question of some interest is whether spending per pupil rises or falls as a result of the centralization of funding induced by *Serrano* and its sometimes invisible offspring.

The answer in California is clear. Fabio Silva and Jon Sonstelie (1995) compared the trend in California spending per pupil to that in the rest of the United States from before *Serrano* to years after Proposition 13. California fell well below the trend-line of growth with the onset of *Serrano*. Silva and Sonstelie concluded that half of California's drop was caused by the state's increasing enrollments, which generally cause spending per pupil to fall (just as falling enrollments cause them to rise). The other half of the decline they attributed to the centralizing effects of the *Serrano* decision. (Sonstelie, Brunner and Ardon [2000, chap. 5] conclude that the spending decline was more likely caused by the loss of nonresidential tax revenues that had previously been earmarked for education under the local property tax.) A noneconometric but numerically transparent study by Bradley Joondeph (1995) also documents California's fall from fiscal grace after *Serrano*.

Whether *Serrano*'s descendents in other state courts increased funding for schools in the rest of the nation is not so clear, which in itself is surprising. The expectation of the plaintiffs in these cases has been that putting the responsibility for funding on the state rather than the local fisc (or, to be more accurate about pre-*Serrano* practice, dividing responsibility between the state and the local districts) should increase resources available to schools. Perhaps not to the very highest spending or richest districts, but generally pulling up the lower tail while not reducing the spending of the average. After all, the state does not have to worry as much as local districts about raising taxes, and the considerable influence of teachers' unions in the state capitols should have added to the prospending forces.

The national, econometric studies of the fiscal effects of the *Serrano*-style decisions in other states have yielded mixed results. The pioneer econometric study by Thomas Downes and Mona Shah (1995) found that sometimes states with *Serrano*-style decisions raised spending per pupil above the national trend, but in other instances it fell, as in California. Similarly mixed results were found by Joseph Manwaring and Steven Sheffrin (1997). Less ambivalent were William Evans, Sheila Murray, and Robert Schwab (1997), who concluded that the average of the eleven *Serrano*-style decisions prior to 1992 caused spending per pupil to rise in those states compared to those without a court decision. Murray, Evans, and Schwab (1998) concluded that these states tended to both equalize and "level up." Neither of the latter two studies separated out individual states, so their conclusions, though not their rhetoric, may be consistent with the mixed results of Downes and Shah and of Manwaring and Sheffrin.

6.2 State Histories Suggest a "Level Down" Response

The mixed results of the aforementioned econometric studies are partly due to lumping all of the plaintiff-victory cases into a single category of "reform." All but Wisconsin's did require more equalization and a larger fiscal role for the state, but the exact nature of that role was not specified in the studies. Caroline Hoxby (1997; 1998) found that legislative responses to *Serrano*-style decisions varied. Some legislatures adopted school-aid formulas that encouraged spending, while others (the majority of those with a plaintiff victory) adopted formulas that penalize higher spending by local districts. (Reasons for this will be discussed in Section 6.9.) The effect of the newly adopted school-funding formula on local districts' incentives, she found, was a good predictor of whether statewide spending fell or rose after it was enacted.

The other problem that afflicts attempts to assess school funding litigation among a group of states is that we do not know how much individual states anticipated the court decision. Some may have lowered spending before the decision in order to collect a reserve for compliance. States in the "control group" of those without court decisions might have increased state funding to forestall an adverse decision, as my stories in Section 5.16 indicated. This is not to say that court decisions do not matter. It does suggest that broad-brush econometric studies are a less appropriate way to assess this movement than a detailed history of individual states.

Most of the individual state accounts indicate that the court decisions reduced or left unchanged previous spending totals. Neil Theobald and Lawrence Picus (1991) titled their introduction to studies of California's and Washington's experience with judge-made reform "Living with Equal Amounts of Less." An econometric comparison of Washington to neighboring Oregon, which did not have a similar court decision, found that Washington's ruling reduced instructional spending growth by 1 percent per year (Deborah Garvey 2000). It was especially hard on the "property-rich" but low-income Seattle school district, which ironically had been the plaintiff in the case (Seattle School District v. State 1978).

Michael Heise (1995) examined the experiences of New Jersey and Wyoming, whose courts had overturned local financing in 1973 and 1980, respectively (though both states had subsequent decisions that again overturned the legislature's response). Heise found that, when other factors that influence per pupil spending are controlled for, the court decisions had little or no effect on spending trends. Russell Harrison and G. Alan Tarr (1996) concluded that New Jersey's considerable rise in spending per pupil after litigation began merely continued previous trends and could not be attributed to court decisions.

An econometric study of all states by Murray, Evans, and Schwab (1998) concluded that *Serrano*-style victories did not result in high-spending districts being held back by the resulting reforms. Studies of individual states suggest that this was not true for the three largest states whose courts ordered reforms in their 1972–1992 sample. (Murray, Evans, and Schwab did not weight the states by size, nor did they break out results for individual states.) The three big states, California, Texas, and Washington, have more than two-thirds of the students in the ten plaintiff-victory states in that period.

- California, as mentioned above, clearly pulled the high-spending districts down after Proposition 13.
- Washington State imposed binding caps on local efforts to supplement the state's constitutionally required (as declared by its supreme court) "basic grant." Most of Seattle's suburban districts

as well as Seattle itself bump up against those caps (Margaret Plecki 1997). While local voters and many legislators would like to lift the caps, insiders to Washington politics believe that doing so would invite a lawsuit that the state would lose (Betty Jane Narver 1990).

- Texas reforms likewise show that high-spending districts were considerably constrained in their spending following the court-ordered Texas reforms (Lawrence Picus 1994). Shawna Grosskopf et al. (1997) were similarly impressed with how the Texas reforms tended to constrain the high-spending districts.

6.3 Most Poor Kids Are Not in "Property-Poor" Districts

The main objection to the local financing of schools has been that the poor are concentrated in certain communities. The Tiebout model seems to countenance more income segregation than reformers think is healthy for the economy as a whole. The school-finance reform movement has largely been motivated by a desire to make sure that poor places are not left without an adequate education. Merging the wealth of the districts with that of the state via statewide funding or property-tax base sharing has been regarded as a way to help the poor.

The most obvious problem with this claim is that a large fraction of the poor live in places that have above-average tax bases per pupil. Poor people often live in "property-rich" districts. The modest value of the homes in which they live is offset by the larger-than-average amount of commercial and industrial property located in such districts. National studies of this distribution are lacking because most data about poverty are not linked to school districts. The evidence from individual states, however, overwhelmingly rejects the idea that most poor people live in property-poor places.

One of the stumbling blocks to New York State's unsuccessful *Serrano*-style suit (Board of Education v. Nyquist 1982) was that New York City was "property rich" even though it had a disproportionate number of students from poor families. Plaintiffs attempted to avoid this problem by saying that the city suffered from the "municipal overburden" of other fiscal obligations. But the "overburden" claim is refuted by Harvey Brazer and Therese McCarty (1989), who found no evidence from national data that cities with large nonschool spending were starving their schools. Even among the suburbs, large amounts of commercial development are located in the less affluent communities (Helen Ladd 1976) in part because those communities are more willing to accommodate them with their zoning and planning laws (Fischel 1976; 1979; William Fox 1981).

The equation of poor people with property-poor communities has actually been discredited for a long time. A much-cited (for example, by Justice Powell in *Rodriguez*) student note in the *Yale Law Journal* (1972) addressed it using Connecticut data in the earliest days of the school-finance litigation movement. The *Yale* note found no correlation between district wealth per pupil (which in Connecticut was the town tax base per pupil) and indicators of student poverty. Poor kids were as likely to live in a property-rich district as a property-poor one. A student project by Karen Negris (1982) that I supervised found almost no correlation (r = .04) between tax base per capita and family income in New Hampshire.

In 1999, New Hampshire adopted a statewide property tax in response to its school-finance decision (Claremont v. Governor 1997), which said that unequal tax rates could not be used to fund basic education expenditures. Twenty-seven "property rich" towns had to disgorge nontrivial sums (between $100,000 and $2 million) to fund schools in other towns. Of the twenty-seven "donor" towns, as the victims are called, sixteen had median household incomes below the median income of the state as a whole. The sixteen lower-income towns had a total population that was a third larger than the eleven donor towns whose income was above the state median. New Hampshire's three richest (by household income) towns were not donor towns, and one of the largest contributors to the equalization effort was Lincoln, one of the poorest towns in the state that was "property rich" by virtue of a nearby ski area.

The response to *Serrano*-style decisions in other states has also put the poor at a disadvantage. The state of Washington's 1977 centralization of school finance reduced revenues in districts with high percentages of poor and minority students (Theobald and Hanna 1991). Michigan's recent centralization and equalization of school funding has resulted in less money for Detroit and other poor, urban districts (Courant and Loeb 1997).

In California during the *Serrano* litigation, a data analysis by John Mockler, whose results were widely reported (but, as Mr. Mockler told me in 1999, not published as a report) found that most of the state's poor lived in districts with an above-average property tax base (*Los Angeles Times*, June 30, 1974). Mockler's study was confirmed and documented years later by Jon Sonstelie, Eric Brunner, and Kenneth Ardon (2000, pp. 20–28), who found that the poor in California were more likely to be in property-rich districts than the rich. This was mainly because Los Angeles, Oakland, Long Beach, and San Francisco, whose tax base per student exceeded the state average, had, like other central cities, a disproportionate number of poor families.

Despite this evidence, several influential economics articles promote the belief that property wealth per student and personal household income are closely correlated (Murray, Evans, and Schwab 1998; Thomas Dee 2000). The problem with these otherwise sophisticated studies is that they use the term "poor district" to refer to districts with low spending per pupil from locally assessed taxes. Low spending from this source usually indicates low property wealth, not low income. It is possible that such places are poorer than average, but that does not change the aforementioned evidence that *most of the poor do not live in such districts.* It is time to abandon the false equations of poor people with poor districts and rich people with rich districts.

6.4 Capitalization Moots Tax Reform's Redistributions

The other problem with attempting to redistribute wealth by evening-out tax bases is capitalization. The distribution of gains and losses by permanent redistribution of the tax base will be offset by the housing market, as Bruce Hamilton (1976) pointed out and economists have consistantly reaffirmed (Paul Wyckoff 1995; Thomas Dee 2000). If reforms really do eliminate the fiscal disadvantages of living in a "property-poor" place, then buyers of housing will bid up the price of houses in such places. This is perhaps one reason that some homeowners in such places might join a *Serrano*-style lawsuit against the state, even if they are perfectly happy with their schools.

Owners of homes in "property-poor" places who acquired them prior to the reform will get a nice capital gain by having lower property taxes, assuming that their public schools are not worse after the reform.

Capitalization works just as well at the low end of the housing market as it does for the high end. Low-income people may be even more attentive to fiscal differences since the purchase of a home represents a larger fraction of their assets than it does for richer people.

The housing market thus quickly wipes out any gains for the poor, even if we assume (falsely) that the poor live only in "property-poor" communities whose tax rates are reduced by the reform. If school-finance reform lowers the property taxes on a modest home and the tax is expected to stick, low-income buyers of that home will pay more for it. The greater mortgage and other homebuying costs will offset the lower taxes, and the buyers will not be any better off financially than if there had been no reform at all. Likewise, buyers of homes in formerly property-rich places will purchase them at a lower price that reflects the loss of fiscal advantages, and they will be no better off or worse off than before.

The point of this nihilistic-sounding recitation is to argue that the proper focus of school-finance reform should be educational efficiency, not taxpayer equity. It is true that capitalization undermines an important judicial rationale—tax base or tax-rate inequality—that is deployed in most of the school-finance reform cases. But capitalization also undermines the rationale for returning to the previous system, if all we are concerned about are the effects of property taxes on the distribution of income and wealth. Expectations by themselves are not a good defense for any fiscal practice. After all, people could expect enormous inequities to persist, and they would, therefore, be capitalized. So we need a better rationale for defending the interests of local homeowners in maintaining a local school system. The defense is simple: Localism seems to produce better schools.

6.5 Nonresidential Property Reduces the "Tax Price"

One reason that local control produces better schools is that the local property tax system channels the revenues of nonresidential property into public education (Sonstelie, Brunner, and Ardon 2000, p. 102) . Commercial and industrial property lowers the "tax price" faced by resident-voters in communities in which they locate. As schools appear "cheaper" to the voters, they will be induced to spend more on education.

The tax price is a misunderstood concept. Many people share the view of *Serrano*-advocate Jack Coons (1978, p. 148), who regarded the property tax *rate* as a price. The tax price is different, however, and is best explained with an example. Assume initially that all school funding is local and that the tax base consists exclusively of homes, each of which contains one child in school. The school board proposes an increase in school expenditures by $500,000 a year to hire more teachers and reduce class size. If there are 1,000 taxpayer-voters, each with an equal amount of property—their homes—the "tax price" of the additional spending for the median voter will be $500. If a majority approve the expenditure in order to get the benefit of smaller classes, the median voter will pay $500 more in property taxes. (Having homes with unequal values alters the outcome slightly, since the values of median holdings are typically less than the mean, but that is not important for the present argument about intercommunity comparisons.)

Suppose now that another group of taxpayers is added so that the property-tax base is doubled, but the new taxpayers do not vote and add nothing to the expenses of education. For example, they might own vacation homes or stores or factories and have their residences in another community. The median voter now faces a tax price of only $250 for the $500,000 in spending, only half of what she previously faced.

Note that this calculation does not depend on the average value of the homes of the resident voters, which would only affect the nominal tax rate. In comparing purely residential communities, the tax price faced by the median voter is the same regardless of whether she lives in a community of mansions or of mobile homes. It is true, though, that the same value of nonresidential property, say a $100 million shopping center, will reduce the tax price of education in a community of mobile homes much more than it would in a community of mansions. That is one reason that shopping centers are often more welcome in poorer communities, even though the centers' developers might prefer the more affluent place.

The confusion of property-tax rates with tax prices is best illustrated by the common example that advocates of statewide tax-rate equalization use. They take a "typical" home that is worth, say, $200,000, and compare what the taxes would be in various communities. In property-rich Vacationville, the rate is 1 percent and the taxes on the $200,000 home are $2,000 per year. In property-poor Plainville, the tax rate is 4 percent and the taxes on the $200,000 home are $8,000 per year. This is said to "prove" that the burden of public services in Plainville is four times that of Vacationville.

It proves no such thing. The owner of the $200,000 home in Plainville has a much larger or better-quality home, which if it were moved to a lot in Vacationville would be worth much more than $200,000. The lower taxes and better public services in Vacationville would cause the house and lot to cost more, provided that the environmental disamenities of Vacationville's nonresidential tax base did not offset that gain. No one can tell without a detailed inquiry what the exact effect will be. The main point here is to reiterate what was demonstrated in Section 3.1 (the Concord-Bow example): Tax rates by themselves tell us nothing about differences in the economic burden of the property tax among communities.

Let us return to the issue of nonresidential property and the tax price. Because nonresidential property must be taxed at the same rate as residential, and because local school districts cannot redirect the funds from such sources to cash payments for residents, a nonresidential property tax base makes schooling look "too cheap." The average (median) voter in a district whose property tax base is one-half commercial will regard an additional $100 expenditure per household on schools as costing her only $50 in taxes, since nonresidents will pay the rest. Because she cannot simply take the $50 payment from the nonresidential taxpayers in cash due to the "public purpose" doctrine (among others described in Section 2.4), she will tend to vote for "too much" schooling.

As an extreme illustration, the school district that hosted the Shoreham nuclear power plant on eastern Long Island, New York, sent their children on trips to Madrid, Spain, at public expense to learn Spanish (*New York Times*, May 19, 1998). It was cheap to do so for the median voter because 90 percent of local school taxes were paid for by the power plant. This calculation neglects that the nonresidential property owners might also respond to the higher tax rates by removing themselves to other jurisdictions, which dampens residents' spending enthusiasm (Helen Ladd 1975). In fact, Shoreham's power plant never did get an operating permit, and the school district eventually had to live within more modest means, though the failure to get a permit was due to environmental anxieties rather than fiscal burdens. For less dramatic cases, William Oakland and William Testa (1998) establish that industrial and commercial developments do reduce tax prices in the way suggested here.

Some economists are willing to forthrightly say that the lower tax price is a bad idea. Helen Ladd and Edward Harris (1995) advocate that New York State ought to disallow the taxation of commercial and industrial property at the local level and have the state tax it at a uniform rate and redistribute the revenues to school districts everywhere. I think this is problematic because it undermines local incentives to accept commerce and industry, which almost invariably cause at least some inconvenience to the host community (Section 7.5). Without some form of compensation, locals would be unwilling to zone for commerce and industry in their midst.

The fiscal problem with the low tax price, however, is not local compensation for putting up with industry. The fiscal inefficiency is the requirement that the compensation come in a particular form, in this case, education spending. If the legal constraints that channeled the funds to education were removed and nuclear power plants (for instance) just paid residents of the districts in which they located $10,000 each and let them spend it however they pleased, the tax-price distortion would be eliminated.

Now, I don't think that this is the best solution to this "inefficiency." (I use the quotes because it's a little embarrassing: "Imagine, wasting all that money on public education!") The reason is that the public-purpose doctrine that causes it still has a role that is useful. It offers some protection for nonresidents from local exploitation by resident voters. It ties the fortunes of all property owners together. By making the voters spend their nonresidential taxes on things that continue to make the community attractive, the doctrine puts all residents in the same political bed and helps overcome free riders.

An illustration of this effect is from the previously mentioned case of the Shoreham nuclear plant. If the plant's developers had simply given each resident $10,000, the residents could have opted out of public life at the local level. By forcing the transfer to come through the public sector, the beneficiaries must continue to cooperate with one another and with the source of their benefits. The Shoreham–Wading River school district was a major public advocate of granting the nuclear plant's operating license. That it did not succeed was a major blow to the school district and the taxpayers.

6.6 Has *Serrano*'s Legacy "Dumbed Down" Education?

If school quality were just as good when the money comes from a statewide source as it is when the money comes from a local source, then the theory that I espouse here—that concern for their home values leads voters to select more efficient local services—would be in trouble. As this section and the next show, however, the weight of the evidence on school quality favors the capitalization theory.

Public education in California has without a doubt suffered from the effects of what I regard as the *Serrano*-induced fiscal regime that has prevailed since 1978 (Sonstelie, Brunner, and Ardon 2000, chap. 7). Almost no one without an office in the capitol has a good word for the state's school system, which in the late 1960s was almost as well regarded as California's university system (Peter Schrag 1998, pp. 69, 87). California's average class size in the 1980s and 1990s has become the second largest (after Utah's) in the United States. The late Charles Benson, a founder of modern school-finance research and a *Serrano* advocate, glumly conceded before a Congressional committee in the early 1990s, "You must be very careful when you wish for things because you may just get what you wish for. We worked hard for equity in California. We got it. Now we don't like it" (quoted in Hickrod et al. 1995).

The evidence from other states is less clear but still generally pessimistic. Average scores on the Scholastic Aptitude Test (SAT) are a reasonable metric for comparing student academic accomplishment among states once differing participation rates are taken into account (Graham and Husted 1993). There is a fair amount of evidence that SAT scores are worse, not better, in states that have gone down the centralization and equalization road farther than others (Sam Peltzman 1993). Peltzman (1996) also found that non–college students in states with more centralized funding did worse on the Armed Forces Qualifying Test. Two studies that focused on other interstate differences among schools found incidentally that states with more centralized financing had lower SAT scores (Southwick and Gill 1997) and lower scores on the National Assessment of Educational Progress (NAEP) (Fuchs and Reklis 1994). Mark Berger and Eugenia Toma (1994) also found that states with more centralized finance had lower SAT scores, but the coefficient was not statistically significant.

The most extensive study of the effects of school-finance reform on interstate SAT score differences is by Thomas Husted and Larry Kenny (2000). They obtained records of individual test-takers and their personal characteristics for the thirty-four states in which the SAT is taken by a nontrivial fraction of high school seniors. (The SAT is bicoastal; college-bound kids in the middle of the country more often take the ACT, for which information about test-takers was not available.) Husted and Kenny constructed a measure not only of average state SAT scores, but also of the variance in SAT scores within the state. Instead of looking at court orders, they looked at how much centralization and equalization of school funding actually changed over the period 1972–1992 and compared it to how much it would have been expected to change (as a result of demographic and political factors) after 1972.

Husted and Kenny's results show that centralization of school funding—more state money, less reliance on local property taxes—appears to have statistically significant, large, negative effects on average SAT scores. They also find that equalization (which is not the same as centralization) of spending likewise reduced SAT scores. On the less gloomy side, Husted and Kenny found that within-state variance in SAT scores was somewhat reduced by both equalization and centralization, though this result was not as robust as the pessimistic result about average scores. They conclude that equalization and centralization may make the previously lower-scoring students better off relative to the higher-scoring students, but it seems largely to be a "dumbing down" effect, since the average scores are clearly reduced by both centralization and equalization.

6.7 Has Equalization Helped Low Achievers?

There is little evidence that the goal of equal opportunity is improved by achieving the goals of the *Serrano* litigation. Students in previously low-scoring districts do not close the test-score gap after spending becomes more equalized, as Thomas Downes (1992) has shown. His much-cited evidence comes from California, where court-induced centralization resulted in an equality of paupers. (See also Sonstelie, Brunner, and Ardon 2000, chap. 10.) Perhaps it worked better in "level-up" states. Connecticut's response to the *Horton* decision did cause expenditures in its largest city, Hartford, to rise above the suburban average, but with no measurable improvement in student performance. As a sympathetic commentator, James Ryan (1999, p. 538), pointed out, "Successful school finance reform did not make a significant difference in the academic achievement of Hartford students."

Two studies suggest a note of optimism. David Card and Abigail Payne (1998) found that poor students did slightly better on SATs in states whose courts ordered more equalized spending. Their most elaborate regression, however, was not statistically significant and is questionable because of low SAT participation by the poorest students. (The previously mentioned studies using SAT scores looked at state averages, not the poor by themselves.)

Thomas Dee (2000) chose a different approach, one more consistent with the theme of this book. He examined states whose courts had undertaken *Serrano*-style reforms. He hypothesized that formerly low-spending districts should have their property values increased as a result of the additional state aid. If their schools were getting better as a result, more people would want to live there and drive up housing prices. His results suggest that at least for the formerly low-spending districts, the reforms improved education. My only objection to his clever study is his labeling of these low-spending districts as the "poor districts," which implies that the reforms helped most poor people. As I mentioned earlier, there is no evidence that the majority of poor people live in the "property-poor" districts that are the focus of *Serrano*-style litigation.

Although the Card and Payne and Dee studies suggest some note of optimism about the educational results of the school-finance cases, the bulk of the evidence seems pessimistic. An important long-range goal of school-finance equalization is to narrow the gap between high- and low-wage workers (Roland Benabou 1996). A study by Eric Hanushek and Julie Somers (1999) concluded that "the three-decade-old movement toward reducing the variation in school spending within states appears to have done nothing to reduce subsequent income variations of workers." Three decades may be too short a period to fully judge the effects, but their finding is certainly not cause for optimism.

The pessimistic results are reinforced by nonacademic commentators in other states. For example, New Jersey is often cited as a state whose response to its court decision was to increase average spending, and it has indeed remained a high-spending state. Former governor Thomas Kean wrote a column on the occasion of New Jersey's (supposedly) final settlement in its school-finance case (*Bergen Record*, March 8, 1998). Kean was not critical of the litigation itself, only its focus on how much the state had to pay. He mentioned the billions of dollars spent by New Jersey to comply with nine court decisions from 1973 to 1994 and concluded, "All this taxpayer money has accomplished nothing. Test scores haven't risen; in fact, in some cases they've fallen. Dropout rates haven't improved much either. In fact, the evidence is clear. After all the rhetoric and money, the poorest children of the state continue to be warehoused rather than taught."

With such negative assessments in the press, one would think that academics, who mostly regard court interventions as desirable, would respond with more systematic evidence. The *Journal of Education Finance* has since its inception in 1975 published scores of articles about the experience of states that have moved toward centralization and equalization. I have looked at all of them through 2000. Not one of these articles reports a single instance of measurable academic improvement from centralization or equalization for anyone, let alone the students from low-income families.

One of the few articles that addressed the accomplishment issue at all reported on Hawaii. Its public schools have long been wholly state financed, although it does not appear that its courts had anything to do with this condition. The measurable academic quality of Hawaii's schools is disappointingly low (John Thompson 1992), which may explain why Hawaii has such an extensive system of nonsectarian private schools. As if to usher school-finance litigation into the second millennium, the *Journal of Education Finance* finally published an article that evaluates the educational aftermath of litigation. A study of Tennessee districts that successfully sued the state for more funds found that after five years there was no trend toward convergence of test scores between the seventy-one plaintiff districts and the rest of the state (Peevely and Ray 2001).

6.8 Public-School Competition Raises Scores

Much of the criticism of public schools from conservative quarters characterizes them as a "monopoly." Such critics usually recommend reforms that would break this alleged monopoly by allowing families to use public funds ("vouchers") to send their children to private schools. But as the Tiebout model supposes, local governments, including school districts, are sufficiently numerous in most areas that footloose households in fact have a range of choices that exceeds that found in most other markets. Public schools in most states operate in a geographic market that is highly competitive.

But does a wider range of choice among public school districts actually produce better educational outcomes? If competition among public schools lowers their quality, the homevoter hypothesis would take a serious blow. Thus one important test of the capitalization model's efficiency is to see whether the number of school districts in a given area by itself promotes better educational results.

The evidence on this is strongly positive. More districts means better results. Evidence on competition comes from studies of in-state scores of tests that are administered on a uniform basis and thus do not require the participation-rate adjustment that one must make in comparing states according to SAT scores. Blair Zanzig (1997) looked at standardized-test scores of school districts in California in 1970 (before the *Serrano* decision). Zanzig found that twelfth-graders in counties in which there were four or more school districts had higher scores. Counties that had fewer districts had lower scores because, Zanzig inferred, there was less competition among the districts.

The same results appear in other states. John Blair and Samuel Staley (1995) found that Ohio school districts that were subject to more competition from other public school districts had better reading scores on a standardized, statewide test. Melvin Borland and Roy Howsen (1993) obtained similar results with a sample of Kentucky school districts, as did Michael Marlow (1997) with statewide scores for the United States as a whole.

The foregoing studies all invoked modern econometric evidence and employed extensive control variables in an attempt to keep other things equal. They all conclude that a more decentralized, localized system of financing education produces better test scores, which is consistent with my hypothesis. The trouble with them is that we do not know what caused the districts in a given area to be numerous or few. Perhaps those areas with only a few districts were created that way to take advantage of scale economies. If that were the case, we could not be sure that the worse test results were not offset by some unobservable reasons for consolidation.

Caroline Hoxby (2000) invented an imaginative test to overcome these problems. She looked for metropolitan areas around the country that had natural features (chiefly bodies of water) that might separate urban areas into school districts. In areas with many such immutable dividers, the fragmentation of school districts would be "natural" in its most literal sense. (Such geographical boundaries would discourage school-district consolidation but not, in most cases, the search by homebuyers for good school districts.) Using this measure as a proxy for fragmentation and deploying the usual econometric controls, Hoxby found that a greater number of independent school districts in a metropolitan area increased her measure of educational accomplishment (high-school graduation rates and college-going). Her most important finding was that in the competitive situation, where there are many school districts in the metropolitan area, all schools, even those serving disadvantaged populations, were better and cost *less* to operate than schools in areas with only a few districts to choose from.

6.9 Why Would State Funding Impair Education Quality?

The evidence that competition improves school quality helps explain why *Serrano*-style decisions have apparently worsened overall school quality. Centralization and equalization of school finance undermine homevoters' influence by, in effect, reducing competition among school districts. Although the number of districts may remain the same after centralization of funding, the ability of local districts to compete is attenuated by their reduced ability to raise additional resources to, say, hire better teachers. Childless voters in such districts also have much less reason to support cost-effective education measures. Nearly every sophisticated study indicates that greater state funding reduces the efficiency of local districts (Caroline Hoxby 1998; Husted and Kenny 1997; Duncombe and Yinger 1997).

How can it be that more state funding, something usually eagerly sought by local school boards, reduces local efficiency? One reason is that the structure of state grants can penalize successful districts by reducing the amount of the grant after a certain level of spending or property wealth is reached. This causes the median voter in the district to perceive that the tax price she pays for education—the increase in her tax bill for a dollar's increase in education spending—is higher. This is in fact what most court-induced reforms have done, according to Caroline Hoxby (1997; 1998), and she finds that disincentives for local spending do reduce a state's spending relative to other states.

Defenders of increased state funding point out that there are ways to do it that do not undermine local district incentives. State funds could be redistributed to school districts in the form of grants that were based on family income, so that districts with many poor people could get more resources (Ladd and Yinger 1994). This would not then prevent local districts from funding education from local property taxes. Other forms of categorical grants (based on categories such as parental education, handicapped status, or poverty levels) would likewise not do much damage to the efficiency aspects of the local property tax system. Even though such formulas are not consistent with most *Serrano*-style court decisions—which, for reasons described in the next section, insist that remedies be based on property wealth rather than demographic characteristics—the legislature might adopt them as a means of forestalling further litigation.

But as important as incentives at the margin are, attention to them overlooks the long-run impact of an increased state role in education. No legislature can sit by and simply let a state-funded school-aid formula do its job. It will eventually be driven to attach more strings to the funds. Liberal legislators will insist on regulations that increase the role of teachers' unions—the mainstay of the Democratic Party since at least the 1980s. While the interests of teachers and students usually correspond in the classroom, at the state level teachers' unions promote work rules that reduce school efficiency (Hoxby 1996). Conservatives will demand curricular reforms under the rubric of "accountability," which further reduce the role of local districts. While in theory such legislative tinkering was always available, even when funding was mostly local, in practice the attention of the state legislature is directed to where the state's money goes.

6.10 Why Court Decisions Are Hostile to Property Taxes

The other reason that increased state aid undermines localism is that the local property tax became a necessary focus for the school-finance litigators. Although the poster children of most litigation are districts that are both income poor and property poor, the constitutional basis for the litigation almost always rests on the tax base issue (Kenneth Wong 1991). Variation in local property tax bases, the very quality that makes the system efficient, was the main point of constitutional attack. Any legislature that subsequently allows this seemingly obvious inequality to persist after losing a school-finance suit will always be at risk of another unhappy day in court.

It is important to understand how this focus came about. The original school-finance litigation in the 1960s did not cast local property taxation as the villain (Joseph Henke 1986, pp. 5–12). The complaint in McInnis v. Shapiro (N. D. Ill. 1968) was that children of poor families were not getting the education that they needed to succeed in life. The issue was poverty and educational outcomes, not property taxes. But this approach failed in the courts. The judges said that the remedy of equal educational outcomes for rich and poor kids was too difficult for them to monitor. They also shrank from the implications of holding inequalities of income to be a constitutionally suspect category (Frank Michelman 1969). If that were so for schools, why not for every other inequality of personal wealth?

After these setbacks, the school-finance litigants then came up with Plan B. Don't focus on educational outcomes. Focus on the easily monitored issue of revenue and expenditure. And confine the inequality argument to something that is both important and publicly financed. The school property tax thus became the object of attack because it was both measurable and confinable to a particular type of public expenditure. Judges could see that there was a definable remedy and a stopping point.

"Plan B" was the invention of three activist law professors, John Coons, William Clune, and Stephen Sugarman. They laid it out in a law journal article (1969) and expanded it in a book, *Private Wealth and Public Education* (1970), which immediately became the Bible of the school-finance litigation movement. Focus on property tax inequalities was, they freely acknowledge, a second-best argument. Their preferred system involves state funding of vouchers for low-income children (Coons and Sugarman 1978). But since the courts could not be induced to require that or any other family-background-based remedy, their strategy was to attack the inequalities of the property tax base. Even if this penalized the poor in some districts (a majority, as it turned out, in California), the resulting funding system would just have to be better than what Coons had called the "pathetic American system of local non-government" (1974, p. 305).

Their strategy has worked with enormous success, at least the part that suppresses the local property tax. And it seems like the only strategy that is likely to continue to work. While some courts, such as that of Kentucky, have shown a willingness to invoke educational standards as remedies, failure to comply with these standards is almost always measured in spending per pupil (Goetz and Debertin 1992). Local funding that results in spending variations related to property-tax base is automatically suspect. To vary an old saw, when litigants say, "It's not the money, it's the educational standards," you can bet it's the money.

The special nature of the centralization induced by *Serrano,* which focused on property-tax base differences, can account for why centralization before *Serrano* had little adverse effect on public schools. Centralization of educational funding began long before *Serrano* and its progeny. The share of spending funded by local property taxes peaked at more than three-quarters in 1930 and has declined steadily to only about one-third in 1990 (Bahl, Sjoquist, and Williams 1990). Almost all of this decline was due to displacement by state funds. But legislatures in the pre-*Serrano* era had the liberty to distribute the state's largesse in a more balanced fashion, one that took account of district variations in income and cost of living as well as property-tax base. Once the *Serrano* decision had elevated the property-tax base—and not income or parental background or other measures of need—to the status of constitutional command, additions to the share of funding by the state became increasingly destructive of the efficiency virtues of the local property tax.

6.11 No-Kids-in-School Voters Are a Majority

So far in this chapter I have described the judicial experiments that seem to confirm the homevoter hypothesis. One aspect of the story remains unexplored in this context: the observed behavior of voters, as opposed to the indirect evidence from housing prices. To get at this, I will explore the problem of the "no kids in school" voters.

Voting-age adults who currently have no children in the public-school pipeline form a majority in most jurisdictions. I infer this from the fact that in 1990 only 38 percent of American adults lived in households with children under age eighteen. From this one should subtract perhaps another five percentage points for the parents of children who attend private schools. (In fact 10 percent of children attend private schools, but they may be in households with siblings in public schools, or they may want the option of moving to public schools in later grades.) By any calculation, the voters with a direct, consumer's interest in public schools are a minority in most jurisdictions.

School budgets are often subject to voter review. Local school board elections are frequent, and "fiscally conservative" candidates have little trouble getting their message out. If the no-kids-in-public-school majority were solely concerned about their tax bills, they could vote down any increase in school expenditures, either directly or through school board elections. But they do not. Budgets are more likely to have problems in districts with a large no-kids-in-school majority, but even in these some budget is eventually passed. I take this as evidence that schooling's effect on home values is an important discipline that keeps the no-kids-in-school voters supporting schools even if they aren't enthusiastic about school taxes.

The home-value motivation should work for any voter who owns a home in which families with children might live. It is also a reason why private communities whose covenants restrict children from occupying homes should be discouraged from locating in regular school districts. In "adults only" subdivisions, better schools do little for the value of one's own home, since it cannot be sold to families with school-age children. The travails of local education in retirement-community states like Florida and Arizona are consistent with this claim.

For most other places, home value is a powerful motivator for voters. Ted Bergstrom, Dan Rubinfeld, and Perry Shapiro (1982) found in their analysis of a voter survey in Michigan that voters over age sixty-five were unusually supportive of local school spending. The authors (all Michigan residents at the time) suggested an explanation for this seeming anomaly: If you are planning to retire to Florida, you need to sell your home at a good price, and bad schools drag down the price. Even if childless homeowners know they will stay in the community for a long time, their home is still the most important asset against which they can borrow money.

This is not to deny that homeowners who currently have children at home have a greater stake in schools than others. They are most likely to vote in school elections, and they have more knowledge of how schools are actually performing, so they are in a better position to monitor them. People who have children in school do have an incentive to vote for more expenditures than others, although the devaluation of their homes from too-high property taxes in the future (assuming that high expenditure levels are difficult to reverse) might temper their enthusiasm for gold-plated educational programs.

Similarly, childless homeowners have fewer (but still some) incentives to vote for school funding, especially if they plan to stay a long time (Brueckner and Joo 1991). It's like home remodeling decisions. If you plan to stay a long time, you are more inclined to suit yourself; if you plan to move soon, you suit the market. But like the remodeling decision, voting for durable local services is always tempered by the prospect that the homeowner will eventually sell the home. Poor investment decisions, whether in the private or local public sectors, will eventually come due.

I don't want to overstate the case, though. It is possible that a community with an especially large number of voters who have no children in the school pipeline and who plan to stay a long time may have less than optimal levels of school funding. The problem may be acute when the oldsters are of a different race or ethnic group than those who have children in school (James Poterba 1997). But the alternative system urged by the heirs of *Serrano* is even worse in this respect. The problem of statewide funding is that it offers childless voters no financial motivation to support efficient levels of education spending. No-kids-in-school voters at the local level at least have the home-value motive. The homevoter motive is eliminated when funding is centralized.

A former Republican Party chairman in Washington State, whose schools are funded almost entirely by the state legislature, drew the implication clearly in a 1991 newspaper interview: "The fact is, there is no political profit in being a crusader for the schools. These guys [state legislators] can count votes, and they understand that parents [of school-age children] account for less than one-quarter of the voters" (quoted in Theobald and Hanna 1991, p. 28).

6.12 No-Kids-in-School Homeowners Are Moved by Capitalization

There is direct, albeit episodic, evidence that home values motivate school voting. Social psychologists Kenneth Rasinski and Susan Rosenbaum (1987) did a survey of voters in a local referendum that proposed to raise property taxes considerably and spend the revenue on local education. The referendum passed—I am pretty sure it was in Evanston, Illinois, though the authors did not specifically reveal it—and the researchers wanted to know why people supported it. One of the most frequently voiced reasons, given by people who had no children in the schools as well as those who did, was that a decline in school quality would hurt their home values.

It is not just Evanston. *Serrano*-advocate Charles Benson noticed, without benefit of a formal survey, that childless voters in Piedmont, California (a suburb of Oakland) also supported school spending in part because of its salutary effects on property values (Benson and O'Halloran 1987). Martha Jones, a Berkeley graduate student and mother who lived in Piedmont, told me in 1992 that she had heard homeowners specifically invoke this reason at school board meetings.

Evanston and Piedmont, the skeptic might point out, are fairly affluent places. Is this behavior typical of other districts? Jon Sonstelie and Paul Portney (1980b) analyzed a school referendum held in 1970 in the more middle-class city of South San Francisco. (This was before the *Serrano* decisions took away most local control over schools.) They concluded that "the larger is the average expected increase in property values in a precinct, the more likely it is that voters in that precinct will support the referendum" (p. 194). They titled their article "Take the Money and Run" to highlight the fact that even voters with no plans to stay in the community and no children will be inclined to approve spending measures that will raise the value of their major asset, their homes.

The influence of no-kids voters helps explain why the "fiscal harness" theory of statewide funding does not work well. The theory goes like this. The Tiebout model allows voters with a high demand for education to obtain it in their own communities. These same voters, it is assumed, then oppose statewide taxes to fund schools in other places. The fiscal harness theory attempts to yoke demand for local spending with statewide spending, so that residents of high-demand districts will be willing to support statewide taxes to fund the low-demand districts (Susanna Loeb forthcoming). If you want to spend $500 extra on your own schools, you have to add something to the coffers of the entire state. Local demand is thus harnessed to the fiscal affairs of other districts.

In response to its 1970s school-finance litigation, the state of Washington moved to a more centralized system of funding. In order to keep the fiscal disparities within the limits of the state supreme court's tolerance, the legislature imposed limits on how much extra money can be raised from local property taxes. Local districts are permitted to vote to "override" these limits in order to spend more, but there is a ceiling by which the high-spending districts are constrained. The architects of the policy deliberately adopted these ceilings in order to induce voters in the high-spending district to support a statewide income tax (Betty Jane Narver 1990, p. 162).

The plan has not worked. Attempts to adopt a state income tax, which requires a majority vote in a statewide referendum, have all failed. Attempts to increase funds by the roundabout method of boosting automobile registration fees were upended by a voter initiative in 1999. Washington's schools have an egalitarian funding system, but the level of spending is low because, as most observers agree, voters will not accept an income tax (Marge Plecki 1997; Narver 1990).

One explanation for this stalemate is that the fiscal harness theory neglects the different motives of voters without children in public school. At the local level, they are willing to support, or at least not oppose, high levels of spending because better schools add to the value of their homes. At the state level, voters without children do not perceive such an offsetting benefit for their taxes. More spending statewide, even if it does improve the schools, has little effect on any individual voter's property values.

6.13 Capitalization Short-Circuits the "Death Spiral"

The anxiety expressed by people to whom I have explained the homevoter hypothesis is that it may be okay for upper-class places like Evanston and Piedmont, but lower-income places with a declining tax base may be stuck in a "death spiral." The idea is that as taxpaying, high-income homeowners and industry depart, taxes must be raised, inducing still more people and industry to depart. Self-help is of no use, according to this pessimistic idea; the Tiebout model works fine for the upper crust, but not for the bottom layer, they say.

The "death spiral" argument makes no empirical sense. If it were true, then every town that ever experienced a tax increase would now be in bankruptcy, and municipal bankruptcy is a rare event. Yet one hears the argument all the time, sometimes even by economists. It was presented on behalf of Claremont, a New Hampshire town that was the lead plaintiff in the school-finance suit in which I testified in 1996. Claremont once had a bustling set of textile mills, but most have closed, and its residents have had to endure higher taxes. But a visit to the town shows that home construction is proceeding and new schools have been opened. There was not any state-sponsored bailout for Claremont at that point, and no one expected one. Instead, the real estate market and the self-help motive have prevented the scenario of helplessness that the "death spiral" notion conveys.

An advertisement that has appeared several times in my local newspaper (Lebanon, N.H., *Valley News,* September 9, 1999, p. C8) compared the price of an eight-room home in Claremont with that of nearby Lebanon and Hanover, which have lower tax rates. The advertisement, originally sponsored by the city of Claremont and now by area realtors, pointed out that the average price of an eight-room home was $90,000 in Claremont, compared to $137,000 in Lebanon and $238,000 in Hanover. Of course, the tax rate on the Claremont home would be higher than in the other towns (a fact that the newspaper advertisement did not mention but that potential buyers would certainly discover), but a buyer who saves $47,000 by buying a house in Claremont instead of Lebanon (or $148,000 compared to Hanover) will have cash left over to pay those taxes. As real estate salespeople say, price cures all.

Claremont, moreover, is not a passive observer of the decline of its industrial base. It has an active economic development office, which has met with some success. The issue of revitalizing the town is also raised at school meetings, at which voters are asked to approve or vote down new school spending. At one such meeting on March 11, 1995, a former mayor spoke in favor of a bond issue that would raise taxes for a new school. He invoked the Sullivan County Citizens for Tax Relief (of which he was not a member), who usually oppose tax increases, in support of the bond issue: "Their goal is property tax relief. The goal is more than just cutting budgets. The goal is to make city hall and the schools more efficient. An environment must be created that will increase the tax base and the average pay of a worker in Claremont. Part of this will be accomplished by having an efficient education system . . .

The school facilities will play a major role in attracting new business to Claremont."

The budget passed.

6.14 Do Homebuyers Really Know about School Quality?

If homebuyers do not know about test scores and other indicia of school quality, it is not for lack of sources of information. Many metropolitan newspapers publish annual surveys of test scores and other data on every school in the city and in the suburbs. There is an annual book listing the one hundred best schools in California, ranked by test scores. Real estate salespeople have similar information for almost every metropolitan area, and when it is to their advantage (they represent the seller in most cases), they put it right on the listing sheet.

But are homebuyers really interested in school quality, or is it just living in an elite neighborhood or community? There are a good number of econometric studies that find that districts with higher test scores have higher home values (Jud and Watts 1981; Hayes and Taylor 1996). I reviewed in Section 3.12 the evidence by political scientists that Tiebout shoppers pay attention to school quality, even if they do not know the objective numbers. William Bogart and Brian Cromwell (1997) found that homebuyers in the suburbs of Cleveland were willing to pay substantial premiums in the form of higher home prices—on the order of 5,000 to 10,000 dollars—to live in higher-quality school districts, even though such districts had higher tax rates. Donald Haurin and David Brasington (1996) found that test scores were actually the most important determinant of variations in house values in their Ohio sample.

The problem with these studies—indeed, the difficulty facing most capitalization studies—is that many of the explanatory variables are correlated with one another. Find a district with high test scores and it is likely to have large homes, high family incomes, low crime rates, good sidewalks, and all the other amenities that make for a good place to live. Modern econometric techniques can control for many of these correlations, but it remains difficult to erase the fact that good test scores and nice neighborhoods do seem to go together.

The study that seems best to have controlled for these problems is by Sandra Black (1999). Rather than compare homes in different communities, she used as her standard of comparison homes within the same community but in different school-attendance zones. She had the 1993–1995 standardized test scores for the elementary schools in each of these attendance zones, which were in eastern Massachusetts communities. (She did not include Boston schools.) Thus Black did not have to worry about differences in tax rates in her comparisons, since the attendance zones were within the same school district. She further confined her comparisons to homes near the edges of the borders of attendance zones, and excluded borders that were obvious neighborhood dividers, such as freeways, rivers, and parks. This controlled almost perfectly for differences in neighborhood quality, since the homes being compared were usually across a residential street from one another.

Black was assured by local officials that attendance-zone boundaries were stable, so homebuyers could rely upon being in the same elementary school zone for a long time. She found 22,000 home sales that met the boundary criteria for her sample. With the value of single-family homes as her dependent variable, she was able to determine the differences in value that could be attributed to being in one attendance zone versus its neighbor. She found that being in an attendance zone whose fourth graders were in the top test-quartile of the state raised the value of the home by $4,000 compared to a nearby home in a zone whose test scores were in the bottom test-quartile of the state. (Housing values in the sample averaged about $190,000.) Although $4,000 is not a huge number—it is about half what previous studies had shown using interdistrict data—it is hardly trivial. It shows without much doubt that homebuyers do notice differences in test scores, or some school quality closely related to test scores, and are willing to pay a premium for them.

6.15 Begging Is a Poor Substitute for the Property Tax

The decline of variation in spending among school districts and the related decline in the use of local property taxation does not mean that homevoters have proportionately less interest in local education. Recall that in Sandra Black's study of the influence of test scores on home values, property taxes were identical in the different attendance zones because the comparison homes were in the same district (which in Massachusetts means the same town.) So homeowners still have an incentive to try to make sure that their schools are good. What's missing when property taxes cannot be varied is that local voters cannot use *local* public spending to improve schools. So they have to find other ways.

California is the leader in finding ways around the equality-of-spending requirement of *Serrano* and the self-imposed property-tax drought of Proposition 13. It is important to understand that both *Serrano* and Proposition 13 were directed specifically to ad valorum property taxes. *Serrano* said spending could not vary as a result of differences in the ad valorum property tax base, and Proposition 13 nailed that down by putting a ceiling of 1 percent on the property tax rate, and a 2 percent annual ceiling on assessment growth. For nearly all California districts, the option of raising money for the school library by increasing property-tax rates is a distant memory.

But California districts still raise money by other means. Private foundations are widespread, though their amount is modest and their funds cannot be deployed to support core instructional activities of the schools. Parcel taxes (based on a physical characteristic, not value), which require a two-thirds voter approval, can also be used to exceed *Serrano* spending limits. But the most important source of spending variations is gifts from Sacramento. According to Thomas Timar (1994), the legislature has created a vast array of categorical grants not based on property wealth, so that their variation is permissible under *Serrano.* Such grants are likely to be guided to districts not on the basis of educational need or poverty levels, but on the ability of individual legislators to channel funds to their constituents (Dennis Leyden 1992). Influence in the state budget is the key to this largesse. Thus California is highly centralized in its school finance, but its spending has become less equal than it had been immediately after Proposition 13, and rankings of per pupil spending inequalities usually place California in the middle range of the states.

As a result of these fiscal inequalities and, perhaps, other sources of school-district differences, Los Angeles–area school districts with better education numbers had higher home values, even though *Serrano* and Proposition 13 had leveled the fiscal differences (Brunner, Murdoch, and Thayer 1999). This may explain an otherwise puzzling phenomenon. If the combination of *Serrano* and Proposition 13 leveled down California schools, wouldn't California voters now be more inclined to accept a voucher system? (Such systems give public funds in the form of per student "vouchers," which recipients can use to pay tuition for private or public schools other than those in their local district.)

Public funding for vouchers as a response to *Serrano* was in fact envisioned by two of *Serrano*'s original intellectual architects, Jack Coons and Steve Sugarman (1978). Their plan was tilted more toward low-income people than those initiatives that were actually on the ballot. But the 1992 and 1996 voucher initiatives in California were badly beaten. Brunner and Sonstelie (1997) found that one contributing factor appeared to be that voters with strong demands for education had already made other arrangements within the public sector. Voters in districts whose home values reflected the value of better schools were especially opposed to vouchers. To adopt such a system would have reduced their home values.

The reader might reasonably ask, so what's the fuss about *Serrano* and Proposition 13? Voters seem to be getting the variation they want through private donations, parcel taxes, and influence on their state legislators. The differences are reflected in home values, just as they are in the pre-*Serrano* era. But the fiscal discipline is much more attenuated in the post-*Serrano* world. Homeowners who do not have children may contribute to school foundations on the principle that good schools will help their home values, but the urge to free-ride on the contributions of others is a considerable problem. Brunner and Sonstelie (1997) have demonstrated that there is surprisingly little free-riding among parents with children in school. (They play down the pessimistic view of my California friends with school-age children that such "voluntary" payments seem a bit like extortion, with your kids as the hostages.) It is difficult to believe that owners of nonresidential property or of homes without school-age children would not be tempted to forgo the fund drive.

Appealing to one's state representatives for special favors such as school funds is a time-honored method of channeling resources to one's district. It has a time-honored name, too: the pork barrel. The problem with pork is not the project, but that the costs are spread to the rest of the state while the benefits are concentrated. Pork lacks the discipline between cost and benefit other than the much looser constraints of legislative vote trading. Thus it should not be too surprising that the expenditures that are made at the state level have not been successful in improving the general quality of education in California. As the soul song says, "God bless the child that's got his own."

6.16 Has Equalization Mixed the Rich with the Poor?

The late Norman Williams began the 1975 edition of his multivolume casebook on land-use law with the *Serrano* decision. *Serrano* is of course a school-finance, not a land-use, case. Williams nonetheless made it the keynote of his book because he believed that this decision and others like it would make the evils of exclusionary zoning obsolete. With uniform funding for schools, towns would have less incentive to zone out low-income housing that did not pay its own way.

There is some evidence that income segregation by census tract is less prevalent in metropolitan areas that have fewer school districts (Hamilton, Mills, and Puryear 1975). With fewer districts, families have less reason to choose neighborhoods on the basis of public schools. Two recent studies have taken advantage of the school-finance litigation movement to see if school districts in states that have had *Serrano*-style decisions now mix the rich and poor more than they used to. Daniel Aaronson (1999) and Thomas Downes and David Figlio (1999) find some evidence supporting this proposition. Neither study claims that the result is strong, and both invoke the problematic proposition that all state court decisions, not just *Serrano*, can be viewed as exogenous events. Their results are best viewed against the finding that income segregation within metropolitan areas became more pronounced during the 1970s and 1980s, even as indicators of racial segregation declined (Abramson, Tobin, and VanderGoot 1995).

Nonetheless, the foregoing studies at least suggest that there may be an up side to the otherwise disappointing results of school-finance centralization. No one reports that the suburbs are actively rezoning to accommodate the poor. There is, however, some evidence of a reverse migration to the central cities so that the metropolitan area is less segregated by income groups. I observed some of this during my year in Berkeley in 1991–1992. A surprising number of younger faculty had purchased houses in Oakland, the down-at-the-heels big city next to Berkeley. It has some pleasant neighborhoods that are close to the university. The professors were not rich, but they could have bought homes in suburbs such as Walnut Creek or Orinda. By choosing Oakland, they contributed to income mixing within Oakland, which seems like a socially desirable thing to do.

One should not put too optimistic a face on this trend, however. All of the Oakland residents that I knew who were Berkeley faculty (including one of the original *Serrano* advocates) sent their children, if they had any, to private schools. I surmise that one of the reasons that they did not live in the suburbs was that the public schools were no longer so attractive there. But they certainly were not about to subject their children to the Oakland public school system. Their behavior is consistent with the findings of Downes and Figlio (1999), who concluded in regard to school-finance reform's influence on location decisions, "The evidence is wholly consistent with the notion of highly educated families moving to central cities in response to school finance reforms and sending their children to private schools" (p. 107).

6.17 Private Schools Have Been Transformed

Thomas Downes and David Schoeman (1998) found that private school enrollment rose in California just after *Serrano II* and Proposition 13. Downes and Shane Greenstein (1996) found that individual private schools in California opened in response to concerns by high-demand residents that public schools had declined. But the increase in private schooling in California, from ten to twelve percentage points, is hardly massive, and its growth does not seem to have persisted into the 1990s (Sonstelie, Brunner, and Ardon 2000, chap. 8). This is perhaps because the high-income suburbs have adjusted to the public constraints with private financing, as Brunner, Murdoch, and Thayer (1999) suggest.

But the stability of private school enrollments after *Serrano* may hide an important nationwide shift. Catholic schools, which are the largest category of private schools, have changed radically over the last twenty-five years (Byrk, Lee, and Holland 1993, pp. 23–34). Their clientele until the 1960s consisted largely of immigrant families who sent their children to parochial schools for religious and cultural reasons. That component of Catholic school clientele is now much reduced. Nowadays Catholic schools are sought by both Catholic and non-

Catholic refugees from urban public schools who seek an education that is, by most measures, better than in the public sector (Evans and Schwab 1995).

Moreover, Catholic schools' share of education enrollments has slipped from 12 percent in 1965 to 5.4 percent in 1990 (Byrk, Lee, and Holland 1993, p. 33). For the national private-school attendance fraction to have remained steady over this period (at around 12 percent of school-age children), other types of private schools, in which matriculation is more likely to be for academic reasons, must have expanded during the period. Some of this represents the effects of public-school desegregation, but even in this case, many if not most of the refugees from big-city busing are families concerned about educational quality, not the race of their children's classmates. Big-city parochial schools are fully integrated with respect to local racial conditions (Byrk, Lee, and Holland 1993). Hence the national stability of overall private school enrollment masks the extent to which public school decline has driven educationally ambitious families to private schools.

The trend toward private schools whose cachet is better education rather than religious environment (though I do not deny that the two may be related) seems to be a legacy of *Serrano*. Indeed, the possibility that parents dissatisfied with the quality of public schools would send their children to private schools in response to *Serrano* was anticipated by none other than the litigation's intellectual architects. "If they do leave, it will be principally because the legislature has decided to have inferior public education" (Coons, Clune, and Sugarman 1969, p. 419). Their conditional prediction seems to have come true, though it seems doubtful that the declining quality of the public schools since 1969 is entirely the fault of the state legislatures.

6.18 Conclusion: A Negative Experiment in Homevoting

Public education is the premier example of a public service that can be financed at both the local and state levels. I have used the judicial revolution in education funding to advance my hypothesis that the homevoter model yields different and more accurate predictions about public decisions than does a unified model that treats local governments as if they were little states. Homeowners' concern about the value of their major asset makes them more attentive to the benefits and costs of education regardless of whether they have children in public schools. My hypothesis explains Proposition 13 and its persistence without relying on a view of voters as irrational or myopic, and it explains why the apparent quality of public education has declined nationwide as the states' share of funding for it has risen.

Although in this chapter I have examined centralization mainly from its effects on the quality of schools, there is evidence that loss of local property taxation reduces civic engagement generally. After California's Proposition 13 undermined the property tax, overall interest in local affairs seems to have dropped (Alvin Sokolow 1998, p. 184). This was especially true for school boards, which now attract people with personal crusades instead of sober-sided business leaders concerned that their tax money was being put to good use. As Peter Schrag (1998, p. 74) deftly put it, "No representation without taxation."

The normative implications, which I do not claim to have worked through entirely, seem to point to the possibility that court-ordered centralization of school finance and the supposed fiscal disparities that have driven it are largely wrongheaded. Centralization produces less effective schools, and equalization of local tax burdens creates temporary capital gains and losses to both rich and poor in a pattern that promotes no coherent principle of wealth redistribution. I have criticized the hubris of the judicial reformers in other places (Fischel 1998b), so I will not explore here the many reasons that courts are clumsy institutions for social change. In fact, I owe some debt to the *Serrano* court for providing the basis for a natural experiment in change that allows insights into the system of local government. But after twenty-five years of judicially induced school-finance centralization, the experiment does seem to be outliving its usefulness even for social scientists.

7
The Race to the Top in Environmental Protection

THIS CHAPTER and the next explore the implications of the homevoter hypothesis for local efforts to promote and protect the environment. The dominant view by social scientists is that local governments are inadequate to this task. Indeed, a large fraction of commentary suggests that local governments make the problem worse by selling their environmental patrimony for a mess of pottage or, worse, by despoiling their neighbors in pursuit of localized fiscal or employment gains.

I argue that this pessimistic view is wrong both in theory and in practice. Because homeowners are such important players in municipal affairs, and because their assets would be devalued by adverse environmental effects, local governments are apt to err on the side of caution in admitting industry. Concern about their property values more likely fuels a "race to the top" among local governments.

7.1 Homevoter "NIMBYism" Promotes Municipal Caution

It has long been an article of faith among environmental policymakers that local governments should not be entrusted with any but the most inconsequential decisions about environmental protection. Anti-localism emerges from a widespread belief that competition among jurisdictions poses a danger of a mutually-destructive "race to the bottom." As Dan Esty, a leading commentator on environmental politics, points out, "Fears of a welfare-reducing race to the bottom represent one of the central underpinnings of federal environmental regulation in the United States" (1996, p. 628).

The story goes something like this. Local officials are always eager to lower taxes and promote jobs by attracting industry. But because there are many other communities eager for industrial development, the owners of an unusually large business can demand concessions in return for settling into their tax-cow and job-creator status. (I say "unusually large" to cover both monopolists and large-but-competitive firms that seek locations episodically. If all businesses were small and their entry continuous, their competition among themselves for sites would undermine their ability to extract special concessions from officials.) In the large-firm scenario, businesses may insist on exceptions to reasonable environmental rules. And though local officials would normally be loathe to grant such concessions, the possibility that another jurisdiction might get the plant induces them to cave in and give away the store.

Although this is sometimes described as an example of game theory's "prisoners' dilemma," the usual story is just local officials who respond to the fact that the firm has alternative sites and can go there if the community's taxes or regulations are not satisfactory. In Chapter 8, I will explore the more sophisticated prisoners'-dilemma version of this story, in which the polluting industry threatens to locate right next door. I start with this bald complaint about competition because it is so often invoked. It is apparently the foundation for the nationalization of American environmental policy (Esty 1996, p. 593).

The contrary story is based on the dominance of homeowners in local politics. An owner-occupied home is the largest asset most people own, and owners cannot insure it against devaluation by neighborhood effects. As I argued in Section 1.5, this fact goes a long way to account for NIMBYism—the "not in my back yard" reaction to land use changes. NIMBYism is not occasioned solely by episodic events such as the selection of sites for waste dumps. The risk aversion that gives rise to it pervades all of local political decisions, and it thus makes local governments the least likely candidates for a "race to the bottom" of the environmental ladder.

Even if the homeowner does not care about local air quality, traffic, and noise from industrial development, she knows that prospective buyers of her house do care about it. If she has any say about the prospective plant's location—and she certainly does at numerous local public hearings at which the plans can be examined—she will fight the development unless its owners offer something that offsets its costs to her. If these promises can be made and enforced without excessive administrative costs, the provision of localized environments will be at a level more consistent with society's goals (which include provision of other goods besides amenable environments) than that accomplished by a more centralized system.

7.2 The Oates-Schwab Baseline Informs the Debate

There has been a lively debate in law journals about the race to the bottom. Daniel Esty (1996) articulates the pessimistic view that localities are not to be trusted. Richard Revesz (1992; 1997) presents the contrary, more optimistic view, but it is not based on the idea of capitalization or homevoter influence, at least not directly. His argument is that government officials who are enticed by the tax and employment benefits of would-be polluters are pressured by another side. Their constituents care about local environmental quality as well as jobs. If public officials are attentive to their citizens' demands for both goods—those purchasable by having good jobs and those available by having a pleasant environment—there is no reason to suppose that competition among jurisdictions will result in a "race to the bottom" of the environmental quality spectrum.

The touchstone of the analysis by Revesz and his critics is an article by Wallace Oates and Robert Schwab (1988). They developed a theoretical model that fits the stylized facts of the "race to the bottom" scenario. The model supposed numerous jurisdictions among which capital—the job provider—was perfectly mobile. But the residents of these jurisdictions were perfectly immobile, at least among jurisdictions. The usual competitive economic assumptions otherwise applied: No single jurisdiction or firm could by itself affect the conditions of supply or manipulate demand.

The novelty that Oates and Schwab introduced was a model of political decision-making. Elected officials were presumed to be able to allow firms in or to deny them access to the jurisdiction. Allowing firms to enter degraded the environment but raised their constituents' wages. In addition, local officials had to raise taxes for other local public services, and they could tax the income of residents (immobile labor), businesses (mobile capital), or both.

As is usual for normative models like theirs, Oates and Schwab worked out an "optimal" solution—one that maximized the joint value of environment, private goods (provided by wages), and public goods (provided by taxes)—and compared it to what a competitive model would produce, given their assumptions. Their key assumption involved the behavior of the public officials. If the public officials were faithful representatives of the median voter, and if voters within each jurisdiction did not differ in their preferences for the environment and other goods, then the competitive model and the optimal solution were the same. There was neither a "race to the bottom" nor a "race to the top" in their median-voter, homogeneous-community baseline.

Optimality in their model did not mean that environmental quality was at its maximum. To do that might require excluding all businesses from all jurisdictions, and that would result in low wages and output of other goods. (This is why "race to top" and "race to bottom" can be misleading terms—they beg the question, top or bottom of what?) The optimum that was achieved in the Oates-Schwab baseline was one in which citizens of each jurisdiction got the mix of environmental quality and other goods that matched their personal demands. The "top" in this instance was the constrained maximum of a utility function of a representative resident (since all are the same) in which environment and other goods are both arguments.

What was avoided was a scenario in which each jurisdiction went too far in the job-creating direction and thus sacrificed too much environmental quality. The discipline on public officials was the electoral apparatus that made them highly responsive to voters. If officials let in too few firms, the voters will turn them out and elect the more prodevelopment types. If the latter go too far, the public will elect environmentalists to chase polluters and their job-creating capital away. (There are no irreversible situations in these models, so my heuristic of a back-and-forth politics does not affect the ultimate outcome.)

7.3 Bureaucrats and Factionalism Upset the Baseline

Commentators have deployed the Oates-Schwab article to support their contention that a race to the bottom is unlikely (Revesz 1992), or they have displayed its extreme-sounding assumptions to argue that the anxiety is justified (Esty 1996). Oates and Schwab, however, used their optimistic result mainly as a starting point for exploring situations in which the optimal outcome might not obtain. One way in which the political market (competition among jurisdictions) might fail, they supposed, was that a government might be dominated by bureaucrats who sought to maximize tax revenues and thereby feather their own nests. Here is how.

One of the seeming oddities of the Oates-Schwab optimal baseline is that business capital is not taxed at all. This is, however, a standard result in economics that follows from capital's perfect mobility. You don't want to tax things that can easily run away from the tax man. In their bureaucratic variation on the model, Oates and Schwab supposed that elected officials might try to extract taxes from skittish capital by bribing its owners with exceptions to environmental regulations. This lust for tax revenue does not serve the interests of the voters, who prefer a better environment to the tax revenue, but voters are assumed in the bureaucratic model to have no clout. The bureaucrats want the taxes to expand the scope of government, a goal not necessarily shared by the voters. So disfranchised voters get stuck with more pollution than they would like in that model.

I once heard Aaron Wildavsky, the late dean of Berkeley's public policy school and one of the most astute observers of American political economy, say that the bureaucratic model did not describe American politics especially well. The useful models were, if I remember him right, the median voter and the pluralistic or interest-group model of politics. The pluralistic model assumes that people are organized by interest groups, and politics consists of politicians trying to win elections by serving a dominant group's interests. Even where bureaucrats do seem important, my own view is that their goals seem much wider than budget maximization. The U.S. Environmental Protection Agency could increase its budget if it were required to compensate landowners burdened by their regulations, but I have never encountered any evidence that the EPA favored Congress's proposed "just compensation" bills for that or any other reason.

So the more interesting (to me) variation that Oates and Schwab proposed was one in which interest groups determined political outcomes. Dropping the assumption that all voters have the same interests, Oates and Schwab supposed that the voters were divided into workers, who gained from jobs, and other residents, who either had no jobs (and no relationship with the workers) or had jobs that did not depend on the amount of capital in their jurisdiction. I'll call the first group the "six-packs" and the second the "white-wines," in honor of the stereotypical beverage of choice of each group. If this rigid division of interests cannot be overcome by intrajurisdictional logrolling or by side payments, then one faction or the other might seek to alter the efficient result.

Note that this model could be interpreted as an interest group model, as I have done here, or a median-voter model in which there are simply differences between the immobile majority and immobile minority's preferences within the jurisdiction. The difference is that in an interest-group model, strength of preference—manifested perhaps by monetary contributions to politicians—might allow a minority to prevail over the majority, which never happens in the median-voter model.

If my "six-packs" were the dominant interest group, they could increase their wages by lowering environmental standards. This might be profitable for six-packs because the state can subsidize firms to enter the jurisdiction by using some of the taxes that are imposed on the white-wines. (Thus the real source of exploitation is the ability to tax people who do not share your preferences.) This would raise the wages of six-packs enough to compensate them (but not the white-wines, whose incomes do not depend on local capital) for reduced environmental quality. Likewise, if the white-wines were dominant, they might impose environmental standards that were too high, since white-wines care nothing for local jobs. In this latter case, the result would be that environment would be "too good" as a result of too little capital in some jurisdictions.

7.4 Pittsburgh's Business-Driven Race *from* the Bottom

A critical assumption in the Oates-Schwab model is often neglected by those who invoke it. Oates and Schwab assume that each jurisdiction is large enough to internalize employment benefits. Thus they are talking about states or a largely mythical (in the United States) metropolitan government. Their model does not track the situation of American local governments, and Oates and Schwab (1988, p. 351) explicitly deny that their model follows Tiebout in this respect. Local governments are usually too small to internalize employment benefits sufficiently, and anyway, the Oates-Schwab model assumes that residents of each jurisdiction cannot migrate, Tiebout-style, to states that match their preferences. Only "voice" is allowed to select environmental quality.

The neglect of local government in the debate about the race to the bottom is in one sense understandable. Much of the policy debate about "environmental federalism" considers the alternative to national standard-setting to be devolution to the states. The primary criticisms of state standard-setting roughly track the Oates-Schwab scenario in which employment and business interests (my "six-packs") triumph over environmental interests.

I will presently argue that the more appropriate model for local environmental competition is one in which NIMBYish homevoters are dominant. But even if it were true that local politics were dominated by business interests, would it follow that environmental quality would be entirely discounted? The following example shows that politicians who are attentive mainly to employment interests nonetheless have an incentive to pay attention to environmental quality. I want to emphasize, however, that it varies the assumptions of the Oates-Schwab model in an important but, I think, realistic way. Instead of only capital being mobile, I assume that capital and at least some key components of labor (in this case, managers) are mobile between regions.

Air pollution from the burning of coal for industry, transportation, and home heating was a pervasive problem in late-nineteenth and early twentieth-century cities. American city governments were keenly aware of the problem and attempted to regulate coal smoke since at least 1880 (Robert Grinder 1980). In most cases, successful regulation involved inducing businesses and households to switch from smoky bituminous coal to clean-burning anthracite coal or even cleaner natural gas.

The city whose struggle with smoke was greatest was Pittsburgh (Grinder 1978). Its steel mills depended on coke made from bituminous coal, and the railroad trains and tugboats that transported its raw materials and its finished product also used bituminous coal. Anthracite was costly to ship from the eastern part of the state and, in any case, made poor fuel for the steel industry's blast furnaces. As a result, Pittsburgh had some of the most wretched air quality of any city in the nation as it approached the midpoint of the twentieth century, when most other large cities had cleaned up their most visible air pollution.

The cleanup of Pittsburgh's air was not induced by the federal government. President Truman declared that pollution was a local problem and was unwilling to promote legislation to help (Charles Jones 1975, p. 30). The Pennsylvania state legislature likewise did not initiate smoke-control legislation, but it did respond to regional concerns once the city had decided to act so as to get the many suburbs of Pittsburgh on board (Roy Lubove 1969). Nor, I must concede, were local homeowners the source of political organization to combat smoke.

Instead, it was business leaders, including steel-company executives, who finally decided that something had to be done about Pittsburgh's smoke. And the reason was simple: Their companies were finding it increasingly difficult to get executives to relocate to Pittsburgh (Lubove 1969, p. 107). The area's smoky reputation repelled at least managerial workers. Smoke abatement was driven by the fact that Pittsburgh firms had to hire in a national job market, and the market was telling the city to clean up its act. Even U.S. Steel, the region's major employer, was considering relocating its headquarters to another region because of its difficulties in getting managers to move to Pittsburgh (Michael Weber 1988, p. 203).

Pause for a moment and contemplate the ironies of U.S. Steel, the world's largest steelmaker at the time, threatening to remove its headquarters from Pittsburgh because there was too much smoke. The most obvious is that U.S. Steel was itself a major polluter. But because it was not the only polluter, it did face a collective-goods problem. Other firms over which it had no direct control also contributed mightily to pollution. U.S. Steel would surely have been put at a competitive disadvantage and fallen short of its goal of making the city more attractive to prospective employees had only it cleaned up its act. Thus collective action had to be taken, and industry leaders joined with local and state officials to overcome the potential for free-riding.

The other irony, more important in my mind, is that U.S. Steel's threat to relocate, and indeed the whole business community's motivation for the cleanup, turns the conventional "race to the bottom" scenario on its head. The businesspeople in Pittsburgh were contemplating relocation not because Pittsburgh's embryonic environmental regulations were too strict, as the usual race-to-the-bottom story has it, but because they were not strict enough. Faced with excessively dirty air, Pittsburgh businesspeople considered moving to more environmentally friendly jurisdictions. All of the smoke-abatement articles mentioned that Pittsburghers held rival St. Louis's successful smoke abatement as a paradigm for them to emulate. Nor was Pittsburgh's situation unique. Boston's mayor was similarly goaded into action in 1940 by the threat of major taxpayers moving out of the city because of excessive smoke (Lloyd Briggs 1941, p. 4). The intermetropolitan race was toward the top of the environmental ladder, not to the bottom.

Why were homeowners not part of the smoke-control story, even though they bore a great deal of the cost of smoke pollution? Part of their ineffectiveness before 1920 might have been that women, whose interest in the home was most direct at the time, did not have the vote. In describing Chicago's failed attempt to reduce smoke in the 1890s, Christine Rosen (1995) mentions that women's clubs in Chicago did lobby for smoke abatement, but they never had a chair at the policy-making table. Even in 1940s Pittsburgh, however, more than two decades after women got the vote, homeowner interests played no mentionable role. And this should not be too surprising. Air pollution does affect home values, but pollution sources are often outside of the municipality's jurisdiction.

In the balance of the chapter, I will argue that homeowner concerns are effective in controlling pollution emanating from within their jurisdiction. The smoke abatement example shows that homeowners are not likely to be effective for more pervasive environmental issues. Pittsburgh's story, however, challenges the idea that employment interests are not interested in pollution issues. Those advertisements in which oil companies depict themselves as friends of the environment might not be just spin. Better environments make it cheaper to get workers to move to regions where they operate.

7.5 Fiscal Benefits, Not Jobs, Persuade Suburban Homevoters

In most metropolitan areas, the majority of residents work in a community other than where their residence is located. The problem faced by commercial and industrial developers is how to get homevoters in any jurisdiction within a metropolitan area interested in job creation. A new factory in one jurisdiction usually has a beneficial spillover: It creates jobs for people who live in other jurisdictions. To be more precise, a new employer raises regional wages (not just in one jurisdiction) by adding to the demand for labor in a setting in which labor supply is not perfectly elastic and by adding to regional agglomeration economies (Ciccone and Hall 1996). If a single jurisdiction encompassed the entire labor market, we would expect its officials to take account of this benefit. But such metropolitan-area governments are rare, and because of their size, they would have other drawbacks, such as being prone to interest-group manipulation.

Dealing with employment spillovers in a fragmented metropolitan area is not a problem if another assumption, one that is more reasonably precluded in the Oates-Schwab statewide model, can be invoked in the local context. Because the number of voters is relatively small in municipalities, it is possible for prospective firms to compensate residents for enduring the local spillovers that cannot profitably be internalized within the boundaries of the firm's property. This idea was the basis for my 1973 doctoral dissertation (Fischel 1975).

I modified the Tiebout model to include firms that wanted to locate in the residential communities. Firms could shop around the numerous municipalities. Residents of these communities were already ensconced and had to be satisfied that the firms' location decisions would not make them worse off. Communities were deemed able to exclude firms by zoning, which implied that they could change the zoning to allow the firms to enter if it seemed worthwhile. As William Oakland (1978) put it, my theory viewed communities as suppliers of commercial and industrial sites by virtue of their ability to establish and modify zoning regulations. The suppliers (the homevoters) do not like the disamenities of businesses, but residents could be persuaded to accept them if property taxes paid by the firms (in excess of services required) were large enough.

In the localized setting that I proposed in my dissertation, the property taxes and development exactions paid by businesses to local governments amount to a local "pollution tax." This seems like a strong statement. Pollution taxes are the holy grail from which economists have vainly sought to persuade state and national policymakers to drink. But in a world in which firms are mobile and local governments do tax them, at least some of those revenues should be viewed as compensation for the adverse effects that those firms have on the resident-voters in the community.

The city of Linden, New Jersey, provides an unusually explicit example of such balancing. Its city council agreed to accept a transfer station for New York City's municipal waste (*New York Times*, May 25, 2000). The garbage would be received from barges and then transferred to rail cars to be shipped to landfills in other states. The Linden city council readily agreed to accept it because the transfer station would be on derelict industrial land, far from any residential areas, and New York would pay Linden more than $4 million per year in extra property taxes and local fees. (Other industrial cities nearby had rejected New York's proposals because the proposed sites were too close to residential areas.) The mayor of a neighboring city, whose residents worried that the increased train traffic from Linden's transfer station would devalue their railside homes, asked rhetorically, "Is Linden ready to be called the garbage capital of the world. . . .? Have they thought about what it would do to their real-estate values?" To which Linden's mayor responded by asserting that "the garbage port might even increase real estate values by keeping taxes down."

7.6 Communities Balance Taxes and Environmental Costs

The rational balancing of local amenities against business side-payments (property taxes plus impact fees) that I took for granted is often overlooked in academic writing about industrial location. Community goals are instead often characterized by rules of thumb such as "minimizing taxes" or the slightly more sophisticated "maximizing fiscal dividends" (Michelle White 1975). The latter supposes that communities seek to attract the firms whose contribution to local revenues exceeds the cost of providing services for the firms by the greatest amount. But these goals are not rational as long-run propositions.

Communities can minimize taxes by not spending anything on local services, but that would irrationally reduce home values in most places. Maximizing fiscal dividends neglects that an excess of revenues over expenditures might nonetheless reduce home values if the wrong types of businesses, such as heavy polluters, are permitted too close to homes. In New Jersey, a proposed low-level nuclear waste storage facility that promised a host community a fiscal dividend of $2 million a year for fifty years found no takers among the state's 567 municipalities. (This was described in Section 1.3). I do not regard the municipalities that spurned the money as irrational. The reputation effects of having the facility could have reduced home values by more than the fiscal benefits would have increased them.

To test my balancing theory, I examined the determinants of housing value in a 1970 sample of Bergen County, New Jersey, municipalities. Bergen County has seventy municipalities packed into a relatively small area next to New York City, so it surely looks like the ideal sample for the "race to the bottom" to happen. My results indicated that the commercial and industrial tax base by itself conferred neither a large gain nor a large loss on median home values in the communities (Fischel 1975, p. 162). That is, there was no statistically significant capitalization, positive or negative, of the percent of property values accounted for by commerce and industry. James Burnell (1985) and William Oakland and William Testa (1998, p. 211) came to the same conclusion in analyzing business location in Chicago-area suburbs.

This is what one would expect in a competitive market. Businesses that paid a lot of taxes without producing many adverse neighborhood effects would get favorable treatment—tax breaks or special services—in many communities, so the net benefits of having them would not be so large as to raise home values. Firms that raise NIMBY anxieties or that demand additional local services would have to pay more in property taxes and side payments to communities that valued such revenues more than the disamenities of the firms. A real polluter would have to pay a lot to offset its deleterious effects on homes in the community.

Lack of capitalization of firms' presence in my regression seems inconsistent with my previous claim that good things and bad things are reflected (capitalized in) housing prices. If nearby traffic from industry lowers housing values and good schools that the industry pays for raise values, how is it that I find no effect? The reason is that I tested solely for the effect of the presence of the firms in the community. Had I looked only at school spending (subsidized by the firms), the effect on home values would be positive. Had I looked only at traffic and noise that were increased by the presence of industry, the effect would have been negative. My theory is that these effects cancel one another out on average, so that in the end industry conveys neither a windfall nor a wipeout (at the sample mean) for the residents of the host communities.

I concede that some business tax payments do seem like windfalls to the community. Property taxes from some nonresidential uses surely do more than simply offset the environmental disamenities and higher cost of services (police and fire protection). Vacation homes and resorts in rural communities are perhaps the most common examples, though one wonders whether the year-rounders would put up with the seasonal visitors if their cottages and chalets did not help pay for the schools. But occasional windfalls from business location are consistent with the lack of capitalization in econometric studies of a large sample of communities, whose estimates are for the mean value of the sample. The windfalls to some may be offset by wipeouts in other communities from firms that turned out to be more problematic than expected.

7.7 Industrial Uses Lower Residential Tax Prices

The reader might think it is a bit sad that there is so little capitalization of business property in home values. All that competition for business, but no gain to homeowners. The answer is that there *are* gains to homeowners from this process, just not at the margin. For example, hedonic price regressions—the type generally used in capitalization studies—usually find that the value that an extra bathroom contributes to the average home's value is just about equal to the cost of building an extra bathroom. That does not mean that the bathrooms that are already in the home add the same value—try selling a home without a bathroom!

For the same reason, an individual community that starts out with no industry might eagerly seek it. The effects of a small industrial park on residential ambiance may be inconsequential and the benefit of having another taxpayer to help pay for schools could be relatively large. But after the industrial park is full, the net benefit of establishing another one might not be so large, since the next-best site might have more adverse spillover effects on nearby homes. Thus in equilibrium, marginal (tax) benefit will equal marginal (environmental) cost for an additional industrial firm. But that does not mean that removing the first industrial park would be a matter of indifference to community residents.

My conclusion about local taxes on business in my model is, incidentally, the same as the Oates-Schwab result. They found that taxes on capital (business) should be zero, since capital is the mobile factor. In my model, the taxes that businesses pay are not truly on capital, but arise only because their activity gives rise to some offenses to residents that the businesses cannot profitably eliminate and because they generate a need for extra municipal services. The taxes paid are for benefits received, and, on average, no more.

A second, more important problem with nonresidential property arises if the sole means by which it compensates homeowners for its disamenities is through the property tax. If this were the case, the apparently lower "tax price"—the lower cost of local services perceived by the median voter when businesses are paying much of the bill—might cause "too much" local public expenditure. If homeowners see that businesses will pay 30 percent of local taxes, the price of getting local services looks to the median voter as if it is only 70 percent of its true cost.

The low tax price created by commercial development is the product of one of the institutional constraints on municipal opportunism that I discussed in Section 2.4. The "public purpose" doctrine prevents municipalities from simply negotiating a cash settlement with commercial developers, in which those seeking permission to locate in the community simply offer cash for it, with the proceeds to be distributed to residents.

Although I made this distortion and its resolution a major part of my earlier work (Fischel 1975), I have since concluded that the tax-price distortion is not important for municipalities. Local governments have plenty of ways besides the property tax to extract side payments from prospective firms. Exactions and impact fees are only the most obvious means of charging new development (Altshuler and Gómez-Ibáñez 1993). Such side payments are essentially like cash to the median voter, and for that reason they do not distort local decisions. Moreover, municipalities have multiple means by which to spend largesse from the public sector. Cities with extremely low tax prices, such as Commerce, California, have found not-too-subtle ways of converting public spending into perfectly legal, above-board private expenditures. These cities provide services for residents, such as vacation camps, that are essentially private goods.

School districts, as opposed to municipalities, are more subject to the tax-price distortion. Exactions pay only a small fraction of their costs, and school districts have less opportunity to convert public sector money into private expenditures. As I suggested in Section 6.5, this "inefficiency" is hardly a catastrophe. Indeed, it is one way by which lower-income people can obtain high-expenditure schools, since higher-income communities are usually even more skittish about accepting nonresidential land uses that create the "problem" of too much school spending.

7.8 Tax Competition Theory Must Account for Zoning

Several other researchers added to my modest statistical evidence for the rationality of the trade-off between environmental amenities and tax revenue. Instead of testing for variation in property values, they looked at the other side of the transaction, location decisions by business. A necessary implication of my theory is that in choosing communities in which to locate, businesses respond to the *net* burden of taxes and local regulation.

Businesses like low taxes, but they also need land that is zoned to accommodate them. Before scholars paid attention to the zoning constraint, however, it was difficult to see much relationship between taxes and business location (William Oakland 1978; Newman and Sullivan 1988). The earlier studies were inconclusive, I submit, because they overlooked that firms cannot get into the low-tax places to which we would expect them to gravitate unless they can pass environmental muster.

William Fox, who developed a theory of business location parallel to mine, examined the location patterns of industry among Cleveland's suburbs (Fox 1981). He found that higher-income communities tended to zone out industrial uses entirely. Whether such communities had high or low tax rates did not matter to prospective firms—these suburbs did not want the businesses anyway.

Once Fox cleared his sample of communities that made no accommodation (via zoning) for industry, he found that having lower local taxes did attract firms. Results consistent with Fox's were obtained by Rodney Erickson and David Wollover (1987) and Warren McHone (1986). These studies imply that many communities deliberately forgo industrial development and keep their residential taxes high because they do not want to suffer the adverse environmental effects. They are interested in home values, not just fiscal benefits.

It has long been this way. Jon Teaford's histories of American local government describe as many instances of cities incorporating to deter business and industry as to attract it (1979, p. 84; 1997, p. 17). Some communities—usually not the most affluent—eagerly annexed territory on which commerce and industry either were already located or could easily be located without much annoyance to homeowners. The "industrial park" was born and acquired its oxymoronic name during the post–World War II period (1997, p. 52).

As Teaford describes it, intermunicipal competition for industry was hardly an environmental "race to the bottom." Homeowning residents had to be well insulated from industry, and plenty of other communities used their zoning and annexation powers to prevent the development of commerce and industry too near to their homes, deliberately forgoing the fiscal benefits in order to preserve the local environmental benefits. The communities that do get the firms must be getting fiscal compensation that offsets their disamenities. In other words, at least some part of firms' local property taxes are pollution taxes.

An implication of this view is that fiscal competition for property tax base is not wasteful. Many otherwise sensible economists condemn fiscal competition because it supposedly distorts the choice of location of businesses, inducing them not to choose the least costly area in which to operate. The Federal Reserve Bank of Minnesota has actually gone on record to denounce this activity (Burstein and Rolnick 1995), and there are proposals to have Congress or even the federal courts intervene to limit competition for business among states and cities (Peter Enrich 1996).

None of these proposals to limit competition considers the preferences of local homeowners and other residents for jobs, tax base, or environmental quality. It may be true, for example, that the "least costly" location for a shopping center is in the midst of a high-income residential area because that will minimize trips by potential shoppers. But that calculation of cost ignores the adverse effect that the shopping center has on the nearby residents, and it ignores that some other communities might be more willing to accept such spillovers in return for the shopping center's fiscal benefits.

To take another common example, residents of a large city that has lost industry might in fact be willing to trade the full loaf of tax benefits for a half-loaf of some tax benefits plus employment opportunities. The resulting tax breaks that the city gives to attract and retain industry may look like a giveaway, but the value of the city's residential property may still rise because prospective workers will want to move there. Only if residents of all places have the same demands for employment, fiscal, and environmental conditions can it be said that exchanging one benefit for another is an example of wasteful competition.

7.9 An Aside on the Unfairness of Tax-Base Sharing

In Chapter 6, I described the school-finance reform movement's attack on differences in property tax bases among communities. Coons, Clune, and Sugarman (1970) argued that unequal local property-tax bases were unfair because one community could pay for schools at a lower tax rate than another. At least sixteen state courts, beginning with Serrano v. Priest (Cal. 1971), have overturned their school-finance systems in part for this reason. Nor is the desire to share tax bases advocated solely by attorneys. Economists Helen Ladd and Edward Harris (1995) argue for removing commercial and industrial property from local taxation and having the state tax it for all districts' benefit.

My criticism of these claims in Sections 6.3 and 6.4 focused on two phenomena. One was that "property-rich" school districts were often populated by "income-poor" people who had settled in commercial and industrial areas or deliberately invited such development. Equalization of tax bases would as often harm the poor as benefit them. My other criticism was that the differences in tax base are reflected in home values, so that the residents of property-rich places have to pay in advance for the privilege of lower taxes or better schools. My claim in this chapter adds a third criticism to tax-base sharing: It penalizes communities that accepted industry in the past only on the understanding that this industry would be fiscally profitable. Here is an example.

When Vermont and New Hampshire were recently compelled by their state supreme courts to level fiscal differences among school districts due to differences in local tax bases, governors of both states sought to exclude from tax base sharing the towns that had nuclear power plants. (Each state has one: Vernon, Vermont, and Seabrook, New Hampshire.) Both governors pointed out that it would be unfair to redistribute the enormous tax base that these towns had acquired. No other town or city had been willing to accept a nuclear plant, which, when they were planned, were regarded as a necessary response to the region's extremely high electricity costs. "Recapturing" their tax base would in effect renege on a deal and leave both communities to endure an otherwise unwanted neighbor without compensation.

My theory simply extends the governors' view to all nonresidential uses. Some nonresidential uses may be more benign than others, but few can be thought of as having no disruptive effects on the residential character of communities. Tax-base equalization from this viewpoint is not simply taking a windfall away. It is leaving "property-rich" communities worse off than they would have been had they not accommodated the commercial and industrial development.

Tax-base sharing also complicates future attempts to locate problematic land uses, although this seems less important for individual communities because land-use exactions can be substituted to compensate the host community. Even if this works out, however, new firms end up paying an additional tax to the state or regional government. The additional tax has deadweight loss because it is not tied to the "benefit" of being allowed into the community. States or regions that adopt tax-base sharing may end up being less attractive to business (Fischel 1976). Even if many firms are not deterred, evidence shows that the burden of statewide taxes on businesses is rapidly shifted back to workers in the form of reduced wages (Feldstein and Wrobel 1998).

7.10 Cities Cannot Be Forced to Take Industry

An important environmental problem has been how to find homes for a region's "necessary nuisances" in an era of heightened environmental awareness. If the detritus of society can no longer be dropped anywhere (if it ever could), new sites for both hazardous and ordinary ("municipal") wastes must be developed. The problem is where to locate these necessary nuisances, whose ubiquity has spawned another acronym: LULU ("locally unwanted land use"). NIMBYs don't want LULUs.

Attempts in the 1970s and 1980s to site LULUs such as dumps employed top-down tactics. Many states adopted "preemption" laws that permit the state government to override local opposition to such sites. The right of the state to do this is usually clear, as courts everywhere continue to recite the mantra—true in texts, dubious in practice—that local governments are "creatures of the state."

Kent Portney, who studied attempts to locate unpopular land uses in

Massachusetts, observes that it is "very difficult, if not impossible, to pre-empt local authority in practice" (1991, p. 51). The reason is that the local interests get themselves on state commissions and manage to scuttle the idea. Lawrence Susskind and Stephen Cassella (1987) reviewed the attempt by California to preempt local opposition in order to locate a liquid natural gas facility along the Pacific coast. Despite the vigorous promotion of the facility by Governor Jerry Brown, it was never built. The state's heavy-handed attempt made local opponents dig in their heels. Michael Gerrard, an attorney whose national clientele includes commercial hazardous-waste facilities, states flatly that preemption of local government "never works" (1994, p. 170).

Studies of how hazardous waste sites are promoted sometimes point out that the state had offered the communities compensation, but that did not work, either (Vicki Been 1994a; Kent Portney 1991). I think it is important to understand the difference between state-dictated compensation and the compensation that is arrived at through voluntary negotiation with locally controlled institutions. It is the same as the difference between the forced compensation you would receive from eminent domain proceedings that took your home and the compensation that you would get from a buyer to whom you sold voluntarily.

People who would willingly sell their property when they are ready and at a price to which they have agreed are often much aggrieved by the government's insistence that they sell their property immediately and at the market price (Jack Knetsch 1983). In the language of academic law, your ownership is protected from government takings only by a "liability rule," while your ownership is protected from most other buyers by a "property rule" (Calabresi and Melamed 1972; Krier and Schwab 1995). Property rule protection—the right to just say no, or to demand whatever terms you want—is clearly preferable to most owners, including municipalities (Michael Schill 1989). Those who crafted the state-dictated compensation schemes for LULUs apparently underestimated the importance of that distinction.

It isn't simply the dollar amount of compensation that is important to communities; it is compensation arrived at by the consent of the community. Studies of successful LULU sitings indicate that community involvement, which I take to mean as situations in which residents can veto terms they do not like, is a critical feature (Bacot, Bowen, and Fitzgerald 1994). This may explain why private LULU developers seem to have better luck with compensation schemes than does the public sector (Been 1994a). Private developers usually lack the right of eminent domain, and the community authorities thus may feel less threatened. Sovereign power—in this case, the judicially declared power of the state over its municipalities—can be a Midas-like curse.

7.11 "Environmental Justice" Overlooks Local Consent

My contention that local governments can control the entry of unlovely land uses runs contrary to claims of the "environmental justice movement." Its adherents claim that poor communities are stuck (involuntarily, it is implicitly assumed) with polluting uses such as hazardous waste facilities. It is true that lower-income communities are more likely to accept problematic land uses, but this is almost always the result of a process that involves the consent of local authorities.

It is worth pointing out that while there may be dissenters at the end, as there are in all public decisions, the process of locating LULUs favors the status quo. Opponents typically get several times at bat in the numerous public forums that any nonstandard land use must pass. And the sober-sided research that evaluates the claims of the environmental-justice movement finds that there is almost no evidence for them. Vicki Been's several articles have shown that the poor often move to the site after it was located there (Been 1993), and that there appears to be no racial bias in the siting of hazardous waste facilities (Been 1994b; Been and Gupta 1997; Gupta, Van Houtven, and Cropper 1996). Been and Gupta's more worrisome finding, that Hispanic communities have a disproportionate number of sites, is balefully consistent with my view that enfranchised citizens get what they want. Many Hispanics are not yet citizens.

What is clear, though, is that lower-income communities are more likely to accept the low-level polluters such as industrial sites and power plants. I have long argued that this is a desirable thing, a manifestation of voluntary exchange of local amenities for fiscal and employment rewards (Fischel 1975; 1979). To randomize the location of such sites would make everyone worse off. Fiscal and employment benefits would go to communities that did not value them as much as those that would voluntarily accept such businesses, and communities that were eager to bootstrap themselves into fiscal solvency would be denied the opportunity. Voluntary exchange makes municipalities better off in the same way that it makes individuals and consensual organizations better off.

An inverted confirmation of my view arose in 1998 when the U.S. Environmental Protection Agency, invoking new "environmental justice" rules, vetoed permits for a proposed chemical plant in a poor, largely African-American community in St. James Parish, Louisiana (*Pittsburgh Post-Gazette*, June 15, 1998). (Parishes are Louisiana's name for counties.) Although some parish residents applauded the EPA's veto, the majority were reported to be upset that their opportunity to get better jobs and improve their tax base had been foreclosed.

According to the article, the local government had actively sought the plant, and a Louisiana official cited "polls indicating local and countywide approval of the plant, and endorsements from the NAACP and nearly every public official in St. James Parish as evidence that Shintech is welcome." One wonders why denying such places the opportunity to get what even opponents to the project concede are much better jobs—$12 an hour plus benefits versus $6 an hour in the sugarcane fields—is not itself a civil rights issue.

Yet I recognize that such exchange is anathema to many. Environmental rights are said to be inalienable, like voting and childbearing (Susan Rose-Ackerman 1985). According to that argument, we do not allow people to sell those rights. A closer analogy might be military service, whose parallel to environmental issues I explored a few years ago (Fischel 1996b). Many people argued that an all-volunteer military would be morally wrong (the United States had a draft from 1940 to 1973) because it would induce a disproportionate number of poor and minorities to choose a dangerous occupation.

The success of the all-volunteer service since it was adopted and reasonably funded (around 1980) has muted this criticism, but it is still there. If we do conclude that rights to even low-level environmental disamenities cannot be surrendered by the communal consent of those affected, then another process for distributing such disamenable uses must be decided upon. The controversial history of the military draft does not suggest that such a process would be easily implemented or happily accepted.

7.12 Conclusion: Compensation by Consent

The risk aversion that homeowners feel because of the concentration of their assets in one place makes them eager to participate in local environmental decisions. They are among the least likely groups to give away their environmental birthright. I have argued in this chapter that local governments are, if anything, inclined to accept too little garden-variety industry, let alone the unlovely but necessary nuisances such as power plants, landfills, and quarries. Since the onset of zoning, the placement of such uses has almost always required consent of a municipality. In most cases, part of this consent was obtained by the prospect that the use would generate additional property taxes. For the state to expropriate this base because it makes the community look "property rich" seems fundamentally unfair.

Consent is best obtained by compensation offered in a system in which local governments can decline to accept the use. Schemes that force communities to accept compensation and the unwanted use are apt to meet much more resistance. The higher government that can force the compensation today can change its mind tomorrow and simply force the city to accept unwanted uses without compensation. Being able to say no is a crucial part of the process of assuaging homevoters' concerns.

8
"Beggar Thy Neighbor" and Landfill Location

THE PREVIOUS CHAPTER dealt with the claim that municipalities will trash their own environments, a claim disputed by both theory and evidence. This chapter deals with the possibility that one city might opportunistically foist the costs of its profitable but environmentally problematic land uses onto its neighbors. The notion that adjacent municipalities pursue "beggar thy neighbor" policies is similarly dubious, and I offer a fine-grained examination of an instance in which it was said to occur.

The constraints on "beggar thy neighbor" policies turn out to be similar to the reasons that individual property owners value neighborliness. The permanence of geographic neighbors makes them think about future as well as present relationships. They are locked into a web of mutually beneficial exchanges at both the political and the personal levels. A major default from neighborly behavior on one front would invite retaliation on other fronts. The same example demonstrates, however, that these constraints can fail when neighboring communities do not have regular contacts with one another.

8.1 The "Beggar Thy Neighbor" Proposition

State-sized jurisdictions, the type that Wallace Oates and Robert Schwab (Section 7.2) were concerned with, do not have to worry much about spillover effects from localized environmental policies. Most of their territory is several miles from the borders of other states. For in-state decisions about problematic land uses, the trade-off is a political game of "we against us." But in smaller jurisdictions, the in-town decision is more likely to be "we against them." The smaller area of local government makes it more likely that local land-use decisions will have effects that spill over to the next jurisdiction.

In generating employment spillovers, the small size of municipalities is usually a good thing. Firms can find a municipality willing to accept them more easily when jurisdictions are numerous (and thus small), and workers in other municipalities in the metropolitan area can commute there. But those same job centers may in turn generate excess traffic, noise, unsightliness, and smells that annoy people in neighboring towns who are not getting the benefit of whatever compensation the firms are paying their host community.

Economists have suggested that communities might deliberately engage in a beggar-thy-neighbor policy (Michelle White 1975, p. 198). They could place their less-than-neighborly land uses on the borders where the costs will fall on other communities, while the fiscal benefits stay home. I have for years searched in vain for a systematic study of this proposition. This is why I took such interest in an article in the *Journal of Environmental Economics and Management* by Daniel Ingberman (1995). His largely theoretical article takes the strongest position that I have read in favor of the inevitability of an inter- and intramunicipal beggar-thy-neighbor syndrome. David Spence and Paula Murray (1999) invoke his findings in support of federal preemption of state and local law in order to prevent an environmental race to the bottom.

In Ingberman's political model, voters in one community are so self-interested that they eagerly foist profitable but disamenable uses either onto their outvoted fellow residents in remote sections of town or onto the neighboring community's residents. This creates an incentive to accept too many polluting firms because the majority of voters do not perceive the full costs of their actions.

The scenario that Ingberman paints for the *intra*municipal excess assumes that self-interested voters in one part of town will vote to locate profitable but polluting developments in a lightly populated part of town. This is inefficient because the economic losses to property in the lightly populated area might not be exceeded by the economic gains to the community at large by having the polluting industry. Now under the conditions of the famous Coase (1960) theorem, this scenario would not happen. People in the lightly populated area would simply pay the majority to forswear such activity and write an iron-clad covenant, running with the land, to prevent it from happening there in the future. But the present book (unlike my last two) is not about the Coase theorem. I will instead assume that the transaction costs of such side payments are too large and look to other institutions.

8.2 Property Taxation Promotes Mutuality within Cities

The property tax is one institution that helps forestall majoritarian transfers within communities. This is because having property as a tax base makes voters interested in maintaining it in the future. Devaluing one person's property means that others must take on the tax burden (assuming uniform taxation requirements). This is why rent control is usually opposed by homeowners, as I described in Section 4.7. Uniform property taxation makes each taxpayer interested in the value of property held by every other taxpayer. In upholding an early zoning law, a Minnesota judge pointed to the erosion of the property-tax base in residential districts invaded by nonconforming uses: "The loss is not only to the owners, but to the state and municipality by reason of the diminished taxes resulting from diminished values" (Twin City Building v. Houghton 1920, p. 162).

As a concrete example of the property tax's protective incentives, consider a proposal to site a profitable landfill within a community. The dump's profit will be shared with the community by means of land-use exactions, money paid by the developer in exchange for a rezoning that permits the dump. The dump, however, will devalue nearby homes of a small group of residents. If the devaluation of the homes is taken into account, the dump should not be built, even though a majority of the community would benefit.

The ad valorum property tax provides an automatic signal to all voters that the dump may not be the best use of the land. The reduction in the value of the homes near the dump will shift the burden of the tax to other residents of the community. Because they anticipate this, the majority will be more cautious about allowing land uses that reduce the aggregate value of property in the community. Such a signal would not be present (except under the conditions of the Coase theorem) if taxes were assessed on the otherwise more efficient basis of heads or land area.

A real-world example of the benign incentives of property taxation can be seen in the behavior of California municipalities after Proposition 13 was passed in the 1978 tax revolt. With the property tax no longer much of a source of revenue, municipalities have sought land uses that produce sales tax revenue, part of which is rebated to the point-of-sale jurisdictions. This skews land-use decisions toward commercial uses rather than those uses that raise property values generally (Lewis and Barbour 1999; Jonathan Schwartz 1997). In a twenty-year retrospective on Proposition 13, the *San Francisco Chronicle* (May 20, 1998) interviewed Lenny Goldberg, leader of the "liberal California Tax Reform Association, no fan of Proposition 13." The article went on:

> A few years ago, a Southern California town had a Price Club store and an Eastman Kodak research center competing for the same piece of city-owned land, Lenny Goldberg said. The city instantly took the Price Club and its $800,000 a year, even though the research center was an attractive, nonpolluting source of new jobs. . . "Increases in homes and offices now are seen as bringing no benefits, but only costs and more strain on the local infrastructure," such as schools, roads and public services, Goldberg said.

A formal model that encompasses the main idea behind this principle was developed by Edward Glaeser (1996). He starts with the observation that informs this book: Voters are interested in activities that enhance property values. But his public officials are not responsive to the median voter, as they are in my view. Instead, Glaeser assumes a worst-case scenario in which the local public officials are "kleptocrats" who simply try to maximize tax revenues, which they divert for personal gain. He supposes that voters know this tendency in advance and want to select a tax base (embedded in an unalterable constitution) that will nonetheless give the kleptocrat incentives to maximize their property values. In Glaeser's model, the community must choose between a head tax and a property-value tax.

The tax that is most likely to maximize property values will generate the greatest demand for housing (the only taxable property) in the community. In other words, to get more tax revenues, the kleptocrat has to make the community attractive to potential immigrants. Kleptocrats can also use some of the tax revenues to provide amenities to attract potential taxpayers, but their sole interest in doing so is to maximize net tax revenues.

Glaeser finds that, under a variety of circumstances, the property tax is superior to the head tax in aligning the interests of homeowners and "kleptocratic" officials. The reason is that the head tax in several cases generates more taxes but, because of overcrowding, lowers the level of amenities and thus lowers property values. Under a head-tax regime, tax-hungry officials ignore that new residents may lower aggregate property values, just as the California city officials in the example above discounted the effect on property values of a sales-tax generator (the Price Club).

The more "incentive-compatible" tax in Glaeser's analysis is the property tax. The incentives of the decision-makers are made compatible with the objectives of the majority. Even officials who are indifferent to residents' well-being will be induced to adopt land-use and spending policies whose effect is to maximize property values, for only in that way will they maximize property-tax collections. (Recall that the officials do not get to select the tax base—the residents do—but the residents cannot control officials' behavior afterward.)

I do not assume that public officials are kleptocrats. Majority voting, however, raises a similar anxiety about oppression of a minority within the municipality. Glaeser's model shows that a uniform property tax constrains majoritarian decisions to take account of the minority. But there is probably a more important constraint in most communities. Residents of such places are seldom strangers to one another. They meet on multiple fronts: Their children go to school together; they shop in the same places; they are involved in civic activities. As I will suggest in Section 8.10, such interactions constrain opportunistic behavior in the local political realm. Even if a majority of residents were so cynical as to exploit fellow community members, it seems to me that they would not be acting in their own self interest. Who would want to buy a home in such a place?

8.3 Does the Prisoners' Dilemma Overproduce Dumps?

The *inter*community spillover-effect invoked by Ingberman (1995) is the more interesting and policy-relevant issue. In Ingberman's framework, a large, monopolistic, and well-heeled polluter plays one community off against the other. By purchasing land along the border of both communities, it can threaten each of them with the prospect of moving to the other side. If the polluter locates in your community, you get the taxes (or other side payments) from the firm, and half of the pollution. If it locates in the other community, you still get half of the pollution but none of the side payments. By threatening each community with the prospect of being the sucker who gets the dirt without the dollars, the firm induces the eventual host community to lower its demand for side payments.

In this version of game theory's famous prisoners' dilemma, neither community ends up with much compensation. (For contextual explanations of the prisoners' dilemma and how it can be avoided in close-knit groups, see Robert Ellickson 1991a, chap. 9.) The inefficiently low level of compensation in turn encourages too many firms to enter the polluting industry because they do not have to pay for their pollution. It is as Hobbesian a situation as one can imagine, and Ingberman proposes Hobbes's solution: The higher sovereign takes over the siting of polluters to prevent this war of all against all. This is the more sophisticated justification for federal environmental policy. It does not rest on local irrationality, but instead on too much (apparent) calculation by local officials in the face of intermunicipal spillovers.

Ingberman presents two examples to support his thesis. (This is two more than most other game theorists offer in arguments like this.) One is simply a map of Pennsylvania with county boundaries overlaid with the location of the state's forty-six official municipal waste landfills in 1992. A majority appear to be near the borders of an adjacent county, suggesting a pattern of imposing costs on unrepresented outsiders. Ingberman's finding impressed Richard Revesz (1996, p. 2354), who is otherwise skeptical of race-to-the-bottom scenarios. But the scale of

Ingberman's map is too gross to determine anything about intercounty spillover effects. Even hazardous waste sites cease to have deleterious effects on property values beyond a range of about two to four miles, according to Stephen Farber's (1998) survey of empirical studies. It is not evident from Ingberman's Pennsylvania map that anyone in an adjacent county suffers from any spillovers or that the process did not involve the consent of adjoining municipalities. (An e-mail from a spokesman for the Pennsylvania Department of Environment in February 1999, assured me that siting a landfill is a process involving all communities in the area, though I do not know how long such rules have been in effect.)

Ingberman's more persuasive and extensive example concerns a landfill in the borough of Tullytown, Pennsylvania, which adjoins the Delaware River about fifteen miles northeast of Philadelphia. The blue-collar borough has a population of 2,200 on two square miles. Its landfill, which opened in 1987, covers nearly a third of a square mile in area. The dump is owned and operated by Waste Management, Inc. (WMI), the nation's largest for-profit company that accepts municipal (not hazardous) waste on this site from haulers in Pennsylvania, New Jersey, and, more recently, New York City.

Two miles east of Tullytown's landfill is an equally large dump called by the acronym GROWS. Located in Falls Township, Pennsylvania, it is also owned by WMI, though a different company had established the landfill in the early 1970s. Ingberman deploys the juxtaposition of the two landfills to illustrate his proposition that competition among weak municipalities (Tullytown and Falls Township) and a monopoly-like landfill developer (WMI) will result in a race to the bottom of the environmental heap.

To his considerable credit, Ingberman undertook some site-specific research to explore his example. He cited a newspaper article (*Philadelphia Inquirer*, November 18, 1990, p. A1), communications with Tullytown officials, and the borough's public documents. The two-page picture he paints seems to support his example. A Falls Township resident is quoted in the news article as declaring, "The [Tullytown] landfill is practically in our backyard, yet we get nothing out of it." Ingberman then notes, though, that Falls Township also has a landfill owned by WMI and is paid $2.5 million annually in host fees. The message, as I hear it, is that neither Tullytown nor Falls Township would have taken its landfill if it had not been worried that the other would grab it, and both settled for lower compensation than they would have but for that threat.

Ingberman goes on to note that Tullytown was in a weak bargaining position vis-à-vis WMI. It faced a large municipal deficit in 1987 and lacked a land-use plan (though it did have zoning) when approached by WMI to site its landfill. Poor Tullytown was unable to put up more than a token legal fight. Ingberman was told by Tullytown officials that even if they did resist, WMI would just expand right next to their border, leaving them with all the spillovers and none of the cash. The borough council president stated in the November 18, 1990, newspaper article that "since the landfill was something we couldn't stop, I think we've made the best of the situation." Although Tullytown receives $1.5 million annually in host fees, Ingberman notes that this is less than the $2.5 million received by Falls Township.

From these sources Ingberman offers a "possible explanation" for the rape of Tullytown, one that fits his basic beggar-thy-neighbor, race-to-the-bottom scenario. As he enumerates this explanation: (1) Tullytown lacked bargaining power, (2) WMI could credibly threaten to develop in Falls Township, right next to Tullytown, and (3) the existence of potential dump sites along their joint border "may have disciplined the reservation values of both localities downward" because "WMI could have feasibly expanded in either Tullytown or Falls Township."

8.4 Tullytown's Landfill Location Looks Sensible

Ingberman's intrepid search for facts with which to illustrate his theory inspired me to do some additional research. I obtained U.S. Geological Survey maps (Trenton-East and adjacent quads) of the Tullytown area and located the landfill sites with the aid of an online map provided by a Bucks County–based landfill opponent, an environmental group called "B-PURE." My chief source, however, was the online archives of the *Philadelphia Inquirer*, which go back to 1982. The *Inquirer* covered the landfill issue extensively and intensively. Keywording "Tullytown" or "Falls Township" and "landfill" produced more than a hundred articles between 1982 and 1998. I read the first paragraphs of each of these articles and purchased the complete text of sixteen that appeared to give especially thorough background coverage. I also visited Tullytown and

Falls Township and looked at the landfills from a number of vantage points in July and December of 1999.

The picture that emerges from my longitudinal and close-up look is not completely at variance with Ingberman's remote-camera snapshot. Both Falls Township and Tullytown were in a much poorer position to defend themselves from a landfill siting than other boroughs and townships in Bucks County. But the factors leading to this weakness do not appear to be irrational or unfair.

A stylized map (Figure 2, adapted from the aforementioned USGS maps) might help explain this. I have indicated Tullytown as a pentagon (its approximate shape) and the three landfills as rounded boxes marked G, T1, and T2. The area east of the railroad tracks is dotted with lakes and coves (near the tracks). The rest of the eastern side (nearer the river) is industrial. The remaining operations of U.S. Steel Corporation's Fairless Hills plant and related businesses dominate the landscape. USX, as the steel manufacturer is now known, has downsized the plant and sold nearly eight square miles of its nearby land to WMI. Falls Township had permitted the landfill called GROWS

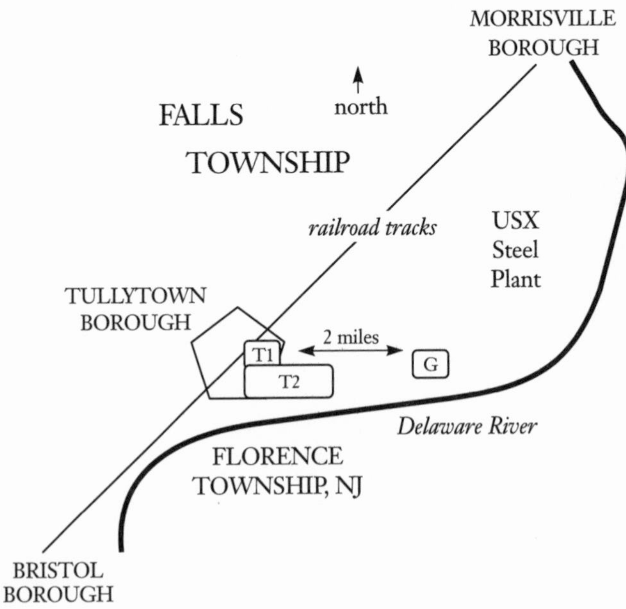

Figure 2 Environs of Tullytown, Pennsylvania

(marked as G on the map) to be established in 1972 between the steel plant and Tullytown. A landfill that served both the steel mill and municipalities was established at the GROWS site sometime before 1972.

The GROWS site seems like a logical place for a landfill. It does not take much acquaintance with steel mills (I grew up near one about forty miles north of this area) to know that they are somewhat messy, and that land nearby is probably best used for something that is similarly messy. The 1983 USGS map indicates few residential structures anywhere near the plant or the dump site. On my 1999 visits, I saw no residential structures in the vicinity other than those in Tullytown itself. There is a structure that appears to be a former farmhouse located between the landfill sites. It is now an office building for WMI. Behind it, on an inlet that separates most of Tullytown from the landfill, are seasonal recreation sites that are, according to the security person I talked to, avidly sought by boaters.

Tullytown's zoning apparently recognized that the area on which its landfills were placed (denoted T1 and T2 on the map) was poorly suited for residences. The land was zoned for industrial development. This designation specifically permitted landfills when WMI purchased the site. If Tullytown was being gamed by WMI, it had set itself up to be taken advantage of.

Had Tullytown possessed deep pockets, it might have been inclined to hire a lawyer to defend a change in its zoning after WMI had bought the land. But even with the best lawyers around, it would have been an uphill fight, especially in Pennsylvania, whose courts subscribe to the unusual theory that all communities ought to be zoned for all things (Ellickson and Been 2000, pp. 896–899). As an example, when Falls Township denied a variance to WMI to expand its original landfill site, the Pennsylvania appellate courts actually reversed the township zoning board (WMI v. Falls Township 1986).

8.5 Tullytown and Falls Township Won a Fiscal Jackpot

The courts were not the only ones to nudge Tullytown and Falls Township toward having a landfill on their industrial-zoned land: government agencies were also involved. Note that the anxiety-ridden "race to the bottom" that supposedly motivates the municipalities is said by Tiebout pessimists to be prevented only by appeal to higher governments. As Robert Inman and Daniel Rubinfeld put it, "The final outcome of Tiebout's competition among small governments will be a race to the bottom and economically inefficient public policies. The solution is to find a more centralized government to manage these misallocations" (1997, p. 1222).

Representing the larger public interest and possessing resources greater than the municipalities, regional and state governments are supposed to be the referee or big brother (depending on the problem) who prevents the municipalities from mutually trashing each other or being trashed by the likes of big WMI. Both Bucks County and the Pennsylvania Department of Environmental Resources had oversight in these matters. Bucks had to have a plan to dispose of its regional garbage, and the state's department had an elaborate set of command-and-control rules for landfills to prevent air and water pollution. Either agency could have stopped either landfill.

But in fact, both agencies pre-approved the landfill sites and their subsequent expansion in both Tullytown and Falls Township. Bucks County in particular was eager to have a disposal facility to deal with its 1980s garbage crisis. It accepted a "host fee" (thirty-five cents per ton of waste accepted by the landfill, projected at about $1 million per year) from WMI for all out-of-county garbage that it accepted. Bucks County officials promised to earmark much of those revenues for special facilities to benefit the area that was adversely affected by the landfill—which included Tullytown and Falls Township.

All of this pressure from the county and the state makes it look as if Tullytown was a reluctant bridegroom. But even allowing for the possibility that its original, industrial zoning designation that permitted landfills was a mistake, Tullytown officials' protestations of powerlessness as noted by Ingberman have the look of trying to justify their actions to a potentially envious outside world. In the November 18, 1990, article that Ingberman cites, the *Philadelphia Inquirer*'s reporter characterized Tullytown as "positively rolling in dough. So much dough the Bucks County borough has paid off its Fire Department's $200,000 debt and purchased a brand-new pumper. So much dough officials plan to repair and repave every street and curb in town. So much dough the borough of fewer than 2,500 people is renovating Main Street, building a $1.3 million municipal hall, beefing up its police force and spending a cool $50,000 on next year's centennial celebration."

The mayor of Tullytown is quoted in the same article as saying, "A lot of people are very jealous of the wealth we have." My visit to the town confirmed that Tullytown's public capital is new and exceptionally attractive for a small borough.

In addition to improving town facilities, WMI's side payments have enabled the borough to give grants to local property owners of at least $1,000 per year for most of the 1990s. There is enough left over from these expenditures that Tullytown has invested it with the objective of seeing to it that it will never have to levy any local property taxes after the landfill is closed. Some of these side payments appear to have been used by property owners to spruce up their homes, though it is not clear that they were earmarked for that purpose. My impression from walking down the borough's main street was that a vinyl-siding company had bequeathed the village free siding for life. No one would mistake Tullytown for an affluent suburb, but its appearance suggests that its residents had recently won a medium-sized lottery prize.

The neighboring municipality, Falls Township, gets even larger payments from WMI, since its landfills (GROWS and part of the expanded Tullytown dump, T2, that now crosses the township line) are even more extensive. Ingberman tries to put a glum face on the township's larger payments by noting that Falls Township has many more residents, so that the per capita payments are lower. But nearly all Falls Township residents live on the western side of the railroad tracks and endure almost none of the disamenities from either dump. From Fall's Township's side of the tracks, it is difficult even to see the mountain of trash, which, as it is deposited, is covered with topsoil and seeded with grass. WMI's payments finance half of Falls Township's government operations, which result in lower taxes and better services for the entire township. The township's website points with pride to a new park built without tax financing.

A good fraction of Tullytown residents live on the east side of the railroad tracks, where the dump is a visible presence. At more than two hundred feet in height (WMI gained permission from both municipalities in the 1990s to pile it higher than originally permitted), the artificial mountain is more than twice the height of the nearest hills in the area. Except for this, however, the dump seemed hardly noticeable when I visited. Garbage trucks streamed to the landfills while I was there, but all were routed over the main highways and avoided residential areas in Tullytown and Falls Township. (The Tullytown borough manager confirmed that WMI purposely avoids the settled areas.) Although it was a hot day when I visited in July, my normally sensitive nose did not at any point notice unusual odors.

The verdict for Tullytown's bargain thus seems unclear. The landfill is visible from Tullytown, and people do wonder whether it will cause pollution at some later time. But for Tullytown, taxes are no problem anymore, and residents have much better public infrastructure and a modest annual addition to their disposable personal income to boot. The cash payment, voted annually by a borough council that has much turnover, has always been somewhat tentative over the years. It will be eliminated once the dump is closed, though then the active working of the dump will cease, too.

8.6 Home Values Did Not Suffer from the Dump

As the theme of this book has suggested, one way to determine whether the localized benefits exceed costs of Tullytown's pact is to look at how its home values have done over the years. The tax reductions, rebates, and new public infrastructure should raise Tullytown's home values relative to those in other towns, while the dump's spillover and reputation effects should reduce them. If Tullytown's home values rise faster than otherwise comparable values in towns without the landfill, then Tullytown has come out ahead. If they have fallen, Tullytown has, on balance, suffered the "frown of the world" for having hosted it.

I selected two other boroughs near Tullytown as control groups. They are Bristol, three miles downriver, and Morrisville, six miles upriver. The advantage of these comparison boroughs is that their circumstances look fairly similar to Tullytown's, but neither hosted a landfill. All three boroughs have a housing stock that has remained stable in size since 1980, so I am reasonably sure that 1980, 1990, and current home values reflect the circumstances of the same properties, not new subdivisions. (This is not true for the adjoining townships of Falls and Bristol, which have continued to grow over the period.) Morrisville Borough annexed some territory from the adjacent township in the 1980s, but it is possible to subtract the annex's influence on the borough's housing stock by using census tracts. Each of the boroughs' racial composition is more than 90 percent white.

A drawback of this comparison group is that Bristol and, to a lesser extent, Morrisville, may have been affected by the Tullytown landfill. Bristol is three miles from Tullytown and Morrisville is six miles away. But the main adverse effects—visibility of the mound, truck traffic, and seagull droppings—were not mentioned as affecting Bristol or Morrisville in the many newspaper stories that dealt with the landfills. This is in contrast to the many stories about such effects on Florence Township, New Jersey, whose travail will be described presently. I walked around both towns during my 1999 visits, and the presence of the landfills was imperceptible.

The Census data show that home values in the two census tracts that make up Tullytown rose almost exactly as rapidly (150 percent) between 1980 and 1990 as those in Bristol and Morrisville. The establishment of the GROWS landfill in Falls Township in 1972 could have telegraphed to homebuyers in 1980 that a similar landfill was about to be established in Tullytown in 1987, which would then compromise this comparison. The scenario seems unlikely, though. Articles about the Tullytown landfill in the *Inquirer*, whose on-line archives go back to 1981, did not appear until 1986. The nearly identical housing-appreciation values in all of the towns therefore suggests that the net effect of the landfill on Tullytown during the landfill's formative years was nil. The bad things that happened as a result of the landfill seem to have been offset by the good things that happened as a result of WMI's side payments. The landfill looks like a wash.

Subsequent data suggest that Tullytown may have done a little better in the 1990s, when the side payments grew along with the height of the mound. The web site for the local Bucks County newspaper, the *Courier-Times* (www.phillyburbs.com) has "home values" for the towns in the area. It does not indicate their source or their date, but if they can be taken as comparable to the 1990 census figures for each borough, they indicate that Tullytown's home values have risen 6.2 percent and Morrisvilles's (including its annexed territory in 1990) have risen by 3.0 percent. Values in the borough of Bristol declined by 7.6 percent. (Bristol has a markedly poorer population than either Tullytown or Morrisville, and the average income of all three boroughs is below the average for Bucks County, which is the most upscale of Philadelphia's suburban counties.)

By this evidence then, it does not seem that the landfill and its operation have done any damage—or provided much advantage—to Tullytown homeowners. The parity may understate Tullytown's advantage, however, since its fiscal affairs and the public infrastructure prior to the 1986 WMI agreement may have been on a downward trajectory. Without the infusion of WMI's cash, the town in 1990 might have had home values that were lower.

I do not have comparable housing-price data for Falls Township because, as I mentioned, the township's housing stock grew over the period. But it seems reasonable to suppose that Falls Township was a net winner from the landfill development. Nearly all of its residents live farther from the dumps than most of Tullytown's residents. Moreover, Falls got little adverse publicity from the dumps because its original landfill (G on the map) was called and continues to be called by the acronym "GROWS," and Falls Township's share of the expanded dump (T2 on the map) is invariably designated as the Tullytown landfill. Falls Township does have to endure garbage-truck traffic, but this is confined to the main roads that parallel the railroad track and are thus removed from residential neighborhoods.

The net effect of the landfills from this calculation seems positive. In one respect, focus on Falls Township and Tullytown understates the region's gain, since without their landfills, communities in Bucks County and other area towns and cities would have to send their municipal waste to even more remote sites, at presumably greater cost, or develop them within their own borders on sites that would seem to be at least as problematic.

8.7 Do Unto Others?

My mission here is not to undertake a benefit-cost analysis of the municipal landfill. The issue relevant to this chapter is that raised by Ingberman: Was the siting of the landfills in Tullytown an example of a beggar-thy-neighbor policy, and did it result in too many sites being developed for landfills and adverse effects on each community?

The home-value evidence that I just presented seems to confute the last charge. At worst, neither community was made worse off by the combination of spillover effects and side payments. It could be argued that their home values should have risen more than those of otherwise comparable communities as a result of the landfill's host payments. (I admit that I thought they would, given the glowing newspaper accounts of Tullytown's fiscal prosperity.) But in that case, the dump would become too attractive to other communities, and they would be eagerly sought by them, which could result in yet more landfills being developed. So leaving the community only slightly better off on net seems more consistent with an efficient allocation of landfills.

Ingberman's suggestion that WMI bargained down its compensation to Tullytown by threatening to move to Falls Township (or vice versa) is belied by WMI's eagerness to develop landfills in both communities. The reason for its eagerness is obvious. Siting a landfill, municipal or hazardous, in any location is extremely difficult (Kent Portney 1991). Pennsylvania, a leader in rationalizing landfills (and hence the leading importer of out-of-state waste), passed a law in the early 1980s requiring that private operators had to pay host counties twenty-five cents a ton as compensation for the waste. WMI ignored this floor and immediately offered Bucks County thirty-six cents a ton. Subsequent requests for expansion of the landfill upward and outward have elicited even more generous compensation for Falls Township and Tullytown, reported in 1992 as $4.00 per ton.

As I noted in Section 8.3, Ingberman quoted one Falls Township resident as saying, "The [Tullytown] landfill is practically in our backyard, yet we get nothing out of it." This person was described in the same *Inquirer* article (November 18, 1990) as "a Falls Township resident who lives just shy of the Tullytown border." But if he does, he is unrepresentative of Falls Township's 35,000 residents. The resident's claim also neglects that Falls Township was (as Ingberman did mention) actually getting more aggregate side payments from WMI than Tullytown was, and that Falls Township had the original landfill next to the steel plant. At any rate, the issue being examined here is not that landfills will be acceptable to everyone. Ingberman's hypothesis is that municipalities will foist fiscally profitable disamenities on the borders with their neighbor that they would not do unto themselves.

What would be more convincing evidence of a beggar-thy-neighbor policy? Either that Tullytown or Falls Township had an alternative site, not near the other's border, that looked equally attractive for a landfill, or that the landfill sites could have been more profitably developed in an alternative use. I cannot say that I have surveyed all of Falls Township, but nothing on the USGS maps of the area suggests a similarly suitable nonresidential area. Nor did anyone cited in the many newspaper articles on the siting process suggest that the landfills would be better located elsewhere in Falls Township or Tullytown. It looks as if geography and history—particularly the early establishment of the GROWS landfill next to the steel mill—not game theory, best accounts for this case.

8.8 Township and Borough Comity

Another approach to the beggar-thy-neighbor theory would be to look for it in other behavior by the two municipal land-use decision-makers. If there had been a deliberate, tit-for-tat policy of dumping unwanted but profitable land uses on municipal borders, one would expect to see unneighborly behavior show up elsewhere. A clear opportunity to do so was reported in the *Philadelphia Inquirer* on September 14, 1989. The Falls Township zoning board was asked to grant a variance for a shopping center to be developed along Tullytown–Fallsington Road, which forms the border between Tullytown and Falls Township at the proposed development. The only abutting neighbors to the proposed strip mall were residents of Tullytown, and they showed up at the Falls Township zoning hearing and expressed their opposition. The township zoning board tabled the request despite a recommendation by its planning board that it should be granted. (The owner had a lot seventy-seven feet wide at its narrowest point, and he could have built without a variance if the lot had been eighty feet wide.)

The *Inquirer*'s next story on the shopping-center proposal was on January 14, 1990. It reported that the Falls Township board of supervisors had turned down a request to rezone the land to allow the center to be built. I infer from the request for a rezoning that the variance had been denied after being tabled. When I visited the site in July 1999, there was no shopping center, just a few stores that appeared to have been there for more than ten years.

If the Falls Township zoning board or its board of supervisors had felt that they had been played the fools by Tullytown officials on the landfill issue, they seemed to be in a position to do a little payback at this time. They could have allowed the shopping center to be built, and the only apparent opposition came from Tullytown residents. Yet the

Falls Township officials, acting against their own apparent fiscal self-interest and contrary to the recommendation of their own planning staff, disallowed the shopping center.

8.9 Florence Township, New Jersey: Out of the Loop

The Tullytown–Falls Township relationship does not fit the beggar-thy-neighbor theory. Neither community seems to have lost out from the landfill decisions, and neither seems to be at odds with the other. Of course, a few residents of both places are not happy with the outcome. But that is no different from any other collective decision that is made on the basis of less than unanimity—even the best school districts have parents who are dissatisfied with them.

In the process of examining the Tullytown–Falls Township relationship, I came across an example that seems to fit the beggar-thy-neighbor proposition better. As one can see on the map (Figure 2), the residential area closest to the expanded Tullytown landfill is not Falls Township or Tullytown itself, but across the Delaware River (south of the dump, since the river bends westward in this area) in Florence Township, New Jersey.

Florence residents anticipated that they would be on the short end of the landfill decision from the beginning of the regulatory process. At a Tullytown zoning hearing on the proposed landfill on October 29, 1986, 150 Florence Township residents (of a crowd of 350) vigorously protested allowing the dump. They expressed anxieties that their wells would be polluted and that their air quality would be degraded.

As it turned out, one of their fears was well founded. As the dump expanded toward the river in the 1990s (with both Tullytown's and Falls Township's approval), seagulls that feasted on the garbage fouled waterfront properties in Florence. In addition, odors from the landfill's methane-recovery system occasionally waft across the two hundred yards of river that separate the states at that point.

More obvious were the visual disamenities. Many Florence homes have backyards on a bluff above the river. Their view of what had formerly been undeveloped riverine area on the Pennsylvania side was now a working landfill two hundred feet high. Allegations that home values in Florence dropped as a result cannot be easily confirmed, since the census tract in which it is located is much larger than just the area along the river. Nonetheless, the tribulations of Florence seem to be a more plausible example of a beggar-thy-neighbor policy.

I offer three conjectures as to why Florence's interests seem to have been disregarded in the planning of the Tullytown landfill. One is that Florence is out of the intergovernmental loops that bind Falls Township and Tullytown together. Falls Township and Tullytown officials sat on the Bucks County commissions that had to give permission to locate the Tullytown landfill. Indirect governmental relationships also hold them together: They elect the same state and Congressional representatives (although their Congressman was prominently opposed to any landfills in his district). Falls Township and Tullytown officials rub shoulders when roads have to be planned, and their fire and police departments maintain a mutual-aid pact. Tullytown and Falls Township are part of the Pennsbury school district, which encompasses four municipalities. Florence Township, New Jersey, is part of none of these relationships. When any informal horse trading went on among public officials in planning the landfill, Florence was mostly out of the loop.

Intergovernmental contact is in fact pervasive in Pennsylvania and other states whose local governments are highly fragmented. Roger Parks and Ronald Oakerson (1993) offer a detailed account of how the 130 municipalities in Allegheny County (the center of the Pittsburgh metropolitan area) cooperate to take advantage of scale economies in police, fire, streets, and schools. With cooperative arrangements on many fronts, it would be strange to find that, in the land-use area, local officials would act uncooperatively. The overall evidence suggests in fact the opposite. Elinor Ostrom (1990) and Vincent Ostrom (1991), whose lifetime of work on local institutions is well known among political scientists, conclude that local governments are capable of generating relationships that can overcome the temptations of the prisoners' dilemma.

8.10 Environmental Order without Law

The second reason that Falls Township and Tullytown did not pay much attention to Florence's interests may have been the interactions of the townspeople. Here I lean on the work of Robert Ellickson (1991a), who investigated how neighbors settled disputes—chiefly over cattle trespass—in rural Shasta County, California. He found that dispute resolution was seldom governed by the law—few in fact knew the rules—but by bottom-up norms that Ellickson argued were actually more efficient than resort to the law. (Hence the title of his 1991 book, *Order without Law.*) Most important for my present purposes, Ellickson found that being an established neighbor—owning property and living on it—almost always forestalled opportunistic behavior that gives the prisoners' dilemma its doleful conclusion. Adjoining landowners know that the neighbor they might spite today is the neighbor they might need tomorrow.

I submit that Falls Township and Tullytown residents, not just their public officials, were bound in similar long-term relationships. Of course, these are urban people, not the residents of Shasta County's ranges, ranches, and ranchettes. But there are surely many opportunities for personal contact in the urban setting, too. Falls Township and Tullytown parents send their kids to the same schools. The Levittown neighborhood in the north of Tullytown (the part west of the railroad tracks) continues seamlessly into Falls Township. Residents of both towns probably see each other at work, in social situations, at PTA meetings, at Little League games, and in civic clubs almost as much as they see people from their own towns.

Neighboring towns in the same state and same county may not always get along, but a respect-thy-neighbor characterization is surely closer to the truth than the Hobbesian view that sees them perpetually on the prowl to get short-term gains from others. Moreover, even the prisoners' dilemma does not have to result in its tragic ending if there are opportunities for repeat play, as Robert Axelrod (1984) has shown in imaginative experiments and historical accounts. Falls Township's unwillingness to permit the small shopping center because of Tullytown residents' opposition (Section 8.8) is consistent with the idea that long-time neighbors do not normally take advantage of one another.

Residents of Florence Township, New Jersey, by contrast, probably encounter residents of Tullytown and Falls Township, Pennsylvania, only occasionally. Being in another state is not an insuperable barrier, but there is a river between them and no bridges conveniently connect Florence with its Pennsylvania neighbors. The nearest local bridges are downriver in Bristol and upriver in Morrisville. The Delaware Memorial Bridge is closer to Tullytown, but it connects the two state's turnpikes and is not a convenient, everyday route. Local suburban newspapers do not overlap in their territory, so a Pennsylvania town's local news is not likely to be read about in New Jersey towns. The school systems of the two states, needless to say, are completely separate.

Thus there were fewer opportunities for the everyday interaction that might have made the 150 Florence residents at the 1986 Tullytown zoning hearing more familiar faces. It may explain why no similar Florence turnout was reported at the many subsequent hearings on the landfills. As true outsiders, Florence residents may have supposed that Tullytown and other Pennsylvania public officials would not pay much attention to their concerns.

8.11 Federal Courts Helped Out-of-State Homeowners

A third reason for the apparent derogation of Florence's interests may have been that Pennsylvania state and local officials anticipated that the landfill developer, WMI, would make its peace with Florence in federal court. Several suits were instigated by Florence Township residents as soon as the Tullytown landfill was given state and local permits. The litigation was finally settled out of court in December 1998. WMI agreed to pay $2.1 million to Florence Township for public facilities and $3.1 million to individual residents whose homes had been devalued by the dump.

As part of the settlement, WMI agreed to undertake a nuisance-reduction program that would make less of the working face of the landfill visible to Florence residents and diminish the appeal of the landfill to seagulls. It also promised to help finance a cleanup of waterside facilities in Florence that had been fouled by the birds. When I visited Florence's waterfront area in July 1999 the seagulls were not an obvious problem, even though the landfill was then actively receiving trash.

I do not know if this settlement leaves Florence residents whole, but the $5.2 million lump sum (plus WMI's internalization activities, and less Florence's legal bills, which exceeded $1 million) is much less than the total of $5 million *a year* that Falls Township and Tullytown get in host fees. My informal survey of a statistically insignificant number—two, to be exact—of Florence residents at a tavern near the river in December 1999, elicited a mixed response. One man said that the dump was a terrible imposition on the community with no redeeming features. The other respondent (the barkeep) was more fatalistic. She did not care for it, but she thought that waste had to go somewhere. Tullytown takes much of the municipal waste of Burlington County, New Jersey, in which Florence is located. For some New Jersey officials, Tullytown was the answer to their prayers.

But all in all, the apparent discounting of Florence's interests by Tullytown and Falls Township does suggest the limits of a self-policing system of intermunicipal restraint. Over the river and out of state, maybe there is something to the beggar-thy-neighbor proposition. It hardly seems so pervasive, though, as to justify the enormous intellectual load that American environmental policy puts on it.

8.12 Conclusion: Do Homevoters Constrain the States?

Local governments responsive to homeowners are among the least likely candidates to produce an environmental race to the bottom. Whether their hypersensitivity to environmental risk is caused by psychological concerns or by rational risk aversion, homeowners are, if anything, too reluctant to trade environmental amenities for fiscal gains. Because local governments are geographically permanent and interact regularly with most of their neighbors, they are unlikely to pursue mutually destructive, beggar-thy-neighbor policies. When there is some deviance from neighborly norms, existing legal and legislative institutions seem capable of correcting them without wholesale preemption of local authority.

Interstate spillovers are a more serious problem, but again, existing legal institutions and doctrines do not seem so fossilized that they could not be adapted to dealing with them (Ellickson 1979). More widespread pollution issues are not well handled by local governments, and my argument in this chapter does not suggest abolishing state or national review of such issues. My position is simply that higher-government preemption of local land-use decisions is not justified by the usual academic theorizing about a race to the bottom or a supposed inclination of one municipality to beggar its immediate neighbors.

If my view that local governments are highly sensitive to environmental issues is credible, it could suggest another reason why there is so little evidence that states engage in any serious race to the bottom

(McConnell and Schwab 1990; Richard Revesz 1997). It may not be that state governments are attentive to their residents' wishes, as suggested by the median-voter model invoked as a baseline by Oates and Schwab (1988). As numerous critics have argued, concentrated interest groups with much to gain from development would seem more likely to be served at the state level. The scenarios in which environmental quality is sacrificed in exchange for taxes, jobs, and political favors seem more likely to be developed in the cloakrooms of the statehouse.

I think that this scenario is exaggerated in that state legislators and governors do seem sensitive to reputation effects. They may also be restrained by the interactions that they and their citizens have with those of other states, though because of the size of states, the proportion of people who interact is much smaller than for adjacent municipalities. But even when states are inclined to go too far to attract problematic industry, where are the offending polluters to be located? Most states are covered with local governments, and most local governments have zoning laws. Even municipalities that lack zoning can quickly implement an interim zoning law if their residents get wind of an unwanted land-use proposal.

The state government has the right to override local laws, but in practice, such preemptive laws are hardly ever effective. Local governments are simply too strong a force in most statehouses. So the would-be polluter, although licensed by the state government, has to appease the local government and the homeowners at a local hearing. The prospect of this review, rather than state-level concern for reputation, may be what restrains the interstate race to the bottom.

9
How Homevoters Remade Metropolitan Areas

MOST CRITICAL REVIEWS of American local government strongly imply, when they do not say it outright, that metropolitan fragmentation is an "accident of history" or "an accident of geography." The term "accident" leads one to ask what can be done to cure the unfortunate condition into which hapless cities have fallen. It precludes serious inquiry into whether local fragmentation might have served, and thus might still serve, some desirable purpose.

This chapter will review the history of municipal incorporation. The legal mechanics were limned in Chapter 2, but such descriptions seldom account for the forces that have led homeowners to become the dominant players in most municipalities. In describing this history, I offer a new explanation for why zoning came to America when it did. Zoning's rise in turn explains why the consolidation of local governments declined at about the same time. The incorporation rage in the Los Angeles area in the 1950s and 1960s confirms this account. It also explains how the city of Baldwin Park, California, became the poster child of the school-finance reform movement.

9.1 Municipal Formation Was Decentralized in the 1800s

Jon Teaford's *City and Suburb: The Political Fragmentation of Metropolitan America, 1850–1970* (1979) is a wide-ranging history of how local governments became so fragmented. His unassailable conclusion is that it was no accident. The people on the ground at the time wanted it that way. Fragmentation was the result of a bottom-up political process, democracy in one of its rawest forms. Moreover, this bottom-up process was not inevitable in any constitutional sense. Every state, from its earliest beginnings, had the authority to create localities by whatever means it chose—centralized or decentralized.

Teaford's conclusion is all the more convincing to me because he does not much care for fragmentation. His first page opines that "the result of this fragmentation is inefficiency, confusion of authority, and disparity in shouldering the burdens of the metropolis." His sympathies are with consolidation or, failing that, strong federations. But he is an honest recorder of facts, and he acknowledges that the political actors at the time often did not agree with his point of view. I review his work in some detail in this and the next several sections to show that fragmentation was what people wanted, and, more important, that consolidation and federation were in fact proposed and rejected. Modern advocates of metropolitan government tend to elide the fact that metropolitanism is a path that has been explored in the not-so-distant past.

"The Fragmentation of the Metropolis, 1850–1910" is Teaford's second chapter. The industrial revolution, which dates from about 1830 in the United States, promoted a migration to cities and the creation of brand new local governments. Before 1850, most state legislatures would create cities by special charters, just as they created private business associations. These charters described the location and powers of the local government, much as the same legislature might charter a railroad by describing where it could build and what its permissible activities might be.

Teaford briefly mentions the parallel between private and municipal incorporations (1979, p. 34). In the middle third of the 1800s, legislatures were being overwhelmed with requests for special charters by new businesses. In response, legislatures created more general and automatic procedures for incorporation both for businesses and for municipalities. This devolution was deliberate; legislatures could have gone on tailoring municipal-corporate charters to individual and local circumstances. A few eastern states persisted in this practice long after most others had taken a hands-off position with respect to most local government incorporations.

The underlying cause of municipal decentralization was "partially a reflection of the social and economic particularism emerging in industrializing America" (Teaford 1979, p. 10). In other words, people decided to resolve their differences by setting up different communities. It was a Tiebout world from the beginning. A demand for newly developed urban services, such as sanitary sewers, paved roads, and piped water, was often most easily realized by incorporating a small part of a township or county as an independent unit. The separation avoided the otherwise inevitable conflict between townsfolk and rural residents, who had little need for such services.

Some of the differences were literally matters of taste: Local regulation of alcoholic beverages was an important divide among communities throughout the 1800s. Less-frequent (though sometimes related) divides concerned local preferences for gambling, prostitution, architectural style, and public schools. Racial issues occasionally played a role in incorporation, sometimes with the twist of blacks incorporating in order to govern themselves without whites' control (p. 27).

Businesses also tried their hands at municipal incorporation both to keep taxes down and to keep regulators at bay. Owners of factories and their workers were more tolerant of the noxious side effects of activities that provided their profits and wages than people not connected with those industries. Smoky factories and smelly meatpackers sometimes found that it was cheaper to incorporate than fight residents not connected with the industry. Some entrepreneurial residents would also incorporate to accommodate concentrations of industry as tax havens. Both residents and the firms would keep taxes low by declining to include within their boundaries tax-exempt property and larger numbers of residential users. Even though zoning did not exist in the 1800s, the establishment of municipal boundaries was often clearly influenced by fiscal considerations.

9.2 Consolidation Followed Fragmentation

"The *Consolidation* of the Metropolis, 1850–1910" (my italics) is Teaford's chapter 3. It embarks on a path that seemingly contradicts his previous chapter. Over the same time period that riotous fragmentation was going on, central cities were gobbling up the nascent suburbs that had grown up around them. Some of this was annexation of territory that had not previously been organized, but a significant amount was the merger of two municipal corporations, which is what consolidation meant. Friendly consolidations resulted from a local process in which voters of both municipalities consented to the merger. Town A voted by a majority to merge with Town B, and Town B did the same for the merger. Failure of either town to get a majority stopped the consolidation.

Hostile consolidations could result if the state legislature forced the consolidation without the consent of a majority of the local voters in the smaller town. The 1854 merger of the suburban boroughs and townships of Philadelphia County into the city and county of Philadelphia was accomplished by the state legislature despite the protests of at least some of the local governments that were headed for extinction. The rules for annexation and consolidation varied by state, and some were hybrids of consent. For example, the vote might be local, rather than decreed by the state legislature, but simply require a majority of both municipalities combined. In this case, a small city that was strongly opposed might nonetheless be taken over by its larger neighbor.

Top-down, legislatively decreed consolidations like that of Philadelphia and its then-suburban cities became increasingly rare after 1850. So did the combined-majority approach. Consent of both parties was the usual rule. And even where the state continued to arrange the marriage, it seldom did so in the teeth of opposition by one of the cities (Teaford 1979, pp. 36, 62). One of the few substantial departures from this rule was the merger of Pittsburgh with the city of Allegheny (both were in Allegheny County, Pennsylvania) in 1907. The taxpayers of Allegheny City sued in federal court on the grounds that their property had been unconstitutionally devalued by having to take on the large municipal debts of Pittsburgh. The U.S. Supreme Court would have none of it. In Hunter v. Pittsburgh (1907), it famously opined that states could do anything they pleased with municipal boundaries.

Law professors such as Gerald Frug (1980) often decry the legal "powerlessness" of cities. They point to *Hunter* as both a source and a manifestation of it, contrasting legislative manipulation of city affairs with the greater autonomy enjoyed by business corporations. As is often the case, however, the legal rule does not describe political behavior. Teaford notes (without discussing the *Hunter* case) that the Pittsburgh-Allegheny merger was the "last time Pennsylvania's legislature would authorize an involuntary merger in the Pittsburgh region" (1979, p. 94).

A city's consolidation bait for its suburbs was usually access to the big city's water supply (pp. 39, 58). A central city (or what was to become the central city) would build a large reservoir and distribution system. The excess capacity of such a system made it possible to provide a reliable supply of water to nearby suburbs at a modest cost. The price of provision was often that the suburban government had to give up its separate existence and consent to consolidation.

The low quality and chancy quantity of most small-town water systems was a serious problem as urbanization proceeded. Surface and sometimes groundwater sources became polluted. Fire fighting became more important as the suburbs developed more city-like densities. Withholding of water was a serious problem, and it was the big carrot for inducing formerly separate municipalities to consolidate with their bigger neighbor.

9.3 Why Did Municipal Consolidation Decline from 1910 to 1930?

In the years between 1910 and 1930, the city-suburb consolidation process stopped almost dead in its tracks. Teaford describes it in his chapter 5, "Suburban Ascendancy, 1910–1940." Central cities continued to annex unincorporated territory when it was nearby, but such land became increasingly scarce as incorporated suburbs continued to proliferate and—what was new—balk at consolidation. The consolidations that did take place were with suburbs that were small or fiscally weak, and they were no great prizes. This phenomenon of 1910–1930 has been noticed by other historians of urban development (Kenneth Jackson 1972, p. 454). Even the city of Los Angeles, among the most aggressive in pursuit of territory by both consolidation with nearby cities and annexation of unincorporated territory, had by 1930 found itself "a city surrounded" by incorporated cities that were disinclined to join their fortunes with their water-rich neighbor (Gary Miller 1981, p. 12).

Seattle was another example of the great divide. Between 1908 and 1910 all eight of Seattle's adjoining suburban cities voted to consolidate with the city of Seattle. (My source is a table of incorporations at www.mrsc.org/library/inctable.htm.) They were the last consolidations of the century. The eight suburbs—all small in land area compared to Seattle—had been incorporated between 1890, when Ballard was established, and 1906, when Southeast Seattle was incorporated. By 1910, every one of these new cities was just a neighborhood within Seattle. Ballard and some others were induced to join Seattle by the promise of water from the city's expanding works, but all had the option of remaining independent. Seattle continued to annex adjacent territory from unincorporated King County after 1910, but no consolidations of Seattle with a previously existing city ever took place again.

Teaford offers three explanations for the national reluctance of viable suburbs to consolidate with cities after 1910.

1. The threat of withholding water diminished as suburbs developed their own water sources or joined special-purpose districts that did not require them to surrender their corporate existence (Teaford 1979, pp. 78–80).
2. The reputation of big-city politicians soured by the turn of the century as muckrakers such as Lincoln Steffans proclaimed *The Shame of the Cities* in his 1904 bestseller (p. 83).
3. All of the differences in preferences and fiscal conditions that had promoted fragmentation in the first place remained in place and, if anything, grew wider after 1910 (p. 91). The suburbs with stronger preferences for local control and with a viable fiscal base no longer had to succumb to the city's blandishments, and most major consolidation efforts failed (p. 103).

Teaford's explanations are reasonable but unsatisfying for an event of this magnitude. The decline of consolidation was a sharp break with the past. It requires stronger explanations. Why did special-purpose water districts not arise at some previous time? Was big-city politics ever played according to Marquis of Queensbury rules? Why were suburban differences becoming larger?

My explanation has to do with the rise of homevoters. The decades of 1890–1920 saw large advances in urban commuting technology—the streetcar and the automobile—which in turn promoted suburban homeownership (Sam Bass Warner 1962). People did not have to live near their jobs anymore. Those who could afford it—initially only the rich, later the middle class—could commute from suburban locales.

The commuters bought homes (not, I would note, with any help from the federal government), and suburban homeownership grew rapidly during this period (Robert Barrows 1983; LeRoy and Sonstelie 1983).

Homes became a powerful focus for the suburbanites' savings and their affections. Teaford is well attuned to this feeling. In describing the failure to create the "Federative Metropolis" in chapter 6, he describes the ambivalence of suburban businesspeople about getting into political bed with the central city. The suburban businessman with an office in Cleveland was eager to see Cleveland grow both by adding population and territory. But he also dearly valued the independent suburb in which he lived (1979, p. 115).

9.4 Zoning Was Induced by Footloose Development

Teaford (1979, p. 84) mentions in passing that after 1910, the independent suburb acquired a new and valuable tool to maintain its existing character: zoning. Zoning was sweeping the country in that era; contemporary accounts of its spread among the suburbs make it sound a bit like the spread of dance crazes (W. L. Pollard 1931). Its popularity at the time arose, I believe, from the separation of work and home that had recently been made available by the streetcar and automobile. Zoning provided the means by which suburbs could retain their autonomous character.

Consider, as Teaford does, the view of the suburban homeowner toward amalgamation with its adjacent neighbor, Cleveland, prior to zoning. In 1900 Cleveland's suburbs were certainly different than Cleveland, and the differences were perhaps increasing. But in the absence of zoning, there was little to prevent most suburbs from eventually becoming developed to resemble Cleveland. Without collective controls, conversion of a home to a store, rebuilding a store as an apartment house, and development of factories that did not quite fall into the nuisance category (and thus be enjoinable by the courts) would have been perfectly possible in most suburbs.

There is direct evidence that such threats were real. A respected book on real estate by Stanley McMichael and Robert Bingham (1923) offered two chapters (of thirty-six) on the new institutions of zoning and planning. The authors, a real estate professional and an attorney in Cleveland, discussed the pros and cons of zoning in a way that seems thoroughly modern. Among its advantages was protection of home values, especially in the suburbs, because zoning forestalled the threat of apartments and commercial and industrial uses settling in the neighborhood. To illustrate this possibility, the book displays pictures of two residential neighborhoods invaded in this way during the prezoning era—one by a natural-gas storage tank and the other by a warehouse (pp. 316, 318). That this sort of problem was endemic at the time is suggested by a Harvard professor's mention of it in his widely used textbook (Chester Hanford 1926, p. 234) as well as by state supreme court opinions that upheld zoning at the time (Martha Lees 1994, pp. 404–406).

Private covenants might have prevented suburban changes in land use, but their establishment was cumbersome and, even where they were installed by the original developer, they almost never covered the entire community. As Los Angeles residential developers had found in the early 1900s, covenants in one neighborhood did nothing to prevent other developers from placing incompatible uses nearby (Marc Weiss 1987, p. 68). Nor could covenants protect a municipality's fiscal situation from adverse development on uncovenanted land.

The development of the automobile was an important impetus for zoning. The original commuter suburbs developed along the lines of street railroads. As automobiles came into the hands of the middle class, the areas between the streetcar lines filled in (Eric Monkkonen 1988, p. 177). Streetcar fares dropped and more lower-income families could afford to commute, so developers built high-rise apartments along the lines. This was not a great threat to single-family homeowners, though, because the routes of streetcars could be regulated and hence avoided by most homeowners, as Andrew Cappel (1991) established in his nuanced study of prezoning New Haven, and Charles Cheape (1980, pp. 29–32) showed for prezoning New York City.

Homeowners could thus avoid conflicts by building out of the reach of the streetcar, assuming they had an automobile, and by using their political influence to control the routes of new streetcar lines. But the makers of automobiles soon brought forth over-the-road buses and trucks. Truck transportation was especially important in liberating manufacturers from the confines of downtown docks and railroad stations (Moses and Williamson 1967, p. 215). The motor vehicle that liberated homeowners from the central city and the lines of fixed rail transport also soon liberated apartment builders and industrial developers. The motor bus, which became the chief competition for the streetcar, could not be confined to a fixed route as easily. By the 1920s, zoning was the only practical way to protect residential neighborhoods from the newly footloose industrial and apartment developments. Henry Ford should perhaps be acknowledged as the true instigator of zoning in America.

9.5 Euclid v. Ambler Reflected Cooley's Vision of Local Autonomy

Before they obtained the comprehensive control of municipal territory that zoning provided, close-in suburbs must have viewed consolidation with their central cities with a sense of inevitability. Even if they did not join with the city, they would soon become just like the city. Without zoning, the fiscal and environmental differences that made the suburb preferable to the city would not long persist. With such bleak prospects in the prezoning era, the blandishments of water and the economies of administration made merger with the city a reasonable proposition.

After zoning was established, however, the suburbs did not have to bow to the inevitability of convergence with their neighbors. They could control their own destiny. Independence from the bigger city was now worth fighting for. This did not mean, I hasten to add, that the suburbs could resist change entirely, even if they were so inclined. Zoning's birth was difficult and its growth, though rapid, was often constitutionally problematic.

Some state courts initially resisted zoning's novel restraints on the use of private property. This induced a short-lived attempt by some cities to compensate owners for zoning restrictions by invoking eminent domain (William Anderson 1927). Most state courts fell in line after the U.S. Supreme Court's 1926 decision in Euclid v. Ambler, which upheld zoning against the charge that it had unconstitutionally restricted the property rights of development-minded landowners. That the Court's most conservative member, Justice George Sutherland, wrote the *Euclid* opinion undermined almost all state-court opposition to zoning.

Sutherland is an illustrative figure for the homevoter explanation of zoning's origins. Both his academic admirers and his more numerous detractors commonly regard *Euclid* as an aberration in Sutherland's jurisprudence, even though he wrote three opinions in the following year that upheld zoning (Keith Revell 1999, p. 122). Hadley Arkes (1994) offers an explanation for Sutherland's seemingly liberal inclination on this issue. Arkes is bent on rescuing Sutherland from his notoriety as an implacable opponent of the New Deal and other regulatory schemes. (The title of a 1950 biography by Joel Paschal summed up the common view: *Mr. Justice Sutherland: A Man against the State.*) Arkes singles out *Euclid* as being consistent with Sutherland's mildly paternalistic, "natural law" outlook (pp. ix, 70). For the origins of this outlook, Arkes points out that Sutherland was a University of Michigan law student under the tutelage of Michigan Supreme Court Justice Thomas M. Cooley and was much influenced by him (pp. 41–43).

In his widely used *Constitutional Limitations*, Cooley maintained that there was an inherent right of "local self-government" that, even though it was not explicitly stated in their constitutions, state governments should not abridge (1868, p. 35; Paul Carrington 1997, p. 535). Cooley's influence seems apparent from Sutherland's recognition in *Euclid* that "the village [whose zoning was under attack], though physically a suburb of Cleveland, is politically a separate municipality, with powers of its own and authority to govern itself as it sees fit within the limits of the organic law of its creation and the State and Federal Constitutions" (272 U.S. at 389). These are not words suggested by "Dillon's Rule" and other doctrines that see municipalities as entirely derivative of the state. Sutherland goes on to note that the village of Euclid could control its own destiny: "Its governing authorities, presumably representing a majority of its inhabitants and voicing their will, have determined, not that industrial development shall cease at its boundaries, but that the course of such development shall proceed within definitely fixed lines." With the Court's approval of zoning, Dillon's view of municipalities was implicitly ousted in favor of Cooley's.

Even before *Euclid*, zoning was recognized as a major change in the municipal landscape. It provided an additional reason for municipal independence from larger cities as well as a means of maintaining it. The new reason was that the value of existing homes could be enhanced by appropriate zoning. Homeowners were becoming conscious that the attractiveness of their entire community, not just their own structures and those of their neighbors, made a difference in the value of their homes. The City Beautiful movement of the turn of the century reinforced this idea and helped make city planning respectable.

9.6 Developers Substituted Zoning for Covenants

The influence of planners and judicial decisions on zoning's development is often overstated, though. Marc Weiss (1987, p. 28) points out that the developers who pioneered large-scale residential subdivisions in Southern California were the prime movers behind the U.S. Commerce Department's promulgation of the Standard State Zoning Enabling Act in 1928. It was not a top-down process. It was motivated by the experience of developers, who found that voluntary covenants were insufficient to protect their property's value from incompatible uses on their borders.

The large-scale developers embraced zoning as an alternative to covenants because it "would maximize aggregate land values, and stabilize values at each location, but would not maximize values everywhere" (Weiss 1987, p. 101). The California developers thus agreed with their Cleveland contemporaries McMichael and Bingham (1923, p. 324), who concluded, "Home neighborhoods which had no protection from business encroachment have [after zoning was adopted] taken a sudden spurt and have built up rapidly as soon as it was apparent that only residences were to be allowed therein." Far from regarding zoning as an intrusion on their property rights, developers at least initially saw public regulation as a mechanism to attract buyers eager to protect their investments.

Several modern scholars have cast doubt on the validity of the claims that zoning enhanced property values. They point to the viability of covenants elsewhere and the lack of evidence that nonresidential uses were harmful to residences at the time (Andrew Cappel 1991; McMillen and McDonald 1993). Although the aforementioned examples from Los Angeles and Cleveland suggest the opposite, it may still be true that 1920s New Haven (Cappel's example) and Chicago (McMillen and McDonald's) were not suffering much from unzoned development. My demurrer is that their evidence from the era just before zoning was established is suspect because it reflected land-use patterns of the era before motor vehicles. Rail transport of both people and goods was no great threat to residential values (as Cappel points out). Rail lines were controllable and avoidable; everyone knew which side of the tracks was the "wrong" side. Zoning was a response to the radical uncertainty created for homeowners by the automobile, the truck, and the motor bus, which had no tracks to be on the right side of.

It is important to note my chain of causation. I do not argue that the invention of zoning by itself made the suburbs resistant to consolidation with the bigger city. Zoning was not thrust upon the suburbs. The first cause in my story is a transportation revolution that enabled separation of home from work by long distances. Homeownership became more widespread as more distant territory was opened up. After self-propelled buses and trucks came into widespread use, homeowners began to look for ways to protect their assets from commercial and multifamily neighbors. Zoning, invented in Germany a few decades earlier, provided a way to prevent or at least regulate neighborhood and community change that would affect their home values. Adoption of zoning after 1910 made the suburbs reluctant to consolidate with other cities.

This story fits, incidentally, with that of Edward Glaeser, Matthew Kahn, and Jordan Rappaport (2000), who argue that the location of the poor in central cities is the product of those cities having public transportation and, to a lesser extent, more services for the poor. The authors' primary objective is to provide a more realistic account than that of conventional urban economics, which for years has supposed that the rich live in suburbs because the income-elasticity of demand for housing exceeds that of commuting cost. Glaeser, Kahn, and Rappaport discount the idea that "exclusionary zoning" in the suburbs is the cause. But if my account of zoning's origins can be credited, one important reason that there is so little public transportation in the suburbs is because of land-use decisions about both transportation systems and housing density.

The layout of the transportation system was always a major concern of local politics (Monkkonen 1988, p. 162). The decision by Robert Moses to build suburban Long Island parkways with overpasses that inhibited the passage of buses and large trucks is only the most famous example of suburban resistance to public transportation. The failure of modern metropolitan passenger rail systems to live up to their promise of reducing automobile congestion is widely attributed to the low-density patterns of suburban development (Melvin Webber 1976). Many suburbs decline to rezone land to accommodate higher-density uses even when commuter rail facilities are built (Boarnet and Crane 1997).

9.7 Metropolitan Government Is an Old Idea

Teaford confirms the reluctance of suburbs to cede their independence in two later chapters of his book (1979, chaps. 7 and 8). In lieu of consolidation, urban reformers, who were often residents of the higher-class suburbs, proposed metropolitan federations. These would empower the larger regional government to make some laws, especially about transportation, and leave local governments with the remaining powers. But the movement was not sufficiently popular to overcome localism, and for the most part, only a few special-purpose districts for water, sewer, and transportation were established on a metropolitan basis.

One of the major stumbling blocks to metropolitan government was who would do the zoning. Teaford's most recent book, *Post-Suburbia* (1997), attends to the history of the maturing suburban economies from 1920 to 1990. Zoning plays an even greater part in this account, with suburbs in all parts of the country incorporating with the explicit desire to wrest land-use controls from counties and other forces of metropolitan consolidation. Summarizing the concerns of a Long Island suburb in the 1920s, Teaford writes, "Fearful of unregulated development that could lower property values, residents of Munsey Park were just as eager to adopt zoning ordinances to protect their half-acre plots as the estate owners of Lake Success or Centre Island were to preserve their one-hundred-acre manors" (1997, p. 16).

The fragmentation of metropolitan areas continued through the twentieth century, and it became especially active after World War II. By the 1950s and 1960s, "Academics, journalists, and reform-minded politicians viewed the multitude of suburban governments as a national disgrace threatening the quality of metropolitan life" (Teaford 1997, p. 85). Yet little was done about it. Part of the reason was that by the 1960s much of the resistance to metropolitan government was coming from within the central cities, not just the suburbs. African-Americans, whose numbers and enfranchisement in big cities had grown steadily, were at the forefront. Blacks came to control the mayor's office and city council in many central cities. They saw little advantage in merging with suburbs and again becoming a political minority (Michael Danielson 1976, p. 278).

9.8 The Lakewood Plan Promoted New Cities

In the balance of this chapter and in part of the next, I demonstrate that the underlying reason for municipal incorporations continues to be the desire by homeowners to become homevoters. Suburban residents form small local governments and reject consolidation with larger units because they want to be governed by a unit of government in which people like them—people who own their own homes and who have similar demands for local services—get to call the shots about local issues. They want smaller rather than larger communities in order to preserve the rule of the median voter.

The modern suburban incorporations that have drawn the most scholarly attention were those of Southern California in the 1950s, especially in Los Angeles County. The fiscal arrangement that facilitated them is the widely known Lakewood Plan. Lakewood was an unincorporated place in Los Angeles County just north of the city of Long Beach. It was already substantially developed, and its municipal services had been provided by Los Angeles County and by special districts, a common arrangement in much of the West.

In the early 1950s the city of Long Beach sought to annex Lakewood as part of its plan to expand its territory so as to challenge the city of Los Angeles's position as the commercial and industrial center of Southern California. Although Long Beach had a substantial tax base from its port and oil wells, Lakewood residents were not inclined to join. But the idea of incorporation was not attractive, either, because of the cost of providing urban services.

To solve this problem, Lakewood got Los Angeles County to agree to continue providing municipal services on a contractual basis. (The city and county of Los Angeles have entirely separate governments, though residents in the city also vote for county officials.) The new city of Lakewood would elect officials and hire a small city-hall staff, but police, fire, and other services would continue to be provided by Los Angeles County on a fee basis. Los Angeles County officials and managers agreed to this arrangement because the alternative was not for the county to continue running the unincorporated area, but to have

Lakewood become annexed by Long Beach. Long Beach had its own departments to provide services, so Los Angeles County personnel would have that much less work, and Los Angeles County elected officials would have that much less power.

Lakewood voters accepted this plan in 1954, and it became the model for other unincorporated areas that had cityhood on their minds. Incorporation moved from a hand-crafted affair to an assembly-line process. Between 1954 and 1963, thirty new cities were formed in Los Angeles County under the Lakewood Plan.

9.9 Incorporators Sought Control of Taxes and Zoning

The Lakewood Plan attracted the attention of several political scientists. In a book that enthusiastically applied economic analysis to metropolitan organization, Robert Bish (1971) devoted part of a chapter to the Lakewood Plan. He specifically invoked the Tiebout model (among others) in concluding that the new incorporations were a good thing. Like-minded people were able to provide a more satisfactory level of services for themselves and keep their taxes down.

The most extensive analysis on the Lakewood Plan, and perhaps the only book-length work by a social scientist devoted exclusively to municipal incorporations, is Gary Miller's *Cities by Contract* (1981). Miller comes to just about the same conclusion as Bish did ten years earlier: The Lakewood Plan allowed like-minded people to provide a more satisfactory level of services for themselves and keep their taxes down. But Miller concludes that this was a bad thing. He regards these incorporations as little more than exercises at tax avoidance and a way to use land-use controls to shirk from metropolitan income redistribution.

Like Bish, Miller is a political scientist and is well versed in economics. He has read Tiebout and the related literature. He deploys the graphical tools of economics to frame his analysis. This background, coupled with Miller's fine-grained description of the political background of individual incorporations, make his book a source to be reckoned with.

Miller's analysis confirms the centrality of residential voters in establishing the new municipalities (1981, pp. 31–33). Although the entrepreneurs who got the incorporation movements rolling had a mixed bag of motives, they always had to get their proposals approved by the votes of cold-eyed residents. As Miller notes, plenty of incorporation votes failed because the majority of homeowners were unpersuaded of their merits.

The incorporations that succeeded had to show the resident homeowners that there was something to be gained. The something was lower taxes or better services and protection of their home values by locally controlled land-use regulations. The fear that motivated most of them was that county officials or those of an established municipality that annexed them would either use their taxes to fund services they did not value or change land use in ways that would adversely affect the residential character of their neighborhoods. County officials were generally much more eager to promote development than were the residents of the immediate area (Miller 1981, p. 86; Richard Cion 1966).

9.10 Lakewood Cities Produced Tiebout Communities

Miller's descriptions of other incorporations illustrate their ad hoc nature, the constant concern about tax base, and the use of zoning to manage the tax base and protect residential homes. While Miller denies that the cities were formed to facilitate different preferences for public services, his evidence seems largely to the contrary. The cities he describes are really different in their character: Some are exclusively residential; others are business enclaves. One, Dairy Valley, was formed to protect dairy farmers from urban encroachment, but these same landowners later used rezonings to facilitate the highly profitable transformation of their enclave into the city of Cerritos (Miller 1981, p. 60).

Even if the Lakewood-era municipalities had no special identity upon incorporation, they seem to have acquired one in the subsequent years. Eric Heikkila (1996) used factor analysis of census-tract characteristics to see if Los Angeles County municipalities were distinct from one another. If Miller's characterization of them were true, then the characteristics of the population that would give rise to differences in demands for public services would be randomly distributed. Census tracts dominated by families with children, say, would be as likely to be within the same municipality as tracts dominated by households without children. Tracts with high-income people would be as likely to be in the same municipality as tracts with low-income people, if there were no Tiebout sorting.

Heikkila found that there was extensive Tiebout-sorting in the 1990 census data. Census tracts with similar characteristics were much more likely to be found within the same municipality than in adjacent or nearby municipalities. The characteristics that accounted best for tract sorting were the scale of development (such as "small town"), ethnicity ("East Asian"), household type ("married with children"), and employment category. Thus even if Miller is correct in saying that municipalities formed under the Lakewood Plan were not formed to satisfy different public service demands, after thirty years they certainly look as if they have distinctive characteristics that are likely to cause differences in demand.

As I have argued throughout this book, fragmentation of local governments causes property owners, who are mainly homeowners, to seek a mix of local services that maximizes the value of their holdings. The financing of local services from the property tax is a key element of this efficiency-seeking activity. Homevoters will vote for property tax increases if the expenditures they finance will increase their home values. By the same token, they will avoid living in jurisdictions in which their property taxes are used to finance things that they do not want.

This process benefits central city residents as well as those in the suburbs. Competition from other places in which residents can select homes makes central city officials more responsive to their constituents. When examining the forty-nine largest U.S. cities in 1967–1982, Philip Grossman, Panayiotis Mavros, and Robert Wassmer found that "the greater the number of cities in a central city's metropolitan statistical area and the greater the average population of suburban cities in the metropolitan area, the more technically efficient the central city is" (1999, p. 297). Their measure of technical efficiency was property value, with higher values implying more efficient government. Competition, it appears, is good for central cities even if their mayors do not like it.

The evidence that Gary Miller offers from the Lakewood Plan's history is consistent with this notion. He points out that many incorporations were undertaken to resist annexation by older cities whose expenditures were of little interest to the would-be residents. It was not mindless tax minimization. The existing cities whose annexation proposals they rejected often had a tax base considerably larger and a tax rate lower than the municipality they formed. Had they leaned back and accepted annexation, their tax payments would have gone down. Incorporationists did not so much object to paying taxes—not that anyone considers it a great honor. They wanted to pay taxes for services that enhanced the attractiveness of their major asset, their homes. It seems no more insidious than a desire to have the plumber do the work for which you pay her.

9.11 The Irony of Baldwin Park

Miller's most valuable service is to describe the incorporation process. One group of new cities he classifies as "commercial incorporations," in which the apparent motive was to grab as much taxable property as possible in order to keep taxes low. The frankly named two cities of Commerce and Industry are surely the apotheoses of this motive.

The city of Industry is especially bizarre, because it has never had more than about six hundred residents but contains an enormous industrial park situated on either side of the Southern Pacific Railroad tracks. In fact, to meet the minimum population for incorporation, Industry's organizer, a municipal lawyer named Graham Ritchie, had to include a nearby mental hospital so that the patients could be counted among the residents. I visited the city in February of 1999, and it still is strange to see. Miles of large warehouse-style buildings and almost no houses in sight except those across a boulevard in adjacent municipalities. Local roads are nicely maintained, and the city has an exquisitely manicured historic building, but the place seems lifeless. It's as if invisible extraterrestrials ran the local government.

Other efforts to incorporate around a large commercial tax base in the 1950s were not so successful, according to Miller. One that caught my eye was the story of Baldwin Park, which Miller had curiously categorized under "commercial incorporations," as were Commerce and Industry. Baldwin Park is the city whose school district served as the poster-child of the *Serrano* litigation described in Section 5.1. It was described by the plaintiffs as the archetypal "property-poor" district and paired unfavorably with Beverly Hills. Yet Miller categorized it as a tax-base-grabbing "commercial incorporation," which should have made it "property rich." What had gone wrong?

The area that became Baldwin Park was near several gravel pits owned by Consolidated Rock Company. Gravel trucks streamed through Baldwin Park residential neighborhoods, and a group of homeowners had sought to incorporate so as to ban the trucks. (Los Angeles County officials were not sympathetic to efforts to hobble the quarry's operations.) Consolidated Rock funded a group that opposed Baldwin Park's incorporation, and the incorporation failed.

After a time, however, a local water-district official convinced Consolidated Rock that incorporation of Baldwin Park, followed by annexation of their gravel pits, would actually be in the company's interest. With the gravel pits as part of its tax base, the official reasoned, Baldwin Park residents would see that the property taxes paid by the company were worth the nuisance from the trucks (Miller 1981, p. 55). Nothing like a clear opportunity cost to stay the hand of unreasonable regulation.

Following this line, Baldwin Park incorporated around its already developed residential area. It became the second Lakewood Plan city, incorporating in 1956. It then turned its attention to annexing the nearby gravel pits, as Consolidated Rock had wanted, and the nearby industrial area along the Southern Pacific tracks. The latter area was to become the city of Industry, the richest tax base in the area. It was Baldwin Park's for the taking. Had it succeeded, Baldwin Park's tax base might have exceeded that of Beverly Hills, assuming it had been as successful in attracting industry as Industry later was.

But Baldwin Park's plans failed. I quote Miller's description of how things fell apart so that I cannot be accused of making this up:

> To the dismay of local leaders such as Holmes [the water company official who brokered the Consolidated Rock deal], however, the newly elected city council did not make annexation of the vacant tax base to the south its first order of business. Instead, the city council insisted on first attending to the issue of developing a municipal zoning ordinance. While the reasons for this were not clear at first, they became evident within two months of incorporation. Within that length of time, three city councilmen were indicted for taking bribes to corrupt the zoning ordinance to which they had insisted on giving priority. As it turned out, two of the councilmen had asked for bribes of $200 each from the promoter of a

local massage parlor. The promoter, evidently guessing from the small size of the bribes requested that he was dealing with green, untrustworthy officials, decided to report the bribes before one of them did. Before the dust was settled from the case, the tax base to the south had incorporated as Industry, and Consolidated Rock Company had definitely eliminated the possibility of annexation to Baldwin Park.

Here then is how Baldwin Park became the epitome of the property-poor district in the *Serrano* litigation. It was not an "accident of geography," as the advocates of court-ordered school reform often put it. The "accident" was of human volition, the result of human frailties on the part of the city's founders. Had its public officials been more honest, Baldwin Park might have been numbered among the property-rich districts and been spared its notoriety as a paragon of education failure.

On my visit to Industry in February 1999, I also took a swing through Baldwin Park. It is not in a state of collapse. It's not East Saint Louis, Illinois, which I visited in the summer of 1999 and which is the most alarmingly desolate city I have ever laid eyes on. (By coincidence, I was there on the same day that then-president Clinton visited as part of a national campaign to call attention to poor areas. I noticed that even the poorest have their pride: East Saint Louis was busily sweeping its streets in preparation for its day in the national spotlight.) No, Baldwin Park was a lower-income area with low-rise apartment buildings and modest single-family homes on small lots. There were few signs of physical deterioration, and the streets did not seem forbidding. The new community center I passed at dusk had an outdoor basketball game going and, were I a few years younger and without promises to keep, I'd have been inclined to stop and get into a game.

In case my impressionistic views missed something important, I checked the census data for housing quality and found that Baldwin Park in 1970 had no more in the deteriorated category ("lacking some plumbing") than the average for Los Angeles County. (Later census data did not include this category.) Its owner-occupancy rate was about the same as the state average, and, while incomes are low compared to its neighbors, its poverty rate is no greater than that of the state.

9.12 The City of Industry Bred LAFCO

It seems likely, though not certain, that the well-being of the Los Angeles region would have been higher had Baldwin Park managed to annex the prime industrial area that became the city of Industry. Baldwin Park's residents would have had lower taxes, better schools, and better municipal services. Of course, they would have had to pay more for their houses as a result—Thomas Dee (2000) inferred this from a national sample—and some current residents would likely not have been able to afford to live there.

There might have been less industrial development in the area had Baldwin Park done the zoning and taxing of the industrial area. The present city of Industry advertises its low taxes as a lure along with its probusiness services and protective (in this case, antiresidential) zoning. The expanded Baldwin Park would have had less of those attractions. But probably not much less. The location itself—next to a railroad, near major freeways, and accessible to markets and the labor force—accounts for much of Industry's attraction. The success of the city of Commerce in attracting businesses to a city run largely by lower-income residents of Hispanic heritage suggests that Baldwin Park could have done the same (Boone and Modarres 1999).

Oddities such as the city of Industry are the evolutionary sports that crop up in the free-wheeling, bottom-up municipal incorporation process that the Lakewood Plan epitomized. Miller's other successful "commercial incorporations" do not amount to a large fraction of the region's nonresidential tax base, so it seems wrong to judge the incorporation process by such peculiarities. At any rate, the Lakewood Plan era came to an end in 1963. The state legislature established the Local Agency Formation Commission to supervise the creation of new cities and annexation activities by existing cities. At least eleven other states have formed similar boards (ACIR 1992), and their effect has been to retard municipal incorporation from its 1950s heyday (Teaford 1997, p. 97). Incorporations in California still occur, but the era of tiny, idiosyncratic municipalities has largely passed.

LAFCO, as California's agency is mirthlessly known, is a county-based agency with two city members, two county members, and a fifth chosen by the other four. It appears to operate as an uneasy cartel to deter competition in the provision of municipal services. After its establishment, existing cities found it easier to annex adjacent territory, because they did not have to worry that that the territory's residents would incorporate. At least one serious study found that LAFCO resulted in more costly local government in California when compared to other states that did not adopt a LAFCO-like structure (Martin and Wagner 1978).

9.13 Conclusion: Exuberant Incorporations

This chapter has advanced a historical thesis. The rise of zoning and the end of municipal consolidation in the 1910–1930 era can be explained by the homevoter hypothesis. Automobiles, buses, and trucks allowed metropolitan decentralization. As homes became the locus of most families' net worth, residents seized the institutions of local government and used zoning to protect single-family homes from footloose developers of apartments and commercial uses. In doing so, the new homevoters seemed to have appreciated that smaller units of government were more likely to protect their interests. Metropolitan fragmentation was a logical result of homeowners' desire to protect their otherwise uninsurable assets.

In the wake of the local political shift to homeowners, the city-suburb consolidation movement fell by the wayside. Even modest manifestations of regionalism have foundered on the question of local control of land use. Instead, metropolitan governance started to go the opposite direction. The bottom-up incorporation process of most states engendered a proliferation of local governments. The Los Angeles Lakewood Plan was only the most famous of the spurts of incorporations. Boundary review boards have retarded new incorporations since then, but they have not put a stop to them, as the next chapter will demonstrate.

10
Sprawl, Metropolitanism, and Local Control

IN THIS CHAPTER I turn to an issue in which homevoters play a less sanguine role. The charge here, which I have addressed in numerous previous works, is that most suburban governments, particularly the smaller ones in which homevoters are most clearly in charge, zone for excessively low-density residential uses (Fischel 1985, chap. 12; 1995, chap. 9). When enough of them do so, it contributes to metropolitan area sprawl and deters lower-income households from finding homes in the suburbs (Anthony Downs 1994; Fischel 1999).

One approach to the excesses of local zoning is to establish a regional government that has the power to override parochial concerns. The bulk of this chapter describes how Washington State, particularly the Seattle metropolitan area, has tried to deal with the twin problems of excessively low-density suburban development and suburban resistance to housing for low-income people. I argue that this has been undermined by municipal incorporations. But these incorporations also demonstrate the ongoing desire by homeowners to form communities that promote a distinctive identity and provide a better level of local public services.

10.1 Sprawl Is Caused by Homevoter Anxieties

Homeowners are more likely than other property owners to say "not in my back yard" to any development that poses even the slightest chance of environmental degradation. The NIMBY does not distinguish between industrial developments and housing developments, even when the houses proposed are no more harmful to the environment than those in which the preexisting residents live. The nature of the neighborhood effects may be different for housing than for factories, but the common denominator is that existing residents worry that higher-density development of any sort will devalue their own homes. NIMBY anxieties are not just expressed at zoning hearings. They work themselves into long-term plans, which are then expressed as zoning ordinances that require multiacre lots and related controls.

Homeowners' preference for low-density zoning in the remainder of their community is not irrational. Suburban homeowners believe that such zoning will maximize the value of their homes. Open-space, low-density zoning adds to existing home values in many ways. Open space may be a substitute for parks and viewscapes. Low density may keep congestion down, at least within one's own community. Larger lots may price out supposedly undesirable residents and promote own-lot privacy. Less development means fewer substitutes for existing housing and thus the possibility of larger capital gains when the home is sold. There isn't any way to slice off the motives you do not like without slicing off the ones that you do (William T. Bogart 1993). Few public officials are so stupid as to say that they do not really care about preserving farmland but rather just want to keep out the denizens of public housing.

In my judgment, NIMBYism and the public officials who respond to it cause excessively high home prices, induce lower-than-optimal development patterns, and cause metropolitan areas to be too spread out (Fischel 1990). Here is the scenario: Developers frustrated by the regulations of close-in (to central cities), partially developed suburbs head for the more rural areas in search of buildable land. Rural governments are more friendly to developers because a larger proportion of their voters own developable land and because many residents work in the jurisdiction and stand to gain from development (Alan Hahn 1970; Sherrill Spies et al. 1998).

As a result of pushing development prematurely to rural areas, housing that should have been placed closer to existing highways and other metropolitan infrastructure is removed to land-extensive subdivisions farther away. The exurban communities in turn adopt zoning similar to that of suburbs (Thomas Rudel 1989, p. 63), which drives development still farther afield. A national study of metropolitan growth in the 1980s by Rolf Pendall (1999) is largely consistent with this scenario: Counties whose municipalities adopted large-lot zoning and growth moratoria did experience lower-density development patterns.

10.2 Sprawl Is Not Caused by Speculation or Subsidies

There are other candidates for causes of low-density sprawl. I have dealt with them extensively in my review of the issue for the National Research Council (Fischel 1999), so I will mention only the two most common charges. They are that land speculators cause leapfrog development patterns by not building adjacent to existing development and that the federal government's homeowner subsidies induce excessive suburbanization. The first is just wrong, and the second is small compared to land-use regulation.

Land speculators are said to hold land off the market from willing developers, thus sending them farther away and keeping land idle. This is actually a good thing for them to do if in a few years another developer comes along and puts in higher-density development (David Mills 1981; Richard Peiser 1989). If the landowner had sold too soon, the initial development would have been lower density, and it is nearly impossible to raze the old, low-density housing and put in higher-density units. Land speculators thus assist in preventing urban sprawl in the long run. They do this because waiting for the higher density development is profitable.

Now, it could be that speculators guess wrong about later development's density, and they end up losing money and causing unnecessary sprawl. I am sure that this is not the cause of sprawl. If it were, the undeveloped tracts that have been skipped over would be at least as valuable when they were sold as comparable tracts next to them. Even foolish speculators eventually sell their properties to the highest bidder. But the nearly universal observation of these tracts is that they have a much lower value than their already developed neighbors, adjusting for the infrastructure and buildings on the nearby tracts (Brownstone and DeVany 1991; James White 1988). These lower values are the result of land-use regulations that prevent their more intensive use.

The federal government's treatment of owner-occupied housing for tax purposes does promote suburbanization. People become owner-occupants more often than they would if the income and capital gains from home ownership were taxed at the same rate as other forms of personal investment. The magnitude of this effect for the national homeownership rate is large, but its effect on sprawl is not.

The homeownership advantage can be had for high-density units (for example, condominiums and row houses) as well as for homes on three-acre lots. Sprawl is caused by using an excessive amount of *land* for housing. Nearly every study shows that extra acres of land on a multiacre lot add very little to the value of the home (David Chicoine 1980; White 1988). It is common knowledge among suburban realtors that one-acre lots that were subdivided before three-acre minimum lot size zoning took effect (and thus are still legal lots) sell for almost the same price as three-acre lots. Thus the tax advantage of owning excessive acreage is correspondingly small. The reason that people live on multiacre lots in the suburbs is not because of the tax advantages, but because multiacre lots are imposed upon developers by local land-use regulations.

There is one sense, however, in which the homeownership subsidy does create sprawl. Homeowners are more likely to oppose development because of the nature of their asset. They must live in it, so there are personal stakes to be reckoned, and they cannot insure it against devaluation from neighborhood effects. A nation of homeowners is likely to be a nation of NIMBYs, and their anxieties are likely to be manifest in zoning laws.

10.3 The Metropolitan Alternative: My Year in Seattle

I spent the academic year 1998–1999 in Seattle at the University of Washington's Graduate School of Public Affairs. I chose Seattle for my sabbatical in part because it is on the frontier of metropolitan growth-management issues. Washington State had, in 1990, adopted a comprehensive governance reform called the Growth Management Act. It established urban growth boundaries and a regional governance system to override local parochialism. Its goal was to promote high-density housing, which in turn would make regional mass transit—buses and an ambitious new fixed-rail transit system—economical. I had expected to get information about the act's operation through informal and serendipitous contacts as a result of being there. After I arrived, however, I discovered something that channeled my interest into a more systematic inquiry.

Between 1990 and 1999, ten new cities incorporated in King County, Washington, of which Seattle is the largest and oldest city. Ten cities in ten years is remarkable. From 1969 to 1989, only two new cities in the entire state of Washington were incorporated. My feelings about King County's wave of incorporations might be similar to those of a geologist who traveled to the Aleutians to study volcanic islands only to discover that new ones had been added to the last map she'd seen.

Actually, my surprise might have been greater than the geologist's. Fragmentation of local government is regarded as a major evil among metropolitanists (Myron Orfield 1997; David Rusk 1993). Seattle is part of one of the most politically progressive metropolitan areas in the country. (A mark of its progressiveness is that King County, which is 5 percent African-American, has decided that its name should honor Martin Luther King, Jr., not the now obscure vice president for whom it was originally named.) Yet its suburbs are actively fragmenting into the smaller units of government that are decried by professional planners and many social scientists.

The ten new cities are not trivial in size, either, as the map (Figure 3) indicates. Their aggregate population in 1999 was over a quarter of a million. More interesting is that this fragmentation was occasioned by the Washington State Growth Management Act, passed in 1990. (It is actually two laws, passed in 1990 and 1991. For accessible details and sources, see Jared Black [1998].)

After I got to the University of Washington in September 1998, I volunteered to teach in spring 1999 a seminar for graduate students in public affairs and in planning called "The Political Economy of Municipal Incorporations." I ultimately had a dozen students to help me investigate the new municipalities and the metropolitan consequences of their formation. All of the students interviewed local officials and, for the most part, at least some citizens who were involved in the incorporation effort. I visited and explored each of the ten cities, and I systematically read newspaper accounts of all of their incorporations from the online archives of both Seattle newspapers, the *Times* and the *Post-Intelligencer*. I also invited four local officials to address the class about the

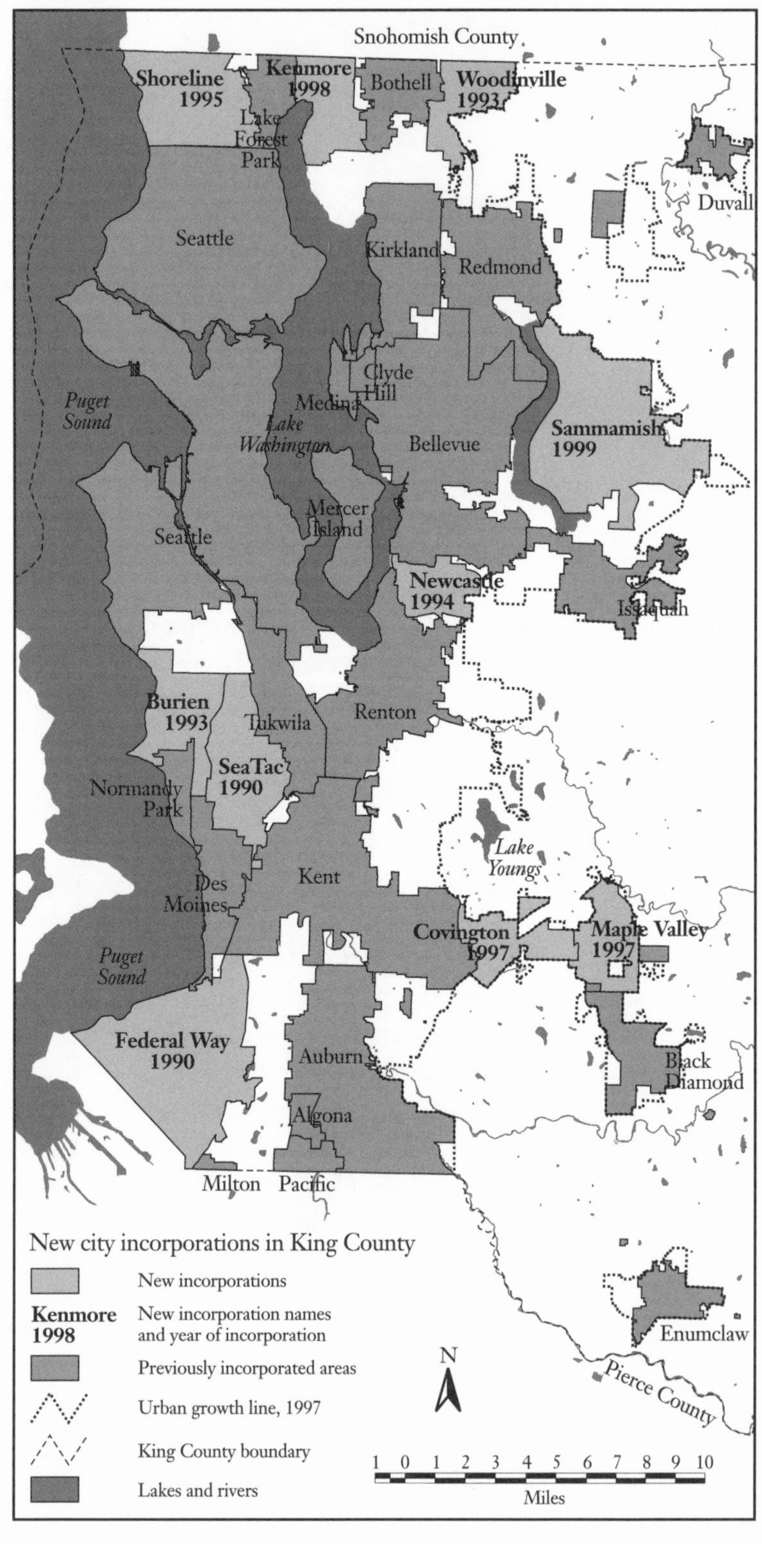
Snohomish County
Shoreline
1995
Kenmore
1998
Bothell
Woodinville
1993
Lake
Forest
Park
Duvall
Seattle
Kirkland
Redmond
Clyde
Hill
Medina
Puget
Sound
Lake
Washington
Bellevue
Sammamish
1999
Mercer
Island
Seattle
Newcastle
1994
Issaquah
Burien
1993
Tukwila
Renton
SeaTac
1990
Normandy
Park
Lake
Youngs
Des
Moines
Kent
Covington
1997
Maple Valley
1997
Puget
Sound
Federal Way
1990
Auburn
Black
Diamond
Algona
Milton
Pacific
New city incorporations in King County
New incorporations
Kenmore
1998
New incorporation names
and year of incorporation
Previously incorporated areas
Urban growth line, 1997
King County boundary
Lakes and rivers
N
1 0 1 2 3 4 5 6 7 8 9 10
Miles
Enumclaw
Pierce County

issue of new incorporations, and I kept careful notes on their talks. These officials were:

Mary McCumber, executive director of the Puget Sound Regional Council, a four-county governmental organization created to respond to the Growth Management Act;
Greg Nickels, a long-time King County council member (one of thirteen) whose district includes two of the new cities;
Anne Pflug, a local-government consultant who has served as assistant city manager for two of the new cities and who teaches a local-government management course at the Evans School; and
Paul Tanaka, King County's deputy executive, its highest nonelective position.

10.4 Fiscal Background and Incorporation Procedures

King County, on the eastern shore of Puget Sound, is the state's most populous county. In 1990, its population of 1.5 million was divided about equally among the city of Seattle, the twenty-eight incorporated suburban cities, and unincorporated portions of King County. Most residents of the unincorporated part of the county were provided with urban public services (police, parks, and zoning) by King County and its now-defunct hybrid, Metro King County, as well as by a patchwork of special districts that provided water, sewer, and fire protection. ("Metro" was an urban service area that was folded into the county's jurisdiction because it was held in 1990 to violate the one-person, one-vote rule.) This arrangement is similar to that of many other western-state metropolitan areas.

Incorporation in Washington State is a bottom-up procedure. The state cannot declare a place to be a city without its residents' consent. A petition to have an incorporation election requires the signatures of 10 percent of the registered voters in the proposed area. A minimum population of 1,500 or, within urban areas, 3,000, is required for incorporation. Prior to the election, a body called the Boundary Review Board

Figure 3 Map of the ten new cities incorporated in King County, Washington, 1990–1999 (from King County Department of Development and Environmental Services Geographic Information System; map by Susan Olsen)

must evaluate the proposed incorporation for geographic reasonableness and financial feasibility and make a recommendation. Financial feasibility typically means that the new city can provide the same level of services as the county without increasing local taxes.

Boundary review boards are similar in function to California's Local Agency Formation Commission (LAFCO), which I described in Section 9.12. Washington's boards are organized by county, and members are appointed by the governor. The board's incorporation recommendations are advisory, though its fiscal feasibility studies are seldom ignored by the voters. Its major substantive power is the ability to add or subtract territory from the proposed city prior to the referendum on cityhood. This authority helps prevent new cities from leaving isolated islands of unincorporated area within its midst, and it discourages new cities (and, in annexation proceedings, existing cities) from grabbing high-tax-base territory while neglecting nearby and contiguous low-tax-base territory.

The fiscal base of both the county and the cities rests on a shifting tripod. It is one part property tax, one part sales tax rebated by the state to the point of sale (although there is some sharing with other jurisdictions), and one part a mixed bag of business taxes and fees largely aimed at nonresidential activity. When a new city is incorporated, it takes with it that part of the county's property tax base whose revenues were earmarked for local roads. For most cities this is a gain, even though they have to now do the road work themselves. Most cities spend less on roads than the county and are thus able to divert some of the revenues to other projects or to lower taxes. (Various statewide initiatives of the past have limited property tax rates, but local governments can override them by referenda, which are usually successful.)

The other big gain to a new city is sales tax revenues. These are not earmarked for any particular expenditure, and their loss to the county's coffers is the county's major complaint about the system. The county, however, makes up most of this loss from contracts for police and other services with the new cities. County-government employment has not suffered since the new cities have run off with some of its tax base.

The table lists the ten new cities along with three indicators of their fiscal well-being: median household income (constructed from the 1990 Census tract data); in-city jobs per resident population, which provides a rough indicator of how much the city can "export" its property, sales, and miscellaneous taxes; and taxable property value per cap-

New cities in King County since 1990, by 1990 household income

City name	Median household income, 1990	1998 jobs per capita	1998 taxable property value per capita	1998 est'd population
SeaTac	$32,300	1.17	$91,000	23,500
Burien	$36,700	.35	$65,000	28,100
Shoreline	$37,900	.28	$69,000	50,400
Woodinville	$38,300	.95	$97,000	10,100
Federal Way	$38,400	.36	$56,000	76,800
Kenmore	$43,000	.21	$74,000	17,000
Maple Valley	$43,500	.15	$61,000	12,000
Covington	$43,800	.19	$55,000	12,900
Newcastle	$57,500	.07	$68,000	8,600
Sammamish	$60,700	.09	$98,000	28,400
For comparison:				
Seattle	$29,400	.85	$96,000	540,000
King County	$36,200	.60	$85,000	1,666,000

ita. I have arranged the table by household income, lowest on top, so that the generally inverse relation between income and nonresidential property (jobs / population) can be clearly seen.

In general, the lower-income cities have proportionately more nonresidential property to tax. This is not an accident. The lower-income cities could not have incorporated without some commercial property to help pay the taxes. As a result, there is no clear relationship between taxable property value per capita and household income. It is notable that only two new cities, Woodinville and Sammamish, have property values per capita that are on a par with Seattle's, even though median household income in all of the new cities exceeds Seattle's.

10.5 Growth Management Promotes Higher Densities

The Growth Management Act of 1990 required Washington's metropolitan counties to adopt an urban growth line around their existing developed areas plus some adjacent rural area to accommodate a state forecast of population growth. Outside of the growth line, each county was required to restrict housing and commercial development to rural densities and preserve farmland and forests. Inside the line, the act sought to promote higher-density development. The idea was not to restrict overall development of the region, but to channel it to areas in which development had already begun and for which public infrastructure was readily available. This approach has been hailed as a means of preventing sprawl by keeping new development close to existing cities. The act also requires all cities within the growth line to plan for low- and moderate-income housing, so that development is not exclusively for the rich.

The state Growth Management Act was to a large extent modeled on plans adopted by King County in the 1980s, which established the first urban growth line in the state. King County was motivated, according to Mary McCumber, who was active in the movement from its birth, by a number of regional concerns about the quality of life in the area. The conversion of farmland and woodland to developments was the chief rural concern, though one prominent advocate recently admitted that exclusion of development, even if the land could not be farmed profitably, was the primary objective of farmland preservation (*Seattle Times*, October 11, 1999). Complementing that was growing traffic congestion in the urban parts of the Seattle metropolitan area. The act was thus a working example of a metropolitan governance structure that commentators see as the middle way between political consolidation and fragmentation (Richard Briffault 1996; Anthony Downs 1994, chap. 9).

Among the Seattle area's scenic assets are its extensive waterways, but they also amount to its chief drawback for traffic. Instead of building additional highways and bridges, which stir enormous neighborhood resistance, regional planners have proposed a fixed-rail transit system, in addition to extending its existing system of express buses and making improvements to existing highways. Most planners are aware (at least in private) that the fixed-rail, urban transit systems built in the United States since the 1960s have been economic failures. Few of them achieve more than half of the ridership that would be necessary to make them economically viable (Kenneth Small 1992, p. 8). The only reason that they continue to operate is that federal and state taxpayers finance subsidies, which on a per rider basis are much higher than those received by automobile or bus passengers. Even with these subsidies, they have had only the tiniest effect on urban automobile congestion (Gordon, Kumar, and Richardson 1989).

The failure of rail transit to attract riders is largely attributable to the low residential and employment densities of American metropolitan areas. To make rail transit economically viable, there must be a large number of people who live close to the stations, and a high density of jobs in a central place. American metropolitan areas have been decentralizing both homes and jobs for at least a hundred and twenty years. Seattle's planners, taking their cue from Portland, Oregon, proposed to make fixed-rail transit viable by reversing this trend. The urban growth line is seen in these influential circles as a way to herd residential development into established areas, which would then make the urban rail lines viable and reduce the demand for new highways. (This is analogous to the way in which recycling is made economically viable by requiring producers of new paper, say, to use a certain amount of recycled material.)

In order to accommodate the influx of "infill" development, local zoning laws had to be modified. Large-lot zoning and restrictions on apartment houses had to be lifted. Regional plans were drawn up, and the county established numerical goals for housing construction in existing communities. Under these rules, each community must draw up a master plan and, if necessary, revise its zoning laws to meet these goals, which are negotiated and set by the county and cities.

10.6 Hearings Boards Enforce Growth Management Goals

Enforcement of these commands is undertaken by the Growth Management Hearings Board, a three-member panel established for multicounty regions of the state. (Hearings boards are entirely separate from the county's Boundary Review Board.) This board does not directly certify municipal plans. Its role is quasijudicial. It hears complaints by interested parties—builders, housing advocates, landowners, environmentalists—that a particular city's plan does not conform to the goals of the Growth Management Act. To enforce its rulings, it can recommend that the governor impose fiscal sanctions against a city whose plan it concludes is inconsistent with the Growth Management Act's goals (RCW 36.70A.340).

The power of the hearings boards is highly unusual in American metropolitan areas. Most other regional and statewide zoning review boards, such as those in Vermont and Florida, have been of the "double-veto" type (Ellickson and Tarlock 1981, p. 926). A developer who is approved by the local government can then be vetoed by the regional or state review board. But if he is turned down by the local authorities, the regional board cannot grant him approval in the face of local opposition. Developers can go from "yes" to "no," but not from "no" to "yes." Washington's hearings boards are not of the double-veto style; they can make municipalities take some developments that their local boards have rejected.

The only metropolitan arrangement of which I am aware that can regularly override a wide range of local zoning and planning decisions, particularly density of development, is in Portland, Oregon (Gerrit Knaap 1985). (Other Oregon cities have the same arrangement, but the action is in Portland.) Massachusetts and New Jersey have state commissions that can override local regulations that restrict low-income housing, but they do not deal with overall density. Portland's Metro arrangement actually exceeds Seattle's in authority (Carl Abbott 1997). The Portland Metro board has the power to override local zoning laws if it finds that they do not meet the goals of the metropolitan land-use authority. Unlike Washington's hearings boards, which review plans only after they have been established, and which must presume that those plans are valid unless proven otherwise, Oregon municipalities must get their plans approved before they go into effect. If a community zones for single-family lots where the board deems apartments more appropriate, Portland's board can order the change.

The Oregon boards' powers are unprecedented in the United States, and most Washington growth management advocates are envious. In fact the Washington boards are in retreat from the Oregon model. State laws adopted in 1997 curtailed the power of Washington's hearings boards (Jared Black 1998, p. 575). Under their original powers, boards could reverse a community's decision if a "preponderance of evidence" warranted that it was inconsistent with the Growth Management Act. Under the revised law, the hearings boards must uphold local decisions unless they are "clearly erroneous," a standard that favors the local governments against both pro- and antidevelopment challengers.

10.7 Unincorporated Areas Were to Be Annexed

Washington's decision to establish urban growth boundaries was accompanied by a decision to get the counties, at least those in the Puget Sound region, out of the business of providing urban services. The Growth Management Act envisions that areas within the urban growth line will eventually be within incorporated cities. The major role of the counties will be to provide regional governance. Counties would continue to provide roads, planning, police, and parks in the rural areas outside the growth line. The growth line is intended to expand periodically in response to population projections, but only in areas adjacent to existing municipalities, which are then expected to annex the territory under guidelines established by the act and by the boundary review boards.

Because the advocates of the Growth Management Act supposed that almost all of the unincorporated areas within the urban growth boundary would be annexed by *existing* cities (Washington State Growth Strategies Commission 1990, p. 39), King County carved all of its unincorporated urban area into "potential annexation areas" that would eventually be taken by existing cities. Annexation in Washington and in most other states must be mutual. Both the existing city and either a majority of the annexation area's residents or owners of 60 percent of the property value in the area must agree.

In order to discourage urban development outside of the urban growth boundary, legislation adopted as part of the Growth Management Act made it nearly impossible to establish new municipalities in rural areas. The legislation did not alter the basic municipal incorporation laws of the state. But city founding is not a trivial exercise, since an entirely new governance structure must be established. Before the Growth Management Act, most incorporation votes failed in Washington. It was clear that the authors and promoters of the act both expected and preferred that all unincorporated areas would have been annexed by existing cities. Yet at least half of the population that was in the unincorporated urban area of King County is now within a new city.

10.8 Land Use Was Incorporation's Common Denominator

Despite the absence of any encouragement (at least initially) on the part of regional and county officials, ten new cities formed in King County during the 1990s. The main reasons for their formation were, in order of importance, residents' desire to (1) control land-use decisions, (2) direct police services to local concerns, and (3) protect the school district.

Control over land use was paramount because the Growth Management Act had decreed that land use had to change within the affected communities. I found the frankest expression of this on the website "Citizens for Incorporation of Kenmore," representing residents of a suburb of about 17,000 just north of Seattle. Under the rubric "What's in it for all of us" is a lengthy discussion of advantages that incorporation would bring. Its first argument is worth repeating verbatim, though the italics are mine:

> *Control over Growth Management Planning*
>
> Kenmore is one of the fastest growing areas of King County. The King County Council has designated Kenmore as an Urban Growth Area and allocated us the highest densities of anywhere in unincorporated King County (up to 45 units per acre). *As a city, we can negotiate growth and density targets*, allowing us to better manage transportation, housing, and infrastructure needs. *Although we will still have to accept some growth, we can better control how, when and where it goes and what it looks like.* (www.accessone.com/~traci/kenmore/ The website became inactive in November 1999; for a time the address automatically referred one to Kenmore's official website.)

Every newspaper article about incorporations in other cities also mentioned that control of development was a major, if not the major, factor in the drive to become a city. Other factors, such as control over police and, sometimes, congruence with a school district, were also mentioned for several cities, but land use was universal.

10.9 King County's Size Favored Development Interests

The procedural issue that propelled incorporations was the desire to establish a government that was more responsive to local concerns. This manifested itself in the term "local control." Because that term is so often invoked favorably by localities and so often derided by metropolitan reformers and not a few academics, it is worth looking more carefully at the situation in which the issue arose.

Residents of the unincorporated areas had always had King County as their primary local government. Although special districts for water, sewer, and fire services are technically "governments," almost no one expressed opinions about their quality. Nor was there much controversy about the competence or standards of King County public officials in delivering local services. The strongest evidence for this is that after incorporation, nine of the ten new cities have contracted with King County to provide police services along the lines of California's Lakewood Plan. The county police simply put on local insignia and drive cars marked "[new city] Police." The new cities select a chief from a panel of senior officers on the county police force. In other words, the new cities are essentially "Lakewood Plan" cities. (I found that King County officials were thoroughly familiar with the Lakewood Plan, but they were reluctant to mention it, perhaps because Seattle residents seem to regard anything from Los Angeles as the devil's handiwork.)

For the residents of unincorporated areas, the drawback of being governed by King County was its remoteness. This had both a physical and political aspect. King County offices were in downtown Seattle, which made a trip for a permit into an all-day affair for many people in the unincorporated territory.

More important was the sense of political remoteness. King County is governed by a council of thirteen members who are elected by geographic districts, and by a county executive who is elected at large. The districts are set up to be contiguous and equal in size, so that each councilmember is elected from a district that has about 120,000 people. Of the cities, only Seattle has a population larger than 120,000. Thus nearly all of the suburban areas are represented by a councilmember whose district encompasses more than their city or what was to become their city if they became incorporated or annexed. In short, the geographies of county councilmembers and subcounty local governments—existing or potential—were not closely aligned.

As a result of both the council districts' size and their lack of alignment with other governments, both prospective and incumbent councilmembers have a difficult time getting local citizens interested in county elections. There is what economists characterize as a median voter somewhere in the district, but candidates have found it hard to communicate with her. County Council candidates thus have to rely heavily on advertising for their campaigns, and this requires fundraising.

The most eager providers of funds are developers and their allies.

This seems to have something to do with why the county council is a good deal more prodevelopment than any other local government except perhaps Seattle itself. In other words, the median-voter model applies much less accurately to the King County Council. Given that incorporation advocates' most common objection to King County governance was its tendency to rezone to allow higher-density zoning, it seems clear that the motivation for incorporation was, in its most general terms, to reassert the primacy of the median voter. That's what local control means.

The reader might recall that while King County was the current service provider for unincorporated areas, the Growth Management Act contemplated that it would not be the provider for long. The alternative to incorporation was thus not to remain unincorporated, but to be annexed by a preexisting municipality. Sooner or later citizens of Newcastle, say, would become part of the long-established cities of Renton or Bellevue. They could join the self-governing polity of these places, all of which were considerably smaller in population, of course, than King County. And many residents of unincorporated areas regarded that outcome as just fine. At least as much territory and population from the formerly unincorporated areas have been annexed to existing cities (recall that annexation must be mutual) as have been incorporated in new cities.

Thus I need to tell a more nuanced story than one in which people choose a smaller unit over gigantic King County. The next four sections describe in chronological order the formation of the ten cities that formed during the 1990s, and particularly why they rejected annexation to nearby cities. In the telling, it will become clear that the size and shape of the new cities is not some random event, but reflects a community of interest that was determined by long-standing historical and institutional factors. The median-voter story will still stand up, but it requires a deeper probe into the desire for "local control" than just rejection of governance by King County.

10.10 Sex and Zoning: Federal Way and SeaTac in 1990

The two pioneers of the King County Ten have the strangest names. The old name for what is now Highway 99 was "the Federal Way," because it was the first highway in the area built with federal funds. When a school district was established in the suburbanizing area just north of Tacoma in the 1940s, it took the name of the highway. The new municipality then took the name of the school district that it is almost coterminous with.

The city of SeaTac took its name from Seattle-Tacoma International Airport, which it nearly surrounds. (The airport is known as Sea-Tac, the hyphen now distinguishing it from the city.) The area near the airport has a large commercial tax base because of hotels and airport-support facilities. These are eminently taxable both for their property values and for the fraction of the state sales tax that is rebated to point-of-sale municipalities.

SeaTac's ostensible reason for incorporation was prostitution. The strip of Highway 99 that runs through SeaTac had become a notorious stroll for prostitutes, and county police were said to be insufficiently vigorous in combating this and other quality-of-life crimes. Once incorporated, SeaTac beefed up its police force, which consisted now of county police in SeaTac uniforms, and drove the streetwalkers off of Highway 99. SeaTac also used its newly acquired control over zoning to close down massage parlors and restrict the spread of other illicit businesses.

A more cynical view of SeaTac's incorporation is that it wanted to grab a large chunk of tax base from the county and direct it to its own purposes. There is undoubtedly some truth in this, but that truth is not so cynical. SeaTac has, by a considerable margin, the lowest household income of any of the ten new cities. It simply could not have afforded to incorporate without a substantial nonresidential tax base. It uses much of its plentiful tax revenues for social services needed by its own lower-income population and by transients.

All observers agree that Federal Way incorporated in 1990 because it wanted to stop the county from approving apartments and commercial development in areas that had previously been exclusively single-family homes. This has created a tension that persists to the present between local preferences and the Growth Management Act's goals of higher-density development and affordable housing within the urban growth line.

County officials have pointed out that Federal Way has fallen far off the pace needed to achieve the housing goals that were set by the county for each municipality within the urban growth line. Developers complain that the city has not been sufficiently accommodating since it incorporated and immediately took over zoning and planning from the formerly compliant county. But they have not been able to make any of these charges stick at the Growth Management Hearings Board.

Federal Way offers a forecast of how well the Growth Management Act will function in its affirmative side. It is pretty clear that an urban growth line can retard development on the rural side of its boundaries. But enforcing an affirmative duty inside the line is much harder. It is especially so when the duty devolves to a multitude of parties, including local-government officials who are beholden to watchful voters, whose chief asset is their already existing home.

This is not to say that any of the local governments simply stonewall the county's quotas. I noticed a curious shift in tone after cities incorporated. Preincorporation rhetoric was dominated by criticisms of the excesses of development and how the new city would get a handle on it. The tone of the antidevelopment statement by Citizens for Incorporation of Kenmore can be easily inferred from many preincorporation comments in newspaper articles about any of the new cities. After incorporation, however, local officials in the same cities were circumspect in their statements. None would admit outright to my student investigators that they thought the county's development goals were unreasonable or that they did not intend to comply with affordable housing goals. The student who analyzed Federal Way's zoning changes, however, came to the unmistakable conclusion that the new city made higher-density, infill development more difficult to accomplish.

10.11 Runway and Jail: Burien and Woodinville in 1993

Like SeaTac, Burien abuts the region's major airport. Unlike SeaTac, Burien gets little in return from its noisy neighbor. Relatively little hotel and other airport-related commercial development has located in Burien. Instead, Sea-Tac Airport, particularly its two runway expansions in its direction, is blamed for blighting much of the city's housing stock and for occasioning the construction of limited-access highways that sliced up the community in the 1960s and 1970s. As in Federal Way, the last straw was a plan by King County to develop additional high-density housing in Burien. Four previous incorporation attempts had failed, but the success of Federal Way and SeaTac galvanized activists for another try, and they succeeded in 1993.

Burien has a mix of high- and low-income residents, the rich living on the west by the shores of Puget Sound and the poor on the east close to the airport. It has only a modest nonresidential tax base, and it has joined with several other communities in a costly legal battle to halt construction of a third runway for Sea-Tac Airport. The student who investigated Burien concluded that the losing battle with the airport has sapped most of the community's fiscal and volunteer strength, and it has had to delay other projects, including rewriting its master plan, as a result. Students in my seminar agreed that Burien does seem like a sad case, but its difficulties stem from the fate of having a major airport nearby.

Residents of Woodinville had, like Burien, rejected incorporation efforts four times before 1993. The galvanizing factor that overcame obstacles was a proposal to place a new jail in the area. In this case, the incorporation successfully fought the jail.

Since its incorporation, Woodinville has built up its tax base by being highly accommodating of light industry and commercial development. In this respect it is an anomaly among the new cities. Its residents are relatively high-income, yet Woodinville is hospitable to nonresidential development. This is perhaps because the city's relatively undeveloped terrain allows for a convenient separation of residential areas along the ridges from the commercial development along the Sammamish River valley. As in the other new cities, then, Woodinville was formed to deal with land-use issues, although its goals were less antigrowth than those of any of the others except perhaps SeaTac.

10.12 Shoreline and School-District Protection

The area north of Seattle and short of the Snohomish County line is indistinguishable from the northern area of Seattle itself. The Shoreline school district was established there after World War II. In the early 1960s, the southern portion of the district, which was unincorporated territory, voted to annex itself to Seattle. The city thereby added about five square miles to its municipal territory. Residents of the annexed area were said to have been assured that they would remain in the Shoreline school district, not in Seattle's. Soon after annexation, however, the Seattle school district's lines were moved north to correspond with the city's new boundary.

School-district lines are controlled by a state board, not the city, but no one takes seriously the idea that Seattle officials had no influence on the school-district annexation. Thus when a Seattle City Council member brought up the possibility of annexing the rest of Shoreline in 1988, the residents "just went ballistic," according to a news story, and an incorporation drive was soon in place. That incorporation took until 1995 to accomplish may reflect the fact that, aside from the school district, there is not much that unites the community. It has no obvious center or geographic markers to set it off from its neighbors, nor does it have an especially distinct history, like that of Woodinville, Maple Valley, or Newcastle, that would make for a strong community identity.

School-district boundaries were established long before most municipalities were incorporated, and district boundaries are adjusted by a state board that is at least nominally independent of local politics. Nonetheless, it is clear that school-district boundaries matter a great deal in community formation, and not just in Shoreline. As I mentioned, Federal Way took both its name and most of its territory from the preexisting school district. A school-district boundary forms the dividing line between the new cities of Maple Valley and Covington, and district boundaries form long segments of the borders of SeaTac, Burien, and Kenmore, as well as those of long-established cities. The unofficial Kenmore-incorporation website noted, "Kenmore city boundaries have been selected to ensure that all residents would remain within the Northshore School District." Of the ten new cities, only Newcastle and Sammamish are divided between two school districts.

District boundaries matter for the municipalities for several reasons. One is that the municipality itself can channel some resources into the schools. SeaTac, for example, funds a special program for professional travel education in the high school located within its boundaries. Seattle assists its school district with after-school activities and other enrichment programs. In smaller cities, schools also provide meeting and recreation facilities for local organizations and sometimes for the municipality itself.

It seems likely, too, that a district that corresponds with a municipality would find it easier to pass school budgets and undertake other decisions. Washington allows local districts to have annual plebiscites to add to the basic grant given by the state, though these special levies are subject to a ceiling so as not to create too much inequality in spending and run afoul of the state courts. Rallying voters for an override is probably easier if most of the voters also live within the same municipality. And to the extent that municipal land-use decisions affect schools, it is easier to coordinate them if the district and the municipality are coterminous. Exactions from developers can only be extracted by municipal planning authorities, and these exactions are often earmarked for local schools.

The overlap of district and municipal boundaries is also likely to assist in incorporation. For most residents, their children's schools are where they get to know people who are not their immediate neighbors. In petition drives for annexation or incorporation, it is undoubtedly easier to get the cooperation of people you already know than of strangers. My students who identified incorporation activists in Shoreline found that many of them had also been involved in local school affairs. School boards are where many political leaders get their first experience with elective office.

10.13 Keeping Local Identity and Community Character

The cities of Newcastle (incorporated 1994), Maple Valley (1997), Covington (1997), Kenmore (1998), and Sammamish (1999) were not incorporated in response to a specific alarming event, such as a proposed jail (as in Woodinville) or a threat to the school district (as in Shoreline). Incorporation had become a more attractive alternative to annexation as it became apparent that SeaTac and Federal Way, which had embarked on independence in 1990, did not fall into a fiscal abyss. In all of the remaining five cities, the public debate centered on the merits of local control, particularly of land use, and whether to annex to an adjacent community or to incorporate.

The most contentious of these incorporations was Newcastle. The city of Bellevue, the second largest (after Seattle) in the county, had wanted to annex much of the territory. Renton, the industrial city to the south of Newcastle, sought to annex the rest. The fact that the school district boundaries of the two larger cities ran through the middle of Newcastle made the annexations, which were supported by King County, an easy call.

Newcastle residents managed to fight off both suitors. As an upscale residential community, it did not want to share an address with industrial Renton. Bellevue, as the seat of the affluent "East Side" (of Lake Washington) was in that respect a more congenial match. But Newcastle residents were wary because Bellevue, with over 100,000 people, had nearly ten times its population. They did not want to go from having almost no voice in a large county to having only a tiny voice in a large city. (Bellevue has since responded to the latter concern by allowing some newly annexed areas to retain veto power over city zoning changes that affect their district, an arrangement that required an amendment in the state's zoning enabling acts.)

Maple Valley and Covington formed in 1997. Maple Valley's incorporation was motivated by a long-time identity as a rural market town, even though it now has a more suburban look. King County's annexation proposals would have divided Maple Valley between Kent and Black Diamond, and this threat plus a desire to control its own land use made incorporation an easy sell within the community. Its simultaneously formed neighbor, Covington, was in a different school district than Maple Valley, which seems to be the only reason the two areas did not join to form a single city.

Covington incorporated so as not to be annexed by its large neighbor, Kent, even though the communities are in the same school district. Land use was the definitive issue. Although it is nominally a suburban city, more than two-thirds of Kent's households live in rental units. Covington has no apartments whatsoever, and all observers agree that its desire to maintain its single-family character was its reason for incorporation. King County planners expect Covington to become a city of some 40,000 people by 2010, but in 1999, accommodating that infill development did not seem to be high on the agenda of many of Covington's 13,000 residents.

Kenmore incorporated in 1998 for reasons similar to those of Maple Valley. Its options as a small community were annexation by one or more of its neighbors, and its residents wanted to preserve its identity and small size. Anxiety about the higher densities demanded by the Growth Management Act were mentioned prominently in press accounts as well as on the unofficial web site that promoted Kenmore's incorporation, which I quoted in Section 10.8.

Sammamish voted to incorporate while I was in Seattle. The county had been issuing many building permits in the semirural area on the

"Plateau" east of Lake Sammamish, so it was included within the urban growth boundary. Its annexation options were with Issaquah to its south and Redmond, home of Microsoft, to its north. Roads in the area have become congested as development proceeded rapidly. Sammamish's motives were transparent and widely reported: It wanted to stop growth. Like Newcastle, Sammamish has little commercial tax base but a large stock of high-value homes, so the Boundary Review Board gave its incorporation its fiscal seal of approval. Local developers sponsored a last-minute (and amazingly inept) campaign to stop incorporation, but it was overwhelmed by popular sentiment.

10.14 Local Voters Chose the Median-Voter Model

Some generalizations about the nature of local government and the American attachment to a bottom-up "local control," so often derided by academics, can be inferred from the foregoing look at municipal incorporation. The sizes and shapes of the new cities were not arbitrary. They were shaped in part by geography, history, and the decisions of their neighbors. But they are also shaped in large part by the decisions of residents—mostly homeowners—to join or reject a particular community.

Most of the King County Ten had previously attempted to incorporate. For example, Sammamish had attempted in 1992 to form a city around a larger area than it ultimately wound up with. The largest source of opposition was a neighborhood on the southern side of the proposed city that had ties to the existing city of Issaquah. In the next Sammamish vote, the petitioners proposed a city that excluded the dissenters, and the new city's incorporation easily passed. Federal Way had three votes between 1971 and 1985 that failed before its incorporation succeeded in 1990. Kenmore's incorporation efforts had failed five times since 1950. Several proposed cities within the urban growth line have likewise rejected incorporation since 1990. No one should suppose that voters treat a major political change lightly.

Voters' circumspection is also evident in annexation debates. One of my students examined annexations by Lake Forest Park, which had formed in the 1960s. As the Growth Management Act was put in place in the 1990s and Shoreline had formed to its west, Lake Forest Park began to annex unincorporated territory, and it eventually tripled its area and population. This led to some battles with the new city of Shoreline over residential and commercial territory that both coveted. As my student's account made clear, people in the contested territories had definite ideas about which city they wished to be annexed to, though on paper the two cities do not look much different. As odd as the shapes of the communities may seem on paper (and some of those shapes will change as the new cities annex more territory), they are the result of deliberate, on-the-ground decisions, not the whims of faraway politicians and bureaucrats.

The issue of city size was also present in nearly all of the incorporation debates. Even where there was a neighboring city whose policies and makeup seemed congenial, voters often chose the potentially costly route of forming their own city. The term "local control" in this context meant an ability for the majority of voters to understand and have access to local government. They wanted, in other words, a median-voter model.

This means more than just a statistical probability of affecting an election. It means control of an area by more-or-less like-minded people with whom one has the possibility of interacting. In a small city, almost every long-time resident knows someone who knows the mayor or another elected official. Paul Tanaka, the King County deputy county executive, said that he thought the metropolitan area would be better governed by a single municipal government. (I presume he meant the one he worked for, but he did not say so specifically.) He nonetheless conceded that he would probably have voted for incorporation, too, if he lived in faraway Maple Valley. Manageable size and physical proximity to their government are important to people, even in (or is it especially in?) the region that is home to Microsoft, Adobe, and other purveyors of the technology of placelessness.

10.15 New Cities Seem Successful and Diverse

I was not able to obtain much information about the satisfaction of residents with their new city governments. The difficulty with both my students' papers and news reports is that they focus on activists and local officials. In most of the new cities, those who worked for incorporation often ended up on the new city council or some other local government position. Nonetheless, there were people who voted against incorporation, and one would expect at least some news from them if it had worked out badly. The silence is deafening. I do not mean to say that the new cities lack controversy or invariably had smooth sailing. Shoreline in particular had a problematic start-up in part because of a controversial city manager.

What I mean is more fundamental. I could not find a single source (interview or article) in which a resident of a new city lamented the incorporation decision or wished that a neighboring city had annexed its territory. The least successful of the new cities, Burien, has quixotically fought the Sea-Tac airport expansion, but it shares its obsession with the long-established cities of Normandy Park and Des Moines. Had Burien's residents remained part of King County, it seems unlikely that they would have had a governmental channel to voice their concerns about the airport, since King County as a whole is eager to promote the airport expansion.

Perhaps there is a "Tiebout bias" in my rosy assessment, meaning that those who did not like the new city government have left for places more to their liking and are not around to complain. But even if this were true, it would point to the advantages of living in an area in which there are other places to go.

The evidence that my students did assemble indicates that almost all of the new cities modified some aspect of services that were formerly undertaken by the county. It was not just planning and zoning, though that was the common denominator. Although nine of the ten new cities contract for police services with the county (Federal Way does not), several of them hired more police than the county had previously assigned. All of them, not just SeaTac, have made their police forces more attentive to local affairs. Special services such as helicopters and SWAT teams are provided by contract with the county, but every city proudly marks its police vehicles and insignia with its own name, even though the fine print reveals that the cars are driven by county officers.

Anne Pflug, the local government consultant who spoke to my class, mentioned another important change in cities after incorporation. Most of the new cities have rewritten or begun to rewrite their planning and zoning documents that they inherited from the county. This was an opportunity for the new city to do what they told their citizens they would do, which was to lower densities, albeit in ways subtle enough to avoid legal challenge. Ms. Pflug, however, noted that most of the new plans also envisioned development of a town center, in which public buildings, offices, and commercial development would become the focus of the new city. I mention this to dissuade the reader from supposing that the new communities formed solely to prevent development. Channeling development in ways that created a community focus and perhaps reduced residents' commuting and shopping-trip distances was an important goal.

It is also worth mentioning that all close observers of the new cities regard them as remarkably diverse, both in the sense of being different from one another and, to a lesser extent, having a diversity of housing and income levels within their borders. Ms. Pflug, the consultant, argues that there is as much diversity among them as there is within the city of Seattle. Paul Tanaka, the deputy county executive, confirmed the intercommunity differences despairingly, since it made his job of reaching regional agreements more difficult.

My own impressions from visiting the new cities (and others) indicate that the image of a homogeneous, bland suburban landscape can only be maintained by people with the classic *New Yorker*–cover vision of the country, applied in this case to the suburbs. (You know, the Steinberg drawing that pictures the nation west of Manhattan as a few scattered icons of American folklore.) Kenmore harbors the region's largest seaplane base. Woodinville is home to the region's largest commercial greenhouse, Molbak's. Newcastle's new, privately developed (but open to the public) golf course sits atop a former coal-mine spoil (hence the city's name) and has one of the finest views in the region. Maple Valley has a rural festival that began in 1950. The people who live in these communities have civic preferences at least as refined as those of the citizens of central cities. The King County Ten demonstrate that the desire for local self-governance is as vital now as it ever has been in American history.

10.16 New Cities Retard Infill Development

There is a downside to incorporations, though. The more serious metropolitan problem created by the new cities is housing cost. Their ability to retard infill development raises housing prices. Now, I must admit that this was not an issue that local officials in the Seattle area regarded as having anything to do with the incorporations. Housing prices in the region were rising rapidly, but this was attributed by most observers to shifting demand, not supply constraints. After all, housing construction is proceeding rapidly. Only Federal Way has been criticized (so far) for lagging behind schedule in achieving the infill housing goals set by the Growth Management Act.

Yet Federal Way represents the future scenario of many of the new cities, as well as areas that annex themselves to existing cities. It is useful to compare Federal Way, incorporated in 1990, with Sammamish, which incorporated in 1999. Sammamish immediately issued a moratorium on building permits. This had no immediate effects on the rate of construction, since King County had issued permits for thousands of units before incorporation, and these permits are legally vested and are not subject to the moratorium. Eventually, however, the moratorium will be a binding constraint, and anticipation of that drives up prices now.

The reason for developers' permit rush in Sammamish is easy to see. Developers read the newspapers, too, and they anticipated that the new city would soon be formed and that its major objective was to slow development. Any owner of land in the soon-to-be city of Sammamish who wanted to develop it in the near future would anticipate that getting a permit from the county would be a good idea. There is some cost to premature permitting, since subdivisions must be platted and approved, but the cost of waiting until the demand ripens in, say, five years might be that permits would then be much more difficult to obtain.

Not all cities are as antidevelopment as Sammamish and Federal Way, and even if they were, there is still plenty of land within the urban growth line that is zoned by the ever-prodevelopment county. Most of this land, however, is less attractive for homeowners, is already developed, or is likely to be annexed to an adjacent city soon. There are some prodevelopment cities besides Seattle. My impression is that Renton, Kent, and Auburn are more eager for growth than other cities. But there appear to be no cities as friendly to developers as King County. As more of the territory inside of the urban growth line is annexed and incorporated, the current residents will have more say in land use than the developers.

10.17 Hearings Boards Do Little to Offset Local NIMBYs

If I am right that the new cities in King County were born to fight density, perhaps their efforts are offset by the Puget Sound Growth Management Hearings Board. The board has the power to undo local plans that do not conform with the Growth Management Act. There has been no systematic effort to evaluate the extent to which the enforcement side of the Growth Management Act has offset local efforts to retard development within the urban growth line, where it is supposed to occur. Federal Way's failure to meet its quotas has caused county officials to seek state legislation that would allow it to penalize jurisdictions that did not comply. (*Seattle Times*, August 8, 1999. The effort has so far been unsuccessful.) This suggests that the Growth Management Hearings Boards are not especially effective.

The hearings boards are not, however, entirely toothless, as is illustrated by a controversy that was resolved in 1999, when I was in Seattle. Two developers in the city of Woodway, an affluent, one-square-mile city just north of Shoreline (and thus in Snohomish County), had purchased a sixty-one-acre wooded tract and proposed building eighty-six homes. The eighty-six homes were allowed as of right when they bought the land, but Woodway quickly changed the zoning and put other regulatory barriers in the developers' path. After negotiations failed, the developers brought a complaint to the hearings board. Woodway is well within the urban growth line, and its zoned densities were already lower than the Growth Management Act had contemplated for cities in its situation.

The hearings board ruled in favor of the developers. It held that the appropriate density would allow 240 homes to be built, almost triple the original entitlement. After the ruling, Woodway negotiated with the developers to purchase some of their land so that no more than one hundred homes would be built. The city has an option to buy and preserve lots on which ten of the one hundred units could be constructed, so it is not clear how many will ultimately be built.

So this is a success. The hearings board surely helped the developers avoid a massive downzoning. But what they finally agreed to was only a few more units than they were originally entitled to when they bought the land. The density of those units is far below what the Growth Management Act contemplates as needed to make rail transit feasible. (No one expects rail transit in Woodway itself, but higher densities within the growth line are necessary for the region's bus and rail plans to succeed.) Indeed, all reports were that the developer would have been satisfied with the original zoning that allowed eighty-six units. It simply is not clear from this that the hearings boards are capable of overcoming the large-lot zoning that nearly all the suburbs already have in place.

It may seem unfair to criticize the hearings board process on the basis of a single event. This was, however, the only prodevelopment, infill-oriented decision that the Puget Sound Hearings Board had ever issued. The *Seattle Times* later referred to it as the board's "first ruling on urban densities" (January 13, 1999) since the board had been established in the early 1990s. (There were numerous reports of occasions in which a hearings board struck down plans for higher-density development *outside* of the urban growth line.) It could be that the mere existence of review has forestalled downzonings by cities with less chutzpah than Woodway. But if developers are counting on the Growth Management Hearings Boards to come to their aid to promote infill, they might have to wait a long time.

10.18 High Housing Prices Retard Employment Growth

The long-run problem that an antigrowth bias creates is a mismatch between job creation and housing construction in the Seattle region. For the most part, businesses have not been affected as much as housing development by the Growth Management Act. Seattle and most older cities have plenty of land zoned for business development. The urban controversies in which growth management is invoked involved home building far more often than commercial development.

Housing prices are rising rapidly in the area. Even the units set aside for "affordable" housing are soaring in price upon resale. Most officials, however, denied that there was any connection between growth management and housing costs. They pointed out that there is much undeveloped land within the urban growth line and that housing starts were growing.

It is well established that owners of developable land within an urban growth line anticipate that they will have less competition from other lots because of new restrictions on development. Claude Gruen (1977, p. 16) found this from his detailed interviews with landowners and land brokers in the San Jose area. Owners of land within the urban growth line in the Seattle area are surely no less aware of their favored status, and the knowledge that developers must come to them first makes them reluctant to sell unless the offer price is high.

Moreover, it is clear that developers in the most rapidly growing areas such as Sammamish had banked building permits in the past. Thus the rapid building in the current period is in part working down a stock of permits that is not likely to be refreshed. But even if the supply restriction from homevoter dominance has yet to affect the price of housing, it will eventually affect the economy of the region. Firms are deterred from locating in a region when their employees face excessive housing prices (Gabriel, Shack-Marquez, and Wascher 1993; Johnes and Hyclak 1999).

10.19 Conclusion: Don't Tread on My Zoning

Dick Babcock, the late dean of American land-use lawyers, used to say at a scholarly conference convened to decry zoning's shortcomings, "Nobody loves zoning but the people." This chapter and the one before concur. Zoning is an important, if not the most important, reason for the existence of most cities formed in the twentieth century. It is at the center of the "local control" issue. Zoning is not a technical planning issue. At no point was it suggested that King County planners were incompetent or that the county's zoning rules were not enforced. The objection to county rule was that rezonings were too permissive.

Residents wanted local control because they knew that in a smaller municipality, their voice—the voices of homeowners—would govern, not the voices of developers. The reason that incorporating cities resisted annexation was in most cases because the annexing city would not have shared the same preferences about land use as the residents of the annexed territory. Either the annexing city was too big or its residents did not share a common experience such as a school district or a long-standing commercial center. These affirmations of local democracy played out time and again in King County, Los Angeles County, and every other group of incorporations that historians of twentieth-century urban life have examined.

Metropolitan governance in King County is an ongoing test of whether a region can implement a policy that offsets restrictions on rural growth with infill development in close-in suburbs. The incorporation of new local governments within the infill area whose primary goals are to frustrate that development indicates the hazards of that approach. It is possible that the enforcer of the Growth Management Act, the hearings board, will step up its so-far anemic efforts to promote infill. And it is likely that pressure from the county and the state legislature will prevent massive downzonings. But the record so far indicates that metropolitanism is more effective in stopping growth on its outskirts than in promoting it within its urban growth line. As a manifestation of the "smart-growth" movement, the Growth Management Act has little to recommend it so far. It seems to act more like a cartel for those already in possession of suburban homes than as a rationalizer of metropolitan development patterns.

11
Reforming and Reaffirming Local Government

I BEGAN the previous chapter with a promise to examine a less sanguine aspect of local governments, their tendency to use zoning powers to exclude too much. The empirical focus, however, ended up sounding more like a cheering section for the ten new Seattle-area municipalities that I studied. As obvious as their motives to stop development were, I found it hard not to admire the pluck of their founders and the apparent success in the uniquely American process of bottom-up, local self-governance.

In part not to end on this pollyannaish note, I will in this chapter reexamine the four questions from Section 1.1 that motivated the book. They concerned (1) the efficiency of the property tax, (2) funding for education, (3) finding sites for environmentally problematic land uses, and (4) exclusionary zoning. There are, of course, many other issues that could be raised about local government, including the structure of federalism and the response of local governments to grants and subsidies by higher levels of government. These are neglected because my task has been to promote a model to understand the internal workings of local government.

My major theme is that residents of owner-occupied homes have a special interest in local affairs that makes local behavior much different than that of the same actors at the state or national level. This insight will be deployed as a tool to examine reform proposals. The principal novelties in this discussion are a plan for home-value insurance that would promote acceptance of less desired land uses and my suggestion that vouchers are not as effective a solution for school finance as a system that subsidizes the poor in their Tiebout search for better school districts.

11.1 The Scholarly Schizophrenia about Localism

A good portion of the scholarship on local government suffers from what seems to be a kind of schizophrenia. When the issue at hand is environmental protection, local governments are deeply mistrusted. Competition among them results in a "race to the bottom," goes this story, and higher government officials are urged to step in to protect homeowners and other residents from their own witless decisions. The policy that epitomizes this view is the federal program for drinking-water safety. Most of the American population is served by local water companies, which are usually an appendage of local government. Federal policy requiring costly safety measures is apparently motivated by a belief that local officials are so indifferent to their constituents (not to mention ordinary tort liability) that they will allow water quality to drop below safe standards (Dan Tarlock 1997).

Many of the same people who subscribe to the "race to the bottom" also worry about the problem of "exclusionary zoning," in which suburbs allocate too little land for low- and moderate-income housing. The conventional explanation for exclusionary zoning, however, is that local governments calculate that lower-income people will become a fiscal drag on the community. In this case, it seems, local governments are too rational, too worried about the well-being of their existing residents. How can it be that when the issue is exclusion, local governments are thoroughly (though unattractively) rational, but when the issue is environmental protection, they are heedless of the consequences?

This intellectual inconsistency suggests the lack of a unified theory of local government behavior. Whatever other defects it might have, the homevoter hypothesis does not suffer from this. Homeowners care a great deal about environmental effects on their homes (contrary to the "race to the bottom" assumption) and about the impact of new residents on the value of their homes (consistent with the "exclusionary zoning" view). Indeed, the main problem with homevoters is that they care too much about the value of their homes. Because homes represent such a large fraction of their wealth, and because this form of wealth cannot, for most people, be diversified, homeowners tend to promote policies that involve too few environmental and fiscal risks. The riskiness of homeownership accounts for both environmental fussiness (the NIMBY syndrome) and exclusionary zoning.

11.2 Property Tax Reform: Land-Value Taxation and Uniformity

The traditional (pre-Tiebout) problem that economists had with the property tax is that it discourages local capital formation. If I add another room to my house, my taxes go up, but I am still entitled to the same benefits from local services. Even though fiscal zoning prevents developers from wholesale free-riding on local services, the subsequent owners of those homes still have some incentives to withhold capital improvements in order to avoid a tax increase.

One answer to the inefficiencies of taxing local capital is to shift the property tax to a land-value tax. Land-value taxation is the goal of a long-standing and somewhat quirky reform movement. It was promoted with millennial zeal by Henry George (1879), and Georgist thought still influences modern economic thought. The Georgists' program is not to abandon the property tax but to shift taxation toward land value and away from building and other real estate improvements. The obvious wisdom of this is that land cannot move away from the taxman the way capital and labor can.

Much of the modern criticism of land-value taxation emphasizes its administrative difficulties (Mills and Hamilton 1989, p. 92). To be workable, property-tax assessors have to come up with valuations without the land-market's help, and the assessors themselves say they are not up to the task (Daniel Holland 1970, chap. 1). Dogged and technically sophisticated Georgists such as Nicolaus Tideman (1990) continue to challenge this pessimistic view, and there is some evidence that untaxing buildings (not quite the same as taxing land value) had some beneficial effects in reviving the fortunes of the city of Pittsburgh (Oates and Schwab 1997). Most economists, however, remain unconvinced that widespread adoption of the Georgist taxation scheme would yield important gains.

The homevoter read on the land-value tax is that the Georgist millennium has arrived via the back door (Fischel 1998a). I have suggested, without having converted any Georgists, that the Tiebout-Hamilton model actually accomplishes by zoning much of what Henry George sought to accomplish by general land taxation. Effective zoning makes the "moveable" part of real estate into something akin to land by removing the ability of the nominal owner to build something other than what the zoning allows. This is not a complete answer to Georgists, who usually think of their tax as a national rather than local tax, but the partial, backdoor success of local zoning in mimicking the Georgist outcome may help explain why land-value taxation has not taken off in the United States.

The other group of reforms of the local property tax allow nonuniformity of taxation, typically to benefit some favored group (homeowners and the elderly) or to promote an admired land use, such as farms and open space. The homevoter hypothesis suggests that these may be justified for reasons other than promoting the interests of the favored group. Exemptions may be necessary to induce farmers or the elderly to support programs desired by homeowners.

If households have no children in local schools and do not plan to sell their homes soon (and thus capitalize on the quality of local schools), they may be less inclined to support public education. Exemptions for the elderly from part of local school taxes might prevent these voters from opposing school spending. Exemptions might thus be less a matter of fair distribution of wealth than a matter of efficient political economy. They are like the discounts older people get for consuming many leisure activities, such as movies and theme parks. The age of the resident is an easily observed, difficult-to-evade basis for discriminating among taxpayers on the basis of demand for some services. This form of price discrimination may, like the more traditional form, promote efficiency in an otherwise competitive market.

Accommodating different demands can also account for the practice of reducing assessments for farmland and other land-extensive holdings. Such tax expenditures are usually justified as a means of preserving farmland, but evidence suggests that its efficacy is modest at best (Adele Morris 1998). It may be that farmland assessment is a way of aligning the political incentives of homeowners with those of owners of undeveloped land. The latter demand fewer services (per taxable dollar) than do owners of developed properties, so reducing their taxes aligns their incentives to vote for public expenditures of interest to the homeowning majority. In other words, if owners of open space are an important factor in local elections, giving them a tax break may help the other voters get what they want.

Another uniformity issue is whether local governments themselves should be able to negotiate tax assessments with businesses. Most state constitutions require uniformity of rate and assessment, which inhibits this process. The advantage of negotiated local assessment is that it allows for less distortion from taxation. All taxes could be administered like land-use exactions, tailored to match the fiscal costs of a given property with the benefits that the property owner realizes (Fischel 1975). Unfettered bargaining generally is more efficient than having to jerry-build compensation through a set of taxes, exactions, and gifts-in-kind.

Yet there are important drawbacks to such discretion, drawbacks that gave rise to Dillon's Rule, the public purpose doctrine, and other constitutional and judicial constraints on local government (Section 2.8). Real estate development involves durable, difficult-to-reverse commitments. If all land-use decisions are up for grabs, it is difficult to see how local governments could convince potential developers that they would not be played for suckers after they were enticed into the community. A tax break dangled today could be jerked away after the development was completed. Knowing this, the developer and the community could not come to satisfactory terms.

Community worries about reputation in future dealings would constrain some opportunism. But where the use in question is highly durable—like real estate—the reputation consequences may be too remote to constrain the community. State-imposed doctrines such as uniformity of assessments and tax rates, and requirements to use tax revenues only for public purposes, give some assurance to immobilized political minorities that the community will not renege on its promises.

11.3 School-Finance Reform: Help People, Not Places

The main reform that the homevoter hypothesis suggests is to change the focus of school-finance reform as it is currently understood. Nearly all criticisms of school-finance reform begin by condemning the "unfairness" of inequalities in local property tax rates or tax bases. Reformers with this in mind have convinced the courts in many states to expend a good portion of their political capital to remove school-tax inequalities. As I submitted in Chapters 5 and 6, the outcome has not been the unalloyed success that litigators had hoped for, and there are serious signs that the more extreme interventions, most obviously that of the *Serrano* court in California, have made nearly everyone worse off.

People who agree with me that *Serrano* caused (or at least had something to do with) Proposition 13 go on to ask, What about the true inequalities in education? Should it be constitutionally permissible for some to get better public educations than others? If *Serrano* and related attacks on localism do not produce the right result, what should be done?

My primary answer is to point out that we have a fairly good system of representative democracy in all of the states. Any time the large majority of voters who have less than the mean level of income or wealth or tax base choose to do so, they can select representatives who will adopt a more equalitarian policy along the lines they choose. I don't have to act as dictator on their behalf, and neither do state court judges. That the system of representative democracy in the states might be flawed in certain ways is undeniable, but to leap from those flaws to the conclusion that judges, who are almost entirely removed from the electorate's choices, should then make the decision strikes me as a non sequitur with pernicious consequences.

This approach of leaving the issue to the voters and their elected representatives is derived from what is called "process theory" among constitutional scholars (John Hart Ely 1980; Michael Klarman 1991). But it begs the question of what advice the homevoter hypothesis suggests to *legislative* reformers. If they are convinced by the economic theorists who submit that a level-up equalitarianism in education is more efficient as well as more just in an otherwise unequal world, what is the best way to accomplish it?

The most discussed way to help out disadvantaged students is to offer them vouchers. The *Serrano* movement's most influential academic advocates, Jack Coons and Steve Sugarman (1978; 1992) in fact urge this solution, though most other *Serrano*-advocates are died-in-the-wool centralists. (The plaintiffs' lawyer in my home state's *Serrano*-style litigation opined in a public forum that the ideal remedy would be for New Hampshire to be one big school district.) There is a problem with vouchers, however, that advocates have yet to face seriously.

One of the virtues of local property taxation is that it brings childless voters into the picture. Homeowners who have no children in the public schools nonetheless have some incentive not to trash their local schools at the ballot box. To do so would reduce their net worth. I pointed out in Section 6.12 that this helps to explain why states that have displaced the property tax with statewide funds have gone on to have less successful schools, at least insofar as we can judge success by test scores. At the state level, no-kids-in-school voters care less about school quality.

The same disadvantage adheres to a state-funded system of vouchers. If vouchers can be used in any community or even in private schools, why would childless voters support candidates who sought to increase funding for vouchers? A better-funded, more successful system of vouchers will not do much for home values. It may be that a system of locally funded vouchers would work better along these lines, but local funding runs into the inequalities of local *incomes* that are a legitimate concern of school-finance reform.

My criticism of vouchers does not deny the many virtues of school choice and competition for students among both public and private schools. In areas where there are few Tiebout choices among local governments, such as states that have totally centralized school funding (Hawaii and California, for example), vouchers are a substitute for location choice. Large central cities are another example, especially for populations whose location choices are constrained by the remaining racism in the housing market (John Yinger 1995). In most other settings, though, it is reasonable to predict that vouchers are not likely to be adopted, since only a minority of voters, those with children currently in school, perceive any special benefit from them.

Whatever state aid for education is intended to boost the opportunities for the poor should aim it at people, not places. In particular, aiming it at "property poor" places is likely to overlook the large number of poor people who live in places that are property rich or nearly so (Section 6.3). State aid formulas that penalize districts for being or becoming property rich are both inefficient and unfair, in that they discourage local voters from accepting locally unwanted but regionally desirable land uses, and they renege on past promises to communities that accepted especially problematic uses. Moreover, aiming aid at poor people, regardless of where they live, has a "magic bullet" quality to it, in that it encourages affluent places to accept low-income housing, as I will discuss in Section 11.10.

11.4 Getting NIMBYs to Accept LULUs

The most important reform of environmental policies that the homevoter hypothesis suggests is to reject the widespread assumption that there is a "race to the bottom" by communities and that they will "beggar their neighbors" in pursuit of a profitable tax base. The evidence from Chapters 7 and 8 suggests the real problem: that municipalities will be too reluctant to accept regionally necessary industry and infrastructure.

The problem is how to get NIMBYs to accept LULUs (locally unwanted land uses) in a reasonably expeditious fashion. Promoting such acceptance is itself an environmental issue. Having waste facilities that are located only in the most remote areas, where there is no one around to complain, increases the transportation costs of relocating waste, whether for final disposal or recycling. The same is true for power plants and other energy facilities. Locating LULUs far away from anyone who might be offended by them imposes economic and environmental costs on everyone.

I suggest in the next section an insurance mechanism to promote consensual exchange between residents within metropolitan areas and the developers of LULUs. It is worth noting at this point that the problem of LULUs and the more subtle problem, exclusionary zoning, derive from the same anxiety: What will it do to voters' home values? Thus the mechanism that I will describe presently—home-value insurance—can be applied to developments involving housing as well as those used for nonresidential purposes.

Home-value insurance, however, *rewards* existing homevoters for allowing the inconvenient use. Most people believe that there should be no penalties imposed on a community for not accepting an industrial LULU. Being free of industrial pollution, or even minor inconveniences from it, has become a status quo that is verging on a constitutional right. Thus communities that volunteer to be subjected to it expect to be compensated. This is unlike the norm for new housing development, which is much less widely agreed upon: Some believe that every community should accept a quota of low-income housing, and others regard it as acceptable to have municipal specialization by housing types.

The obvious answer for NIMBY concerns regarding LULUs is compensation, and this is the usual practice. It is important to recognize that the most practical way to begin any compensation program is to give the municipality in which the LULU is to be located the right to say no. This means "property rule" protection, not "liability rule" protection for municipal zoning decisions (Section 7.10). The state should bind its own hands as much as possible to forgo its indubitable right to override municipalities. If the legal weaponry of state preemption is not parked outside the door, few municipalities will negotiate in good faith. Homevoters will invariably overstate their aversion to a LULU if they suspect that an honest assessment of its effect will result in its being forced upon them.

11.5 Home-Value Insurance Would Assuage NIMBYs

The more novel proposal that I advance here pertains to the form of compensation to be offered to homevoters for accepting LULUs. It is not enough to offer compensation to nearby property owners for expected adverse effects of the new development. There should also be a more general policy of home-value insurance to assuage homeowners' anxieties. (The idea was proposed originally by Marcus and Taussig [1970], who suggested a broader coverage of risks than just land-use changes.)

I mentioned in Chapter 1 that an important instigator of the homevoter hypothesis was my realization that NIMBYs were sensibly worried about the *risk* of unanticipated spillover effects as well as the expected outcome that appears on the immaculately drawn plans. Most homeowners have too much of their net worth tied up in their homes to be able to diversify the rest of their portfolio to offset this risk.

Asset risk is a good thing when it makes homeowners pay attention to the quality of schools and municipal services. It helps overcome the free-rider problem that is otherwise endemic to boring, local political concerns. But for some local decisions, like finding sites for LULUs and other desirable but risky land uses, the risk aversion that breeds NIMBYism is arguably a bad thing.

Not all opposition to nearby development is bad. *Efficient* NIMBYism deters LULUs and other developments whose spillover costs exceed their benefits (including compensatory actions by the developer). *Inefficient* NIMBYism goes further and deters otherwise desirable land uses because homeowners have no way to insure against the risk that the outcome of the project will turn out badly for them (Fischel 2001). Although it is arguable that risk aversion might be desirable in dealing with environmental issues, most NIMBYs' concerns go way beyond that, since neighbors often oppose land-use changes such as day-care centers and public parks that have no long-term environmental impacts.

One way to deal with risk anxiety is for the developer (private or public) to offer home-value insurance to those who might be affected. Here is the insurance contract that would do the trick: In the event that the insured's property does not rise by the amount that it would have had the development not taken place, the insurer (the developer or a sure-to-stay-solvent agent) will pay the owner the difference at the time the owner of the property (or his heirs or legatees) chooses to sell it. Once this difference is paid, the succeeding owner acquires no further claim for adverse effects of the development on the property. (The reason the purchaser has no further claim after the insurance claim has been paid to the seller is that the purchaser has been compensated for the now-revealed adverse effect in the form of the lower price of the house.)

To state the contract's basic terms is to illustrate why such insurance is difficult to write. If this were an insurance contract for fire damage to the home, the baseline event that triggers the insurance compensation is easy to identify. The house catches on fire and physically damages the property. There are plenty of collateral issues that follow from this event: Did the owner work hard enough to prevent it? What is the value remaining if the house was not entirely consumed? But the baseline event, at least, is easy to determine, and the "but for" scenario reasonably clear. Either there was a fire or there was not.

Devaluation of a home's value, however, can follow from many neighborhood, community, and national events besides the nearby development for which the insurance is written. The appropriate "but for" comparison group may also have changed over time. Even if it did not, the selection of the price index on which the insurance contract can be based is problematic. Karl Case, Robert Shiller, and Allan Weiss

(1993) have tried to establish *metropolitan* price indexes to allow people to hedge against regional price changes. The limited success of their enterprise suggests that it would be even more difficult to establish the *neighborhood* price indexes necessary for NIMBY insurance.

I should note one existing insurance program that addresses the issue of home-value decline. Some neighborhoods in the Chicago area offer home-equity "assurance" programs to help deter panic selling in the face of racial change in their neighborhoods (Maureen McNamara 1984). (It was dubbed "assurance" instead of "insurance" in order to escape the elaborate regulations of Illinois insurance companies.) Home-equity assurance was invented in Oak Park as part of a larger (and successful) program to prevent panic selling during racial transition (Carole Goodwin 1979), but it has been adopted most widely in precincts of the city of Chicago (Michelle Mahue 1991). In a phone conversation on April 19, 1999, the director of one of Chicago's programs mentioned that developers sometimes used it to assure neighbors that their projects would not devalue their homes. The developer would pay for the homeowners' appraisals and the fees to enter the program, and this, I was told, headed off the usual NIMBYism.

The primary economic problem with Chicago's program, however, is that it insures only the nominal price of homes at risk. Without a local housing-price index, any adjustment for general inflation must be made by the costly process of reappraising the home to be insured. On top of this are the usual economic problems with insurance, such as the insured's tendency to drop his guard. Such "moral hazard" problems seem especially difficult to overcome in the context of land-use regulation (Shiller and Weiss 1998). But the existence and apparent success of Chicago's program, although motivated by a different issue, does suggest that home-value insurance might become a viable means of dealing with NIMBYism.

11.6 Farmland Preservation Can Obscure Exclusionary Motives

Probably the most complicated and intractable of the problems of localism deal with land-use controls affecting housing. Ever since zoning was adopted early in this century (Martha Lees 1994), and probably long before that (Nancy Burns 1994, p. 35), residents of many municipalities have been concerned that new entrants to the community will devalue their homes. There is nothing new about exclusionary zoning and existing residents' desire to protect their home values.

It is important to understand that homeowners do not care about the source of the devaluation of their homes. They do not make academic distinctions between "externality zoning" and "fiscal zoning." Development of a noisy factory that devalues their homes by $20,000 is the same to them as a tax increase (unaccompanied by better services) that devalues their homes by $20,000. Nor is it easy to identify motive. Even if the motive for low-density zoning is mainly to exclude the poor and racial minorities, local officials will find justification for it in terms of preserving farmland, wetlands, historic districts, endangered species, or, if all else fails, "character of the community."

I suspect that the popularity of otherwise dissonant land uses can be explained by their efficaciousness in providing a rationale to prevent local development of housing. How else to explain the special suburban affection for both the natural environment and commercial farmland? Commercial farming is essentially an applied chemical factory. Its practitioners cannot tolerate diversity of plant species, and wild animals and birds are also often suppressed by a profit-minded farmer. Farming's noises, smells, and chemical residue are sufficiently offensive to nonfarming residents that farmer-dominated communities often pass "right to farm" laws, which suspend the law of nuisance for such offenses. That nonfarming residents tend to oppose such local laws suggests that their affection for farmland is as a device to preserve open space, not really to preserve farming (Adelaja and Friedman 1999).

I will admit that farmland is often pleasant to look at, at least when it is broken by some other scenery such as villages, woods, and hills. The pastoral aesthetic, however, does not explain why the same environmental organizations that promote farmland preservation near cities oppose common farm practices such as open-range cattle grazing in rural areas. The only way that inconsistency makes sense to this observer is that farmland preservation is the best available rationale for suburban and exurban communities that are ripe for development to pull up the drawbridge.

This is not to say that local activists are cynically using farmland preservation as a cover for less attractive goals. My guess is that most could pass a polygraph test that asked whether they truly thought farmland ought to be preserved. (If the questioner asked whether they would be willing to shoulder their share of buying the development rights from farmland owners, the result might be in more doubt.) My point here is that one cannot disentangle motives for most land-use policies. Like the desire for most things, motives for hampering development in one's community are a mixed bag.

The indeterminacy of motives helps to explain why the usual approach to dealing with excessive zoning standards so seldom yields any relief from them. The court that has been at the forefront of the battle against zoning motivated to exclude low-value housing is New Jersey's supreme court. Its *Mount Laurel* decisions (1975; 1983) have been among the most aggressive in attacking local parochialism. The court reinvented the "builders' remedy," in which judges awarded building permits for builders who were willing to build a certain amount of lower-income housing along with their market-rate housing. As I mentioned in Section 3.10, this was so effective that suburban communities induced the state to pass legislation that took the remedy out of the court's hands. In creating the Council on Affordable Housing, the New Jersey legislature reduced but did not eliminate the threat of nonlocal control over zoning.

The popularity of farmland preservation was given a boost by the *Mount Laurel II* decision. The New Jersey Supreme Court was concerned only about the mix of low- and moderate-income housing, not the total amount of development in the community. Once a community was certified as having a *proportion* of new housing that satisfied its "fair share" of low-income housing, it was virtually invited by the New Jersey Court to be as exclusive with the rest of its undeveloped land as it wanted to be: "Finally, once a community has satisfied its fair share obligation, the *Mount Laurel* Doctrine will not restrict other measures, including large-lot and open area zoning, that would maintain its beauty and communal character" (456 A.2d at 421). Towns that do grow after meeting their *Mount Laurel* obligation have found that they are obliged to accept more low-income housing. Local officials now know this and plan not to grow by using such devices as extra-large lot zoning for the ostensible purpose of preserving farmland.

11.7 Why Not Regulatory Takings?

Statistical studies show that New Jersey's "fair share" remedy has failed to change the demographic mix of its municipalities (Alessandro Giovannotto 1994; James Mitchell 2000). The *Mount Laurel* approach has the collateral damage of encouraging "no-growth" regulations that increase housing prices and cause urban sprawl (Fischel 1999, p. 155). The remedy that avoids this is "regulatory takings," a doctrine I explored in an entire book (Fischel 1995) and whose application to suburban areas was first proposed by Robert Ellickson (1973; 1977).

The doctrine as we have advanced it sets a "no compensation" baseline of "normal behavior." A suburb that proposes to develop along the lines that are consistent with its historical growth patterns or that are held to be consistent with regional housing norms does not have to pay development-minded landowners for accepting restrictions consistent with this baseline. Suburbs that wish to accept "subnormal" uses—nonresidential LULUs—can do so at their own discretion. But communities that seek to zone significant amounts of land for "supernormal" standards—ten-acre lots and the like—can do so only if they pay "just compensation" to landowners.

The amount of the compensation would be the difference between what would have been permitted under "normal-behavior" zoning—like development on half-acre lots—and what the community had zoned it for. If the unconstitutional restriction were rescinded, the developer would still be eligible for forgone profits during the period the illegal regulations were in force. This prevents the community from simply stalling the developer with repeated "maybe next time" denials until his planning, litigation, and interest costs induce him to give up.

As far as I know, no state or federal court has used the regulatory takings doctrine as the primary vehicle to strike down any municipality's zoning laws. Courts do strike them down sometimes, but most often on nebulous due process grounds or by declaring the regulation in question not to have been within the powers delegated to the community. In such cases, the community just has to repair the zoning law, not pay any damages to the landowner-plaintiff, except perhaps for attorneys' fees.

Community authorities thus know that time is their friend. Pass a restrictive ordinance, let the landowners sue, then if you lose, adjust the law ever so slightly. Two state courts, those of Pennsylvania and, to a lesser extent, Illinois, are willing to step in and order the community to give the litigating landowner a rezoning or a building permit (Dennis Coyle 1993, p. 11). In most other states, the famous advice that a California municipal attorney gave his brethren who, against all odds, might lose a zoning case still applies: "IF ALL ELSE FAILS, MERELY AMEND

THE REGULATION AND START OVER AGAIN." (Quoted, with emphasis in original, on behalf of the landowner's position by Justice William Brennan in San Diego Gas and Electric v. San Diego, 450 U.S. at 655 [1980].) As Justice Brennan—hardly an enemy of regulation—pointed out, lack of monetary compensation for delay encourages the cynical manipulation of landowners by land-use agencies.

Why have the courts been unwilling to deploy the regulatory takings doctrine in situations where it is singularly appropriate for them to do so? The doctrinal basis is clear. Every state constitution has or implies something like the U.S. Constitution's Fifth Amendment, which concludes, "nor shall private property be taken for public use without just compensation." The common response that this was intended only to apply to physical invasions by the government is historically incorrect; there is little to indicate what the framers intended by it (William Treanor 1985; Robert Brauneis 1996). It is also logically incoherent. If one accepted the distinction—compensable physical invasions, noncompensable regulations—highways could be obtained by rezoning the desired land for "open space," then acquiring it in its devalued state for a nominal payment and then changing the zoning to "highway." Don't think it hasn't been tried.

The idea that regulations are more difficult to value than physical takings is wrong on both sides. On the one hand, physical takings often present complicated valuation issues, especially when a highway splits a parcel of land in two. On the other hand, regulations are often transparently easy to value. In several states, there are programs to purchase development rights from farmland owners, and transactions are made all the time (Kline and Wichelns 1994). It is exactly such rights that are at issue when suburbs rezone farmland from a three-acre minimum lot size to ten, twenty-five or even forty-acre lot sizes for a single residence. It is no more difficult to value the loss of those rights than it is to quantify the loss of a segment of a cornfield to the state highway department.

The homevoter hypothesis suggests one reason why regulatory takings are so abhorred by municipalities and, consequently, withheld by judges. It has to do with the risks to homevoters of increased property taxes. Higher property taxes will lower the value of homes in the community. This threat is, of course, one of the desirable features of a regulatory takings doctrine. If homevoters truly believe that farmland preservation will make the community more attractive, then they should be willing to tax themselves at a higher rate to obtain the farmers' development rights. This not only equalizes the burdens of public life (rather than just dumping them on the farmland owners), it provides a check on the exclusionary consequences of farmland preservation. Community residents have to decide whether it is worth the pain (of higher taxes) to get the gain (of preserving open space).

The problem with the regulatory takings approach is that, because it involves monetary damages, it invites excessive entry into litigation (Blume, Rubinfeld, and Shapiro 1984). The contingency-fee system peculiar to American law, visible most recently in the tobacco litigation, would be turned on regulatory takings law once zoning laws were found to be a source of damages. While a regulatory taking would not involve punitive damages—the source of the tobacco-litigators' billions—the potential claims of injury from government regulation are even broader than for mass torts.

The serious contention that the consequences of deregulating electric utilities amount to a taking of the former monopoly's property begins to suggest the creative range of regulatory takings unbound (Sidak and Spulber 1996). Appellate judges would fear that because of the uncertainty of liability, land-use litigation would be translated into higher taxes for communities whose regulations were perfectly reasonable. This in turn would threaten home values in all communities. Most judges, I would wager, are themselves homeowners.

It is also worth noting again that judicial threats to zoning can bring political retaliation. The New Jersey Supreme Court's aggressive review of zoning in the 1920s and 1980s brought on a constitutional amendment in the former instance and the threat of judicial removal in the latter (Section 3.10). When the U.S. Supreme Court in the late 1970s made municipal activities subject to antitrust law and its triple-damages remedies, Congress quickly swung into action to remove the threat of triple damages in 1982 (Deutsch and Butler 1987). As if to atone for its overreaching, the Court in 1990 virtually eliminated any threat of antitrust liability for municipalities (Brent Kinkade 1992).

11.8 Pragmatic Alternatives to the Regulatory Commons

The failure of so many zoning reforms to have their intended effect counsels a tone of modesty and pragmatism. Courts that adopt sweeping reforms to overcome localism risk the wrath of a state legislature whose geographic selection process makes it highly responsive to the concerns of homevoter-dominated municipalities. Regional governance such as the metropolitan experiments in Oregon and Washington, and statewide overrides of local decisions, have by themselves had a mixed result. While they sometimes get local governments to accept uses that they would otherwise not accept, they also can be evaded by finding novel reasons not to accept development. Regional governance of zoning also runs more of a risk of behaving, perhaps unintentionally, as a monopoly supplier of land-use permits (Louis Rose 1989; James Thorson 1996).

A more pragmatic approach avoids relying on any single reform to make the suburbs more accountable to the outside world. I shall divide the reforms into "carrots"—rewards for community compliance—and "sticks"—penalties for failure to accommodate development. The rewards involve side payments by developers to the community, home-value insurance for nearby property owners, and a state-funded system of compensation for the school-district costs endured by accommodating communities. The sticks are court review of zoning regulations under a variety of doctrines, including regulatory takings, and state and regional review of, but not displacement of, local land-use decisions.

Before discussing these reforms, it is important to consider the more general issue of federal and state government layers of review. Much of what appears to be local exclusion is not caused by the ordinary local political process. A municipality may be in favor of some development, but a minority within that community who live near it or are financially affected by it manage to tie it up in court by invoking environmental and related issues mandated by higher government authorities. I have characterized this problem as that of a "regulatory commons," in which no single group can claim exclusive rights, with the result that there is excessive entry into regulatory negotiations (Fischel 1995, p. 251). Thus a community may approve of a project that involves apartments and commercial development, but because it is being built on a wetland area or some other environmentally problematic site, its residential neighbors (or its commercial competitors) manage to tie it up in court so long that it never gets built.

One way to combat this is to make local governments solely responsible for complying with higher-government regulations. A community that has adopted a set of wetlands regulations, for instance, should be given sole responsibility for administering them within its own borders. Of course, there may be spillover effects to other municipalities, but the liability for that should rest with the municipality (Robert Ellickson 1979). The parties entitled to sue the offending municipality should mainly be other municipalities. The expansion of legal standing to large numbers of groups that are not accountable to any geographically settled group of voters has promoted legislative and judicial gridlock in many instances. It is extremely difficult to balance interests in a setting in which no settled group of parties can come to final agreements (Clifford Holderness 1998).

The argument that localities are incompetent to manage their own environmental interests and respond to the concerns of their immediate neighbors is contrary to much of the evidence adduced in Chapters 7 and 8. This is not, of course, to suggest that state and national regulations should be abolished. Municipalities can visit spillover effects on more than their immediate neighbors. For these far-flung effects—high altitude air pollution or contamination of a major river—the transaction costs among a multitude of municipalities or even states may be so high as to justify a federal role in the process. But simply to say that every local action affects every other geographic area is to surrender to a busybody mindset that ultimately centralizes all decision-making. To modify a bumper-sticker rule: "Think locally; act locally. Think globally; act globally."

11.9 "Carrots" to Promote Community Development

This section describes two of the three types of rewards that municipalities should get for accepting higher-than-normal densities or low-income housing.

Side payments by developers. Side payments by developers to municipalities or to nearby homeowners are the grease by which much of development takes place (Joseph Gyourko 1991). Yet many analysts regard them as if they were a development-retarding tax. Both views can be correct. Like zoning itself, exactions and impact fees can promote orderly development or act as an exclusionary barrier.

As developers discovered long ago, selling homes in communities without zoning-like protections can be quite difficult (Section 9.4). But having opened the Pandora's box of zoning, developers later found that it could be used contrary to their interests. So it is with exactions. An exaction that compensates the community for the inconveniences of development is often less costly for the developer than attempting to remove all of its spillover effects. The exaction can be set sufficiently high, however, that it becomes even more costly than internalizing the spillover effect, yet the developer may be required to pay it. In the latter case, the exaction becomes exclusionary. It is in fact difficult to determine which role exactions play, which may account for why so much commentary on exactions is thoroughly ambivalent about the process.

My chief recommendation about exactions, then, is to tolerate them as long as the developer has some realistic default option. The default option should be something akin to Ellickson's normal behavior. That is, if a developer needs zoning and planning permission to build an apartment house in a suburb with mostly single-family homes, the community can ask for whatever exactions it wants as long as the developer has the option of developing homes more or less like those already there.

The exaction should be for true changes in local land use patterns, not for permission to develop homes similar to those in which current residents already live. (Exaction financing would be fair, however, where most of the development had previously been financed by exactions [Ellickson 1977, p. 458].) A thoughtful article that explores this issue is by Lee Fennell (2000), although her criticism of how current U.S. Supreme Court doctrine appears to limit some gains from trade may be overstated. Developers and community officials who want to make a deal can often get it done.

Home-value insurance. As indicated in Section 11.5, it is possible to establish home-value insurance for neighbors who will be adversely affected by a more intensive residential development nearby. I regard this principle as relatively uncontroversial for commercial and industrial developments, but it is more controversial for residential development. To regard occupants of nearby homes as akin to a nuisance against which neighbors should be indemnified is, when you put it that way, not something that one wants to say in most political settings.

As an example, the initial development of home-equity "assurance" in Illinois was to keep white homeowners from selling their homes in a panic when blacks began to purchase homes. When the program was proposed in Chicago, African-American political figures (one of whom was Mayor Harold Washington) took offense at the idea, and it was defeated. It was only made available at the option of neighborhoods when the Illinois legislature passed special bills allowing it (Mahue 1991).

Once it got past its controversial birth stage, home-equity assurance in Illinois appears to have been both reasonably effective and relatively uncontroversial. As I mentioned earlier, developers in Chicago actually have used it to get acceptance of low-income developments. High transaction costs might preclude a general home-equity program to deal with suburban resistance to higher-density development. In selective situations, however, the costs might not be excessive, especially when the number of neighbors who might be adversely affected is not large.

11.10 Public-School Supplements, Not Vouchers

The most ambitious of carrots for communities to accept higher density or low-income housing would be a state-funded program to reduce the adverse effects of more children in the schools. That this is a major stumbling block for housing is suggested by the nearly universal acceptance (by communities if not neighborhoods) of low-income housing for the elderly. Besides not attending schools, the elderly also are less liable to commit crimes or engage in other unneighborly behavior.

As I noted in Section 6.16, one of the expected benefits of the *Serrano* decision was that it would help break down suburban resistance to low-income housing. *Serrano*-style litigation has been aimed at districts with low property wealth, which is not where most low-income people live. The decisions do not help the poor in any systematic fashion, and their collateral damage to local fiscal control has undermined the beneficial aspects of local property-tax financing.

There is a better way, and it has something of a "magic bullet" effect in that it deals with two problems at once. The state government (or the federal government) should give special public-school funds to low-income families with children. It might best be called a "public-school supplement" to distinguish it from voucher programs. (It would be more accurate but too arcane to call it a "Tiebout voucher.") Unlike vouchers, the school supplement would be payable only to the public schools that the family's children are normally entitled to attend. It thus avoids the controversy about subsidizing private and religious schooling via vouchers. The public-school supplement gives the poor a boost in their Tiebout-search for their preferred community.

This is a "magic bullet" because it deals with two problems simultaneously. First, it is purely a "level-up" expenditure that does not detract in any way from local fiscal control of schools. Unlike tax-base sharing or other state aid that is based on local fiscal behavior, the school supplement does not penalize any community for obtaining additional tax base or spending more on education. Second, it reduces local anxiety about land-use issues in that it provides some assurance that low- and moderate-income housing will not be a burden on the tax base (Schwab and Oates 1991). In effect, the school supplement is a portable endowment. Some school districts might in fact become eager to attract low-income housing in order to obtain the benefits of the endowment.

The drawback of the school supplement is that, like all "magic" remedies, it is costly. Most state programs that aim money at the poor (as opposed to at the tax base) try to limit the cost by excluding from their formulas the poor who live in "property-rich" districts or in otherwise affluent areas in which spending per pupil or tax base is above some cut-off point. It is important to understand that the "magic bullet" aspect of the school supplement is that it travels with poor, public-school children regardless of where in the state they reside. Only if this condition is met will the high-spending and property-rich districts be willing to tell their land-use authorities not to worry about the fiscal effects of proposed low-income housing projects. If the school supplement is denied to families that live in such districts, the same incentives to zone out the poor remain in place.

The public-school supplement could be transformed into a voucher system by paying it to public schools in which the poor family was not resident or by making private schools eligible. The homevoter hypothesis would counsel against such an extension, though. This is because if the poor families live in the district in which they send their children to schools, they will have a fiscal incentive to monitor the schools.

The benefit of "local control" is not just in selecting the schools, but in having a vote and a voice in local politics. Under a voucher system for the poor, a low-income family that located in one community but sent its kids to private schools would have little incentive to vote for or otherwise encourage the local schools. Local school taxes would, for that family, largely be viewed as a waste of its money, because other low-income families who might buy their homes would also not care much about local public schools. It comes down to the same problem as a general voucher system: Because the funding for vouchers does not depend on living where taxpayers' children attend schools, it severs the link between homeownership and education that keeps even childless voters interested in school quality.

11.11 "Sticks" to Discourage Local Misbehavior

The other side of the pragmatic set of devices to moderate zoning's excesses is to maintain some penalties for communities that deviate from wider social norms. It is worth noting at the outset that extra-legal pressures against exclusionary zoning can sometimes obtain voluntary compliance. As I mentioned in Sections 3.16 and 3.17, numerous suburbs take pride in their heterogeneous population, and privately planned new towns seem to find a mix of housing types to be a profitable strategy. Nor is the Tiebout model adversely affected by such heterogeneity, provided that the mix is foreseeably limited. Many communities seem willing to accept some share of the region's lower-income population as long as the development itself remains under local control and is not simply leverage for further expansion of that liability.

The optimistic scenario aside, the problems of excessive restrictions on housing development require more than school supplements, fiscal side-payments by developers, and equity assurance for neighbors. To allow those carrots to be the only device to induce suburbs to accommodate residential development would make the development that does occur so costly as to exclude all but the richest buyers. There must be some "sticks" whose threat brings municipalities to the bargaining table and makes them willing to accept reasonable terms.

Higher-government pressures. Chapter 10 detailed the Seattle area's attempt to herd development inside an urban growth boundary and the inducement it gave to incorporate municipalities whose primary desire was to retard that infill process. But the new and existing cities in King County did not stymie all infill development. While the legislature did weaken the enforcement mechanisms, the suburban cities have not eliminated the obligation. They seem willing for the most part to accommodate new development for low- and moderate-income housing along a fair-share formula. That formula seemed uncontroversial, at least when compared with battles about overall density standards, perhaps because it did not focus on housing for the lowest-income groups.

There is something to be said, then, for having some monitoring of local decisions by a state or metropolitan body. Even if there are few penalties for noncompliance, I suspect that there may be a kind of "shaming" penalty for suburbs that flout the goals. Even loose regional federations engender numerous reciprocal obligations among communities, and subnormal, exclusionary behavior can be penalized in other dimensions.

Substantive due process. The Pennsylvania Supreme Court has long had the most aggressive stance opposing exclusionary zoning. In its landmark decision, National Land v. Kohn (1965), the court struck down a four-acre minimum lot size regulation in the suburban township of Easttown, just off of Philadelphia's upscale Main Line. The court had previously upheld the same township's rezoning of its land to one-acre minimum lot size in Bilbar Construction v. Easttown (1958). Apparently emboldened by that victory, Easttown soon downzoned the land again, this time to four acres.

With a change in court personnel, however, the Pennsylvania Supreme Court embarked on a fairly consistent "due process" review of local zoning. Striking down Easttown's four-acre lot minimum in *National Land* was followed by decisions that have seldom upheld a minimum lot size in excess of one acre (James Mitchell 2000). It has also found that suburban attempts to exclude apartment dwellings and commercial uses are unconstitutional.

Most importantly, the Pennsylvania courts have followed up their due process decisions with remedies that reward the successful litigants. Following Appeal of Girsh (1970), in which the court ruled that a town could not exclude apartments, the losing town rezoned some property for multifamily use. But it did not include the land of the petitioner in *Girsh*. In a subsequent case, Casey v. Warwick Township (1974), the court ordered the township to rezone to accommodate apartments on Girsh's property, specifically mentioning that not to grant such relief would discourage litigation to challenge unconstitutional zoning.

All of this seems to be effective. I found some econometric evidence that Pennsylvania has lower suburban housing prices than other comparable states (Fischel 1980), and oral reports from local realtors indicate that it is still a comparatively low-cost state. Two student studies have found that Pennsylvania suburbs have a greater mix of housing types than comparable New Jersey communities (Giovannotto 1994; Mitchell 2000). With this kind of success, one would think that legal scholars concerned with suburban exclusion would hold Pennsylvania as a model for other courts to imitate.

It is not so. Aggressive "due process" intervention on behalf of development-minded landowners is regarded by most law professors as a vestige of the officially discredited Lochner v. New York (1905), which struck down labor legislation on the nebulous grounds of "freedom of contract." Even for those professors sympathetic to landowner rights, the hands-on, equitable remedies of *National Land* and its successors are regarded as generally inferior to the regulatory takings remedy (Berger and Kanner 1986; Ellickson 1977). They are skeptical of the efficacy of a doctrine that does not penalize delay, and they regard the doctrinal basis of substantive due process as weak compared to the takings clause.

While I have been an enthusiast of the regulatory takings doctrine in the past, I suggested in Section 11.7 that there may be some sound reasons why courts have been reluctant to apply it. A pragmatic approach leads me to believe that due process deserves more respect than it has been accorded. James Ely (1999) has demonstrated that due process in defense of property rights has a more respectable historical pedigree than the *Lochner* critics would have it. Applied to local government zoning, it may be regarded as a useful alternative for courts that are concerned about both the excesses of zoning and the excessive zeal of litigants and attorneys in pursuing monetary damages under the regulatory takings doctrine.

11.12 The Takings Stick Is Still Necessary

Having conceded that a wider range of remedies is needed to combat exclusionary, low-density zoning, I nonetheless want to point out why the threat of monetary damages is still needed. The U.S. Supreme Court has reviewed several regulatory takings cases in the last decade. The most influential so far is Lucas v. South Carolina Coastal Council (1992), which held that the council's denial of a building permit in a beachside resort that was already heavily developed was a taking of property. (The state subsequently bought the land to settle the case, and then turned around and sold the land to a developer, who has since put up a house on one of the two lots at issue.) Broadly speaking, *Lucas* holds that if a regulation (usually a change in regulation) deprives the owner of "all economic use" of otherwise developable land, and the regulation cannot further be justified in the state's "background principles" of nuisance and related legal principles, it will be held a taking requiring just compensation.

As a *sufficient* condition for a regulatory taking, this is not a bad rule. My view of the U.S. Supreme Court's pattern of decisions is that the Court is seeking to prevent state courts from abandoning all review of regulation under the takings clause (Fischel 1995, chap. 1). To do this, it cannot just admonish the states not to discard the doctrine, as it did in First English v. Los Angeles (1987). It has to set some substantive limit on regulatory behavior, and this is what *Lucas*'s "denial of all economic use" standard does. (Note that it does not say denial of all economic *value*. This is because the value of a property is in part a consequence of what a court is expected to decide.) The Court's reference to "background principles" of law was an attempt to keep other state legislatures from simply declaring, as South Carolina's had, that all beachfront development was tantamount to a nuisance, which traditionally would insulate the government from having to pay.

The trouble with *Lucas* is that what was meant to be a minimum standard for states to adhere to has become in many instances the sole standard for the states. The U.S. Supreme Court is understandably reluctant to intervene in land-use decisions. The Justices are at least two trials and many hearings removed from the facts, and what constitutes property in land has always been a state-court matter. Thus in New Jersey, a downzoning of rural land from a three-acre minimum lot size to a ten-acre minimum lot size was held not to be a taking for the obvious reason that a ten-acre lot has some economic use—a house can be put on it (Kirby v. Bedminster 2000). Yet this singling out of a class of landowners to provide a community benefit (open space) without compensation is what commentators across the political spectrum say is a fundamental concern of the takings clause (Richard Epstein 1985; Frank Michelman 1967).

It might be a stretch for a court to strike down a three-acre minimum lot size that had been in existence for a long time (Fischel 1995, chap. 9). Owners' reasonable expectations might plausibly adjust to such standards over time. But the radical change in regulations to standards far more restrictive than the normal suburban lot—which averages about half an acre in size—is something else again. I have been consulting on a farmland rezoning case in New Jersey, and I have met with the plaintiffs. In my writing I have often invoked Frank Michelman's (1967) term "demoralization cost," which sums up the losses of well-being that follow from uncompensated takings. The term was, I must report, insufficient to describe the mixture of frustration, disappointment, perplexity, sorrow, and outrage on the part of older men and women whose local government has deliberately reduced the value of their assets by at least 50 percent without compensation.

Something more than the *Lucas* criterion is needed to prevent the incremental acquisition of property rights by uncompensated regulation. The risk aversion of most municipalities plus the eagerness of the plaintiff's bar for damages may militate against the most vigorous application of regulatory takings. But to leave the government as much latitude as the *Lucas* standard does invites cynical, self-serving manipulation of land-use regulation by local governments and NIMBY opponents of reasonable development.

11.13 Municipal Secession Should Be Easier to Do

The least-talked-about reform of local government is to create new municipalities by allowing secession from those previously established. Most reformers would go in the opposite direction—toward consolidation—and current institutional arrangements discourage further subdivision. As I mentioned in Section 2.3, incorporation virtually guarantees that a city will not go out of business or surrender any of its existing territory to residents who seek to secede to form another city. Landowners within unincorporated areas sometimes can choose which city to be annexed to or to incorporate as a new city, but once they are in, it is like a roach motel: They almost never get out.

Despite the institutional barriers, there are popular rumblings that secession from existing municipalities might enhance the well-being of cities. The best-known examples come from our two largest cities. San Fernando Valley residents talk seriously of seceding from the city of Los Angeles (Peter Schrag 1998, p. 182). Staten Island residents likewise seem to want out of New York City. In Staten Island's case, the proximate cause was the U.S. Supreme Court overturning Staten Island's disproportionate representation on the Board of Estimate, which had an important fiscal and land-use role in the city's governance (Richard Briffault 1992, p. 785). Now completely dominated by the other boroughs of New York, Staten Islanders have sought to withdraw, so far unsuccessfully, from the city (Joseph Viteritti 1995).

The homevoter hypothesis would seem to give a green light to these secessionist efforts. Not only does the statistical evidence indicate that smaller cities give the voters what they want, but, as my Seattle-area investigations indicate, voters are consciously aware that smaller towns will be more responsive to their concerns. The rapidly growing number of quasi-governmental "business-improvement districts" in big cities and the surge of private, residential community associations are examples of what might be called "partial secessions." Why not let them go all the way and form entirely independent municipal governments?

My argument against secession in Section 3.14 suggested that legal subdivision of municipalities was resisted because of homeowners' risk aversion. The risk to be considered is not simply that of those who secede. If it were, there would be little reason to discourage it. The risk also accrues to those who remain in the city. Their home values depend in part on a municipal infrastructure that was tailored to boundaries that were expected to last indefinitely. Bonds were issued on the basis of a tax base that typically included the entire city. Making cities more elastic could make borrowing costs higher and real capital decisions more difficult, to the detriment of homevoters in all municipalities.

Another reason for stable boundaries might apply to large, central cities. In most metropolitan areas, they lead metropolitan-wide development efforts. Central cities promote efforts to attract businesses because their large size gives employment interests, which are subordinate to neighborhood issues in smaller communities, a stronger voice. It may be in the suburbs' interest to maintain a large central city that will do the heavy lifting in promoting the larger economic interests of the region.

Neither of the foregoing strike me as so decisive as to justify the current legal apparatus that stifles nearly all municipal secessions. A system of secession that allows for geographically distinct sectors of a city to seek their own destiny has serious merits. In many cases, the reason for the secession is that the unhappy area has not been integrated well into the rest of the city. Separation in such instances would make public capital expenditures more efficient, because they could be tailored to a more sensibly defined area like Staten Island or the San Fernando Valley.

The importance of big cities' job-seeking leadership has been reduced as jobs and people have decentralized. Los Angeles might have a slightly smaller voice as a regional economic promoter if the San Fernando Valley (which is largely residential) were to depart, but consensual federations of local governments and Los Angeles County seem well poised to take up any slack in that regard. The New York metropolitan region likewise would not seem to be at much of a disadvantage if Staten Island were to become independent. As the Ostroms (Section 8.9) and their students and associates have long argued, metropolitan cooperation does not have to come only from a unified metropolitan government.

11.14 Conclusion: Federalism Requires Tough Love for Local Governments

William Safire, a political commentator for the *New York Times*, also writes a column on language for its Sunday magazine. In the January 30, 2000 issue, he addressed the ambiguous nature of the word "federalism." It denotes a unified state (as opposed to a "federation") whose component geographic parts nonetheless have some degree of political autonomy. That seems clear enough, but Safire wanted to know the meaning of a headline that characterized a court decision as a "blow to federalism." The headline writer took it to mean a reduction in the authority of the national government and a victory for states' rights. I would have taken it as just the opposite, but Safire, while acknowledging that possibility, came down in favor of the headline writer.

The members of the Federalist Society, a group of lawyers with a conservative bent, would have read "a blow to federalism" as a victory for centralization, as would most authors of law review articles on the subject. Federalism connotes "decentralization" to legal scholars. But, as Safire pointed out, members of the long defunct Federalist Party and the authors of the Federalist Papers, one of whom (Madison) graces the logo of the modern Federalist Society, probably would have taken a "blow to federalism" to mean what the *New York Times* takes it to mean: a decision reducing the power of the national government.

Safire's essay suggests that the implication of "federalism" varies by whether centralization or decentralization is the dominant model of political economy. In the early 1800s, a Federalist party and Federalist Supreme Court Justices (the doyen being John Marshall) promoted a stronger central government. The states at the time were on top. In the twentieth century, especially following the Great Depression and the world wars, the national government became the dominant player. Those who want to sail against that wind and increase the authority of state and local governments now call themselves federalists.

Safire's position on the connotation of "federalism" suggests that the winds may be changing. The U.S. Supreme Court's recent "federalism" decisions revive some of the pre–New Deal doctrines of states rights and the related doctrine of separation of powers (Roderick Hills 1998). Perhaps the cessation of the Cold War and the apparent decline in the need for Keynesian, large-national-budget fiscal policy has so diminished America's attention to national affairs that "federalism" will once again take on its nineteenth-century connotation. Decentralization may be on its way to becoming the dominant political assumption.

The decentralization that I have advocated in this book is informed less by constitutional theory than by my belief that local governments are underappreciated actors in the federal system. I submit that local government is a distinct layer of government deserving of independent analysis. I have made no claim, however, that cities require political independence from the states. To the contrary, I submit that the efficient functioning of local governments is founded on their submission to some external controls. These include acceptance of the principle of regulatory takings (and related doctrines) by the courts and support for educational supplements for poor people, funded by state and federal legislatures.

The preface of this book addressed Professor Carol Rose's charge that my advocacy of the regulatory takings doctrine was an example of "localism bashing." As the reader has no doubt noticed (and as my friend Carol knows), I actually like local government. The reforms and remedies discussed in this chapter might best be called "tough love." If we are not to see local governments swallowed by their states or by large-size regional governments, municipalities' indubitable faults must be addressed in a meaningful way. Frustration with localism's parochial land-use politics is already engendering state and federal interventions that sacrifice many of the true virtues of localism.

The reforms limned in this chapter are offered in much the same spirit that John Dillon pronounced his seemingly restrictive rules more than a century ago. As I described in Section 2.4, Dillon is often depicted as being against local government for his insistence on a narrow construction of their delegated powers in his influential *Treatise on the Law of Municipal Corporations*. It is worth remembering, though, that Dillon's multiple editions (1871–1911) spanned local government's apogee in American affairs. He was, like the "federalists" earlier in the nineteenth century, leaning against the wind of decentralization. To cast him as against local government would be as historically wrong as saying that James Madison, whose ideas framed much of the U.S. Constitution, opposed states' rights, which, of course, he did not (Paul Finkelman 1990). Madison advocated a stronger national government only in the context of a polity in which states had almost all the rights already.

My reading of Dillon and his times suggests that he shared many of the same principles as his supposed opposite, Thomas M. Cooley, who conceived of an inherent right of local self-government. Both of them, along with American federalism's most influential observer, Alexis de Tocqueville, believed that local self-governance is an essential part of a functioning federal system. Americans would hardly consider themselves a free people without it.

Case References

The numbers in brackets refer to sections within this book.

Appeal of Girsh, 263 A.2d 395 (Pa. 1970) [§11.11]
Avery v. Midland County, 390 U.S. 474 (1967) [§§2.1, 2.2, 11.13]
Baker v. Carr, 369 U.S. 186 (1962) [§5.5]
Board of Education v. Nyquist, 453 N.Y.S.2d 643 (1982) [§6.3]
Brown v. Board of Education, 347 U.S. 483 (1954) [§§5.3, 5.5, 5.6]
Casey v. Zoning Warwick Township, 328 A.2d 464 (Pa. 1974) [§11.11]
Claremont v. Governor, 635 A.2d 1375 (N.H. 1993) *("Claremont I")*, 703 A.2d 1353 (N.H. 1997) *("Claremont II")* [§§3.1, 5.12, 6.3, 6.13]
Construction Industry Association v. City of Petaluma, 522 F.2d 897 (9th Cir. 1975) [§3.8]
Dartmouth College v. Woodward, 17 U.S. 122 (1819) [§2.4]
Derolph v. State, 677 N.E.2d 733 (Ohio 1997) [§§5.12, 5.16]
Dolan v. City of Tigard, 512 U.S. 687, 114 S.Ct. 2309 (1994) [§3.15]
Edwards v. California, 314 U.S. 160 (1941) [§3.8]
Euclid v. Ambler, 272 U.S. 365 (1926) [§§1.9, 3.10, 9.5]
First English Evangelical Lutheran Church v. County of Los Angeles, 482 U.S. 304 (1987) [§11.12]
Governor v. State Treasurer, 203 N.W.2d 457 (Mich. 1972) [§5.16]
Hills Development Co. v. Township of Bernards, 510 A.2d 621 (N.J. 1986) *("Mount Laurel III")* [§3.10]
Hunter v. City of Pittsburgh, 207 U.S. 161 (1907) [§§2.4, 9.2]
Kirby v. Township of Bedminster, (N.J. Appellate Division, June 23, 2000, docket A-1682.98T5) [§11.12]
Lochner v. New York, 198 U.S. 45 (1905) [§11.11]
Lucas v. South Carolina Coastal Council, 505 U.S. 1003 (1992) [§11.12]
Lumund v. Board of Adjustment, 73 A.2d 545 (1950) [§3.10]

McDuffy v. Secretary, 615 N.E.2d 516 (Mass. 1993) [§5.17]
McInnis v. Shapiro, 293 F. Supp. 327 (N.D. Ill. 1968) [§6.10]
Mount Laurel I, II, and III: See Southern Burlington County NAACP v. Mount Laurel, and Hills Development Co. v. Township of Bernards.
National Land and Investment v. Kohn, 215 A.2d 597 (Pa. 1965) [§11.11]
Oxford Construction v. Orange, 137 A. 545 (N.J. 1926) [§3.10]
Pauley v. Kelly, 255 S.E.2d 859 (W.Va. 1979) [§5.12]
Plessy v. Ferguson, 163 U.S. 537 (1896) [§5.6]
Reynolds v. Sims, 377 U.S. 695 (1964) [§2.8]
Robinson v. Cahill, 303 A.2d 273 (N.J. 1973) [§5.6]
Rose v. Council, 790 S.W.2d 186 (Ky. 1989) [§5.6]
Salyer Land Co. v. Tulare Lake Basin Water Storage District, 410 U.S. 719 (1973) [§2.1]
San Antonio v. Rodriguez 411 U.S. 1 (1973) [§§5.14, 5.15, 6.3]
San Diego Gas and Electric v. San Diego, 450 U.S. 621 (1981) [§11.7]
Seattle School District No. 1. v. State, 585 P.2d 71 (Wash. 1978) [§6.2]
Serrano v. Priest, 96 Cal. Rptr. 601 (1971) *("Serrano I")*, 135 Cal. Rptr. 345 (1976) *("Serrano II")* [§§5.0—5.18, 6.0—6.12, 6.15—6.18, 7.9, 9.11, 11.3, 11.10]
Serrano v. Unruh, 186 Cal. Rptr. 754 (1982) [§5.15]
Southern Burlington County NAACP v. Township of Mount Laurel, 336 A.2d 713 (N.J. 1975) *("Mount Laurel I");* 456 A.2d 390 (N.J. 1983) *("Mount Laurel II")* [§§3.10, 11.6, 11.7]
State v. Nutley, 125 A. 121 (N.J. 1924) [§3.10]
Twin City Building v. Houghton, 176 N.W. 159 (Minn. 1920) [§8.2]
Unified School District No. 229 v. State, 885 P.2d 1170 (Kans. 1994) [§5.13]
U.S. v. Carolene Products, 304 U.S. 144 (1938) [§5.5]
Wilson v. McHenry County, 416 N.E. 2d 426 (Ill. App. 1981) [§3.10]
WMI v. Falls Township, 517 A.2d 1378 (Pa. Commw. 1986) [§8.4]

General References

The numbers in brackets refer to sections within this book.

Aaronson, Daniel. 1999. "The Effect of School Finance Reform on Population Heterogeneity." *National Tax Journal* 52 (March): 5–29. [§6.16]

Abbott, Carl. 1997. "The Portland Region: Where City and Suburbs Talk to Each Other—and Often Agree." *Housing Policy Debate* 8 (1): 11–51. [§10.6]

Abramson, Alan J., Mitchell S. Tobin, and Matthew R. VanderGoot. 1995. "The Changing Geography of Metropolitan Opportunity: The Segregation of the Poor in U.S. Metropolitan Areas, 1970 to 1990." *Housing Policy Debate* 6 (1): 45–72. [§6.16]

ACIR [U.S. Advisory Commission on Intergovernmental Relations]. 1992. *Local Boundary Commissions: Status and Roles in Forming, Adjusting and Dissolving Local Government Boundaries.* Washington, D.C.: ACIR. [§§2.1, 9.12]

———. 1993. *State Laws Governing Local Government Structure and Administration.* Washington, D.C.: ACIR. [§§2.1, 2.2]

Adelaja, Adesoji O., and Keith Friedman. 1999. "Political Economy of Right to Farm." *Journal of Agricultural and Applied Economics* 31 (December): 565–579. [§11.6]

Adrian, Charles R., and Ernest S. Griffith. 1976. *A History of American City Government: The Formation of Traditions, 1775–1870.* New York: Praeger. [§2.6]

Alchian, Armen A. 1950. "Uncertainty, Evolution, and Economic Theory." *Journal of Political Economy* 58 (June): 211–221. [§4.5]

Altshuler, Alan A., and Jose A. Gómez-Ibáñez, with Arnold M. Howitt. 1993. *Regulation for Revenue: The Political Economy of Land Use Exactions.* Cambridge, Mass.: Lincoln Institute of Land Policy. [§§3.15, 7.7]

Anderson, William. 1927. "Zoning in Minnesota: Eminent Domain vs. Policy Power." *National Municipal Review* 16 (October): 624–629. [§9.5]

Arkes, Hadley. 1994. *The Return of George Sutherland: Restoring a Jurisprudence of Natural Rights.* Princeton, N.J.: Princeton University Press. [§9.5]

Asabere, Paul K., Forrest E. Huffman, and Seyed Mehdian. 1994. "The Adverse Impacts of Local Historic Designation: The Case of Small Apartment Buildings in Philadelphia." *Journal of Real Estate Finance and Economics* 8 (May): 225–234. [§3.3]

Augenblick, John G., John L. Myers, and Amy B. Anderson. 1997. "Equity and Adequacy in School Funding." *Future of Children* 7 (Winter): 63–78. [§5.16]

Avault, John, Alex Ganz, and Daniel M. Holland. 1979. "Tax Relief and Reform in Massachusetts. *National Tax Journal* 32 (June supplement): 289–304. [§5.17]

Axelrod, Robert M. 1984. *The Evolution of Cooperation.* New York: Basic Books. [§8.10]

Baar, Kenneth. 1983. "Guidelines for Drafting Rent Control Laws: Lessons of a Decade." *Rutgers Law Review* 35 (Summer): 723–885.

Bacot, Hunter, Terry Bowen, and Michael R. Fitzgerald. 1994. "Managing the Solid-Waste Crisis: Exploring the Link between Citizen Attitudes, Policy Incentives, and Siting Landfills." *Policy Studies Journal* 22 (Summer): 229–244. [§7.10]

Bader, Robert Smith. 1986. *Prohibition in Kansas: A History.* Lawrence: University Press of Kansas. [§4.1]

Bahl, Roy, David Sjoquist, and W. Loren Williams. 1990. "School Finance Reform and Impact on Property Taxes." *Proceedings of the Eighty-Third Annual Conference on Taxation.* Columbus: National Tax Association–Tax Institute of America [§§5.2, 6.10]

Banfield, Edward C. 1965. *Big City Politics.* New York: Random House. [§4.15]

Barkume, Anthony. 1976. "Criteria for Voting Judgments on a Property Tax Initiative: An Analysis of the Watson Amendment." *National Tax Journal* 29 (December): 436–447. [§5.9]

Barrows, Robert G. 1983. "Beyond the Tenement: Patterns of American Urban Housing, 1870–1930." *Journal of Urban History* 9 (August): 395–420. [§9.3]

Bartik, Timothy. 1986. "Neighborhood Revitalization's Effects on Tenants and the Benefit-Cost Analysis of Government Neighborhood Programs." *Journal of Urban Economics* 19 (March): 234–248. [§4.9]

Barzel, Yoram. 1997. "Parliament as a Wealth Maximizing Institution: The Right to the Residual and the Right to Vote." *International Review of Law and Economics* 17 (December): 455–474. [§2.8]

Barzel, Yoram, and Tim R. Sass. 1990. "The Allocation of Resources by Voting." *Quarterly Journal of Economics* 105 (August): 745–771. [§§2.6, 2.9]

Beito, David T. 1989. *Taxpayers in Revolt: Tax Resistance during the Great Depression.* Chapel Hill: University of North Carolina Press. [§5.4]

Been, Vicki. 1991. "'Exit' as a Constraint on Land Use Exactions: Rethinking the Unconstitutional Conditions Doctrine." *Columbia Law Review* 91 (April): 473–545. [§4.2]

———. 1993. "What's Fairness Got to Do with It? Environmental Justice and the Siting of Locally Undesirable Land Uses." *Cornell Law Review* 78 (September): 1001–1085. [§7.11]

———. 1994a. "Compensated Siting Proposals: Is It Time to Pay Attention?" *Fordham Urban Law Journal* 21 (Spring): 787–826. [§7.10]

———. 1994b. "Locally Undesirable Land Uses in Minority Neighborhoods: Disproportionate Siting or Market Dynamics?" *Yale Law Journal* 103 (April): 1383–1422. [§7.11]

Been, Vicki, and Francis Gupta. 1997. "Coming to the Nuisance or Going to the Barrios? A Longitudinal Analysis of Environmental Justice Claims." *Ecology Law Quarterly* 24: 1–56. [§7.11]

Benabou, Roland. 1996. "Heterogeneity, Stratification, and Growth: Macroeconomic Implications of Community Structure and School Finance." *American Economic Review* 86 (June): 584–609. [§§1.1, 3.17, 6.7]

Benham, Lee, and Philip Keefer. 1991. "Voting in Firms: The Role of Agenda Control, Size, and Voter Homogeneity." *Economic Inquiry* 29 (October): 706–719. [§3.16]

Benson, Charles S. 1972. *Final Report of the [California] Senate Select Committee on School District Finance.* Sacramento. [§5.11]

Benson, Charles S., and Kevin O'Halloran. 1987. "The Economic History of School Finance in the United States." *Journal of Education Finance* 13 (Spring): 495–515. [§6.12]

Berger, Charles. 1998. "Equity without Adjudication: Kansas School Finance Reform and the 1992 School District Finance and Quality Performance Act." *Journal of Law and Education* 27 (January): 1–46. [§5.16]

Berger, Mark C., and Eugenia Toma. 1994. "Variation in State Education Policies and Effects on Student Performance." *Journal of Policy Analysis and Management* 13 (Summer): 477–491. [§6.6]

Berger, Michael M., and Gideon Kanner. 1986. "Thoughts on the White River Junction Manifesto: A Reply to the 'Gang of Five's' Views on Just Compensation for Regulatory Taking of Property." *Loyola of Los Angeles Law Review* 19 (May): 685–754. [§11.11]

Bergstrom, Theodore C., and Robert P. Goodman. 1973. "Private Demand for Public Goods." *American Economic Review* 63 (June): 280–296. [§4.11]

Bergstrom, Theodore C., Daniel L. Rubinfeld, and Perry Shapiro. 1982. "Micro-Based Estimates of Demand Functions for Local School Expenditures." *Econometrica* 50 (September): 1183–1205. [§§4.11, 6.11]

Berkovec, Jim, and Peter Zorn. 1998. "Households That Never Own: An Empirical Analysis Using the American Housing Survey." Freddie Mac working paper, January. [§4.6]

Berle, Adolf A., and Gardiner C. Means. 1932. *The Modern Corporation and Private Property.* New York: Macmillan. [§4.14]

Berry, Jeffrey M., Kent E. Portney, and Ken Thompson. 1993. *The Rebirth of Urban Democracy.* Washington, D.C.: Brookings. [§§1.9, 4.16]

Bewley, Truman F. 1981. "A Critique of Tiebout's Theory of Local Public Expenditures." *Econometrica* 49 (May): 713–740. [§4.17]

Bickers, Kenneth N., and Robert M. Stein. 1998. "The Microfoundations of the Tiebout Model." *Urban Affairs Quarterly* 34 (September): 76–93. [§3.12]

Binney, Charles C. 1894. *Restrictions upon Local and Special Legislation in State Constitutions.* Philadelphia: Kay & Bro. [§2.4]

Bish, Robert L. 1971. *The Public Economy of Metropolitan Areas.* Chicago: Markham Publishing. [§9.9]

Black, Jared B. 1998. "Note: The Land Use Study Commission and the 1997

Amendments to Washington State's Growth Management Act." *Harvard Environmental Law Review* 22: 559–606. [§§10.3, 10.6]

Black, Sandra E. 1999. "Do Better Schools Matter? Parental Valuation of Elementary Education." *Quarterly Journal of Economics* 114 (May): 577–599. [§6.14]

Blaesser, Brian W., and Christine M. Kentopp. 1990. "Impact Fees: The 'Second Generation.'" *Washington University Journal of Urban and Contemporary Law* 38 (Fall): 55–113. [§3.15]

Blair, John P., and Samuel R. Staley. 1995. "Quality Competition and Public Schools: Further Evidence." *Economics of Education Review* 14: 193–198. [§6.8]

Blomquist, Glenn C., Mark C. Berger, and John P. Hoehn. 1988. "New Estimates of Quality of Life in Urban Areas." *American Economic Review* 78 (March): 89–107. [§3.4]

Bloom, Howard S., and Helen F. Ladd. 1982. "Property Tax Revaluation and Tax Levy Growth." *Journal of Urban Economics* 11 (January): 73–84. [§4.13]

Blume, Lawrence E., Daniel L. Rubinfeld, and Perry Shapiro. 1984. "The Taking of Land: When Should Compensation Be Paid?" *Quarterly Journal of Economics* 99 (February): 71–92. [§11.7]

Boarnet, Marlon, and Randall Crane. 1997. "L.A. Story—A Reality Check for Transit-Based Housing." *Journal of the American Planning Association* 63 (Spring): 189–204. [§9.6]

Bogart, William T. 1993. "'What Big Teeth You Have!': Identifying the Motivations for Exclusionary Zoning." *Urban Studies* (December): 1669–1681. [§10.1]

Bogart, William T, and Brian A Cromwell. 1997. "How Much More Is a Good School District Worth?" *National Tax Journal* 50 (June): 215–232. [§6.14]

Boone, Christopher G., and Ali Modarres. 1999. "Creating a Toxic Neighborhood in Los Angeles County—A Historical Examination of Environmental Inequity." *Urban Affairs Review* 35 (November): 163–187. [§9.12]

Borcherding, Thomas, and Robert Deacon. 1972. "The Demand for the Services of Non-Federal Governments." *American Economic Review* 62 (December): 891–901. [§4.11]

Bork, Robert H. 1990. *The Tempting of America: The Political Seduction of the Law.* New York: Free Press. [§5.6]

Borland, Melvin V., and Roy M. Howsen. 1993. "On the Determination of the Critical Level of Market Concentration in Education." *Economics of Education Review* 12: 165–169. [§6.8]

Bowen, Howard. 1943. "The Interpretation of Voting in the Allocation of Economic Resources." *Quarterly Journal of Economics* 58 (November): 27–48. [§4.11]

Brauneis, Robert. 1996. "'The Foundation of Our Regulatory Takings Jurisprudence': The Meaning and Myth of Justice Holmes's Opinion in Pennsylvania Coal v. Mahon." *Yale Law Journal* 106 (December): 613–702. [§11.7]

Brazer, Harvey E., and Therese A. McCarty. 1989. "Municipal Overburden: A Fact in School Finance Litigation?" *Journal of Law and Education* 18 (Fall): 547–566. [§6.3]

Brennan, Geoffrey, and James Buchanan. 1979. "The Logic of Tax Limits: Alternative Constitutional Constraints of the Power to Tax." *National Tax Journal* 32 (June): 11–23. [§5.7]

Brennan, William J. 1977. "State Constitutions and the Protection of Individual Rights." *Harvard Law Review* 90 (January): 489–504. [§5.15]

Breton, Albert. 1973. "Neighborhood Selection and Zoning." In *Issues in Urban Public Economics*, ed. Harold Hochman. Saarbrucken: Institute Internationale de Finance Publique. [§1.5]

Briffault, Richard. 1990a. "Our Localism: Part I—The Structure of Local Government Law." *Columbia Law Review* 90 (January): 1–115. [§3.10]

———. 1990b. "Our Localism: Part II—Localism and Legal Theory." *Columbia Law Review* 90 (March): 346–454. [§4.1]

———. 1992. "Voting Rights, Home Rule, and Metropolitan Governance: The Secession of Staten Island as a Case Study in the Dilemmas of Local Self-Determination." *Columbia Law Review* 92 (May): 775–850. [§11.13]

———. 1996. "The Local Government Boundary Problem in Metropolitan Areas." *Stanford Law Review* 48 (May): 1115–1171. [§10.5]

———. 1997. "The Rise of Sublocal Structures in Urban Governance." *Minnesota Law Review* 82 (December): 503–534. [§4.16]

Briggs, Lloyd V. 1941. *Smoke Abatement.* Boston: The Old Corner Book Store. [§7.4]

Brooks, Richard O. 1974. *New Towns and Communal Values: A Case Study of Columbia, Maryland.* New York: Praeger. [§3.17]

Brownstone, David, and Arthur DeVany. 1991. "Zoning, Returns to Scale, and the Value of Undeveloped Land." *Review of Economics and Statistics* 73 (November): 699–704. [§§3.10, 10.2]

Brueckner, Jan K. 1982. "A Test for Allocative Efficiency in the Local Public Sector." *Journal of Public Economics* 19 (December): 311–321. [§4.17]

———. 1983. "Property Value Maximization and Public Sector Efficiency." *Journal of Urban Economics* 14 (July): 1–15. [§4.17]

Brueckner, Jan K., and Man-Soo Joo. 1991. "Voting with Capitalization." *Regional Science and Urban Economics* 21 (November): 453–467. [§§4.17, 4.11]

Brunner, Eric J., James Murdoch, and Mark Thayer. 1999. "School Finance Reform and Housing Values: Evidence from the Los Angeles Metropolitan Area." Working paper, Department of Economics, San Diego State University, May. [§§6.15, 6.17]

Brunner, Eric J., and Jon Sonstelie. 1997. "Coping with *Serrano:* Voluntary Contributions to California's Local Public Schools." *1996 Proceedings of the Eighty-Ninth Annual Conference on Taxation.* Washington, D.C.: National Tax Association. [§§4.8, 6.15]

Buchanan, James M., and Charles J. Goetz. 1972. "Efficiency Limits of Fiscal Mobility: An Assessment of the Tiebout Model." *Journal of Public Economics* 1 (April): 25–43. [§4.5]

Burchell, Robert W., David Listokin, and William R. Dolphin. 1993. *The Development Impact Assessment Handbook and Model.* Washington, D.C.: Urban Land Institute. [§3.15]

Burkhardt, Lynne C. 1981. *Old Values in a New Town.* New York: Praeger. [§3.17]

Burnell, James D. 1985. "Industrial Land Use, Externalities, and Residential Location." *Urban Studies* 22 (October): 399–408. [§7.6]

Burns, Nancy. 1994. *The Formation of American Local Governments: Private Values in Public Institutions.* New York: Oxford University Press. [§2.1]

Burns, Nancy, and Gerald Gamm. 1997. "Creatures of the State: State Politics and Local Government, 1871–1921." *Urban Affairs Review* 33 (September): 59–96. [§2.8]

Burstein, Melvin L., and Arthur J. Rolnick. 1995. "Congress Should End the Economic War among the States." *1994 Annual Report*, Federal Reserve Bank of Minneapolis. [§7.8]

Byrk, Anthony S., Valerie E. Lee, and Peter B. Holland. 1993. *Catholic Schools and the Common Good.* Cambridge: Harvard University Press. [§6.17]

Calabresi, Guido, and A. Douglas Melamed. 1972. "Property Rules, Liability Rules, and Inalienability: One View of the Cathedral." *Harvard Law Review* 85 (April): 1089–1128. [§7.10]

California State Assembly, Revenue and Taxation Committee and Local Government Committee Staffs. 1980. *No-Property-Tax Cities after Proposition 13.* Rolling Hills Estates, Calif.: Joint Committee Interim Hearing Briefing Book, November 6. [§5.10]

Campbell, Colin D., and William A. Fischel. 1996. "Preferences for School Finance Systems: Voters versus Judges." *National Tax Journal* 49 (March): 1–15. [§5.12]

Caplin, Andrew, Sewin Chan, Charles Freeman, and Joseph Tracy. 1997. *Housing Partnerships: A New Approach to a Market at a Crossroads.* Cambridge: MIT Press, [§1.6]

Cappel, Andrew J. 1991. "A Walk along Willow: Patterns of Land Use Coordination in Pre-Zoning New Haven (1870–1926)." *Yale Law Journal* 101 (December): 617–642. [§§9.4, 9.6]

Card, David, and A. Abigail Payne. 1998. "School Finance Reform, the Distribution of School Spending, and the Distribution of SAT Scores." NBER working paper no. W6766. [§6.7]

Caro, Robert A. 1998. "The City Shaper." *New Yorker*, January 1, 1998, pp. 38–55. [§4.7]

Carrington, Paul D. 1973. "Financing the American Dream: Equality and School Taxes." *Columbia Law Review* 73 (October): 1227–1260. [§5.12]

———. 1997. "Law as 'The Common Thoughts of Men': The Law-Teaching and Judging of Thomas McIntyre Cooley." *Stanford Law Review* 49 (February): 495–546. [§§2.7, 9.5]

———. 1998. "Judicial Independence and Democratic Accountability in Highest State Courts." *Law and Contemporary Problems* 61 (Summer): 79–126. [§§5.2, 5.4]

Carroll, Robert J., and John Yinger. 1994. "Is the Property Tax a Benefit Tax? The Case of Rental Housing." *National Tax Journal* 47 (June): 295–316. [§4.6]

Case, Karl E., and Robert Shiller. 1989. "The Efficiency of the Market for Single Family Homes." *American Economics Review* 79 (March): 125–137. [§3.4]

Case, Karl E., Robert J. Shiller, and Allan N. Weiss. 1993. "Index-Based Futures and Options Markets in Real Estate." *Journal of Portfolio Management* 19 (Winter): 83–92. [§1.6]

Cash, Wilbur J. *The Mind of the South.* New York: Knopf. 1941. [§1.10]

Chapman, Jeffrey. 1981. *Rent Controls in Los Angeles: A Response to Proposition 13.* Los Angeles: University of Southern California School of Public Affairs. [§4.8]

Cheape, Charles W. 1980. *Moving the Masses: Urban Public Transit in New York,*

Boston, and Philadelphia, 1880–1912. Cambridge: Harvard University Press. [§9.4]

Chicoine, David L. "Farmland Values at the Urban Fringe: An Analysis of Sale Price." *Land Economics* 57 (August 1981): 353–362.

Ciccone, Antonio, and Robert E. Hall. 1996. "Productivity and the Density of Economic Activity." *American Economic Review* 86 (March): 54–70. [§7.5]

Cion, Richard M. 1966. "Accommodation Par Excellence: The Lakewood Plan." In *Metropolitan Politics: A Reader*, ed. Michael N. Danielson. Boston: Little, Brown. [§§3.10, 9.9]

Clingermayer, James C. 1993. "Distributive Politics, Ward Representation, and the Spread of Zoning." *Public Choice* 77 (December): 725–739. [§4.15]

———. 1994. "Electoral Representation, Zoning Politics, and the Exclusion of Group Homes." *Political Research Quarterly* 47 (December): 969–984.

Coase, Ronald H. 1960. "The Problem of Social Cost." *Journal of Law and Economics* 3 (October): 1–44. [§§8.1, 8.2]

Cooley, Thomas M. 1868. *A Treatise on the Constitutional Limitations Which Rest upon the Legislative Power of the State of the American Union.* Boston: Little, Brown. [§§9.5, 11.14]

Coons, John E. 1974. "Introduction: 'Fiscal Neutrality' after *Rodriguez*." *Law and Contemporary Problems* 38 (Winter–Spring): 299–308. [§6.10]

———. 1978. "Can Education Be Equal and Excellent?" *Journal of Education Finance* 4 (Fall): 147–157. [§6.10]

Coons, John E., William H. Clune III, and Stephen D. Sugarman. 1969. "Educational Opportunity: A Workable Constitutional Test for State Financial Structures." *California Law Review* 57 (April): 305–421. [§§6.10, 6.17]

———. 1970. *Private Wealth and Public Education.* Cambridge: Belknap Press of Harvard University Press. [§§1.1, 5.5, 5.8, 7.9]

Coons, John E., and Stephen D. Sugarman. 1978. *Education by Choice: The Case for Family Control.* Berkeley: University of California Press. [§6.5]

———. 1992. "The Scholarship Initiative: A Model State Law for Elementary and Secondary School Choice." *Journal of Law and Education* 21 (Fall): 529–567. [§11.3]

Coulton, David L. 1996. "The Weighting Game: Two Decades of Fiscal Neutrality in New Mexico." *Journal of Education Finance* 22 (Summer): 28–59. [§5.16]

Courant, Paul N., and Susanna Loeb. 1997. "Centralization of School Finance in Michigan." *Journal of Policy Analysis and Management* 16 (Winter): 114–136. [§6.3]

Coyle, Dennis J. 1993. *Property Rights and the Constitution: Shaping Society through Land Use Regulation.* Albany: State University of New York Press. [§11.7]

Cronin, Thomas E. 1989. *Direct Democracy: The Politics of Initiative, Referendum, and Recall.* Cambridge: Harvard University Press. [§4.13]

Dana, David A. 1995. "Natural Preservation and the Race to Develop." *University of Pennsylvania Law Review* 143 (January): 655–708. [§3.9]

Danielson, Michael N. 1976. *The Politics of Exclusion.* New York: Columbia University Press. [§9.7]

Danielson, Michael N., and Paul G. Lewis. 1996. "City Bound: Political Science and the American Metropolis." *Political Research Quarterly* 49 (March): 203–220. [§1.9]

DeBartolome, Charles A. M., and Mark M. Spiegel. 1995. "Regional Competition for Domestic and Foreign Investment: Evidence from State Development Expenditures." *Journal of Urban Economics* 37 (May): 239–259. [§3.8]

Dee, Thomas S. 2000. "The Capitalization of Education Finance Reforms." *Journal of Law and Economics* 43 (April): 185–214. [§§6.3, 6.4, 6.7, 9.12]

Demsetz, Harold. 1969. "Information and Efficiency: Another Viewpoint." *Journal of Law and Economics* 12 (April): 1–22. [§4.17]

Deutsch, Stuart, and JoAnn Butler. 1987. "Recent Limits on Municipal Antitrust Liability." *Land Use Law and Zoning Digest* 39 (January): 3–7. [§11.7]

Diamond, Stephen. 1983. "The Death and Transfiguration of Benefit Taxation: Special Assessments in Nineteenth-Century America." *Journal of Legal Studies* 12 (June): 201–240. [§4.16]

Dilger, Robert J. 1992. *Neighborhood Politics: Residential Community Associations in American Governance.* New York: NYU Press. [§§2.2, 4.12]

Dillon, John F. 1871. *Commentaries on the Law of Municipal Corporations.* Boston: Little, Brown. [§§2.4, 2.8, 2.10, 3.16, 9.5, 11.2, 11.14]

DiPasquale, Denise, and Edward L. Glaeser. 1999. "Incentives and Social Capital: Are Homeowners Better Citizens?" *Journal of Urban Economics* 45 (March): 354–384. [§1.6]

Dixit, Avinash. 1991. "Irreversible Investment with Price Ceilings." *Journal of Political Economy* 99 (June): 541–557. [§4.10]

Do, A. Quang, and C. F. Sirmans. 1994. "Residential Property Tax Capitalization: Discount Rate Evidence from California." *National Tax Journal* 57 (June): 341–348. [§3.6]

Dodd, Edwin Merrick. 1954. *American Business Corporations until 1860, with Special Reference to Massachusetts.* Cambridge: Harvard University Press. [§2.4]

Dowding, Keith, Peter John, and Stephen Biggs. 1994. "Tiebout: A Survey of the Empirical Literature." *Urban Studies* 31 (May): 767–797. [§3.12]

Downes, Thomas A. 1992. "Evaluating the Impact of School Finance Reform on the Provision of Public Education: The California Case." *National Tax Journal* 45 (December): 405–420. [§6.7]

Downes, Thomas A., and David N. Figlio. 1999. "Economic Inequality and the Provision of Schooling." *Federal Reserve Bank of New York Economic Policy Review* 5 (September): 99–110. [§6.16]

Downes, Thomas A., and Shane M. Greenstein. 1996. "Understanding the Supply Decisions of Nonprofits: Modeling the Location of Private Schools." *RAND Journal of Economics* 27 (Summer): 365–390. [§6.17]

Downes, Thomas A., and David Schoeman. 1998. "School Finance Reform and Private School Enrollment: Evidence from California." *Journal of Urban Economics* 43 (May): 418–443. [§6.17]

Downes, Thomas A., and Mona P. Shah. 1995. "The Effect of School Finance Reforms on the Level and Growth of Per Pupil Expenditures." Discussion Paper 95–05, Department of Economics, Tufts University. [§6.1]

Downs, Anthony. 1973. *Opening Up the Suburbs: An Urban Strategy for America.* New Haven: Yale University Press. [§1.1]

———. 1983. *Rental Housing in the 1980s.* Washington, D.C.: Brookings. [§4.7]

———. 1994. *New Visions for Metropolitan America.* Washington, D.C.: Brookings. [§10.0]

Dresch, Marla, and Steven M. Sheffrin. 1997. *Who Pays for Development Fees and Exactions?* San Francisco: Public Policy Institute of California. [§3.15]

Duncombe, William, and John Yinger. 1997. "Why Is It So Hard to Help Central City Schools?" *Journal of Policy Analysis and Management* 16 (January): 85–113. [§6.9]

Dunlavy, Colleen A. 1999. "A Quiet Revolution: The Declining Power of Small Shareholders in Nineteenth-Century America." Working paper, Department of History, University of Wisconsin–Madison, October. [§2.7]

Dunn, L. F. 1979. "Measuring the Value of Community." *Journal of Urban Economics* 6 (July): 371–382. [§4.10]

East, John Porter. *Council-Manager Government: The Political Thought of Its Founder, Richard S. Childs.* Chapel Hill: University of North Carolina Press. 1965. [§2.2]

Easterbrook, Frank H., and Daniel R. Fischel. 1983. "Voting in Corporate Law." *Journal of Law and Economics* 26 (June): 395–427. [§4.12]

———. 1991. *The Economic Structure of Corporate Law.* Cambridge: Harvard University Press. [§§2.7, 4.4]

Ellickson, Robert C. 1973. "Alternatives to Zoning: Covenants, Nuisance Rules, and Fines as Land Use Controls." *University of Chicago Law Review* 40 (Summer): 681–782. [§§1.1, 11.7]

———. 1977. "Suburban Growth Controls: An Economic and Legal Analysis." *Yale Law Journal* 86 (January): 385–511. [§§1.10, 4.11, 11.7, 11.9, 11.11]

———. 1979. "Public Property Rights: A Government's Rights and Duties When Its Landowners Come into Conflict with Outsiders." *Southern California Law Review* 52 (September): 1627–1670. [§§8.12, 11.8]

———. 1982. "Cities and Homeowners Associations." *University of Pennsylvania Law Review* 130 (June): 1519–1580. [§§1.1, 2.2]

———. 1991a. *Order without Law.* Cambridge: Harvard University Press. [§§8.3, 8.10]

———. 1991b. "Rent Control: A Comment on Olsen." *Chicago-Kent Law Review* 67: 947–954. [§4.9]

———. 1998. "New Institutions for Old Neighborhoods." *Duke Law Journal* 48 (October): 75–110). [§§1.1, 4.16]

Ellickson, Robert C., and Vicki L. Been. 2000. *Land Use Controls: Cases and Materials.* Gaithersburg, Md.: Aspen. [§§2.6, 2.9, 8.4]

Ellickson, Robert C., and A. Dan Tarlock. 1981. *Land-Use Controls: Cases and Materials.* Boston: Little, Brown. [§10.6]

Elmore, Richard F., and Milbrey W. McLaughlin. 1982. *Reform and Retrenchment: The Politics of California School Finance Reform.* Cambridge: Ballinger. [§5.11]

Ely, James W., Jr. 1999. "The Oxymoron Reconsidered: Myth and Reality in the Origins of Substantive Due Process." *Constitutional Commentary* 16 (Summer): 315–345. [§11.11]

Ely, John Hart. 1980. *Democracy and Distrust: A Theory of Judicial Review.* Cambridge: Harvard University Press. [§§5.5, 11.3]

Engelhardt, Gary V., and Christopher J. Mayer. 1998. "Intergenerational Transfers, Borrowing Constraints, and Saving Behavior: Evidence from the Housing Market." *Journal of Urban Economics* 44 (July): 135–157. [§1.2]

Enrich, Peter D. 1995. "Leaving Equality Behind: New Directions in School Finance Reform." *Vanderbilt Law Review* 48 (January): 101–194. [§§5.3, 5.15]

———. 1996. "Saving the States from Themselves: Commerce Clause Constraints on State Tax Incentives for Business." *Harvard Law Review* 110 (December): 377–468. [§7.8]

Epple, Dennis, and Glenn J. Platt. 1998. "Equilibrium and Local Redistribution in an Urban Economy When Households Differ in Both Preferences and Incomes." *Journal of Urban Economics* 43 (January): 23–51. [§3.10]

Epple, Dennis, and Thomas Romer. 1989. "On the Flexibility of Municipal Boundaries." *Journal of Urban Economics* 26 (November): 307–319. [§§2.3, 3.14]

Epple, Dennis, and Allan Zelenitz. 1981. "The Implications of Competition among Jurisdiction: Does Tiebout Need Politics?" *Journal of Political Economy* 89 (December): 1197–1218. [§4.5]

Epstein, Richard A. 1985. *Takings: Private Property and the Power of Eminent Domain.* Cambridge: Harvard University Press. [§§2.4, 11.11]

Erickson, Rodney A., and David R. Wollover. 1987. "Local Tax Burdens and the Supply of Business Sites in Suburban Municipalities." *Journal of Regional Science* 27 (February): 25–37. [§7.8]

Esty, Daniel C. 1996. "Revitalizing Environmental Federalism." *Michigan Law Review* 95 (December): 570–653. [§§1.1, 7.0, 7.1, 7.2, 7.3]

Evans, William N., Sheila Murray, and Robert M. Schwab. 1997. "School Houses, Court Houses, and State Houses after *Serrano.*" *Journal of Policy Analysis and Management* 16 (January): 10–31. [§§5.2, 6.1]

Evans, William N., and Robert M. Schwab. 1995. "Finishing High School and Starting College: Do Catholic Schools Make a Difference?" *Quarterly Journal of Economics* 110 (November): 941–974. [§6.17]

Fallis, George, and Lawrence B. Smith. 1984. "Uncontrolled Prices in a Controlled Market: The Case of Rent Controls." *American Economic Review* 74 (March): 193–202. [§4.10]

Farber, Stephen. 1998. "Undesirable Facilities and Property Values: A Summary of Empirical Studies." *Ecological Economics* 24 (January): 1–14. [§8.3]

Feldstein, Martin, and Marian Vaillant Wrobel. 1998. "Can State Taxes Redistribute Income?" *Journal of Public Economics* 68 (June): 369–396. [§7.9]

Fennell, Lee Anne. 2000. "Hard Bargains and Real Steals: Land Use Exactions Revisited." *Iowa Law Review* 86 (October): 1–85. [§§3.15, 11.9]

Fernandez, Raquel, and Richard Rogerson. 1996. "Income Distribution, Communities, and the Quality of Public Education." *Quarterly Journal of Economics* 111 (February): 135–164. [§3.17]

———. 1999. "Education Finance Reform and Investment in Human Capital: Lessons from California." *Journal of Public Economics* 74 (December): 327–350. [§5.15]

Figlio, David N. 1997. "Did the 'Tax Revolt' Reduce School Performance?" *Journal of Public Economics* 65 (September): 245–269. [§§5.17, 6.16]

Figlio, David N., Thomas A. Husted, and Lawrence W. Kenny. 2000. "Constitutions, Court Decisions, and Inequality in School Spending." Working paper, Department of Economics, University of Florida, Gainesville. [§5.5]

Finkelman, Paul. 1990. "James Madison and the Bill of Rights: A Reluctant Paternity." *Supreme Court Review* 1990: 301–347. [§11.14]

Fischel, William A. 1975. "Fiscal and Environmental Considerations in the Location of Firms in Suburban Communities." In *Fiscal Zoning and Land Use Con-*

trols, ed. Edwin S. Mills and Wallace E. Oates. Lexington, Mass.: Heath-Lexington Books. [§§7.5, 7.6, 7.7. 7.11, 11.2]

———. 1976. "An Evaluation of Proposals for Metropolitan Sharing of Commercial and Industrial Property Tax Base." *Journal of Urban Economics* 3 (July): 253–263. [§§6.3, 7.9]

———. 1978. "A Property Rights Approach to Municipal Zoning." *Land Economics* 54 (February): 64–81. [§3.9]

———. 1979. "Determinants of Voting on Environmental Quality: A Study of a New Hampshire Pulp Mill Referendum." *Journal of Environmental Economics and Management* 6 (June): 107–118. [§§6.3, 7.11]

———. 1980. "Zoning and the Exercise of Monopoly Power: A Reevaluation." *Journal of Urban Economics* 8 (November): 283–293. [§11.11]

———. 1981. "Is Local Government Structure in Large Urbanized Areas Monopolistic or Competitive?" *National Tax Journal* 34 (March): 95–104. [§3.11]

———. 1982. "The Urbanization of Agricultural Land: A Review of the National Agricultural Lands Study." *Land Economics* 58 (May): 236–259. [§2.3]

———. 1985. *The Economics of Zoning Laws: A Property Rights Approach to American Land Use Controls.* Baltimore: Johns Hopkins University Press. [§§3.9, 10.0]

———. 1989. "Did *Serrano* Cause Proposition 13?" *National Tax Journal* 42 (December): 465–474. [§§5.8, 5.10]

———. 1990. *Do Growth Controls Matter?* Cambridge: Lincoln Institute of Land Policy. [§§1.9, 3.10, 10.1]

———. 1991a. "Discounting in One Lesson." *The Practical Litigator* 2 (September): 27–36. [§1.4]

———. 1991b. "Exploring the Kozinski Paradox: Why Is More Efficient Regulation a Taking of Property?" *Chicago-Kent Law Review* 67 (3): 865–912. [§4.9]

———. 1992. "Property Taxation and the Tiebout Model: Evidence for the Benefit View from Zoning and Voting." *Journal of Economic Literature* 30 (March): 171–177. [§3.16]

———. 1994. "Zoning, Nonconvexities, and T. Jack Foster's City." *Journal of Urban Economics* 35 (March): 175–181. [§3.17]

———. 1995. *Regulatory Takings: Law, Economics, and Politics.* Cambridge: Harvard University Press. [§§1.9, 11.7, 11.8, 11.12]

———. 1996a. "How *Serrano* Caused Proposition 13." *Journal of Law and Politics* 12: 607–645. [§§5.9, 5.10]

———. 1996b. "The Political Economy of Just Compensation: Lessons from the Military Draft for the Takings Issue." *Harvard Journal of Law and Public Policy* 20 (Fall): 23–63. [§7.11]

———. 1998a. "The Ethics of Land Value Taxation Revisited: Has the Millennium Arrived without Anyone Noticing?" In *Land Value Taxation: Can It and Will It Work Today?* ed. Dick Netzer. Cambridge: Lincoln Institute of Land Policy. [§11.2]

———. 1998b. "How Judges Are Making Public Schools Worse." *City Journal* 8 (Summer): 30–42. [§6.18]

———. 1999. "Does the American Way of Zoning Cause the Suburbs of U.S. Metropolitan Areas to Be Too Spread Out?" In *Governance and Opportunity in Metropolitan Areas*, ed. Alan Altshuler, William Morrill, Harold Wolman, and

Faith Mitchell. Washington, D.C.: National Academy Press. [§§10.0, 10.2, 11.7]

———. 2001. "Why Are There NIMBYs?" *Land Economics* 77 (February): 144–152. [§11.5]

Fisher, Glenn W. 1996. *The Worst Tax? A History of the Property Tax in America.* Lawrence: University of Kansas Press. [§1.1]

Flanigan, J. J. 1989. "West Virginia's Financial Dilemma: The Ideal School System in the Real World." *Journal of Education Finance* 15 (Fall): 229–243. [§5.11]

Ford, Deborah A. 1989. "The Effect of Historic District Designation on Single-Family Home Prices." *AREUEA Journal* 17 (Fall): 353–362. [§3.3]

Fox, William F. 1981. "Fiscal Differentials and Industrial Location: Some Empirical Evidence." *Urban Studies* 18 (1): 105–111. [§§6.3, 7.8]

Frantz, Douglas, and Catherine Collins. *Celebration, U.S.A.* New York: Holt. 1999. [§3.17]

Frieden, Bernard J., and Lynn B. Sagalyn. 1989. *Downtown, Inc.: How America Rebuilds Cities.* Cambridge: MIT Press. [§1.9]

Friedman, Lawrence M. 1988. "State Constitutions in Historical Perspective." *The Annals* 496 (March): 33–42. [§5.6]

Friedman, Lee S., and Michael Wiseman. 1978. "Understanding the Equity Consequences of School Finance Reform." *Harvard Educational Review* 48 (May): 193–226. [§5.1]

Frug, Gerald. 1980. "The City as a Legal Concept." *Harvard Law Review* 93 (April): 1057–1154. [§§2.4, 9.2]

Fuchs, Victor R., and Diane M. Reklis. 1994. "Mathematical Achievement in Eighth Grade: Interstate and Racial Differences." NBER working paper no. 4784 (June). [§6.6]

Gabriel, Stuart A., Janice Shack-Marquez, and William Wascher. 1993. "The Effects of Regional House Price and Labor Market Variability on Interregional Migration: Evidence from the 1980s." In *Housing Markets and Residential Mobility,* ed. G. Thomas Kingsley and Margery A. Turner. Washington, D.C.: Urban Institute Press. [§10.18]

Gale, Diana Hadden. 1981. "The Politics of School Finance Reform in Washington State, 1975–1979." Ph.D. diss., Department of Urban Planning, University of Washington. [§5.12]

Garvey, Deborah L. 2000. "Does School Finance Centralization Reduce the Growth of Instructional Spending? The Case of Reform in Washington." Working paper, Office of Population Research, Princeton University. [§6.2]

George, Henry. 1879. *Progress and Poverty.* New York: Appleton. [§11.2]

Gerrard, Michael B. 1994. *Whose Backyard, Whose Risk? Fear and Fairness in Toxic and Nuclear Waste Siting.* Cambridge: MIT Press. [§7.10]

Gillette, Clayton P., and Lynn A. Baker. 1999. *Local Government Law: Cases and Materials,* 2d ed. Gaithersburg, Md.: Aspen. [§§2.1, 2.4]

Giovannotto, G. Alessandro. 1994. "Econometric Analysis of the Mt. Laurel Approach to Providing Affordable Housing in New Jersey." Undergraduate honors thesis, Department of Economics, Dartmouth College. [§§11.7, 11.11]

Glaeser, Edward L. 1996. "The Incentive Effects of Property Taxes on Local Governments." *Public Choice* 89 (October): 93–111. [§8.2]

Glaeser, Edward L., Matthew Kahn, and Jordan Rappaport. 2000. "Why Do the Poor Live in Cities?" NBER working paper no. 7636. [§9.6]

Goetz, Stephan J., and David L. Debertin. 1992. "Rural Areas and Education Reform in Kentucky: An Early Assessment of Revenue Equalization." *Journal of Education Finance* 18 (Fall): 163–179. [§6.10]

Goodman, James E. *Stories of Scottsboro.* New York: Pantheon Books. 1994. [§1.10]

Goodwin, Carole. 1979. *The Oak Park Strategy: Community Control of Racial Change.* Chicago: University of Chicago Press. [§11.5]

Gordon, Peter, Ajay Kumar, and Harry W. Richardson. 1989. "Congestion, Changing Metropolitan Structure, and City Size in the United States." *International Regional Science Review* 12: 45–56. [§10.5]

Graham, Amy E., and Thomas A. Husted. 1993. "Understanding State Variations in SAT Scores." *Economics of Education Review* 12 (September): 197–202. [§6.6]

Greenberg, Jack. 1994. *Crusaders in the Courts: How a Dedicated Band of Lawyers Fought for the Civil Rights Revolution.* New York: Basic Books. [§5.5]

Grether, David M., and Peter Mieszkowski. 1980. "The Effects of Nonresidential Land Uses on the Prices of Adjacent Housing: Some Estimates of Proximity Effects." *Journal of Urban Economics* 8 (July): 1–15. [§3.3]

Grinder, Robert D. 1978. "From Insurgency to Efficiency: The Smoke Abatement Campaign in Pittsburgh before World War I." *Western Pennsylvania Historical Magazine* 61: 187–202. [§7.4]

———. 1980. "The Battle for Clean Air: The Smoke Problem in Post–Civil War America." In *Pollution and Reform in American Cities, 1870–1930,* ed. Martin V. Melosi. Austin: University of Texas Press. [§7.4]

Grosskopf, Shawna, Kathy J. Hayes, Lori L. Taylor, and William Weber. 1997. "Budget-Constrained Frontier Measures of Fiscal Equality and Efficiency in Schooling." *Review of Economics and Statistics* 79 (February): 116–124. [§6.2]

Grossman, Philip J., Panayiotis Mavros, and Robert W. Wassmer. 1999. "Public Sector Technical Inefficiency in Large U.S. Cities." *Journal of Urban Economics* 46 (September): 278–299. [§9.10]

Grubb, W. Norton. 1974. "The First Round of Legislative Reforms in the Post-*Serrano* World." *Law and Contemporary Problems* 38 (Winter–Spring): 459–492. [§5.14]

Gruen, Claude. 1977. *Effects of Regulation on Housing Costs: Two Case Studies.* Washington: Urban Land Institute. [§10.18]

Guntermann, Karl L., and Richard L. Smith. 1987. "Efficiency of Real Estate Markets." *Land Economics* 63 (February): 34–45. [§3.4]

Gupta, Shreekant, George Van Houtven, and Maureen Cropper. 1996. "Paying for Permanence: An Economic Analysis of EPA's Cleanup Decisions at Superfund Sites." *Rand Journal of Economics* 27 (Fall): 563–582. [§7.11]

Gyourko, Joseph. 1990. "Rent Controls and Rental Housing Quality—A Note on the Effects of New York City's Old Controls" *Journal of Urban Economics* 27: (May): 398–409. [§4.7]

———. 1991. "Impact Fees, Exclusionary Zoning, and the Density of New Development." *Journal of Urban Economics* 30 (September): 242–256. [§11.9]

Gyourko, Joseph, and Richard Voith. 1992. "Local Market and National Components in House Price Appreciation." *Journal of Urban Economics* 32 (July): 52–69. [§3.4]

Haar, Charles M. 1996. *Suburbs under Siege.* Princeton: Princeton University Press. [§1.1]

Hahn, Alan J. 1970. "Planning in Rural Areas." *AIP Journal* 36 (January): 40–49. [§10.1]

Hain, Elwood. 1974. "Milliken v. Green: Breaking the Legislative Deadlock." *Law and Contemporary Problems* 38 (Winter–Spring): 350–365. [§§5.12, 5.16]

Hamilton, Bruce W. 1975. "Zoning and Property Taxation in a System of Local Governments." *Urban Studies* 12 (June): 205–211. [§§3.15, 3.16, 4.3]

———. 1976. "Capitalization of Intrajurisdictional Differences in Local Tax Prices." *American Economic Review* 66 (December): 743–753. [§§3.16, 6.4]

———. 1979. "Capitalization and the Regressivity of the Property Tax: Empirical Evidence." *National Tax Journal* 32 (June supplement): 169–180. [§3.16]

———. 1982. "Wasteful Commuting." *Journal of Political Economy* 90 (October): 1035–1053. [§3.13]

Hamilton, Bruce W., Edwin S. Mills, and David Puryear. 1975. "The Tiebout Hypothesis and Residential Income Segregation." In *Fiscal Zoning and Land Use Controls*, ed. Edwin S. Mills and Wallace E. Oates. Lexington, Mass.: Heath-Lexington Books. [§6.16]

Hamilton, Bruce W., and Robert Schwab. 1985. "Expected Appreciation in Urban Housing Markets." *Journal of Urban Economics* 18 (July): 103–118. [§3.4]

Hanford, A. Chester. 1926. *Problems in Municipal Government.* Chicago: A. W. Shaw. [§§9.3, 9.4]

Hanushek, Eric A., and Julie A. Somers. 1999. "Schooling, Inequality, and the Impact of Government." NBER working paper no. W7450. [§6.7]

Harrison, Russell S., and G. Alan Tarr. 1996. "School Finance and Inequality in New Jersey." In *Constitutional Politics and the States*, ed. G. Alan Tarr. Westport, Conn.: Greenwood Press. [§6.2]

Hartog, Hendrik. 1983. *Public Property and Private Power: The Corporation of the City of New York in American Law, 1730–1870.* Chapel Hill: University of North Carolina Press. [§2.6]

Haurin, Donald R., and David Brasington. 1996. "School Quality and Real House Prices: Inter- and Intrametropolitan Effects." *Journal of Housing Economics* 5 (December): 351–368. [§§6.14, 10.2]

Hayek, Friederich A. 1945. "The Use of Knowledge in Society." *American Economic Review* 35 (September): 519–530. [§3.2]

Hayes, Kathy J., and Lori L. Taylor. 1996. "Neighborhood School Characteristics: What Signals Quality To Homebuyers?" *Economic Review of the Federal Reserve of Dallas* (fourth quarter): 2–9. [§6.14]

Heikkila, Eric. 1996. "Are Municipalities Tieboutian Clubs?" *Regional Science and Urban Economics* 26 (April): 203–226. [§9.10]

Heise, Michael. 1995. "The Effect of Constitutional Litigation on Education Finance: More Preliminary Analyses and Modeling." *Journal of Education Finance* 21 (Fall): 195–216. [§6.2]

Helms, L. Jay. 1985. "The Effect of State and Local Taxes on Economic Growth: A Time Series Cross Section Approach." *Review of Economics and Statistics* 67 (November): 574–582. [§3.8]

Henderson, J. Vernon. 1985. "The Tiebout Hypothesis: Bring Back the Entrepreneurs." *Journal of Political Economy* 93 (April): 248–264. [§4.5]

Henderson, J. Vernon, Peter Mieszkowski, and Yves Sauvageau. 1978. "Peer Group Effects and Educational Production Functions." *Journal of Public Economics* 10: 97–106. [§3.17]

Henke, Joseph T. 1986. "Financing Public Schools in California: The Aftermath of Serrano v. Priest and Proposition 13." *University of San Francisco Law Review* 21 (Fall): 1–39. [§§4.8, 6.10]

Henke, Joseph T., and Miles A. Woodlief. 1988. "The Effect of Proposition 13 Court Decisions on California Local Government Revenue Sources." *University of San Francisco Law Review* 22 (Winter): 251–292. [§4.8]

Heyman, Ira Michael, and Thomas K. Gilhool. 1964. "The Constitutionality of Imposing Increased Community Costs on New Suburban Residents through Subdivision Exactions." *Yale Law Journal* 73 (June): 1119–1157. [§3.15]

Hickrod, G. Alan, Ramesh Chaudhari, Gwen Pruyne, and Jin Meng. 1995. "The Effect of Constitutional Litigation on Educational Finance: A Further Analysis." In *Selected Papers in School Finance 1995*. Washington, D.C.: National Center for Education Statistics. [§§5.2, 6.6]

Hills, Roderick M., Jr. 1998. "Federalism in Constitutional Context." *Harvard Journal of Law and Public Policy* 22 (Fall): 181–196. [§11.14]

Hinds, Dudley S., and Nicholas Ordway. 1986. "The Influence of Race on Rezoning Decisions: Equality of Treatment in Black and White Census Tracts, 1955–1980." *Review of Black Political Economy* 14 (Spring): 51–63. [§4.15]

Hirschman, Albert. 1970. *Exit, Voice, and Loyalty: Responses to Decline in Firms, Organizations, and States.* Cambridge: Harvard University Press. [§4.1]

———. 1978. "Exit, Voice, and the State." *World Politics* 31 (October): 90–107. [§4.1]

Holcombe, Randall G. 1989. "The Median Voter Model in Public Choice Theory." *Public Choice* 61 (May): 115–125. [§4.11]

Holderness, Clifford. 1998. "Standing." *New Palgrave Dictionary of Economics and the Law.* London: Macmillan. [§11.8]

Holland, Daniel M., ed. 1970. *The Assessment of Land Value.* Madison: University of Wisconsin Press. [§11.2]

Holtz-Eakin, Douglas, and Harvey S. Rosen. 1989. "The 'Rationality' of Municipal Capital Spending: Evidence from New Jersey." *Regional Science and Urban Economics* 19 (August): 517–536. [§4.13]

Horwitz, Morton J. 1982. "The History of the Public/Private Distinction." *University of Pennsylvania Law Review* 130 (June): 1423–1428. [§2.4]

Hoxby, Caroline Mintner. 1996. "How Teachers' Unions Affect Education Production." *Quarterly Journal of Economics* 111 (August): 671–718. [§6.9]

———. 1997. "How to Do (and Not to Do) School Finance Equalization: The Legacy and Lesson of *Serrano*." *1996 Proceedings of the Eighty-Ninth Annual Conference on Taxation.* Washington, D.C.: National Tax Association. [§§6.2, 6.9]

———. 1998. "All School Finance Equalizations Are Not Created Equal." NBER working paper no. 6792. [§§6.2, 6.9]

———. 1999. "The Productivity of Schools and Other Local Public Goods Producers." *Journal of Public Economics* 74 (October): 1–30. [§4.17]

———. 2000. "Does Competition among Public Schools Benefit Students and Taxpayers?" *American Economic Review* 90 (December): 1209–1238. [§6.8]

Hoyt, William H. 1999. "Leviathan, Local Government Expenditures, and Capitalization." *Regional Science and Urban Economics* 29 (March): 155–171. [§4.13]

Hughes, William T., and C. F. Sirmans. 1992. "Traffic Externalities and Single-Family House Prices." *Journal of Regional Science* 32 (November): 487–500. [§3.3]

Hurst, James Willard. 1956. *Law and the Conditions of Freedom in the Nineteenth-Century United States.* Madison: University of Wisconsin Press. [§1.7]

Husted, Thomas A., and Lawrence W. Kenny. 1997. "Efficiency in Education: Evidence from the States." *1996 Proceedings of the Eighty-Ninth Annual Conference on Taxation.* Washington, D.C.: National Tax Association. [§6.6]

———. 2000. "Evidence on the Impact of State Government on Primary and Secondary Education and the Equity-Efficiency Tradeoff." *Journal of Law and Economics* 43 (April): 285–308. [§6.9]

Ingberman, Daniel E. 1995. "Siting Noxious Facilities: Are Markets Efficient?" *Journal of Environmental Economics and Management* 29 (part 2, November): S-20—S-33. [§§8.1, 8.3—8.5, 8.7]

Inman, Robert P. 1978. "Testing Political Economy's 'As If' Proposition: Is the Median Income Voter Really Decisive?" *Public Choice* 33 (4): 45–65. [§4.11]

Inman, Robert P., and Daniel L. Rubinfeld. 1997. "Making Sense of the Antitrust State-Action Doctrine: Balancing Political Participation and Economic Efficiency in Regulatory Federalism." *Texas Law Review* 75 (May): 1203–1299. [§8.5]

Jackson, Kenneth T. 1972. "Metropolitan Government Versus Political Autonomy: Politics on the Crabgrass Frontier." In *Cities in American History*, ed. Kenneth T. Jackson and Stanley Schultz. New York: Knopf. [§9.3]

Johnes, Gerraint, and Thomas Hyclak. 1999. "House Prices and Regional Labor Markets." *Annals of Regional Science* 33 (February): 33–49. [§10.18]

Joint Economic Committee, U.S. Congress. 2000. *U.S. Employment Trends and Development.* Washington, D.C.: Joint Economic Committee, June. [§2.0]

Jones, Charles O. 1975. *Clean Air: The Policies and Politics of Pollution Control.* Pittsburgh: University of Pittsburgh Press. [§7.4]

Joondeph, Bradley W. 1995. "The Good, the Bad, and the Ugly: An Empirical Analysis of Litigation-Prompted School Finance Reform." *Santa Clara Law Review* 35: 763–824. [§6.1]

Jud, G. Donald, and J. M. Watts. 1981. "Schools and Housing Values." *Land Economics* 57 (August): 459–470. [§6.14]

Katz, Lawrence, and Kenneth Rosen. 1987. "The Interjurisdictional Effects of Growth Controls on Housing Prices." *Journal of Law and Economics* 30 (April): 149–160. [§3.3]

Kiel, Katherine A. 1995. "Measuring the Impact of the Discovery and Cleaning of Identified Hazardous-Waste Sites on House Values." *Land Economics* 71 (November): 428–435. [§3.3]

Kinkade, Brent S. 1992. "Municipal Antitrust Immunity after City of Columbia v. Omni Outdoor Advertising." *Washington Law Review* 67 (April): 479–500 [§5.7]

Kirp, David L., John P. Dwyer, and Larry Rosenthal. 1995. *Our Town: Race, Housing, and the Soul of Suburbia.* New Brunswick, N.J.: Rutgers University Press. [§3.10]

Klarman, Michael J. 1991. "The Puzzling Resistance to Political Process Theory." *Virginia Law Review* 77 (May): 747–832. [§5.6]

Kline, Jeffrey, and Dennis Wichelns. 1994. "Using Referendum Data to Characterize Public Support for Purchasing Development Rights to Farmland." *Land Economics* 70 (May): 223–233. [§11.7]

Kluger, Richard. 1975. *Simple Justice: The History of Brown v. Board of Education and Black America's Struggle for Equality*. New York: Knopf. [§5.6]

Knaap, Gerrit J. 1985. "The Price Effects of Urban Growth Boundaries in Metropolitan Portland, Oregon." *Land Economics* 61 (February): 28–35. [§10.6]

Knetsch, Jack L. 1983. *Property Rights and Compensation: Compulsory Acquisition and Other Losses*. Toronto: Butterworths. [§7.10]

Kohlhase, Janet E. 1991. "The Impact of Toxic-Waste Sites on Housing Values." *Journal of Urban Economics* 30 (July): 1–26. [§3.3]

Kozol, Jonathan. 1991. *Savage Inequalities*. New York: Crown. [§5.8]

Krier, James E., and Stewart J. Schwab. 1995. "Property Rules and Liability Rules: The Cathedral in Another Light." *NYU Law Review* 70 (May): 440–483. [§7.10]

Kuttner, Robert. 1980. *Revolt of the Haves*. New York: Simon and Schuster. [§5.10]

Ladd, Helen F. 1975. "Local Education Expenditures, Fiscal Capacity, and the Composition of the Property Tax Base." *National Tax Journal* 28 (June 1975): 145–158.

———. 1976. "State-wide Taxation of Commercial and Industrial Property for Education." *National Tax Journal* 29 (June): 143–153. [§6.3]

Ladd, Helen F., and Edward W. Harris. 1995. "Statewide Taxation of Nonresidential Property for Education." *Journal of Education Finance* 21 (Summer): 103–122. [§§6.5, 7.9]

Ladd, Helen F., and John Yinger. 1994. "The Case for Equalizing Aid." *National Tax Journal* 47 (March): 211–224. [§§1.1, 6.9]

Lafferty, Ronald N., and H. E. Frech III. 1978. "Community Environment and the Market Value of Single Family Homes: The Effect of the Dispersion of Land Uses." *Journal of Law and Economics* 21 (October): 381–394. [§§3.3, 7.6]

Lawyers' Committee for Civil Rights under Law. 1971. "School Finance Litigation: A Strategy Session." *Yale Review of Law and Social Action* 2 (Winter): 153–166. [§5.11]

Leamer, Edward E. 1983. "Let's Take the Con Out of Econometrics." *American Economic Review* 73 (March): 31–43. [§5.4]

Lee, A. James, and Burton A. Weisbrod. 1978. "Public Interest Law Activities in Education." In *Public Interest Law*, ed. Burton A. Weisbrod. Berkeley: University of California Press. [§§5.3, 5.15]

Lees, Martha A. 1994. "Preserving Property Values—Preserving Proper Homes—Preserving Privilege—The Pre-Euclid Debate over Zoning for Exclusively Private Residential Areas, 1916–1926." *University of Pittsburgh Law Review* 56 (Winter): 367–439. [§9.4]

Leonard, Herman B. 1992. *By Choice or by Chance? Tracking the Values in Massachusetts' Public Spending*. Boston: Pioneer Institute. [§5.17]

LeRoy, Stephen F., and Jon Sonstelie. 1983. "Paradise Lost and Regained: Transportation Innovation, Income and Residential Location." *Journal of Urban Economics* 13 (January): 67–89. [§§1.8, 9.3]

Lester, Richard A. 1946. "Shortcomings of Marginal Analysis for Wage-Employment Problems." *American Economic Review* 36 (March): 63–82. [§3.18]

Levmore, Saul. 1992. "Bicameralism: When Are Two Decisions Better than One?" *International Review of Law and Economics* 12: 145–162. [§4.11]

Lewis, Paul G., and Elisa Barbour. 1999. *California Cities and the Local Sales Tax.* San Francisco: Public Policy Institute of California. [§8.2]

Leyden, Dennis P. 1992. "Donor Determined Intergovernmental Grants Structure." *Public Finance Quarterly* 20 (July): 321–337. [§6.15]

Liebmann, George W. 2000. *Solving Problems without Large Government: Devolution, Fairness, and Equality.* Westport, Conn.: Praeger. [§2.9]

Littlefield, Neil. 1962. *Metropolitan Area Problems and Municipal Home Rule.* Ann Arbor: Legislative Research Center, University of Michigan Law School. [§2.4]

Loeb, Susanna. 2001. "Estimating the Effects of School Finance Reform: A Framework for a Federalist System." *Journal of Public Economics* 80 (May): 225–247 [§6.12]

Lubove, Roy. 1969. *Twentieth-Century Pittsburgh: Government, Business, and Environmental Change.* New York: Wiley. [§7.4]

Mahue, Michelle A. 1991. "Home Equity Assurance Programs." *ORER Letter,* Office of Real Estate Research, University of Illinois, Urbana-Champaign, Summer. [§§11.5, 11.9]

Maier, Pauline. 1993. "The Revolutionary Origins of the American Corporation." *William and Mary Quarterly* 3d ser., 50 (January): 51–84. [§2.7]

Malpezzi, Stephen. 1996. "Housing Prices, Externalities, and Regulation in U.S. Metropolitan Areas." *Journal of Housing Research* 7: 209–241. [§3.4]

Manne, Henry G. 1965. "Mergers and the Market for Corporate Control." *Journal of Political Economy* 73 (April): 110–120. [§2.5]

Manwaring, Robert L., and Steven M. Sheffrin. 1997. "Litigation, School Finance Reform and Aggregate Educational Spending." *International Tax and Public Finance* 4 (May): 107–127. [§6.1]

Marcus, Matityahu, and Michael K. Taussig. 1970. "A Proposal for Government Insurance of Home Values against Locational Risk." *Land Economics* 46 (November): 404–413. [§11.5]

Marlow, Michael L. 1997. "Public Education Supply and Student Performance." *Applied Economics* 29 (May): 617–626. [§6.8]

Martin, Dolores T., and Richard E. Wagner. 1978. "The Institutional Framework for Municipal Incorporation: An Economic Analysis of Local Agency Formation Commissions in California." *Journal of Law and Economics* 21 (October): 409–425. [§9.12]

Martin, John Frederick. 1991. *Profits in the Wilderness: Entrepreneurship and the Founding of New England Towns in the Seventeenth Century.* Chapel Hill: University of North Carolina Press. [§§1.7, 2.6]

Martinez-Vazquez, Jorge, and David L. Sjoquist. 1988. "Property Tax Financing, Renting, and the Level of Local Expenditures." *Southern Economic Journal* 55 (October): 424–431. [§4.6]

Matsusaka, John G. 1995. "Fiscal Effects of the Voter Initiative: Evidence from the Last Thirty Years." *Journal of Political Economy* 103 (June): 587–623. [§4.13]

———. 2000. "Fiscal Effects of the Voter Initiative in the First Half of the Twentieth Century." *Journal of Law and Economics* 43 (October): 619–644. [§§4.13, 5.12]

McConnell, Michael W., and Randal C. Picker. 1993. "When Cities Go Broke: A Conceptual Introduction to Municipal Bankruptcy." *University of Chicago Law Review* 60 (Spring): 425–495. [§2.3]

McConnell, Virginia D., and Robert M. Schwab. 1990. "The Impact of Environmental Regulation on Industry Location Decisions: The Motor Vehicle Industry." *Land Economics* 66 (February): 67–81. [§8.12]

McDougal, Gerald S. 1976. "Local Public Goods and Residential Property Values: Some Insights and Extensions." *National Tax Journal* 24 (December): 436–447. [§5.8]

McEachern, William A. 1978. "Collective Decision Rules and Local Debt Charges: A Test of the Median Vote Hypothesis." *National Tax Journal* 31 (June): 129–136. [§4.11]

McHone, W. Warren. 1986. "Supply-Side Considerations in the Location of Industry in Suburban Communities: Empirical Evidence from the Philadelphia Metropolitan SMSA." *Land Economics* 62 (February): 64–73. [§7.8]

McMichael, Stanley L., and Robert F. Bingham. 1923. *City Growth and Values.* Cleveland: Stanley McMichael Publishing Organization. [§§9.4, 9.6]

McMillen, Daniel P., and John F. McDonald. 1991. "A Markov Chain Model of Zoning Change." *Journal of Urban Economics* 30 (September): 257–270. [§3.10]

———. 1993. "Could Zoning Have Increased Land Values in Chicago?" *Journal of Urban Economics* 33 (March): 167–188. [§9.6]

McNamara, Maureen A. 1984. "The Legality and Efficacy of Homeowner's Equity Assurance: A Study of Oak Park, Illinois." *Northwestern University Law Review* 78 (February): 1463–1484. [§11.5]

McUsic, Molly. 1991. "The Use of Education Clauses in School Finance Litigation." *Harvard Journal on Legislation* 28 (Summer): 307–340. [§5.5]

Meltsner, Arnold J., Gregory W. Kast, John F. Kramer, and Robert T. Nakamura. 1973. *Political Feasibility of Reform in School Financing: The Case of California.* New York: Praeger. [§5.4]

Merrill, Thomas W. 1986. "The Economics of Public Use." *Cornell Law Review* 72 (November): 61–116. [§2.4]

Michelman, Frank I. 1967. "Property, Utility, and Fairness: Comments on the Ethical Foundations of 'Just Compensation' Law." *Harvard Law Review* 80 (April): 1165–1258. [§11.12]

———. 1969. "Forward: On Protecting the Poor through the Fourteenth Amendment." *Harvard Law Review* 83 (November): 7–59. [§6.10]

Michie, R. C. 1987. *The London and New York Stock Exchanges, 1850–1914.* London: Allen and Unwin. [§2.7].

Mieszkowski, Peter. 1972. "The Property Tax: An Excise Tax or a Profits Tax?" *Journal of Public Economics* 1 (April): 73–96. [§1.1]

Mieszkowski, Peter, and George R. Zodrow. 1989. "Taxation and the Tiebout Model: The Differential Effects of Head Taxes, Taxes on Land Rents, and Property Taxes." *Journal of Economic Literature* 27 (September): 1098–1146. [§3.15]

Miller, Gary J. 1981. *Cities by Contract: The Politics of Municipal Incorporation.* Cambridge: MIT Press. [§§4.1, 5.13, 9.3, 9.9—9.12]

Mills, David E. 1981. "Growth, Speculation and Sprawl in a Monocentric City." *Journal of Urban Economics* 10 (September): 201–226. [§10.2]

Mills, Edwin S., and Bruce W. Hamilton. 1989. *Urban Economics*, 4th ed. Glenview, Ill.: Scott, Foresman. [§11.2]

Mitchell, James L. 2000. "Assessing Exclusionary Residential Zoning: A Natural Experiment Approach." Ph.D. diss., Woodrow Wilson School of Public and International Affairs, Princeton University. [§§11.7, 11.11]

Molotch, Harvey. 1976. "The City as a Growth Machine: Toward a Political Economy of Place." *American Journal of Sociology* 82 (September): 309–332. [§1.9]

Monkkonen, Eric H. 1988. *America Becomes Urban: The Development of United States Cities and Towns, 1780–1980.* Berkeley: University of California Press. [§§1.7, 2.6, 2.8]

———. 1995. *The Local State: Public Money and American Cities.* Stanford, Calif.: Stanford University Press. [§§1.7, 1.9, 2.4, 2.6, 2.8]

———. 1996. "A Conversation with Eric Monkkonen." *Journal of Urban History* 22 (January): 231–252. [§1.1]

Moomau, Pamela H., and Rebecca Morton. 1992. "Revealed Preferences for Property Taxes: An Empirical Study of Perceived Tax Incidence." *Review of Economics and Statistics* 74 (February): 176–179. [§4.6]

Moon, Choon-Geol, and Janet G. Stotsky. 1993. "The Effect of Rent Control on Housing Quality Change: A Longitudinal Analysis." *Journal of Political Economy* 6 (December): 1114–1148. [§4.7]

Morgan, Edward. 1985. "Obstacles to Educational Equity: State Reform and Local Response in Massachusetts, 1978–1983." *Journal of Education Finance* 10 (Spring): 441–459. [§5.17]

Morris, Adele C. 1998. "Property Tax Treatment of Farmland: Does Tax Relief Delay Land Development?" In *Local Government Tax and Land Use Policies in the United States*, ed. Helen Ladd. Northampton, Mass.: Edward Elgar.

Moses, Leon, and Harold F. Williamson, Jr. 1967. "The Location of Economic Activity in Cities." *American Economic Review* 57 (May): 211–222. [§9.4]

Murray, Sheila E., William M. Evans, and Robert M. Schwab. 1998. "Education-Finance Reform and the Distribution of Education Resources." *American Economic Review* 88 (September): 789–812. [§§6.1—6.3]

Musgrave, Richard A. 1939. "The Voluntary Exchange Theory of Public Economy." *Quarterly Journal of Economics* 53 (February): 213–237. [§§3.11, 4.3]

———. 1959. *The Theory of Public Finance.* New York: McGraw-Hill. [§§4.3, 4.4]

Musgrave, Richard A., and Peggy B. Musgrave. 1989. *Public Finance in Theory and Practice*, 5th ed. New York: McGraw-Hill. [§4.4]

Narver, Betty Jane. 1990. "Schools for the '90s: Washington's Education Choices." In *Washington Policy Choices 1990s*, ed. Walter Williams, William Zumeta, and Betty Jane Narver. Seattle: Institute for Public Policy and Management, University of Washington. [§§6.2, 6.12]

[National Municipal Review]. 1927. "Editorial Comment." *National Municipal Review* 16 (June): 353. [§3.10]

Negris, Karen A. 1982. "Education Finance Litigation and Economics: The New Hampshire Connection." Independent Study Report, Dartmouth College Economics Department. [§6.3]

Nelson, Robert H. 1977. *Zoning and Property Rights.* Cambridge: MIT Press. [§3.9]

———. 1999. "Privatizing the Neighborhood: A Proposal to Replace Zoning with Private Collective Property Rights to Existing Neighborhoods." *George Mason Law Review* 7 (Summer): 827–880. [§§1.1, 2.9]

Netzer, Dick. 1966. *Economics of the Property Tax.* Washington, D.C.: Brookings. [§1.1]

Newman, Robert J., and Dennis H. Sullivan. 1988. "Econometric Analysis of Business Tax Impacts on Industrial Location: What Do We Know, and How Do We Know It?" *Journal of Urban Economics* 23 (March): 215–234. [§7.8]

Nickerson, Kermit S. 1973. *An Idea Whose Time Has Come: Analysis of an Act Equalizing the Financial Support of School Units.* Washington, D.C.: Bureau of Elementary and Secondary Education, Department of Health, Education, and Welfare. [§5.14]

Niskanen, William A., Jr. 1971. *Bureaucracy and Representative Government.* Chicago: Aldine. [§§2.5, 4.11]

North, Douglas C., and Barry R. Weingast. 1989. "Constitutions and Commitment: Evolution of Institutions Governing Public Choice." *Journal of Economic History* 49 (December): 803–832. [§2.8]

Oakland, William H. 1978. "Local Taxes and Urban Industrial Location: A Survey." In *Metropolitan Financing and Growth Management Policies,* ed. George Break. Madison: University of Wisconsin Press. [§7.5]

Oakland, William H., and William A. Testa. 1998. "Fiscal Impacts of Business Development in the Chicago Suburbs." In *Local Government Tax and Land Use Policies in the United States,* ed. Helen Ladd. Northampton, Mass.: Edward Elgar.

Oates, Wallace E. 1969. "The Effects of Property Taxes and Local Public Spending on Property Values: An Empirical Study of Tax Capitalization and the Tiebout Hypothesis." *Journal of Political Economy* 77 (November): 957–971. [§§3.12, 4.1, 4.5]

———. 1972. *Fiscal Federalism.* New York: Harcourt Brace Jovanovich. [§3.13]

———. 1999. "An Essay on Fiscal Federalism." *Journal of Economic Literature* 37 (September): 1120–1149. [§§2.8, 4.4]

Oates, Wallace E., and Robert M. Schwab. 1988. "Economic Competition among Jurisdictions: Efficiency Enhancing or Distortion Inducing?" *Journal of Public Economics* 35 (April): 333–354. [§§1.1, 7.2—7.6, 8.1, 8.12]

———. 1997. "The Impact of Urban Land Taxation: The Pittsburgh Experience." *National Tax Journal* 50 (March): 1–22. [§11.2]

Oliver, Eric J. 1999. "The Effect of Metropolitan Economic Segregation on Local Civic Participation." *American Journal of Political Science* 43 (January): 186–212. [§§4.12, 4.14]

Olsen, Edgar O. 1991. "Is Rent Control Good Social Policy?" *Chicago-Kent Law Review* 67: 931–945. [§4.7]

Orfield, Myron. 1997. *Metropolitics: A Regional Agenda for Community and Stability.* Washington, D.C.: Brookings, and Cambridge: Lincoln Institute. [§§1.1, 10.3]

Ostrom, Elinor. 1990. *Governing the Commons: The Evolution of Institutions for Collective Action.* Cambridge, Eng.: Cambridge University Press. [§8.9]

Ostrom, Vincent. 1991. *The Meaning of Federalism: Constituting a Self-Governing Society.* San Francisco: Institute for Contemporary Studies Press. [§8.9]

Ostrom, Vincent, Charles M. Tiebout, and Robert Warren. 1961. "The Organization of Government in Metropolitan Areas: A Theoretical Inquiry." *American Political Science Review* 55 (December): 831–842. [§4.5]

O'Sullivan, Arthur, Terri A. Sexton, and Steven M. Sheffrin. 1995. *Property Taxes and Tax Revolts: The Legacy of Proposition 13.* Cambridge, Eng.: Cambridge University Press. [§§4.8, 5.7]

Oswald, Andrew J. 1996. "A Conjecture on the Explanation for High Unemployment in the Industrialized Nations." Working paper, Department of Economics, University of Warwick, Eng. [§4.10]

Pack, Howard, and Janet R. Pack. 1977. "Metropolitan Fragmentation and Suburban Homogeneity." *Urban Studies* 14 (June): 191–201. [§3.16]

Palmon, Oded, and Barton A. Smith. 1998. "New Evidence on Property Tax Capitalization." *Journal of Political Economy* 106 (October): 1099–1111. [§3.6]

Parks, Roger B., and Ronald J. Oakerson. 1993. "Comparative Metropolitan Organization: Service Production and Governance Structures in St. Louis, Missouri, and Allegheny County, Pennsylvania." *Publius: The Journal of Federalism* 23 (Winter): 19–39. [§8.9]

Paschal, Joel F. 1951. *Mr. Justice Sutherland, A Man against the State.* Princeton, N.J.: Princeton University Press. [§9.5]

Peevely, Gary, and John Ray. 2001. "Does Equalization Litigation Effect a Narrowing of the Gap of Value Added Achievement Outcomes among School Districts?" *Journal of Education Finance* 26 (Winter): 319–332. [§6.7]

Peiser, Richard B. 1989. "Density and Urban Sprawl." *Land Economics* 65 (August): 193–204. [§10.2]

Peltzman, Sam. 1971. "Pricing in Public and Private Enterprises: Electric Utilities in the United States." *Journal of Law and Economics* 14 (April): 109–147. [§2.8]

———. 1993. "The Political Economy of the Decline of American Public Education." *Journal of Law and Economics* 36 (April): 331–370. [§6.6]

———. 1996. "Political Economy of Public Education: Non-College-Bound Students." *Journal of Law and Economics* 39 (April): 73–120. [§6.6]

Pendall, Rolf. 1999. "Do Land-Use Controls Cause Sprawl?" *Environment and Planning B: Planning and Design* 26: 555–571. [§10.1]

Perlstein, Bruce W. 1980. "Taxes, Schools, and Inequality: The Political Economy of the Property Tax and School Finance Reform in Massachusetts." Ph.D. diss., Department of Politics, Brandeis University. [§5.17]

Perrin, Alan F., and Thomas H. Jones. 1984. "Voter Rejection of a School Finance Recapture Provision." *Journal of Education Finance* 9 (Spring): 485–497. [§5.14]

Peters, Ellen A. 1997. "Getting Away from the Federal Paradigm: Separation of Powers in State Courts." *Minnesota Law Review* 81 (June): 1543–1564. [§5.15]

Peterson, Paul E. 1981. *City Limits.* Chicago: University of Chicago Press. [§1.9]

Piacentino, Edward J. 1988. *T. S. Stribling: Pioneer Realist in Modern Southern Literature.* Lanham, Md.: University Press of America. [§1.10]

Picus, Lawrence O. 1994. "The Local Impact of School Finance Reform in Four Texas School Districts." *Educational Evaluation and Policy Analysis* 16 (Winter): 371–404. [§6.2]

Plecki, Margaret. 1997. *Conditions of Education in Washington State.* Seattle: Institute for the Study of Education Policy. [§§6.2, 6.12]

Pollard, W. L., ed. 1931. "Zoning in the United States." (Symposium.) *The Annals* 155 (May): 1–227. [§9.4]

Pope, Alexander H. 1979. "The Assessor's Perspective." *Southern California Law Review* 53 (November): 155–170. [§5.10]

Portney, Kent E. 1991. *Siting Hazardous Waste Treatment Facilities: The NIMBY Syndrome.* New York: Auburn House. [§§1.6, 7.10, 8.7]

Portney, Paul R. 1981. "Housing Prices, Health Effects, and Valuing Reductions in Risk of Death." *Journal of Environmental Economics and Management* 8 (March): 72–78. [§3.3]

Post, Alan. 1979. "Effects of Proposition 13 on the State of California." *National Tax Journal* 32 (June supplement): 381–385. [§5.8]

Poterba, James M. 1997. "Demographic Structure and the Political Economy of Public Education." *Journal of Policy Analysis and Management* 16 (Winter): 48–66. [§6.11]

Rabiega, William A., Ta-Win Lin, and Linda M. Robinson. 1984. "The Property Value Impacts of Public Housing Projects in Low and Moderate Density Residential Neighborhoods." *Land Economics* 60 (May): 174–179. [§3.3]

Rabushka, Alvin, and Pauline Ryan. 1982. *The Tax Revolt.* Berkeley: University of California Press. [§5.10]

Rasinski, Kenneth A., and Susan M. Rosenbaum. 1987. "Predicting Citizen Support of Tax Increases for Education: A Comparison of Two Social Psychological Perspectives." *Journal of Applied Social Psychology* 17 (November): 990–1006. [§6.12]

Real Estate Research Corporation. 1974. *The Costs of Sprawl: Environmental and Economic Costs of Alternative Residential Development Patterns at the Urban Fringe.* Washington, D.C.: Department of Housing and Urban Development. [§3.15]

Reichley, A. James. 1970. *The Political Constitution of the Cities.* Englewood Cliffs, N.J.: Prentice-Hall. [§1.9]

Reichman, Uriel. 1976. "Residential Private Governments: An Introductory Survey." *University of Chicago Law Review* 43 (Winter): 253–306. [§2.9]

Renner, Tari, and Victor S. DeSantis. 1993. "Contemporary Patterns and Trends in Municipal Government Structures." *The Municipal Yearbook, 1993.* Chicago: International City Managers Association. [§§2.2, 4.15]

———. 1998. "Municipal Form of Government: Issues and Trends." *The Municipal Yearbook, 1998.* Chicago: International City Managers Association. [§2.2]

Reps, John W. 1965. *The Making of Urban America: A History of City Planning in the United States.* Princeton, N.J.: Princeton University Press. [§1.7]

Revell, Keith D. 1999. "The Road to Euclid v. Ambler: City Planning, State Building, and the Changing Scope of the Police Power." *Studies in American Political Development* 13 (Spring): 50–145. [§9.5]

Revesz, Richard L. 1992. "Rehabilitating Interstate Competition: Rethinking the 'Race to the Bottom' Rationale for Federal Environmental Regulation." *NYU Law Review* 67 (December): 1210–1255. [§§7.2, 7.3]

———. 1996. "Federalism and Interstate Environmental Externalities." *University of Pennsylvania Law Review* 144 (June): 2341–2416. [§8.3]

———. 1997. "The Race to the Bottom and Federal Environmental Regulation: A Response to Critics." *Minnesota Law Review* 82 (December): 535–564. [§§7.2, 8.12]

Roback, Jennifer. 1982. "Wages, Rents, and the Quality of Life." *Journal of Political Economy* 90 (December): 1257–1278. [§3.8]

Roe, Mark J. 1994. *Strong Managers, Weak Owners: The Political Roots of American Corporate Finance.* Princeton, N.J.: Princeton University Press. [§2.5]

Rohe, William M., and Leslie S. Stewart. 1996. "Homeownership and Neighborhood Stability." *Housing Policy Debate* 7: 37–81. [§3.3]

Romer, Thomas, and Howard Rosenthal. 1979. "The Elusive Median Voter." *Journal of Public Economics* 12 (October): 143–170. [§§4.11, 4.13]

Romer, Thomas, Howard Rosenthal, and Vincent G. Munley. 1992. "Economic Incentives and Political Institutions: Spending and Voting in School Budget Referenda." *Journal of Public Economics* 49 (October): 1–33. [§4.13]

Rose, Carol M. 1996. "Takings, Federalism, Norms." *Yale Law Journal* 105 (January): 1021–1052. [preface, §11.14]

Rose, Louis A. 1989. "Urban Land Supply: Natural and Contrived Restrictions." *Journal of Urban Economics* 25 (May): 325–345. [§11.8]

Rose-Ackerman, Susan. 1985. "Inalienability and the Theory of Property Rights." *Columbia Law Review* 85 (June): 931–969. [§7.11]

Rosen, Christine M. 1995. "Businessmen against Pollution in Late Nineteenth Century Chicago." *Business History Review* 65 (Fall): 351–397. [§7.4]

Rosen, Kenneth T. 1982. "The Impact of Proposition 13 on House Prices in Northern California: A Test of the Interjurisdictional Capitalization Hypothesis." *Journal of Political Economy* 90 (February): 191–200. [§5.8]

Rosenberg, Gerald K. 1991. *The Hollow Hope: Can Courts Bring about Social Change?* Chicago: University of Chicago Press. [§5.6]

Ross, Stephen, and John Yinger. 1998. "Sorting and Voting: A Review of the Literature on Urban Public Finance." In *Handbook of Regional and Urban Economics*, vol. 3, ed. Paul Cheshire and Edwin Mills. Amsterdam: North-Holland. [§3.14]

Ross, William G. 1994. *A Muted Fury: Populists, Progressives and Labor Unions Confront the Courts, 1890–1937.* Princeton, N.J.: Princeton University Press. [§5.6]

Rossi, Peter H., and Eleanor Weber. 1996. "The Social Benefits of Homeownership: Empirical Evidence from National Surveys." *Housing Policy Debate* 7 (1): 1–35. [§4.6]

Rothstein, Paul. 1992. "The Demand for Education with 'Power Equalizing' Aid." *Journal of Public Economics* 49 (November): 135–162. [§5.16]

Rudel, Thomas K. 1989. *Situations and Strategies in American Land-Use Planning.* Cambridge, Eng.: Cambridge University Press. [§10.1]

Rusk, David. 1993. *Cities without Suburbs.* Washington, D.C.: Woodrow Wilson Center Press, Baltimore, Md.: Johns Hopkins University Press. [§10.3]

Ryan, James E. 1999. "*Sheff*, Segregation, and School Finance Litigation." *NYU Law Review* 74 (May): 529–573. [§6.7]

Ryan, Mary P. 1997. *Civic Wars: Democracy and Public Life in the American City during the Nineteenth Century.* Berkeley: University of California Press. [§2.6]

St. John, Michael. 1990. "The Impact of Rent Controls on Property Value." Working paper no. 90–178, Institute of Business and Economic Research, Haas School of Business, University of California, Berkeley. [§4.7]

Samuelson, Paul A. 1954. "The Pure Theory of Public Expenditures." *Review of Economics and Statistics* 36 (November): 387–389. [§§3.11, 4.3, 4.5]

Sass, Tim R., and Stephan L. Mehay. 1995. "The Voting-Rights Act, District Elections, and the Success of Black Candidates in Municipal Elections." *Journal of Law and Economics* 38 (October): 367–392. [§4.15]

Scheiber, Harry N. 1989. "The Jurisprudence–and Mythology–of Eminent Domain in American Legal History." In *Liberty, Property and Government: Constitutional Interpretation before the New Deal*, ed. Ellen F. Paul and Howard Dickman. Albany: SUNY Press. [§1.7]

Schill, Michael H. 1989. "Intergovernmental Takings and Just Compensation: A Question of Federalism." *University of Pennsylvania Law Review* 137 (January): 829–901. [§7.10]

———. 1991. "An Economic Analysis of Mortgagor Protection Laws." *Virginia Law Review* 77 (April): 489–538. [§1.6]

Schneider, Mark. 1989. *The Competitive City: The Political Economy of Suburbia.* Pittsburgh: University of Pittsburgh Press. [§1.9]

Schneider, Mark, and Paul Teske. 1993. "The Antigrowth Entrepreneur—Challenging the Equilibrium of the Growth Machine." *Journal of Politics* 55 (August): 720–736. [§4.15]

Schneider, Mark, Paul Teske, Melissa Marschall, and Christine Roch. 1998. "Shopping for Schools: In the Land of the Blind, the One-Eyed Parent May Be Enough." *American Journal of Political Science* 42 (July): 769–693. [§3.12]

Schrag, Peter. 1998. *Paradise Lost: California's Experience, America's Future.* New York: The New Press. [§§5.7, 5.10, 5.12, 6.6, 11.2]

Schwab, Robert M., and Wallace E. Oates. 1991. "Community Composition and the Provision of Local Public Goods—A Normative Analysis." *Journal of Public Economics* 44 (March): 217–237. [§11.10]

Schwartz, Jonathan. 1997. "Note: Prisoners of Proposition 13: Sales Taxes, Property Taxes, and the Fiscalization of Municipal Land Use Decisions." *Southern California Law Review* 71 (November): 183–217. [§8.2]

Sears, David O., and Jack Citrin. 1982. *Tax Revolt: Something for Nothing in California.* Cambridge: Harvard University Press. [§5.9]

Shapiro, Lisa. 1995. "Tax Policy and Voting Behavior in Statewide Elections: The 1992 New Hampshire Gubernatorial Race." Ph.D. diss., Department of Economics, Johns Hopkins University. [§5.12]

Shiller, Robert J., and Allan N. Weiss. 1998. "Moral Hazard in Home Equity Conversion." NBER working paper 6552. [§§1.6, 11.5]

Sidak, J. Gregory, and Daniel F. Spulber. 1996. "Deregulatory Takings and Breach of the Regulatory Contract." *New York University Law Review* 71 (October): 851–999. [§11.7]

Silva, Fabio, and Jon C. Sonstelie. 1995. "Did *Serrano* Cause a Decline in School Spending?" *National Tax Journal* 48 (June): 199–215. [§6.1]

Simon, Stacey. 1998. "Comment: A Vote Of No Confidence: Proposition 218, Local Government, and Quality of Life in California." *Ecology Law Quarterly* 25: 519–546. [§5.7]

Small, Kenneth A. 1992. *Urban Transportation Economics.* Chur, Switz.: Harwood Academic. [§§4.13, 10.5]

Smith, Adam. [1776] 1937. *The Wealth of Nations.* New York: Modern Library. [§2.2]

Smith, Daniel A. 1999. "Howard Jarvis, Populist Entrepreneur: Reevaluating the

Causes of Proposition 13." *Social Science History* 23 (Summer): 173–210. [§5.12]

Smith, Vernon L. 1982. "Markets as Economizers of Information: Experimental Examination of the 'Hayek Hypothesis.'" *Economic Inquiry* 20 (April): 165–179. [§3.2]

Sokolow, Alvin D. 1998. "The Changing Property Tax and State-Local Relations." *Publius* 28 (Winter): 165–187. [§1.1]

Sonstelie, Jon, Eric Brunner, and Kenneth Ardon. 2000. *For Better or for Worse? School Finance Reform in California.* San Francisco: Public Policy Institute of California. [§§5.1, 6.1, 6.3, 6.6, 6.7]

Sonstelie, Jon C., and Paul R. Portney. 1978. "Profit Maximizing Communities and the Theory of Local Public Expenditures." *Journal of Urban Economics* 5 (April): 263–277. [§1.5]

———. 1980a. "Gross Rents and Market Values: Testing the Implications of Tiebout's Hypothesis." *Journal of Urban Economics* 7 (January): 102–118. [§5.8]

———. 1980b. "Take the Money and Run: A Theory of Voting in Local Referenda." *Journal of Urban Economics* 8 (September): 187–195. [§4.17]

Southwick, Lawrence, and Indermit S. Gill. 1997. "Unified Salary Schedule and Student SAT Scores: Adverse Effects of Adverse Selection in the Market for Secondary School Teachers." *Economics of Education Review* 16 (April): 143–153. [§6.6]

Spence, David B., and Paula Murray. 1999. "The Law, Economics, and Politics of Federal Preemption Jurisprudence: A Quantitative Analysis." *California Law Review* 87 (October): 1125–1206. [§8.1]

Spies, Sherrill, S. H. Murdock, S. White, R. Krannich, J. D. Wulfhorst, K. Wrigley, F. L. Leistritz, R. Sell, and J. Thompson. 1998. "Support for Waste Facility Siting: Differences between Community Leaders and Residents." *Rural Sociology* 63 (March): 65–93. [§10.1]

Stigler, George J. 1971. "The Theory of Economic Regulation." *Bell Journal of Economics* 2 (Spring): 3–21. [§4.11]

Stribling, Thomas S. 1934. *Unfinished Cathedral.* New York: Literary Guild. [§1.10]

Susskind, Lawrence E., and Stephen R. Cassella. 1987. "The Danger of Preemption Legislation: The Case of LNG Facility Siting in California." In *Resolving Locational Conflict,* ed. Robert W. Lake. New Brunswick, N.J.: Rutgers University Center of Urban Policy Research. [§7.10]

Tarlock, A. Dan. 1997. "Safe Drinking Water: A Federalism Perspective." *William and Mary Environmental Law and Policy Review* 21 (Winter): 233–263. [§11.1]

Tarr, G. Alan. 1998. "Models and Fashions in State Constitutionalism. *Wisconsin Law Review* 1998: 729–745. [§5.2]

Taylor, Alan. 1995. *William Cooper's Town: Power and Persuasion on the Frontier of the Early American Republic.* New York: Vintage Books. [§1.7]

Taylor, Ralph B. 1995. "The Impact of Crime on Communities." *Annals of AAPSS* 539 (May): 28–45. [§3.3]

Teachout, Peter. 1997. "'No Simple Disposition': The Brigham Case and the Future of Local Control over School Spending in Vermont." *Vermont Law Review* 22 (Fall): 22–82. [§5.5]

Teaford, Jon C. 1973. "City versus State: The Struggle for Legal Ascendancy." *American Journal of Legal History* 17 (January): 51–65. [§2.6]

———. 1975. *The Municipal Revolution in America: Origins of Modern Urban Government, 1650–1825.* Chicago: University of Chicago Press. [§§2.2, 2.6]

———. 1979. *City and Suburb: The Political Fragmentation of Metropolitan America, 1850–1970.* Baltimore: Johns Hopkins University Press. [§§2.6, 7.8, 9.1—9.4, 9.7, 9.12]

———. 1997. *Post-Suburbia: Government and Politics in the Edge Cities.* Baltimore: Johns Hopkins University Press. [§§2.3, 4.4, 7.8, 10.5]

Teske, Paul, Mark Schneider, Michael Mintrom, and Samuel Best. 1993. "Establishing the Micro Foundations of a Macro Theory: Information, Movers, and the Competitive Market for Public Goods." *American Political Science Review* 87 (September): 702–713. [§§3.2, 3.12]

Theobald, Neil D., and Faith Hanna. 1991. "Ample Provision for Whom? The Evolution of State Control over School Finance in Washington." *Journal of Education Finance* 17 (Summer): 17–33. [§§5.12, 6.3, 6.11]

Theobald, Neil D., and Lawrence O. Picus. 1991. "Living with Equal Amounts of Less: Experience of States with Primarily State-Funded School Systems." *Journal of Education Finance* 17 (Summer): 1–6. [§6.2]

Thompson, John A. 1992. "Notes on the Centralization of the Funding and Governance of Education in Hawaii." *Journal of Education Finance* 19 (Spring): 288–302. [§6.7]

Thorson, James A. 1994. "Zoning Policy Changes and the Urban Fringe Land Market." *Journal of the American Real Estate and Urban Economics Association* 22 (Fall): 527–538. [§3.10]

———. 1996. "An Examination of the Monopoly Zoning Hypothesis." *Land Economics* 72 (February): 43–55. [§11.8]

———. 1997. "The Effect of Zoning on Housing Construction." *Journal of Housing Economics* 6 (March): 81–91. [§3.10]

Tideman, T. Nicolaus. 1990. "Integrating Land-Value Taxation with the Internalization of Spatial Externalities." *Land Economics* 66 (August): 341–355. [§11.2]

Tiebout, Charles M. 1956. "A Pure Theory of Local Expenditures." *Journal of Political Economy* 64 (October): 416–424. [§§3.11, 3.12, 4.3, 4.5]

———. 1957. "The Community Income Multiplier: An Empirical Study." Ph.D. diss., Department of Economics, University of Michigan. [§4.3]

Timar, Thomas B. 1994. "Politics, Policy, and Categorical Aid: New Inequities in California School Finance." *Educational Evaluation and Policy Analysis* 16 (Summer): 143–160. [§6.15]

Timmins, Christopher. 1999. "The Redistributive Fiscal Role of Residential Water Bills." Working paper, Department of Economics, Yale University. [§2.8]

Tocqueville, Alexis de. 1835. *Democracy in America.* London: Saunders and Otley. [§§2.2, 11.14]

Tracy, Joseph, Henry Schneider, and Sewin Chan. 1999. "Are Stocks Overtaking Real Estate in Household Portfolios?" *Current Issues in Economics and Finance* (Federal Reserve Bank of New York) 5 (April): 1–6. [§1.2]

Treanor, William M. 1985. "The Origins and Original Significance of the Just Compensation Clause of the Fifth Amendment." *Yale Law Journal* 94 (January): 694–716. [§11.7]

Troesken, Werner. 1997. "The Sources of Public Ownership: Historical Evidence from the Gas Industry." *Journal of Law, Economics, and Organization* 13 (April): 1–25. [§2.8]

Turnbull, Geoffrey K, and Mitias, Peter M. 1999. "The Median Voter Model across Levels of Government." *Public Choice* 99 (April): 119–138. [§4.13]

Underwood, Julie K. 1994. "School Finance Litigation: Legal Theories, Judicial Activism, and Social Neglect." *Journal of Education Finance* 20 (Fall): 143–162. [§5.5]

Verba, Sidney, and Norman H. Nie. 1972. *Participation in America: Political Democracy and Social Equality*. New York: Harper and Row. [§4.12]

Verba, Sidney, Kay L. Schlozman, and Henry E. Brady. 1995. *Voice and Equality: Civic Voluntarism in American Politics.* Cambridge: Harvard University Press. [§§1.6, 4.12]

Vesterby, Marlow, and Ralph Heimlich. 1991. "Land Use and Demographic Change: Results from Fast-Growth Counties." *Land Economics* 67 (August): 279–291. [§2.3]

Viteritti, Joseph P. 1995. "Municipal Home Rule and the Conditions of Justifiable Secession." *Fordham Law Journal* 23 (Fall): 1–68 [§11.13]

Wallis, John Joseph. 2000. "American Government Finance in the Long Run: 1790 to 1990." *Journal of Economic Perspectives* 14 (Winter): 61–82. [§2.8]

Warner, Kee, and Harvey Molotch. 1995. "Power to Build: How Development Persists Despite Local Controls." *Urban Affairs Review* 30 (January): 378–406. [§1.9]

Warner, Sam Bass. 1962. *Streetcar Suburbs: The Process of Growth in Boston, 1870–1900.* New York: Atheneum. [§§1.8, 9.3]

Washington State Growth Strategies Commission. 1990. *Final Report: A Growth Strategy for Washington State.* September. (no city or publisher) [§10.7]

Webber, Melvin M. 1976. "The BART Experience—What Have We Learned?" *The Public Interest* 45 (Fall): 79–108. [§9.6]

Weber, Michael P. 1988. *Don't Call Me Boss: David L. Lawrence, Pittsburgh's Renaissance Mayor.* Pittsburgh: University of Pittsburgh Press. [§7.4]

Wegner, Judith W. 1987. "Moving toward the Bargaining Table: Contract Zoning, Development Agreements, and the Theoretical Foundations of Government Land Use Deals." *North Carolina Law Review* 65: 957–1038. [3.15]

Weiss, Marc A. 1987. *The Rise of the Community Builders: The American Real Estate Industry and Urban Land Planning.* New York: Columbia University Press. [§§9.4, 9.6]

West, Martha S. 1999. "Equitable Funding of Public Schools under State Constitutional Law." *Journal of Gender, Race, and Justice* 2 (Spring): 279–313. [§5.10]

Wheaton, William C. 1993. "Land Capitalization, Tiebout Mobility, and the Role of Zoning Regulations." *Journal of Urban Economics* 34 (September): 102–117. [§3.10]

White, James R. 1988. "Large Lot Zoning and Subdivision Costs: A Test." *Journal of Urban Economics* 23 (May): 370–384. [§10.2]

White, Michelle J. 1975. "Firm Location in a Zoned Metropolitan Area." In *Fiscal Zoning and Land Use Controls*, ed. Edwin S. Mills and Wallace E. Oates. Lexington, Mass.: Heath-Lexington Books. [§7.6]

Wickwar, W. Hardy. 1970. *The Political Theory of Local Government.* Columbia: University of South Carolina Press. [§2.2]

Williams, Joan C. 1985. "The Invention of the Municipal Corporation: A Case Study in Legal Change." *American University Law Review* 34 (Winter): 369–438. [§2.2]

———. 1986. "The Constitutional Vulnerability of American Local Government: The Politics of City Status in American Law." *Wisconsin Law Review* 1986: 83–153. [§2.8]

Williams, Norman, Jr. 1975. *American Land Planning Law.* Chicago: Callaghan. [§6.16]

Winter, Ralph K., Jr. 1972. "Poverty, Economic Inequality, and the Equal Protection Clause." *Supreme Court Review* 1972: 41–102. [§5.4]

Wise, Arthur E. 1967. *Rich Schools, Poor Schools: The Promise of Equal Educational Opportunity.* Chicago: University of Chicago Press. [§5.3]

Wong, Kenneth K. 1991. "State Reform in Education Finance: Territorial and Social Strategies." *Publius* 21 (Summer): 125–142. [§6.10]

Wyckoff, Paul Gary. 1995. "Capitalization, Equalization, and Intergovernmental Aid." *Public Finance Quarterly* 23 (October): 484–508. [§6.4]

[*Yale Law Journal*]. 1972. "Note: A Statistical Analysis of the School Finance Decisions: On Winning Battles and Losing Wars, *Yale Law Journal* 81 (June): 1303–1341. [§6.3]

Yinger, John. 1995. *Closed Doors, Opportunities Lost: The Continuing Costs of Housing Discrimination.* New York: Russell Sage Foundation. [§11.3]

Yinger, John, Howard S. Bloom, Axel Börsch-Supan, and Helen F. Ladd. 1988. *Property Taxes and Housing Values: The Theory and Estimation of Intrajurisdictional Property Tax Capitalization.* Boston: Academic Press. [§§3.5, 3.6]

Zanzig, Blair R. 1997. "Measuring The Impact of Competition in Local Government Education Markets of the Cognitive Achievement of Students." *Economics of Education Review* 16 (October): 431–441. [§6.8]

Zimmerman, Joseph P. 1999. *The New England Town Meeting: Democracy in Action.* Westport, Conn.: Praeger. [§4.12]

Index

Legal cases and authors cited are indexed in the Case References and the General References